Using AppleWorks® GS

Douglas L. Brown

Addison-Wesley Publishing Company, Inc

Reading, Massachusetts • Menlo Park, California • New York • Don Mills,
Ontario • Workingham, England • Amsterdam • Bonn • Sydney • Singapore
Tokyo • Madrid • San Juan

Many of the designations used by manufacturers and sellers to distinguish their products are claimed as trademarks. Where those designations appear in this book, and Addison-Wesley was aware of trademark claim, the designations have been printed in initial caps or all caps (i.e. AppleWorks, or Apple IIGS).

Library of Congress Cataloging-in-Publication Data
Brown, Douglas L.
   Using AppleWorks GS / Douglas L. Brown
         p. cm.
   Includes index.
   ISBN 0-201-19678-6
   1. Apple IIGS (Computer)--Programming. 2. AppleWorks GS
(Computer program) I. Title.
   QA76.8.A1774B76 1989   005.265--dc19   88-13764

Cover design by Doliber Skeffington
Set in 10-point Century Schoolbook by Context, Inc., San Diego, CA

ISBN 0-201-19678-6
First printing, January 1989

Contents

Preface

About this book

This book is a complete introduction to AppleWorks GS, the most exciting software product ever produced for the Apple II series. AppleWorks GS combines the graphic interface familiar to Macintosh users with the color and high resolution familiar to Apple IIGS users to provide a unique program for millions of Apple IIGS owners.

What makes AppleWorks GS so exciting? The new features, the ability to transfer information effortlessly between documents, the emphasis on color and graphics — AppleWorks GS opens up a new world of computer uses! As one of the co-authors of the documentation provided with AppleWorks GS, I have been working with this program for nearly a year, and the more I use the program, the more uses I find for it. Just when I think I have explored every possible feature and use, another new use occurs to me. I am convinced that AppleWorks GS will find an important place in millions of homes and schools around the country and world.

This book complements and supplements the manuals that are provided with AppleWorks GS. The manuals are complete, but terse. This book provides a more conversational, informal approach. Where the manuals are intended to be reference works, this book is designed to be a tutorial that provides a step-by-step approach to using AppleWorks GS.

How does AppleWorks GS compare to classic AppleWorks?

Since 1983 millions of Apple II owners have used classic AppleWorks to handle three important applications: word processing, databases, and spreadsheets. Classic AppleWorks handled these tasks well, but it always had certain limitations. You couldn't see text characteristics like boldface or underlining on screen, you couldn't use pictures as categories in a database, you couldn't produce graphs from spreadsheet data — the list of limitations went on and on.

AppleWorks GS moves beyond classic AppleWorks and opens a new world of possibilities. This book describes the six integrated applications that make up AppleWorks GS and provides information for both new and experienced Apple II users.

Like classic AppleWorks, the new AppleWorks GS program is an integrated software package. It contains six applications: word processing, database, spreadsheet, graphics, page layout, and telecommunications. Like classic AppleWorks, AppleWorks GS makes it easy to transfer information from one document to another and one application to another. But AppleWorks GS goes far beyond classic AppleWorks to take advantage of the special capabilities of your Apple IIGS.

Who should use this book?

AppleWorks GS contains a wealth of features in its six applications, and it can be used productively by both new Apple II users and more experienced users. This book is designed to serve both groups, including both introductory information for new users and many shortcuts and tips for more advanced users.

For new users, each application is introduced with an overview of possible uses for the application, followed by step-by-step instructions for the first use of the application. For example, the word processing application is introduced by demonstrating how to create a new document, enter and edit text, save the document , and print the document. The introductory discussion of each application is followed by sections that demonstrate more advanced uses.

More advanced users can focus on the shortcuts and tips that are provided throughout each section. AppleWorks GS provides so many new features that the number of shortcuts and tips is quite large!

How is the book organized?

Using AppleWorks GS is divided into eight major sections:

- Introduction to AppleWorks GS and the Apple IIGS environment, including an overview of the six AppleWorks GS applications, the use of the graphic interface, and the common commands that are used in all six applications.

- Using the AppleWorks GS word processor, including the creation of new documents, entering text, saving and printing text, and formatting text with different fonts and styles.
- Using the AppleWorks GS database, including the design and creation of a database, sorting and retrieving information, and printing reports that summarize the information in the database.
- Using the AppleWorks GS spreadsheet, including entering and rearranging information, asking "what-if?" questions, and producing graphs that summarize the information in the spreadsheet.
- Using the AppleWorks GS graphics application, including the creation of high-resolution color graphics with the AppleWorks GS graphics tools.
- Using the AppleWorks GS page layout application, including the combination of text and graphics into a polished final document.
- Using the AppleWorks GS telecommunications application, including a discussion of the value of telecommunications and the steps required to connect your Apple IIGS with a remote computer.
- Specialized information, including a chapter on transferring information among AppleWorks GS documents and other programs and four appendices containing more detailed technical information.

A final word

During the production of this book, I have spent hundreds of hours working with AppleWorks GS. As the program grew from a skeleton containing menu bars and few operational functions to a fully-developed product, I grew more and more impressed.

AppleWorks GS combines some of the best features found in programs designed for that computer For The Rest Of Us, and it takes those features several steps further. Some features (like paint objects) are found only in the latest Macintosh graphics programs. Other features, like the revolutionary Control-drag feature, represent important new ideas and are found in no other programs (to my knowledge).

And more than anything else AppleWorks GS is fun to use. After years of waiting for exciting new software that takes advantage of the Apple IIGS hardware, AppleWorks GS fulfills the promise of the machine. The graphic interface, the striking colors, and the wealth of new features make AppleWorks GS just plain fun to use.

And so, enjoy AppleWorks GS! I still remember my first reaction, and I promise you that you'll smile the first time that you boot this program. Turn on your computer, plug in the AWGS disk, and get ready for a whole new world!

Acknowledgements

This book is the product of months of intense work, and it's impossible to acknowledge the help of everyone involved in the project. First and foremost, I thank Dave Macdonald, who invited me to join the AppleWorks GS (nee GSWorks) project on a short-time, part-time basis. Neither he nor I suspected how full-time it would become!

Thanks also to Kevin Harvey and all the programmers at Styleware for their patient and careful explanations of the ordinary and extraordinary features in GSWorks. Without the support of David and Kevin and the rest of the gang at Styleware, this book would never have happened.

It's particularly important to acknowledge the special help of two special people: Paul Jennings and Gail Drago. Paul worked with David and me to produce the AppleWorks GS manuals in record time; if anyone needs a professional team to produce a high-quality manual in record time, this group can do it! Gail, the Styleware "screen queen" literally made this book possible; without her tips to help me produce all of the screen dumps, there wouldn't be any illustrations for this book.

Thanks also to the special folks at Addison-Wesley, who turned this book from a stack of diskettes into a real book. Special awards to Julie Stillman, Debbie Cook, and Lynne Reed for support and patience throughout these months.

And finally, extra special thanks to my favorite physician, Judi, for her endless patience and support. Through all the hours at the computer and all the clutter of production, you've been a champ . . . thanks!

Doug Brown
Houston, Texas
December, 1988

Chapter 1

Introduction to AppleWorks GS

About this chapter

This chapter introduces AppleWorks GS and the six AppleWorks GS applications: word processing, database, spreadsheet, graphics, page layout, and telecommunications. The chapter presents a brief summary of each application and shows you how you could use the application in your home or profession. When you finish this chapter, you'll understand that AppleWorks GS is a uniquely useful program for your Apple IIGS computer.

If you have used classic AppleWorks in the past, this chapter also reassures you that you can continue to use those files with AppleWorks GS. AppleWorks GS converts all of your classic AppleWorks word processing, database, and spreadsheet files automatically into AppleWorks GS files. You can use your classic AppleWorks files immediately with AppleWorks GS.

What is AppleWorks GS?

AppleWorks GS is an exciting new program that combines six computer applications into a single program. These six applications are

- Word processing
- Database
- Spreadsheet
- Graphics
- Page layout
- Telecommunications

Using these six applications, you can create text documents, save and retrieve information, work with numbers, create graphics, design documents mixing both text and graphics, and communicate with other computers.

In addition to meeting your most important computing needs, AppleWorks GS provides a productive and easy-to-learn working environment. You can use the Apple IIGS mouse to select commands from pull-down menus, or you can use the keyboard to select commands if you wish.

This combination of power and ease-of-use makes AppleWorks GS one of the most important productivity tools available for use on microcomputers.

Independent, but integrated

Each of these six applications can be used independently. For instance, you can create letters with the word processor without ever using the other applications. But the applications are also **integrated** and designed to be used together. They use similar commands, and it's easy to transfer text or graphics from one document to another.

The word processing application

Word processing simply means using the computer to create text. You will discover that word processing is a very useful computer application.

The AppleWorks GS word processing application replaces your ordinary typewriter with a powerful electronic writing tool. This application provides a full set of basic word processing operations:

- You can create text on the Apple IIGS screen.
- You can make changes in the text; this is called text editing.
- You can save documents on a storage disk for future use.
- You can print one or more copies of a document on your printer.

In addition to these basic features, the AppleWorks GS word processing application lets you produce attractive and professional documents by providing many special features. These special features include the use of different fonts, in different sizes and styles, and in color.

A text font is the specific shape of a set of characters. On an ordinary typewriter, only one font is available: the particular set of characters that are struck on the paper when you press the keys. AppleWorks GS lets you easily use many different fonts in a single document.

You can use fonts in many different sizes for the text in your document. You can use a large font for a title, a smaller font for the body of the document, and a still smaller font for footnotes.

You can also include many different font styles in your document. A style describes the way that text is displayed. For example, familiar styles include bold, underlined, and italic.

AppleWorks GS also includes styles like outline and shadow, and you can combine these styles with different fonts and sizes to give your documents a distinctive look. (See Figure 1-1.)

The word processing application can check the spelling in your document and can suggest alternate words with the built-in thesaurus. You can also print form letters with the mail-merge feature.

The database application

What is a database? A database is just a collection of information. You've used databases for years. Your telephone book is an example of a printed database that contains a collection of names, addresses, and telephone numbers.

The AppleWorks GS database application lets you store and retrieve information in your computer. You can store lists of names, addresses, telephone numbers, books, videotapes . . . any information that you can place in a list can be easily stored and retrieved in the database. You can even store graphic information, like maps, drawings, or digitized images.

The AppleWorks GS database lets you store information in two ways: as a form or as a list. You can store information that you might store manually on index cards. You can view your database on the screen instead of on paper index cards. (See Figure 1-2.)

You can also use the database to store information that would naturally be arranged in rows and columns. (See Figure 1-3.)

An AppleWorks GS database offers many advantages over a printed database:

- You can find information in the database quickly. If you ask for a specific piece of information, your Apple IIGS can quickly find and display the information on the screen.

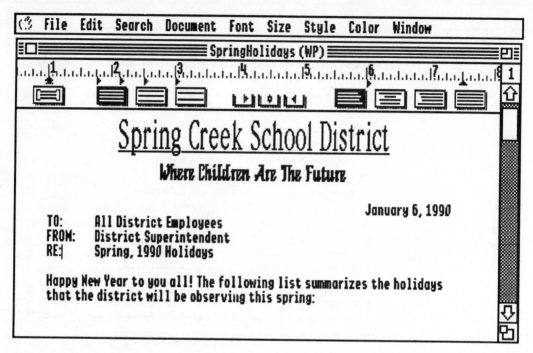

File   Edit   Search   Document   Font   Size   Style   Color   Window

≡ SpringHolidays (WP) ≡

Spring Creek School District
Where Children Are The Future

January 6, 1990

TO: All District Employees
FROM: District Superintendent
RE: Spring, 1990 Holidays

Happy New Year to you all! The following list summarizes the holidays
that the district will be observing this spring:

Figure 1-1   Sample word processing document

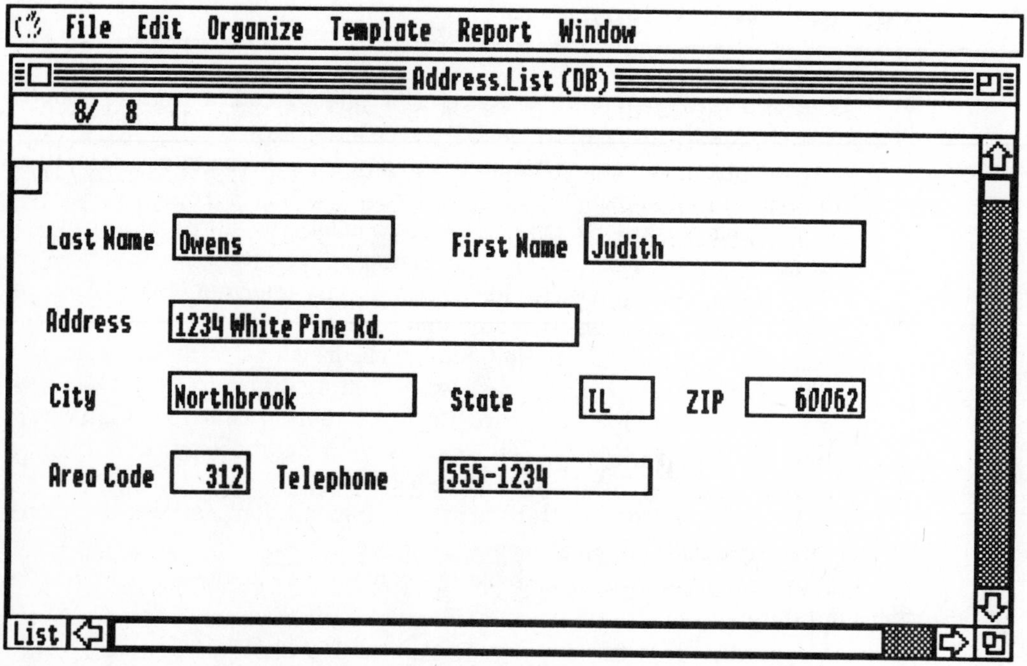

File   Edit   Organize   Template   Report   Window

≡ Address.List (DB) ≡

8/ 8

Last Name Owens   First Name Judith

Address   1234 White Pine Rd.

City   Northbrook   State   IL   ZIP   60062

Area Code   312   Telephone   555-1234

List

Figure 1-2   Database in Form view

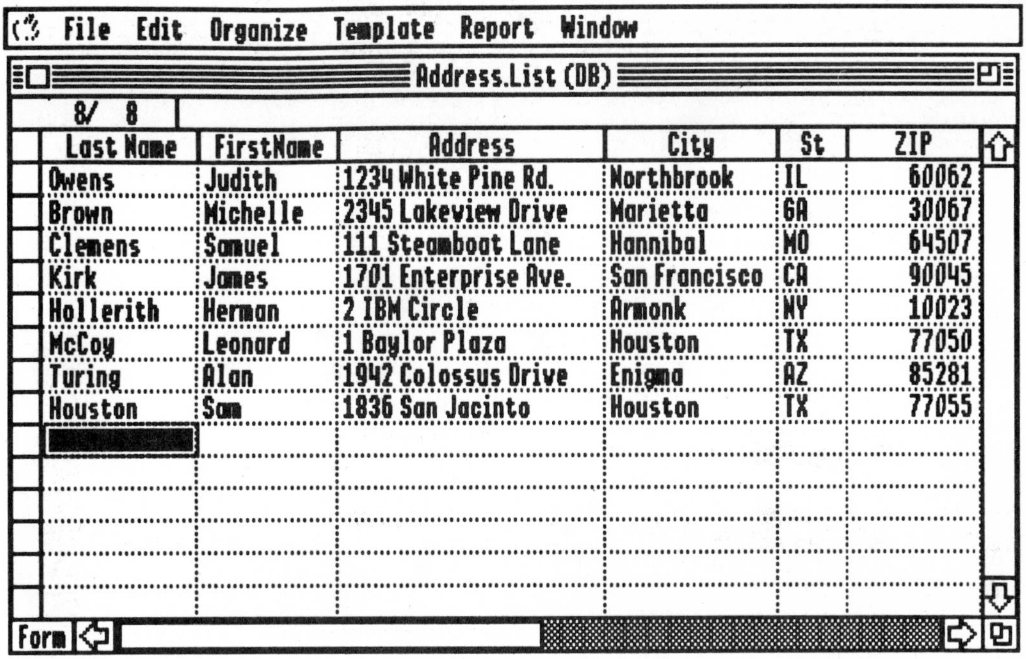

Figure 1-3 Database in List view

- You can rearrange information in the database quickly. You don't need to worry about the order of the information as you type it into the data base. You can always rearrange the information in any desired order later. For instance, you can rearrange names in alphabetical order, regardless of the order in which you entered them.
- You can print out summary reports of the information quickly. For instance, you can print a list that contains a selected part of the database, arranged in any desired order.

The spreadsheet application

A spreadsheet is simply a collection of information that is arranged in rows and columns. In some ways a spreadsheet resembles an AppleWorks GS database, since both can contain information arranged in rows and columns. The spreadsheet offers one important advantage: the power of calculation. It lets you use the computing power of your Apple IIGS to perform both simple and complicated calculations.

When would you use a spreadsheet? You would use a spreadsheet to handle information that is naturally arranged in rows and columns and that requires some calculations. Some typical examples might be

- budget information
- tax information
- student gradebook information
- personnel salary information
- scientific laboratory data

In each of these situations, the information is naturally arranged in rows and columns, and calculations would be performed on the data.

A sample spreadsheet is shown in Figure 1-4.

The AppleWorks GS spreadsheet also provides a special feature: It can produce charts and graphs from your data. You can use the spreadsheet application to produce pie charts, bar graphs, or line graphs of your information. (See Figure 1-5.)

The graphics application

The graphics application is easy to use. Even if you have little experience with graphics, this application lets you produce high-quality color images quickly.

The graphics application lets you create color graphics on the screen that can be printed on your printer or incorporated into other Apple-Works GS documents.

The AppleWorks GS graphics application combines the best features of other Apple IIGS graphics programs. Most other programs are considered either paint programs or draw programs. Paint programs let you sketch freehand on the screen, and draw programs let you create geometric shapes on the screen.

The AppleWorks GS graphics application combines these two kinds of programs into a single, easy-to-use package, resulting in one of the most powerful graphics applications available on the Apple IIGS.

The features found in both paint and draw programs are combined by providing two sets of tools: **paint tools** and **draw tools**.

The paint tools let you sketch freehand on the screen. They include a pencil tool, paintbrush, paintbucket, spraycan, and eraser.

The draw tools let you draw geometric shapes on the screen, including rectangles, rounded rectangles, ovals, and polygons. A text tool lets you include text in your graphic, and all of the usual fonts, sizes, styles, and colors are available.

An example of a graphics document is shown in Figure 1-6.

LoanAm.913 (SS)

A16	A	B	C	D	E	F
1	LOAN AMORTIZATION TABLE					
2						
3	Loan Amount	20000.00		Interest/month ==>		0.96%
4	# Yrs	25		Payment/month ==>		203.29
5	Payments/yr	12				
6	Interest Rate	11.50%				
7						
8	Payment #	Payment	Interest	Principal	Balance	Int rate
9					20000.00	
10	1	203.29	191.67	11.63	19988.37	0.96%
11	2	203.29	191.56	11.74	19976.63	0.96%
12	3	203.29	191.44	11.85	19964.78	0.96%
13	4	203.29	191.33	11.96	19952.82	0.96%
14	5	203.29	191.21	12.08	19940.74	0.96%

Figure 1-4   Sample spreadsheet

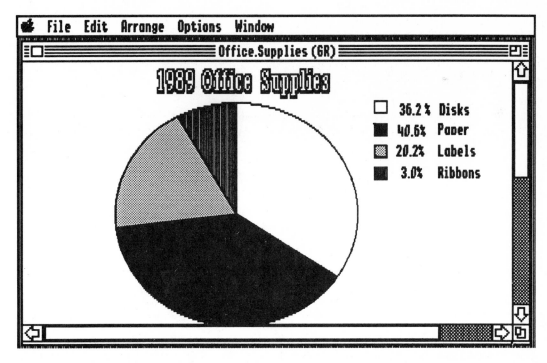

Figure 1-5   Sample spreadsheet chart

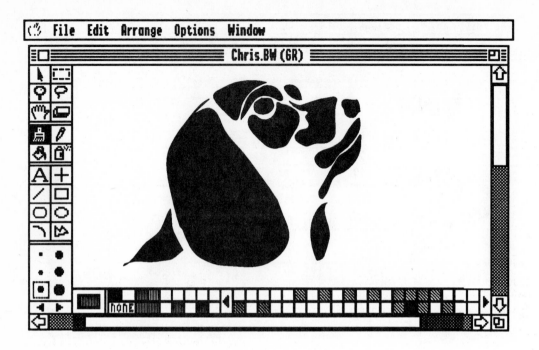

Figure 1-6 Graphics document

The page layout application

The page layout application lets you bring together your text and graphics into a single high-quality document. With this application you can produce a newsletter, a student newspaper, or any other publication that combines text and graphics. (See Figure 1-7.)

In the page layout application you can use text created with the Apple-Works GS word processor or with other programs. You can even create the text directly in the page layout application. You can arrange the text at any location on a page. You can even arrange it into multiple columns if you wish.

You can combine your text with graphics that you created in the Apple-Works GS graphics application or with other programs. The graphics can be arranged at any location on the screen and resized to fit the page. After you have arranged your text and graphics, the finished product is a professional, full-color document.

The page layout application provides many special features. For example, you can use master pages to create text or graphics that you want

Figure 1-7 Page layout document

to appear automatically on every page of your document. You can also use guides to help you align objects on each page.

The telecommunications application

Telecommunications lets you connect your computer to another computer and transfer information back and forth. The other computer may be across the room, across the building, or across the country. Usually your computer is located at some distance from the second computer, with the two computers connected by the telephone system.

The AppleWorks GS telecommunications application handles the transfer of information between the computers, letting you transfer documents from the remote computer to your Apple IIGS and from your computer to the remote computer.

One of the most common uses of telecommunications is to connect a computer like your Apple IIGS to a much larger, more powerful remote computer to transfer information from the remote computer to your system. Many different computer services provide information on a wide

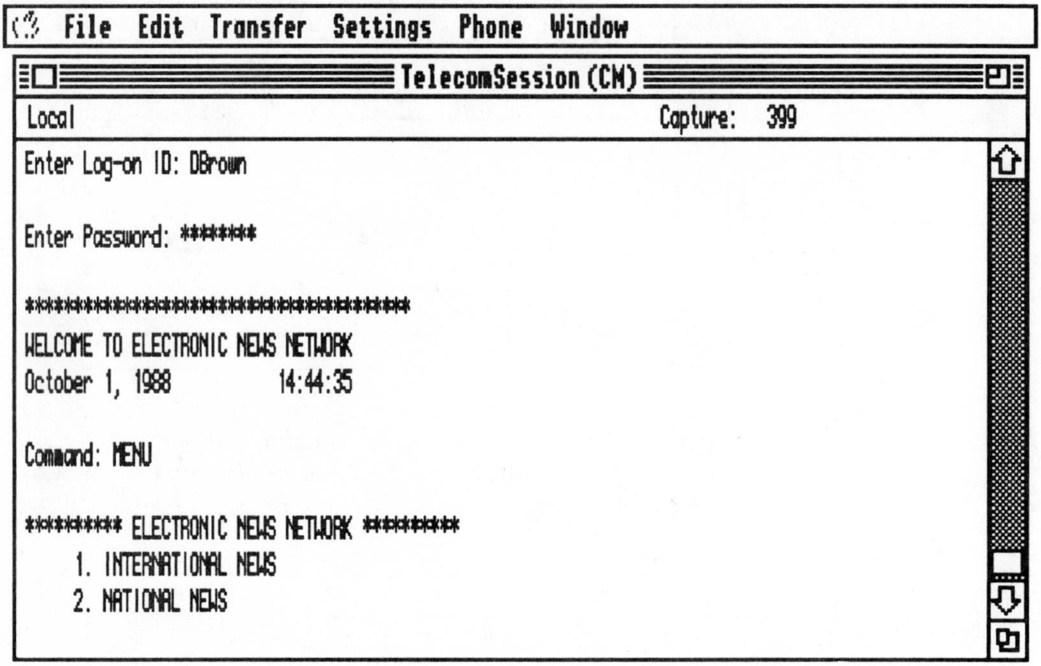

```
 File   Edit   Transfer   Settings   Phone   Window

═══════════════════ TelecomSession (CM) ═══════════════════

Local                                              Capture:    399

Enter Log-on ID: DBrown

Enter Password: *******

*************************************
WELCOME TO ELECTRONIC NEWS NETWORK
October 1, 1988          14:44:35

Command: MENU

********* ELECTRONIC NEWS NETWORK *********
    1. INTERNATIONAL NEWS
    2. NATIONAL NEWS
```

Figure 1-8 Telecommunications session

variety of topics. The AppleWorks GS telecommunications application can connect you to this world of information. (See Figure 1-8.)

Who should use AppleWorks GS?

Before purchasing any software, you should ask yourself: What do I want to do with my computer, and can this software help me to do it?

AppleWorks GS lets you create text and graphics, save and retrieve information, perform calculations, create graphs, print out finished documents containing text and graphics, and communicate with remote computers. In short, AppleWorks GS can handle most of the everyday tasks that you want your computer to do.

AppleWorks GS is designed to be used by every Apple IIGS owner. The six applications can be used by everyone from computer beginners to more sophisticated users. Some applications are more easily mastered than others, but all of the applications can be used almost immediately by most users.

If you have little experience on the Apple IIGS or other computers, you should begin with the word processing and graphics applications. You can use the word processing application almost immediately to create and print text documents, and the graphics application can be used immediately by even young children to create colorful graphics images.

The page layout application is used to place text and graphics into a visually pleasing final document. It requires somewhat more experience. If you begin with the word processing and graphics applications, you will find that many of the same ideas that you learn in those applications are useful in page layout.

The database and spreadsheet applications are a little more specialized. Use the database application when you have lists of information that you need to organize, and use the spreadsheet when you have numeric information that requires calculations.

Finally, the telecommunications application is the most specialized application. If you have a modem for your computer and you need to connect your computer with another computer, you will find that the AppleWorks GS telecommunications application is one of the easiest communications packages available.

What about classic AppleWorks users?

Suppose that you have used classic AppleWorks for years and you have disks full of AppleWorks files. Fortunately, AppleWorks GS lets you move up to these new, more powerful applications without losing your previous work.

AppleWorks GS can open all of your classic AppleWorks files directly, and you can begin to use and modify them with the new applications immediately.

For instance, if you have word processing files that you produced with classic AppleWorks, the AppleWorks GS word processor will open and display those files just as if they were created by AppleWorks GS. Formatting commands like boldface and underlining that are used in your old classic AppleWorks files are recognized, so your old documents are displayed on the screen with those formatting commands. The major difference is that you can now see the boldface and underline formats on the screen, rather than imagine what they would look like!

For more information about using classic AppleWorks files with AppleWorks GS, see Appendix A.

How this book is organized

This book introduces you to AppleWorks GS and provides an overview of the commands used in all six applications. When you've finished this book, you should be comfortable with most of the important commands and operations in the program. The book is organized into the following sections:

Appendix C. AppleWorks GS Functions
Appendix D. Using the Edit Colors Command

The appendices include technical information that you may not need when you begin using AppleWorks GS. Appendix A includes information about using files that you created with classic AppleWorks. Appendix B describes the use of formulas in the database and spreadsheet applications. Appendix C lists the built-in functions that can be used in Apple-Works GS formulas. Appendix D explains the use of the special Edit Colors command that lets you select the colors that you want to use in each application from the thousands of colors available on your Apple IIGS.

The next step

Chapter 2 introduces basic operations on the Apple IIGS, including the Desktop environment, mouse operations, and the menu bar. If you're already familiar with those operations, you may want to go directly to Chapter 3 and begin working with AppleWorks GS.

Introduction to the Apple IIGS Environment

About this chapter

This chapter introduces basic operations on the Apple IIGS.

It introduces basic mouse operations, including how to move a pointer on the screen, how to select text or a graphics object for an action, and how to choose menu commands.

The chapter also introduces the Desktop environment, used by both the Apple IIGS and AppleWorks GS. It introduces icons, windows, and the menu bar found at the top of all six AppleWorks GS applications.

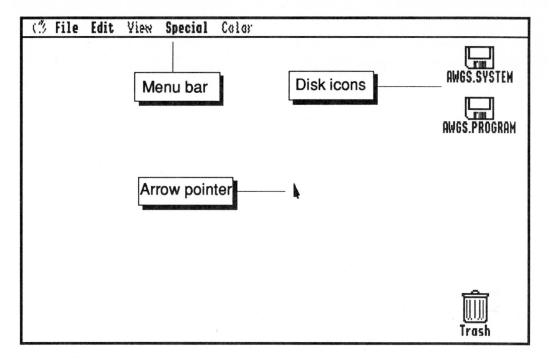

Figure 2-1 The Apple IIGS Desktop

The Apple IIGS Desktop

The AppleWorks GS package includes three disks:

AppleWorks GS System disk
AppleWorks GS Program disk
AppleWorks GS Utilities disk

When you start your computer with the AppleWorks GS System disk and Program disk, the opening screen displays the Apple IIGS Desktop (see Figure 2-1).

Your screen may not look exactly like this. One or more windows may be open already. The screen will display the Desktop in the same condition that you left it.

The screen represents a **desktop**, or a working area where you view your disks and documents. This particular desktop is often called the **Finder desktop**, since a special program called the IIGS Finder is controlling this display.

The Finder Desktop is an example of a **graphic interface**, since you can perform operations by manipulating graphic elements on the screen.

For example, you can copy disks or files by manipulating objects on the screen, rather than typing commands from the keyboard.

The desktop contains several **icons** (or pictures) that represent parts of your system.

The **disk icons** represent the disks in the current (or active) disk drives. A name is displayed beneath each disk icon; this name is the **volume name** of the disk.

At the bottom of the screen is a small icon labeled **Trash**. The Trash icon can be used to remove a document from a disk.

At the top of the screen is the Desktop **menu bar**, which contains commands to manipulate your disks and their contents.

An **arrow pointer** is also displayed on the desktop. When you move the mouse, the arrow pointer moves on the screen. You can use the arrow pointer to select objects on the screen for an action, to choose commands, or to move objects on the Desktop.

Selecting with the mouse

Your Apple IIGS computer follows the current location and movement of the mouse that is attached to the computer. As you move your mouse, some object is moved on the screen. You can use the mouse to move objects, to select the location for an action, or to select a command or choice on the screen.

A small **arrow pointer** is visible on the screen. This arrow pointer is one example of a **cursor**, a graphic element that marks your current location on the screen. In different AppleWorks GS applications, the cursor takes the form of an arrow pointer, a crossbar, or other shapes, depending on the action that is required.

Many AppleWorks GS operations require you to

1. Select an object or text for an action.
2. Choose the action to be taken with the selected object or text.

As you work with AppleWorks GS, your documents will contain both **text** and **objects**. Text is the familiar collection of characters that you probably have created with a typewriter in the past. An object is a graphic on the screen. For example, the disk icons that are displayed on the Desktop are objects.

The mouse is used to select objects and text, and to choose the actions to be taken on the selected objects and text.

Moving the arrow pointer

As you move your mouse, the arrow pointer on the screen follows the direction of the mouse:

- Move the mouse to the left, and the arrow pointer moves to the left.
- Move the mouse to the right, and the arrow moves to the right.
- Move the mouse directly toward you, and the arrow moves down the screen.
- Move the mouse directly away from you, and the arrow moves up the screen.

Selecting an object

An object is a graphic element on the Desktop or in an application. The icons that you see on the Desktop are examples of objects.

You can easily select an object for an action:

1   **Move the arrow pointer to the object that you want to select until the tip touches the object.**

2   **Click the mouse button.**

Clicking on the object selects the object for an action. When you select an object on the Desktop, the **selected** object is highlighted on the screen and displayed in inverse video.

For example, you can select one of the disk icons by clicking on the icon. When you click on the icon, it is selected and highlighted. (See Figure 2-2.)

After the desired object is selected, you can choose a command to operate on the selected object.

Double-clicking

In some cases you can select an object for an action and take a specific action at the same time by double-clicking on an object:

1   **Move the cursor to an object on the screen.**

2   **Click the mouse button twice quickly.**

This is called **double-clicking** on the object. When you double-click an object, you select the object and take some specific action at the same time. For example, when you double-click on a disk icon, the contents of the disk are displayed on the screen.

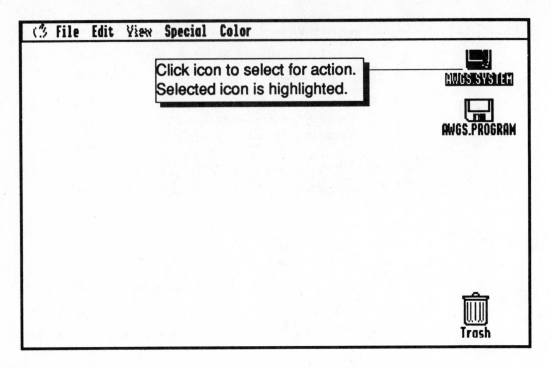

Figure 2-2 Selecting a disk icon

Selecting text

You can select an object for action by simply clicking on it. Once you begin to use AppleWorks GS, you may also want to select text for some action. To select text:

1. **Move the arrow pointer to the beginning of the text that you want to select.**

2. **Click the mouse button, and the text cursor appears.**

   This cursor is shaped like the letter "I" and is called the **I-beam cursor**.

3. **Hold down the mouse button, and move the mouse sideways.**

   Moving the mouse while holding down the mouse button is called **dragging**.

   As you drag the mouse sideways, the text that is touched by the I-beam is selected and highlighted on the screen. If you continue to hold the

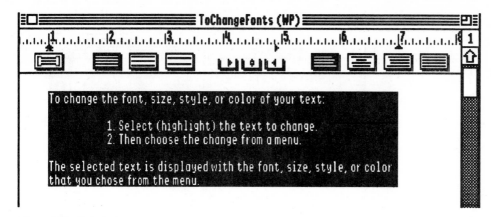

Figure 2-3 Selected text

mouse button down and drag downwards, lines of text below the original point are selected.

☐4☐ **Release the mouse button when the desired text is highlighted.**

After the desired text is selected, you can choose a command to operate on the selected text.

Example: Selecting text to change font and size

For example, in a word processing document, you can select text by dragging the cursor across desired text (see Figure 2-3).

After you select text, you can choose an action for the selected text. You might choose to display the text in a different font and size (see Figure 2-4).

Moving objects on the screen

You can use the mouse to physically move objects on the screen. To move an object with the mouse:

☐1☐ **Move the pointer until the tip touches the object that you want to move.**

☐2☐ **Hold down the mouse button, and drag the mouse sideways.**

As you drag the mouse, the object is moved on the screen.

☐3☐ **Release the mouse button when the object is in the desired new location.**

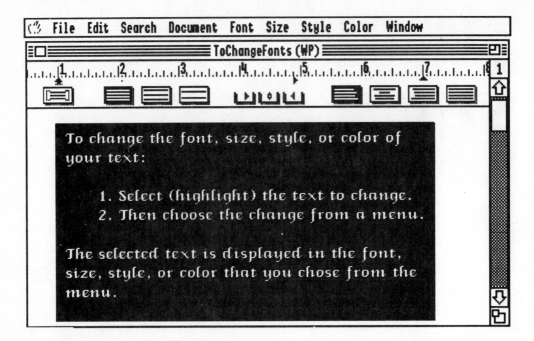

Figure 2-4 Text displayed in different font and size

Example: Moving icons

Any of the icons on the screen can be moved to a desired location.

| 1 | Move the arrow pointer to the icon that you want to move.

| 2 | Hold down the mouse button, and drag the mouse.

As you move the mouse, a ghost image that represents the icon moves with you. (See Figure 2-5.)

| 3 | When the object is in the desired location, release the mouse button. The object remains in the new location. (See Figure 2-6.)

Working with disk icons

When you begin to work with AppleWorks GS, the Desktop displays an icon for each disk. The name of the disk (or volume name) is displayed beneath each disk icon.

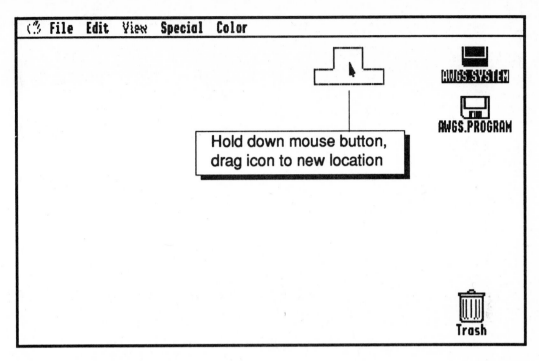

Figure 2-5 Moving disk icons

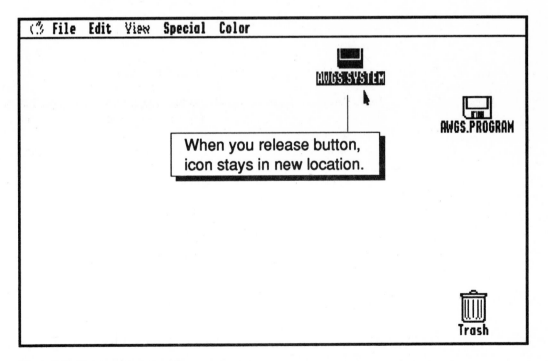

Figure 2-6 Disk icon in new location

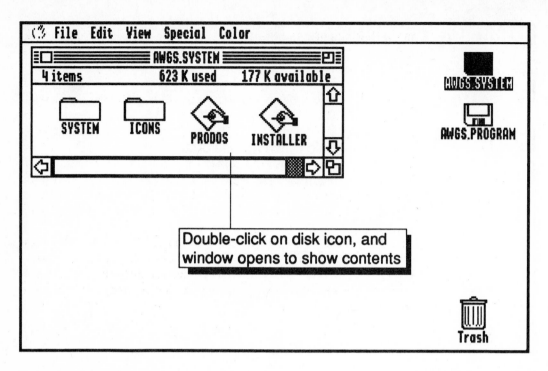

Figure 2-7   System disk window

Viewing the contents of a disk

To see the contents of a disk:

[1]   **Use the mouse to move the arrow to the desired disk icon.**

[2]   **Click the mouse button twice quickly.**

Double-clicking on the disk icon selected the icon and chose an action at the same time. Double-clicking on a disk icon displays the contents of the disk.

The AppleWorks GS System disk window

When you double-click on the AppleWorks GS System disk icon, a window opens on the Desktop and displays the contents of the disk. (See Figure 2-7.)

Note: *The display on your screen will not match this display exactly, since the contents and arrangement of the window may vary.*

This window displays the contents of the AppleWorks GS System disk. The contents of the disk are represented by the icons in the window. These icons can be shaped like small sheets of paper or other objects.

- An icon can represent an **application**, which is a program used to create documents. AppleWorks GS is an example of an application. Icons that represent applications usually have distinctive shapes or markings.
- An icon can represent a **document**, which contains information that you have entered into the computer. Each document that you create with AppleWorks GS will be displayed with its own icon. If you have used classic AppleWorks, a document is equivalent to an Apple-Works file.
- An icon can represent a **folder**. These folders can contain many individual documents, and a folder can also contain other folders. Folders are a convenient way to organize the documents on a disk. Icons that represent folders are easy to distinguish, since they are shaped like manila folders.

Using windows

The AppleWorks GS System disk window contains many of the elements that are found in any window. (See Figure 2-8.)

These elements include

- the **Title** bar, which contains the current name of the disk. The Title bar can be used to move the window on the screen.
- the **Close** box, which can be used to close the window. The box is often nicknamed the Go-Away box.
- the **Zoom** box, which can be used to quickly expand the window to fill the entire screen.
- the **Size** box, which is used to resize the window to a desired size. This box is often nicknamed the Grow box.

Using the Close box

1️⃣ **Move the arrow pointer to the Close box on the window and place the tip of the arrow inside the Close box.**

2️⃣ **Click the mouse button.**

The window is closed and collapses back into the disk icon.

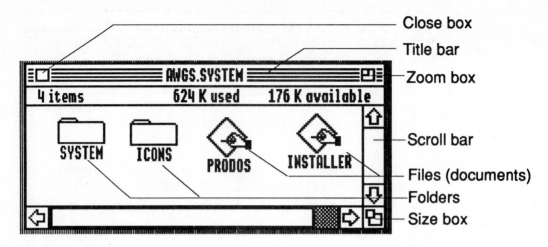

Figure 2-8 Common elements of all windows

Move the arrow pointer to the disk icon, and double-click the mouse button again.

The System disk window is displayed again.

Using the Zoom box

1 **Move the arrow pointer to the Zoom box on the window, and place the tip of the arrow inside the Zoom box.**

2 **Click the mouse button.**

The window display expands to fill the entire screen. (See Figure 2-9.)

To return the window to its original dimensions, move the arrow pointer to the Zoom box and click the mouse button again.

The System disk window is displayed again in its original size.

Using the Size box

1 **Move the arrow pointer to the Size box and place the tip of the arrow inside the box.**

2 **Hold down the mouse button, and drag the mouse sideways.**

As you drag the mouse, the window is resized on the screen. The window can be stretched and resized both horizontally and vertically. (See Figure 2-10.)

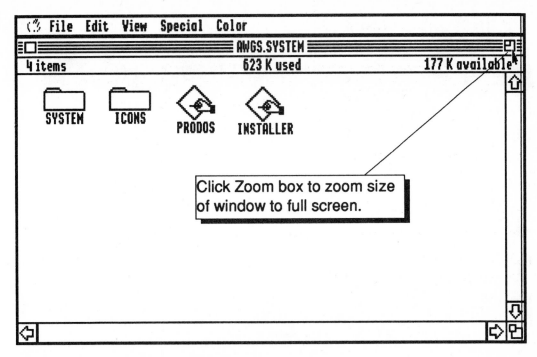

Figure 2-9 Clicking the Zoom box expands the window to the full screen

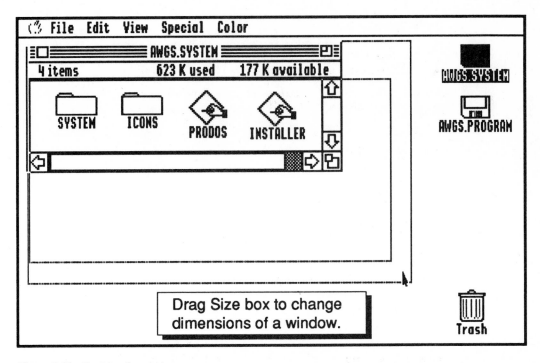

Figure 2-10 Resizing the window

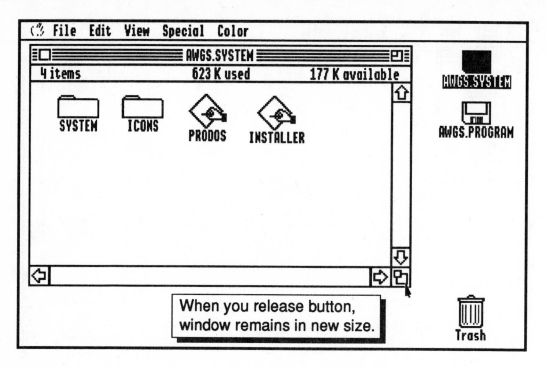

File Edit View Special Color

AWGS.SYSTEM

4 items   623 K used   177 K available

SYSTEM   ICONS   PRODOS   INSTALLER

AWGS.SYSTEM

AWGS.PROGRAM

When you release button,
window remains in new size.

Trash

Figure 2-11   The resized window

3   **Continue dragging the mouse until the window has the desired size and shape.**

Release the mouse button when the window has the desired size and shape. (See Figure 2-11.)

Moving a window

1   **Move the arrow pointer into the lined area of the Title bar of a window.**

Be careful not to place the arrow on the actual title that is displayed. To move the window, the tip of the arrow must be located in the lined area of the Title bar.

2   **Hold down the mouse button, and drag the window on the screen.**

A ghost image of the window moves on the screen as you drag the mouse. (See Figure 2-12.)

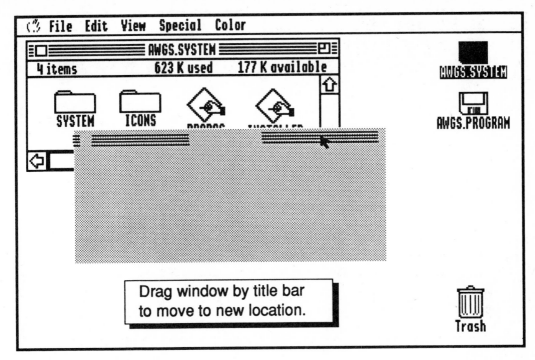

Figure 2-12 Moving the window

3 **Release the mouse button when the window is placed in the desired location. (See Figure 2-13.)**

Using scroll bars

As you resize the window, some of the window's contents may temporarily disappear from the screen. Don't panic . . . the contents are still there, and you can make them visible again by expanding the size of the window later.

You can also use the scroll bars to see window contents that don't fit in the current window.

Many AppleWorks GS applications create documents that are too large to fit in a document window, but scroll bars let you easily browse through the entire contents of a document. (See Figure 2-14.)

• To move upwards in a window, move the arrow pointer to the small arrow at the top of the scroll bar and click the mouse. The window moves upwards one line in the document and displays that part of your document.

• To move down in a window, move the arrow pointer to the small arrow at the top of the scroll bar and click the mouse. The window

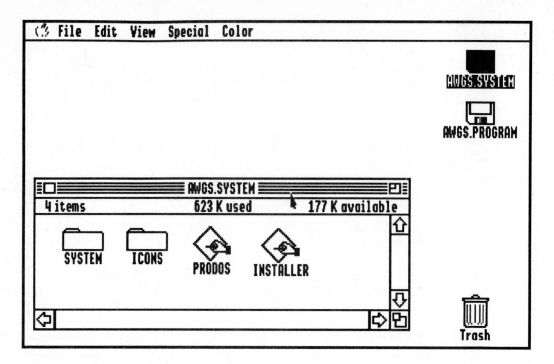

Figure 2-13   Moved window

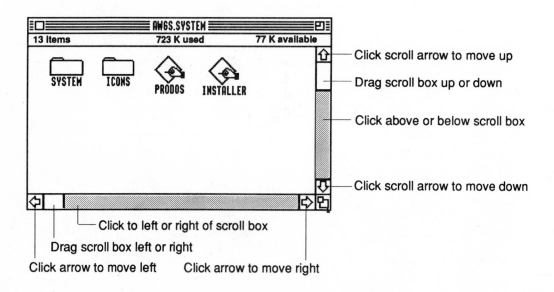

Click scroll arrow to move up

Drag scroll box up or down

Click above or below scroll box

Click scroll arrow to move down

Click to left or right of scroll box

Drag scroll box left or right

Click arrow to move left   Click arrow to move right

Figure 2-14   Scroll bars

moves down one line in the document and displays that part of your document.

As you move through a document, the scroll box moves up and down on the scroll bar to indicate your location in a document.

When the scroll box is at the top of the scroll bar, you are at the very beginning of a document. When the scroll box is at the bottom of the scroll bar, you are at the end of a document. When the box is in the middle of the scroll bar, you are in the middle of your document.

Shortcut: *To move quickly through sections of a window, click the mouse in the gray area of the scroll bar, above or below the scroll box.*

    If you click above the scroll box, the window moves to the previous page. If you click below the scroll box, the window moves to the next page.

Shortcut: *To move quickly to a specific part of a window, move the arrow into the scroll box and hold down the mouse button.*

    Drag the scroll box to a desired location in the scroll bar, and release the mouse button.

    The desired window contents are displayed. For example, drag the scroll box to the bottom of the scroll bar, and the contents at the bottom of the window are displayed.

Working with multiple windows

You can have more than one window open on the desktop at one time.

For instance, you might display the contents of a folder within a disk window, or you might display two windows representing two disks on the Desktop at the same time.

Exploring folders

The AppleWorks GS System disk contains some files collected in folders, and these folders are represented by folder icons in the window.

To see the contents of a folder:

1   **Move the arrow pointer until the tip touches the folder icon.**

    Be sure that the tip is inside the folder icon, and not on the name beneath the folder.

2   **Double-click on the folder icon.**

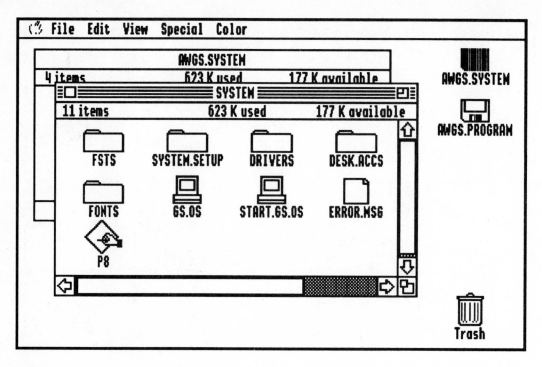

Figure 2-15 System Folder window

A new window is opened that displays the contents of the window. This window contains all of the elements seen in all Desktop windows, including the Close box, Zoom box, and Size box.

For example, if you double-click on the folder named System in the AppleWorks GS System disk, the window shown in Figure 2-15 appears.

3   **After you have viewed the contents of the folder, move the arrow pointer to the Close box and click on the box.**

The window closes and collapses back into the folder icon.

Opening Multiple Windows

You can also open multiple windows to display the contents of different disks on the Desktop.

If you double-click on one disk icon, a window displays the contents of that disk. If you then double-click on a second disk icon, a second window opens to display the contents of the second window.

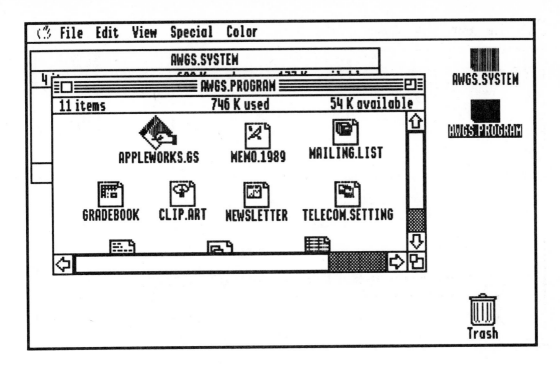

Figure 2-16 AppleWorks GS program disk

For example, if you double-click on the AppleWorks GS Program disk icon, a window opens on the Desktop and displays the contents of this disk. (See Figure 2-16.)

You can only work with one window at a time. This window is called the **active window**.

You can easily tell which window is the active window — the active window displays the lined Title bar. The Title bar in any other window is displayed as entirely white.

To make a specific window the active window, move the arrow pointer into the desired window and click the mouse. That window automatically becomes the new active window.

Overlapping windows

If you open two or more windows, the windows may overlap each other on the screen. Effectively, the windows are arranged in a stack of windows on the screen. Only one window can be the active window at any one time, and the active window is always the window at the top of the stack.

You can quickly move a desired window to the front of the stack of windows.

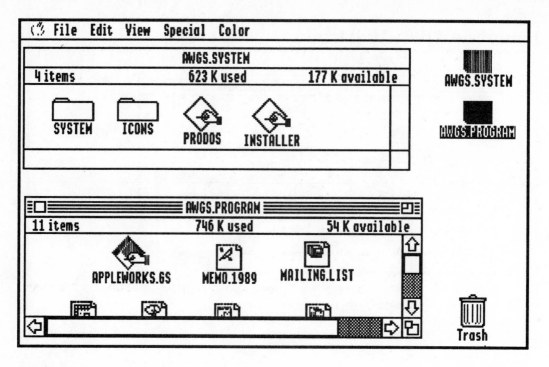

Figure 2-17 . System disk and program disk resized on Desktop

[1] **Move the arrow cursor into the window that you want to send to the front of the stack.**

[2] **Click the mouse button anywhere in the window.**

That window is moved to the front of the stack and becomes the active window.

Resizing and moving multiple windows

When multiple windows are displayed on the Desktop, you can use the Size box in each window to change the size and shape of each window.

You can also drag each window to a different location on the Desktop. With care, you can see the contents of two or more windows at the same time. For example, you can resize and move the System disk window and the Program disk window to view the contents of both windows at the same time (see Figure 2-17).

Remember: You can only work with one window at any one time. To make a specific window the active window, click anywhere in the window.

Using the Apple IIGS Desktop menu bar

At the top of the screen is the Apple IIGS Desktop menu bar. The menu bar contains the set of commands that are available to work with the contents of the Desktop.

These commands are organized into four separate menus: the File menu, the Edit menu, the View menu, and the Special menu.

Since the AppleWorks GS applications use menu bars similar to these, it is important to learn how to view menu commands and to choose menu commands.

Exploring menu commands

To see the commands that each menu contains:

1   **Move the arrow pointer to one of the four titles on the menu bar: File, Edit, View, and Special.**

2   **When the tip of the arrow touches one of the titles, hold down the mouse button.**

A pull-down menu appears beneath the title. For example, if you pull down the commands under File, you see the commands shown in Figure 2-18.

When you look at a list of menu commands, some of the commands are displayed in bold type, and some are displayed in dimmed, gray type.

Only the bold commands are currently available for use; the dimmed commands are not available and cannot be selected at that particular moment. Usually a command is dimmed because some other action must be taken before it can be used. For example, the Print command is dimmed and not available until you select the document to print.

When you look at some menu choices, a checkmark appears to the left of the command. A checkmark indicates that this choice is currently active. For example, on the View menu, a checkmark may appear to the left of the By Icon command. This indicates that you are currently viewing the contents of each window displayed as icons.

The Apple menu

The Apple symbol at the left of the menu bar also contains a pull-down menu. The commands on the Apple menu let you select and activate **desk accessories**, small programs that temporarily suspend your current activity for some special purpose. For example, a typical desk accessory might be a clock to display the current date and time or a calculator that

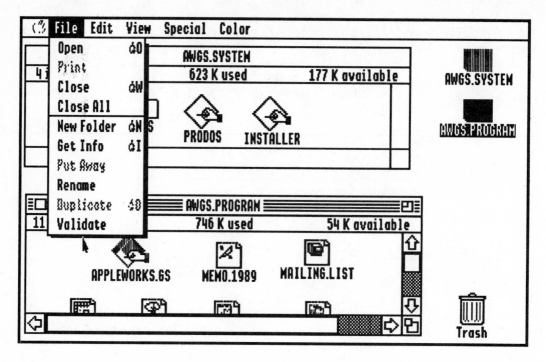

Figure 2-18 The Apple IIGS Desktop File menu

lets you perform calculations quickly on the screen. When you leave a desk accessory, you return to the main application that was temporarily suspended. Information about installing and removing desk accessories can be found in your Apple IIGS system documentation.

Choosing a menu command

1. Move the arrow to the desired title on the menu bar; and hold down the mouse button.

2. When the pull-down menu appears beneath the menu bar, continue to hold down the mouse button and slide the pointer down the menu choices.

As the arrow pointer touches each command on the pull-down menu, the command is temporarily highlighted.

3. When the desired command is highlighted, release the mouse button.

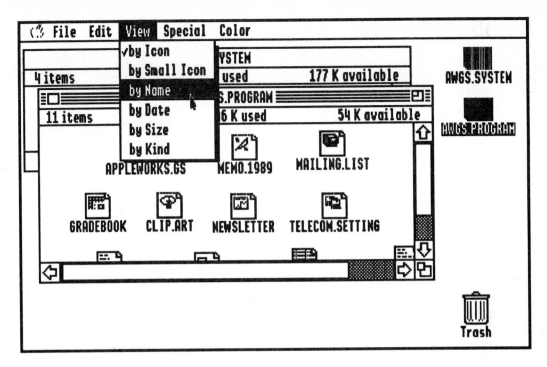

Figure 2-19 Select the View by Name command

The command that is highlighted when you release the mouse button is selected.

Example: Using the View menu

To demonstrate the use of the menu bar, you can change how the contents of the active window are displayed.

1. If the AppleWorks GS System disk window is not open, double-click on the disk icon to display the disk window.

2. Move the arrow pointer to the menu bar, and place the tip of the arrow on the word View. (See Figure 2-19.)

3. Hold down the mouse button, and the View menu is displayed.

4. Continue to hold down the mouse button, and slide the arrow pointer down the menu until the By Name command is selected.

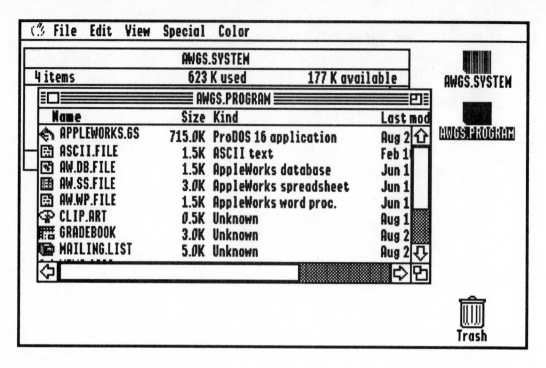

Figure 2-20 Window displayed by name

The contents of the current window are now displayed in a different way. Rather than displaying each document or folder on the disk as an icon, the contents of the disk are displayed alphabetically as a list of document and folder names, along with information about the size and date of each document. (See Figure 2-20.)

To display the contents of the disk by icon again, move the arrow pointer back to the View menu and select the By Icon command. The contents of the window are again represented by icons.

Keyboard equivalents

You can select some menu commands from the keyboard without using the mouse.

Many of the menu commands on each pull-down menu have symbols to the right of them. These symbols are the **keyboard equivalents** for each command.

For example, the New Folder command on the File menu is equivalent to typing Command-N on the keyboard. If you hold down the Command key (the key with the cloverleaf graphic on it) and tap the N key, the same operation is performed as if you had selected the New Folder command with the mouse.

The Apple IIGS Desktop commands

For more information on all of the commands that are available on the Apple IIGS Desktop menu bar, see your Apple IIGS system references.

The next step

Now that you're familiar with basic mouse operations and selecting commands from the menu bar, you're ready to start working with AppleWorks GS. Chapter 3 shows you how to launch AppleWorks GS and discusses the commands that are used in all six applications.

AppleWorks GS Common Commands

About this chapter

This chapter describes how to launch AppleWorks GS, the AppleWorks GS Desktop menu bar, and the common commands that are used in all six applications.

The topics in this chapter include

- Launching AppleWorks GS
- The AppleWorks GS Desktop menu bar
- The File menu common commands
- Printing your documents
- The Edit menu common commands
- The Windows menu common commands

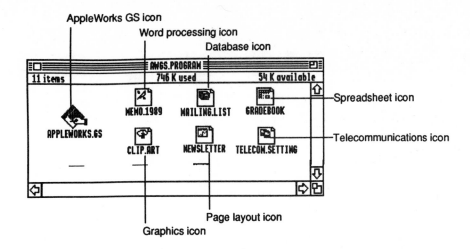

Figure 3-1 AppleWorks GS icons

Launching AppleWorks GS

When you turn on your Apple IIGS computer and load the AppleWorks GS System and Program disks, the Finder desktop displays the contents of the Program disk (see Figure 3-1).

The Program disk window displays the AppleWorks GS application and any documents or files present on the Program disk. The AppleWorks GS application has a distinctive icon, and documents created by AppleWorks GS are displayed with distinctive icons.

Files created with classic AppleWorks are also displayed with distinctive icons.

Note: *The window displayed by your AppleWorks Program disk will not look exactly like this window. Your Program disk window will display the AppleWorks GS application icon, but the documents on your disk will be different from the documents shown in this window.*

To launch AppleWorks GS

1   **Move the arrow pointer until the tip of the arrow touches the AppleWorks GS icon.**

Be sure that the tip is touching the icon and not the name beneath the icon.

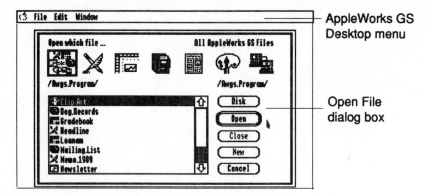

AppleWorks GS
Desktop menu

Open File
dialog box

Figure 3-2 Opening screen after AppleWorks GS is loaded

2   **Click the mouse once, and the AppleWorks GS icon is selected and highlighted.**

3   **Move the arrow pointer to the File menu at the top of the screen, and select the Open command.**

AppleWorks GS is loaded into memory, and the application is ready to use.

The opening screen (Figure 3-2) shows the Open File dialog box, which can be used to create new documents or load documents previously saved. Using the Open File dialog is discussed below.

Shortcut: *Move the arrow to the AppleWorks GS icon, and double-click on the icon. AppleWorks GS is loaded into memory, and the application is ready to use.*

The AppleWorks GS Desktop menu bar

After you launch AppleWorks GS, the AppleWorks GS Desktop appears on the screen. At the top of the screen is the AppleWorks GS Desktop menu bar.

This menu bar is similar to the IIGS Finder Desktop menu bar. It includes the File menu, the Edit menu, and the Windows menu.

As you use each of the six individual AppleWorks GS applications, you will find that each of the applications has its own menu bar. For example, the word processing application has a menu bar, the database application has a menu bar, and so forth. Each application, however, includes a File menu, an Edit menu, and a Windows menu.

AppleWorks GS common commands

All of the AppleWorks GS applications share common commands on the File, Edit, and Windows menus.

The common commands include operations used for opening documents, saving documents, and printing documents. Once you learn to perform these operations in one application, you will use the same commands in all of the other applications.

This chapter discusses those commands that are common to all of the AppleWorks GS applications.

The File and Windows menus are used in a similar way by each application. The Edit menu, however, is somewhat different in each application. Each of the AppleWorks GS applications adds commands to the Edit menu beyond the common commands. These additional Edit commands handle specific operations within the application. The use of these additional Edit commands are discussed in the chapters that deal with each specific application.

The File menu common commands

The File menu in each AppleWorks GS application contains the commands that control file operations. This menu is used to open new documents, open saved documents, save your documents, print your documents, and handle other file operations. (See Figure 3-3.)

File
New...
Open...
Close
Save
Save As...
Delete File...
Import File...
Choose Printer...
Page Setup...
Print...
Print Merge...
Quit

Figure 3-3
File menu

Using the New command

The New command opens a new document for one of the AppleWorks GS applications.

1 **Select the New command from the File menu.**

The New File dialog box appears (see Figure 3-4).

The New File dialog box contains six icons that represent the six AppleWorks GS applications. One of the icons is surrounded by a selection rectangle. The selection rectangle determines the type of new document that will be created.

2 **Move the arrow pointer to the icon that represents the type of document that you want to create, and click the mouse button.**

The selection rectangle appears around the selected icon.

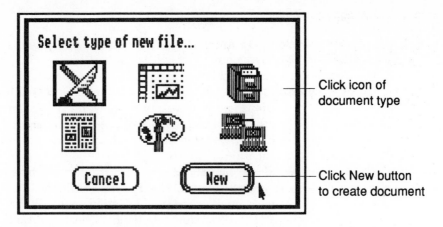

Select type of new file...

Cancel   New

Click icon of
document type

Click New button
to create document

Figure 3-4 New File dialog box

3 **Move the arrow pointer to the New button, and click the mouse button.**

A new document window appears on the screen. The name in the title bar of the document is Untitled; a name is given to the document when you save the document for the first time.

Shortcut: *You can quickly open a new AppleWorks GS document:*

1 **Select New from the File menu.**

2 **Double-click on the icon that represents the desired type of document.**

Using the Open command

The Open command lets you open documents that have been previously saved. You can also use the Open command to create a new document.

When you choose the Open command, the Open File dialog box appears (see Figure 3-5). This box automatically appears when AppleWorks GS is first loaded.

The application icons

At the top of the dialog box is a display of seven icons. These icons represent the six applications that are available for your use. The icon that is selected controls the type of document that is displayed in the document list box.

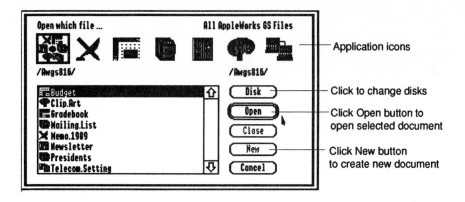

Figure 3-5 Open File dialog box

The first icon is the **AllTypes** icon. This icon represents small versions of the other six icons. When you choose the Open command, this icon is selected and surrounded by a rectangle.

The second icon represents the **word processing** application, used to create text documents.

The third icon represents the **spreadsheet** application, used to enter information in rows and columns, perform calculations on the information, and generate graphs of the information.

The fourth icon represents the **database** application, used to store and retrieve information and print out summary reports.

The fifth icon represents the **graphics** application, used to create full-color graphic images.

The sixth icon represents the **page layout** application, used to combine text and graphics into high-quality multi-page documents.

The seventh icon represents the **telecommunications** application, used to connect your computer to a remote computer and exchange information.

Selecting one of the application icons

When you choose the Open command, the AllTypes icon is selected and surrounded by a rectangle. Documents that can be opened by all six applications are displayed in the document list box.

If you select one of the six application icons, only documents that can be opened by that application are displayed in the document list box.

To select one of the six AppleWorks GS applications, move the arrow pointer to the desired application icon, and click the mouse.

The selected icon is now surrounded by the selection rectangle.

The Open File document list box

Beneath the document type icons is a scroll box that displays the documents on the current disk.

Note: *AppleWorks GS can only work with one disk at a time, and this disk is called the **current disk**. To change the current disk, click the Disk button in the dialog box, and the next available disk becomes the current disk. If the desired disk has not yet been placed in a disk drive, eject the current disk from its disk drive, and click the Disk button.*

If you have selected the AllTypes icon, documents that can be opened by any AppleWorks GS application are displayed in the document list box.

If you select one of the six application icons, documents that can be opened by that particular application are listed in the document list box. For example, if you click on the word processing icon, documents that can be opened by the word processing application are listed in the document list box.

The document list box may contain more names than can be displayed in the box. You can use the scroll arrows on the document list box to see the names that are not currently shown.

The Open File dialog box buttons

The Open File dialog box contains five buttons. A button is an oval that can be clicked to select an action.

- Click the New button to create a new document of the selected type.
- Click the Open button to open the document that is selected in the document list box.
- Click the Close button to close an open document. If the command is dimmed, no documents are currently open and the command is not available.
- Click the Disk button to display the documents found on another disk. The name of the current disk is displayed above the document list box. To use the contents of another disk, eject the current disk from its disk drive, insert the different disk, and click the Disk button until the name of the different disk is displayed.
- Click the Cancel button to cancel the Open File command and return to the AppleWorks GS desktop.

Note: *Most dialog boxes have one button that is surrounded by a double-oval. This is the button that you would select most often. You can choose this button from the keyboard by pressing the Return key.*

Most dialog boxes contain a Cancel button. Click the Cancel button to cancel the current operation. This removes the dialog box from the

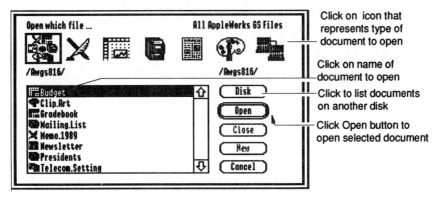

Figure 3-6 Open File Dialog box, saved files

screen and returns you to the active window. You can select the Cancel button from the keyboard by pressing the Esc key.

Opening a saved document

1   **Choose the Open command from the File menu.**

The Open File dialog box appears (see Figure 3-6).

2   **Select the icon that represents the type of document that you want to open.**

The documents that can be opened by the selected application are listed in the document list box. You can select the AllTypes icon, and all document types are displayed.

3   **Click the name of the document that you want to open.**

If the document is not visible in the document list, click on the arrows in the scroll bars to bring the rest of the list into view. If the document is not on the current disk, eject the disk, place the desired disk in the drive, and click the Disk button.

After you click the name of the document that you want to open, the name of the document is selected and highlighted.

4   **Click the Open button in the dialog box.**

A new document window is opened and the contents of the selected document appear in the window.

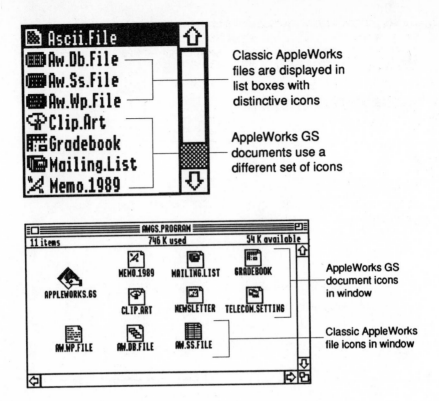

Figure 3-7 Classic AppleWorks files have special icons in a list box or a window

Shortcut: *To open a document quickly:*

| 1 | **Select the Open command on the File menu.** |

| 2 | **Double-click on the name of the document that you want to open.** |

What kinds of documents can be opened?

Each of the six AppleWorks GS applications can open documents previously created and saved by the application.

AppleWorks GS applications can also open files created by other Apple II programs. The word processing application can open files created by classic AppleWorks or MultiScribe GS, or files stored as ASCII text. The database application can open classic AppleWorks database files. The spreadsheet can open classic AppleWorks spreadsheet files. The graphics application can open graphics stored in PICT, APF, Paint, or Screen formats.

These documents are displayed in the document list box with distinctive icons to distinguish them from documents created with AppleWorks GS. (See Figure 3-7.)

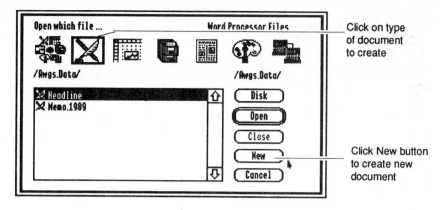

Figure 3-8 Creating a new document with Open File

Creating a new document with the Open command

| 1 | Choose the Open command on the File menu.

The Open File dialog box appears (see Figure 3-8).

| 2 | Select the icon that represents the type of document that you want to create.

| 3 | Move the arrow pointer to the New button, and click the mouse button.

The selected application is loaded into your computer and a new document window of the selected type appears on the screen. The name in the title bar of the document is Untitled; a name is given to the document when you save the document for the first time.

Shortcut: *You can quickly open a new document:*

| 1 | Select Open from the File menu.

| 2 | Double-click on the icon that represents the type of document that you want to create.

Using the Close command

The Close command closes the current active window. To close the active window, select the Close command from the File menu.

If the contents of the active window have not been saved, a dialog box appears (see Figure 3-9).

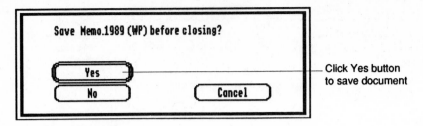

Figure 3-9   Save Before Close dialog box

Click the Save button to save the contents of the active window. Click the No button to close the window without saving the contents of the window. Click the Cancel button to return to the active window.

Using the Save command

AppleWorks GS provides two commands to save your work: the Save As command and the Save command.

The Save As command lets you provide a name for your document and select the drive where a storage disk is located. The Save command saves your work using the name and disk that you last specified with the Save As command.

When you select the Save command, AppleWorks GS repeats the last save operation. Your document is saved with the same name that you last specified and on the disk that you last specified.

If you choose the Save command and the document has not been saved previously, the Save As dialog box is displayed. See the next section for a discussion of the Save As command.

Use with Caution!

Use the Save command with caution. If you are working on a document and use the Save command, the current version of the document is saved and replaces the previous version.

Suppose, for example, that you are working on a document called TermPaper. If you use the Save command, the current version of the document is saved and replaces the old saved version of TermPaper.

If you would like to save the new version of a document without replacing the old saved version of the document, use the Save As command to give the new version a different name from the old version.

How often should you save?

How often should you save your document? There is no hard-and-fast answer to that question, and there are many different opinions. Ask your-

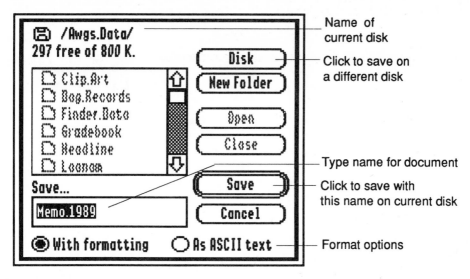

Figure 3-10 Save As dialog box

self this question periodically as you work: "Would I be annoyed to retype the text that I've added since the last Save?" If the answer to the question is yes, then it's probably time to save again.

Using the Save As command

The Save As command lets you provide a name for your document and select the drive where a storage disk is located. You can select the Save command later and your work is saved using the name and disk that you last specified with the Save As command.

To use the Save As command:

1 **Select the Save As command from the File menu.**

The Save As dialog box appears (see Figure 3-10).

2 **The name of the current disk is displayed at the top of the box.**

If you want to store your document on a different disk, click the Disk button until the name of the disk that you want to use appears.

If you want to store your document on a disk that is not currently in a disk drive, eject one of the current disks and insert the storage disk. Click the Disk button until the name of the desired disk is displayed.

Note: *A new blank disk must be formatted before it can be used to save your documents. The documentation that came with your Apple IIGS System Disk tells you how to format a blank disk.*

3   **Type in the desired name for the document.**

You can use any legal name permitted by the Apple IIGS operating system. The current guidelines for names are found in your Apple IIGS system references.

4   **Click on the desired formatting button.**

Different applications provide different formatting options. For example, you can save a word processing document either with all formatting preserved or as ASCII text. ASCII text is a simplified format that removes all special AppleWorks GS formatting; saving a document as ASCII text makes it easier to transfer to other computer systems or other programs, but it removes all special AppleWorks GS features.

Unless you have a special reason to choose ASCII text, save your documents with the AppleWorks GS format.

5   **Click on the Save button.**

Your document is saved on the selected disk with the name that you provided. The name that you provided is also displayed in the title bar of the document.

Saving different versions with the Save As command

Sometimes you may want to save different versions of a document or you may want to save two copies of the same document. For example, if you are working on a document that you saved with the name TermPaper, you might want to save a second copy of the document.

You can save different versions of a document with the Save As command:

1   **Select the Save As command from the File menu.**

2   **When the Save As dialog box appears, type in a different name for the document.**

3   **Click the Save button.**

When you click the Save button, the document will be saved with a different name, and the original version of the document will still be saved with the original name.

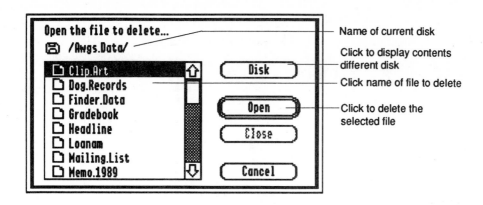

Figure 3-11   Delete File dialog box

Using the Delete File command

The Delete File command lets you remove files from a disk. This is particularly convenient when a storage disk is too full to save the current document. You can use the Delete File command to remove one or more documents from the storage disk and then save the current document without leaving AppleWorks GS.

To use the Delete File command:

1. **Select the Delete File command from the File menu.**

The Delete File dialog box appears (see Figure 3-11).

2. **The name of the current disk is displayed at the top of the box.**

If you want to delete a document on a different disk, click the Disk button until the name of the disk that you want to use appears.

3. **Click the name of the document that you want to delete.**

4. **Click the Open button to open the file to delete.**

A confirming dialog box appears to make sure that you want to delete the file. Click the OK button, and the file is deleted.

Shortcut: *Double-click on the name of the file to delete. The confirming dialog box appears. Click the OK button, and the file is deleted.*

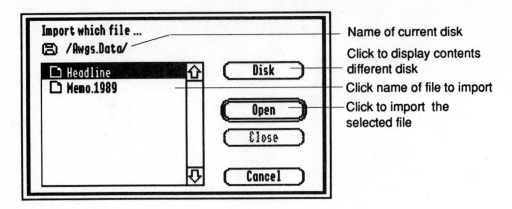

Figure 3-12   Import File dialog box

Using the Import File command

The Import File command pastes the entire contents of a file at your current location in a document. This command is different from the Open File command. The Open command is used to open a saved document into its own document window. You would use the Import File command after you have created a document window, entered some information, and then want to copy the contents of another file at some specific location in the document.

To use the Import File command

1. Open an AppleWorks GS document, and place the cursor at some desired location in the document.

2. Choose the Import File command from the File menu.

The Import File dialog box appears (see Figure 3-12).
The name of the current disk is displayed at the top of the box.
If you want to import a document that is on a different disk, click the Disk button until the name of the disk that you want to use appears.

3. Click the name of the document to import.

4. Click the Open button to copy the contents of the file into the active document at the current location.

Shortcut: *Double-click on the name of the file to import, and the contents of the file are pasted at the current location.*

What files can be imported?

Each of the AppleWorks GS applications can import different files.

The word processing application can import other AppleWorks GS word processing documents, as well as classic AppleWorks word processing files, MultiScribe GS files, or ASCII text files.

The database application can import ASCII text, graphics stored in PICT, APF, Paint, or Screen formats, or graphics created by Apple-Works GS.

The spreadsheet application can import ASCII text files.

The graphics application can import AppleWorks GS graphics, as well as graphics stored in PICT, APF, Paint, or Screen formats.

The page layout application can import AppleWorks GS word processing documents, as well as classic AppleWorks, MultiScribe GS, or ASCII text files. It can also import AppleWorks GS graphics, as well as graphics stored in PICT, APF, Paint, or Screen formats.

The telecommunication application can import AppleWorks GS word processing documents, as well as classic AppleWorks, MultiScribe GS, or ASCII text files.

Additional information about importing files is found in Chapter 18, Transferring Information.

Printing your documents

After you've created and saved a document, you can print out the document on your printer. Four commands on the File menu control printing operations: the Choose Printer command, the Page Setup command, the Print command, and the Print Merge command.

You only have to select the Choose Printer command and the Page Setup command once during an AppleWorks GS session. Unless you need to change the settings later in the session, you don't need to select these commands again.

Using the Choose Printer command

The Choose Printer command is used to select the printer to use.

1 **Select the Choose Printer command from the File menu.**

The Choose Printer dialog box appears (see Figure 3-13).

2 **Click on the type of printer that you are using and the printer port where the printer is connected.**

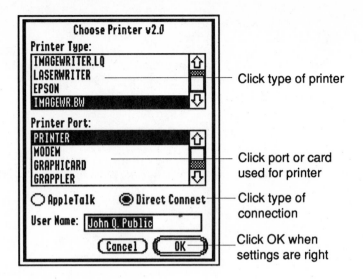

Figure 3-13   Choose Printer dialog box

When you first choose this command, these choices are set to Imagewriter and Printer port.

3   **If your printer is directly connected to your computer, click the Direct Connect button. If you are connected to an AppleTalk network, click the AppleTalk button.**

(If your computer is directly connected to a LaserWriter, you should click the AppleTalk button.)

4   **You can type a name in the User Name input bar; this is optional and only applies if you are using an AppleTalk network.**

5   **When the settings are correct, click the OK button.**

Using the Page Setup command

The Page Setup command lets you specify the type of paper that you are using and certain printing information. There are two different versions of the Page Setup command, depending on the printer chosen in the Choose Printer command.

Page Setup for the Imagewriter

1   **Select the Page Setup command from the File menu.**

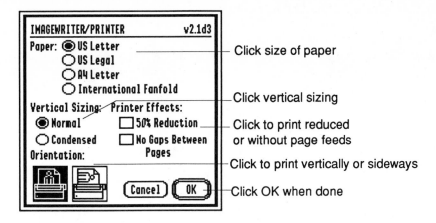

Figure 3-14   Imagewriter Page Setup dialog box

The Page Setup dialog box for the Imagewriter appears (see Figure 3-14).

[2] **Click on the type of paper that you are using, the desired orientation, and any special printer effects that you wish.**

[3] **When the settings are correct, click on the OK button.**

Page Setup for the LaserWriter

[1] **Select the Page Setup command from the File menu.**

The Page Setup dialog box for the LaserWriter appears (see Figure 3-15).

[2] **Click on the type of paper that you are using, the desired orientation, and any special printer effects that you wish.**

[3] **Click on the OK button.**

Using the Print command

The Print command prints your document on the selected printer. When you select the Print command, a dialog box is displayed. There are two versions of the Print dialog box, depending on the printer chosen with the Choose Printer command.

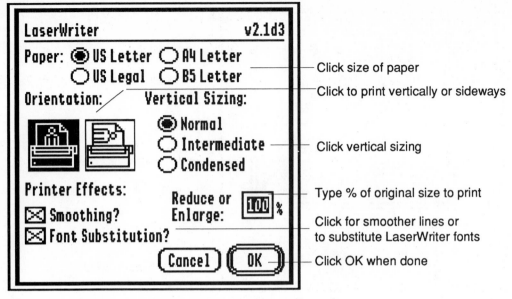

Click size of paper

Click to print vertically or sideways

Click vertical sizing

Type % of original size to print

Click for smoother lines or
to substitute LaserWriter fonts

Click OK when done

Figure 3-15   LaserWriter Page Setup dialog box

Printing with the Imagewriter

1. **Select the Print command from the File menu.**

The Print dialog box for the ImageWriter appears (see Figure 3-16).

2. **Select the desired quality, and enter the pages to print and number of copies.**

3. **Click the OK button.**

Your document is printed on the specified printer.

Printing with the LaserWriter

1. **Select the Print command from the File menu.**

The Print dialog box for the LaserWriter appears (see Figure 3-17).

2. **Select the desired quality, and enter the pages to print and number of copies.**

3. **Click the OK button.**

Your document is printed on the specified printer.

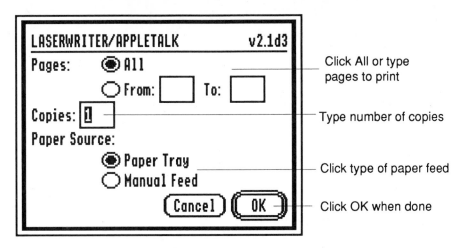

```
IMAGEWRITER/PRINTER
Quality:    ● Better Text
            ○ Better Color ————————— Click desired quality
            ○ Draft
Page range:
            ● All ———————————— Click All or type
            ○ From: [    ] To: [    ]      pages to print
Copies: [1] ———————————————————— Type number of copies
Paper Feed: ● Automatic ○ Manual ———— Click type of paper feed
                                      —— Click if color printer and image
□ Color        ( Cancel )  ( OK ) —— Click OK when done
```

Figure 3-16   Imagewriter Print dialog box

The Print Merge command

The Print Merge command is used to combine information stored in a database with a word processing document. This command lets you produce form letters or other documents that include specialized information in multiple copies of a document.

This command is only available in the word processing application. The command is dimmed and not available in all other applications.

```
LASERWRITER/APPLETALK      v2.1d3
Pages:    ● All ————————————— Click All or type
          ○ From: [    ] To: [    ]       pages to print
Copies: [1] ———————————————————— Type number of copies
Paper Source:
          ● Paper Tray ——————————— Click type of paper feed
          ○ Manual Feed
                ( Cancel )  ( OK ) —— Click OK when done
```

Figure 3-17   LaserWriter Print dialog box

The use of the Print Merge command is described in Chapter 8, Mail Merge and Mailing Labels.

Using the Quit command

This command lets you quit AppleWorks GS and return to the Apple IIGS Finder Desktop.

To select the Quit command, choose Quit from the File menu. If any open windows have not been saved, a dialog box appears for each window to let you save the document before leaving the application.

After all windows are closed, you are returned to the Apple IIGS Desktop.

The Edit menu common commands

Figure 3-18
Edit menu

The Edit menu provides special commands to use the Apple IIGS Clipboard. (See Figure 3-18.) These commands include the Cut, Copy, and Paste commands. These commands are available in all six applications. They let you easily transfer information between documents.

The Edit menu also includes the Undo command to let you reverse the last action taken, and the Select All command to quickly select the entire contents of a document.

Using the Undo command

The Undo command is available in all AppleWorks GS applications except the telecommunications application.

The Undo command lets you reverse the last action taken in the application. To reverse the action, select the Undo command on the Edit menu.

Since each application includes very different possible actions, the actual operation of the Undo command varies in each application. Some actions cannot be undone; if an action cannot be reversed, the command is dimmed on the Edit menu.

The Redo command

After you choose the Undo command, the Undo command is temporarily replaced on the Edit menu by the Redo command. The Redo command lets you reverse the Undo operation.

This command is only available until a new action is taken. Once a new action is taken, you cannot reverse the most recent Undo operation.

The Apple IIGS Clipboard

The Clipboard is a special area of your computer's memory that stores temporary copies of information. It provides an easy way to transfer information from one location to another. The Clipboard can be used in all six AppleWorks GS applications. You can easily transfer text or graphics from one application to another with the Clipboard.

The Edit menu provides the Cut, Copy, and Paste commands to transfer information with the Clipboard. Additional information about the Clipboard can be found in Chapter 18, Transferring Information.

Using the Cut command

When you select the Cut command, any selected text or graphics are deleted from a document and copied to the Clipboard. This operation is similar to using scissors to physically cut information from a paper document and placing the information aside for future use.

To use the Cut command:

1. **Select the text or graphics object that you want to remove from the document and copy to the Clipboard.**

2. **Choose the Cut command from the Edit menu.**

The selected text or objects are removed from the document and copied to the Clipboard. The contents of the Clipboard can be viewed with the Show Clipboard command on the Windows menu.

You can copy the contents of the Clipboard to another location with the Paste command on the Edit menu.

Using the Copy command

When you select the Copy command, any selected text or graphics are duplicated and copied to the Clipboard. This operation is similar to making a xerox copy of text or graphics and placing the copy aside for future use.

To use the Copy command:

1. **Select the text or graphics object that you want to duplicate and copy to the Clipboard.**

2 **Choose the Copy command from the Edit menu.**

A duplicate of the selected text or object is copied to the Clipboard. The contents of the Clipboard can be viewed with the Show Clipboard command on the Windows menu.

You can copy the contents of the Clipboard to another location with the Paste command on the Edit menu.

Using the Paste command

When you select the Paste command, any text or graphics on the Clipboard is placed at the current location in a document.

This operation is similar to taping a paper copy of text or graphics into a document.

To use the Paste command:

1 **Move the location of the cursor in a document where you want to copy the contents of the Clipboard.**

2 **Choose the Paste command from the Edit menu.**

The current contents of the Clipboard are copied at the current location.

Note: *AppleWorks GS provides a special feature called control-dragging that lets you perform an operation similar to Copy and Paste visually on the screen. If you hold down the Control key while dragging selected objects, a copy of the selected object can be visually dragged to a new location.*

Using the Clear command

The Clear command erases the currently selected information.

To use the Clear command, select the information that you want to erase, and then choose the Clear command from the Edit menu.

Using the Select All command

The Select All command usually selects all of the contents of the current active window.

In the word processing, database, spreadsheet, and graphics applications, the entire contents of the current document are selected when you choose the Select All command. The entire document is highlighted and displayed in inverse video.

In the page layout application, the entire contents of the current page are selected by the Select All command, unless you are working with a text object. If an insertion point is selected inside a text object, the Select All command selects all the text in the object and all text linked to the object (see Chapter 14).

In the telecommunications command, the Select All command selects the current review buffer, the most recent 256 lines of text in the session (see Chapter 16).

The Window menu common commands

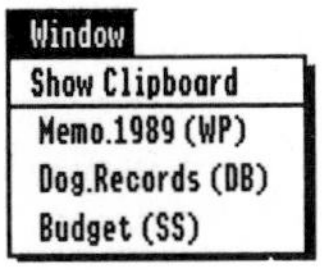

Figure 3-19
Window menu

The Window menu lists all document windows that are open. (See Figure 3-19.) You can use this menu to select any open document to make it the active window. You can also use the Show Clipboard command to view the contents of the Clipboard.

To select a new active window:

1 | **Pull down the Window menu.**

A list of the current open documents is displayed.

2 | **Select one of the documents listed on the menu.**

The selected document is displayed on the screen as the new active document window.

Using the Show Clipboard command

The Cut or Copy command on the Edit menu can be used to copy selected text or graphics objects to the Clipboard, a temporary storage area in your computer's memory. The contents of the Clipboard can be copied to another location using the Paste command on the Edit menu.

The Show Clipboard command lets you review the current contents of the Clipboard.

To use the Show Clipboard command:

1 | **Choose the Show Clipboard command on the Windows menu.**

A window is opened to display the Clipboard contents. You cannot edit the contents of this window. (See Figure 3-20.)

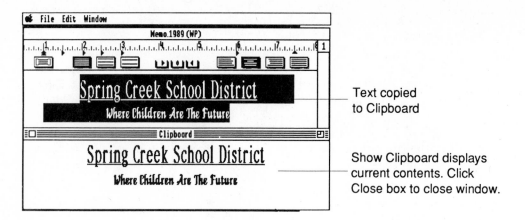

Text copied
to Clipboard

Show Clipboard displays
current contents. Click
Close box to close window.

Figure 3-20   Show Clipboard window

2 **After reviewing the contents, close the window by clicking on the Close box or choosing the Close command on the File menu.**

The next step

This chapter discussed the commands that are common to all six Appleworks GS applications. Now you're ready to begin working with the individual applications, and Chapter 4 begins with one of the most useful — word processing.

Chapter 4

Creating a Word Processing Document

About this chapter

This chapter introduces the use of the AppleWorks GS word processing application. The chapter includes

- Word processing concepts
- AppleWorks GS special features
- The word processing document window
- The word processing menu bar
- The word processing ruler
- Setting the ruler
- Entering your text
- Editing your text
- Saving your text
- Printing your word processing document
- The next step

Word processing concepts

Word processing simply means using the computer to create text, and many people discover that word processing is one of the most useful computer applications. The AppleWorks GS word processing application replaces your ordinary typewriter with a powerful electronic writing tool.

When you create a document on an ordinary typewriter, it is inconvenient to make corrections or rearrange parts of the document. On some typewriters it isn't easy to correct even minor typing mistakes. As a result, most people aren't encouraged to revise and improve a document.

A good word processor is like a super-typewriter, offering all of the features of a typewriter, as well as significant advantages. A word processor makes it easy to draft your document and easy to make changes in your document. Minor typing errors can be erased with the touch of a key, and you can make small (or large) changes quickly anywhere in the document. That makes it easy to revise and improve your work, so that you can concentrate on your ideas, rather than the mechanics of typing.

Basic word processing operations

The AppleWorks GS word processing application provides a full set of basic word processing operations.

- You can create text on the Apple IIGS screen.
- You can make changes in the text; this is called text editing.
- You can save your document on a storage disk for future use.
- You can print one or more copies of your document.

In addition to these basic features, AppleWorks GS provides many special features.

AppleWorks GS special features

The basic word processing features help you create and print basic text documents. The AppleWorks GS word processing application also lets you produce attractive and professional documents by providing many special features. These include the use of different fonts, in different sizes and styles, and color.

Text fonts

A font is a complete set of characters (letters, numbers, and common symbols) in one type face, including caps, lowercase, and punctuation marks.

On an ordinary typewriter, only one font is available: the particular set of characters that are available when you press the keys. AppleWorks GS lets you use many different fonts in a document. The names of fonts that are available include

Courier font

Geneva font

Helvetica font

Monaco font

Shaston font

Times font

Venice font

You can mix these fonts in your documents, and you can add more fonts to this list. For more information on fonts, see Changing Text Fonts in Chapter 5.

Different font sizes

You can also change the size of the fonts used in your document. Font size is measured in points. Some examples of the sizes available are

9 point text   10 point text

12 point text   18 point

20 point   24 point

For more information, see Changing Text Fonts in Chapter 5.

Different text styles

A style describes the way that text is displayed. For example, typical styles include bold, underline, or italic styles. You can include many different styles in an AppleWorks GS word processing document, including

bold

italic

underline

outline

shadow

You can also mix styles. For example, you can specify that text should be bold, underlined, and outlined.

This is bold, underlined, and outline.

Examples of all available styles are shown later under Style menu. The detailed use of fonts, sizes, and styles is discussed in Chapter 5.

Different text colors

AppleWorks GS takes advantage of the color capabilities of your Apple IIGS computer. You can select specific colors for some or all of the text in your documents. The text can be set to any of 16 colors in each document.

Spell-checking and synonyms

AppleWorks GS includes a spelling dictionary, which can check the spelling of words in your document. It also contains a thesaurus, which can be used to suggest synonyms for words in your document. You will find a more extensive discussion of spell-checking and synonyms in Chapter 5.

Mail-merge documents

AppleWorks GS lets you create special documents that combine a word processing document with information stored in the database application. These special documents let you print several copies of a document, with specialized information printed at specific locations within the document.

One use of this feature is the production of form letters, often called mail-merge documents. You can store a collection of names and addresses in a database document, and then print multiple copies of a letter, with a different name and address printed in appropriate locations in each copy.

Merge documents are described in Chapter 8, Merge Documents and Mailing Labels.

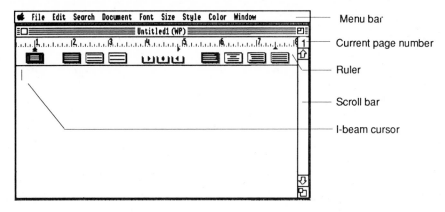

Figure 4-1 New word processing document

Creating a new word processing document

When you are ready to begin a new word processing document, there are two ways that you can create the new document:

- You can create a new document with the New command on the File menu.
- You can create a new document with the Open command on the File menu.

Using the New or Open command to create a new document is described in Chapter 3, AppleWorks GS Common Commands.

Shortcut: *You can quickly open a new word processing document:*

1 **Select New from the File menu.**

2 **Double-click on the word processing icon.**

The word processing document window

When you open a word processing document, a document window appears on the screen. (See Figure 4-1.)

Most of the word processing window consists of blank space. This blank space is equivalent to a blank piece of paper, and you will type your text into this space.

The new word processing document window includes features found on all windows, including the title bar, scroll bars, close box, zoom box, and size box.

The document also includes features that are specific to this application:

- the **word processing menu bar**, which contains the commands that are available in this application.
- the **ruler**, which controls margin settings, tab settings, spacing, and alignment for each paragraph in your document.
- the **I-beam cursor**, which marks your current location in the document. When you type, the letter that you type will appear at the location of the I-beam. This current location is called the **insertion point**, since the letters that you type are inserted at this location. The I-beam cursor tells you where the insertion point is located at any time.

The word processing menu bar

The word processing menu bar is found at the top of the screen. It contains the commands that are available in the word processing application.

The menu bar includes the File menu, the Edit menu, the Search menu, the Document menu, the Font menu, the Size menu, the Style menu, the Color menu, and the Window menu.

This section provides an overview of these menu commands to introduce the kinds of operations that you can perform in the word processing application.

Figure 4-2
File menu

File menu

The commands on the File menu include New, Open, Close, Save, Save As, Delete File, Import File, Choose Printer, Page Setup, Print, Print Merge, and Quit commands. (See Figure 4-2.) These commands are found on the File menu in all AppleWorks GS applications and are described in Chapter 3, AppleWorks GS Common Commands.

The Print Merge command is available on the word processing File menu; in all other applications, this command is dimmed and not available. The Print Merge command lets you print a mail-merge document, combining information stored in a database with a form letter to produce letters containing individualized information. For more information on this command, see Chapter 8, Merge Documents and Mailing Labels.

Figure 4-3
Edit menu

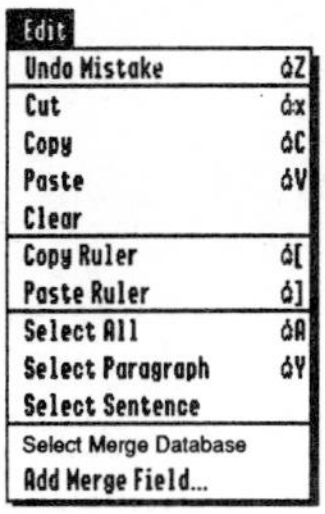

Edit menu

The commands on the Edit menu include Undo, Cut, Copy, Paste, Clear, and Select All. (See Figure 4-3.) These commands are described in Chapter 3, AppleWorks GS Common Commands.

In addition, the word processing Edit menu contains commands that let you select parts of your document quickly, duplicate ruler settings, and produce merge documents. (Producing merge documents is described in Chapter 8.)

Copy Ruler: This command lets you copy the current paragraph ruler settings to the Clipboard.

Paste Ruler: This command pastes the ruler settings stored on the Clipboard and applies them to the currently selected paragraph.

Select Paragraph: This commands selects and highlights the paragraph where the insertion point is currently located.

Select Sentence: This command selects and highlights the sentence where the insertion point is currently located.

Select Merge Database: This command lets you select the database used to produce a mail-merge document. (Merge documents are described in Chapter 8, Mail Merge and Mailing Labels.

Add Merge Field: This command lets you select the information extracted from a database in a mail-merge document.

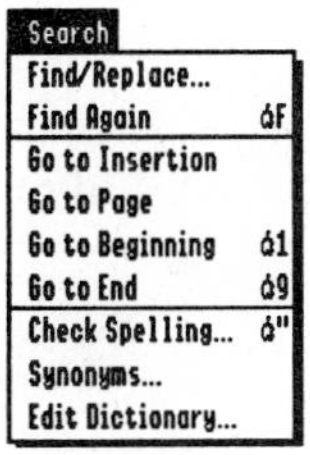

Figure 4-4
Search menu

Search menu

The Search menu commands let you quickly find and move to specific locations in your document. You can also check the spelling of your text or request synonyms for selected words. (See Figure 4-4.)

Find/Replace: This command lets you quickly find a specified phrase or replace one specified phrase with another.

Find Again: This command repeats the last previous Find command.

Go to Insertion: This command brings into view the current location of the insertion point. (If you use the scroll bars to review the contents of your document, this command quickly returns you to the last place where you were typing.)

Go to Page: This command moves you to a specified page number.

Go to Beginning: This command moves you to the beginning of your document.

Go to End: This command moves you to the end of your document.

Check Spelling: This command loads the AppleWorks GS dictionary and checks the spelling of words in your document.

Synonyms: This command provides suggested alternatives for selected words.

Edit Dictionary: This command lets you add or delete any desired words to the AppleWorks GS dictionary.

Document menu

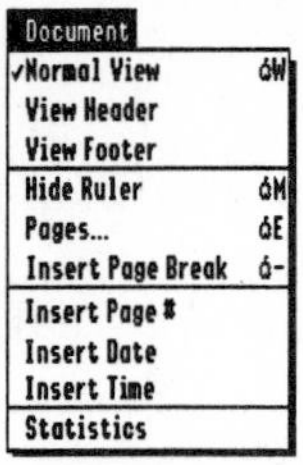

The Document menu contains commands that affect the entire document, including header and footer information, page numbering, and document statistics. (See Figure 4-5.)

Normal View: This command is used to return to your document after creating headers or footers with the View Header or View Footer command.

View Header: This command opens a special header window on the screen. Any text that you type into this window appears at the top of each page of your document.

View Footer: This command opens a special footer window on the screen. Any text that you type into this window appears at the bottom of each page of your document.

Hide Ruler: This command temporarily removes the ruler from the screen. After you choose this command and the ruler is removed, the command is replaced by Show Ruler, and you can choose this command to bring the ruler back into view.

Pages: This command controls certain page specifications, such as the number to use for the first page in the document.

Insert Page Break: This forces the current page to end. The next text that you type will appear at the top of the next page.

Insert Page #: This command places the current page number at a specified location in a header or footer.

Insert Date: This command places the current date at a specified location in a header or footer.

Insert Time: This command places the current time at a specified location in a header or footer.

Statistics: This provides document statistics, including the number of words, lines, paragraphs, and pages in the document.

Figure 4-5
Document menu

Font menu

The Font menu lets you select the font to be used for selected text in your document. (See Figure 4-6.) The Choose Font command is a special short-cut command that lets you select the font, style, and size for selected text in a single operation.

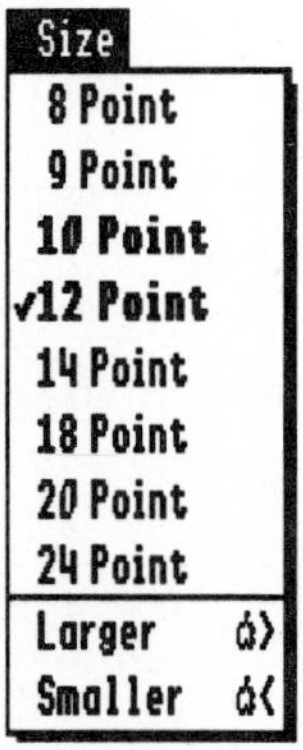

Figure 4-6
Font menu

Size menu

The Size menu lets you select the size of the font to be used for selected text in your document. (See Figure 4-7.) The size is measured in points. (There are 72 points to the inch, so larger sizes are represented by larger numbers on the menu.)

Figure 4-7
Size menu

The Larger and Smaller commands let you increase or decrease the size of selected text. The Larger command increases selected text one point in size, and the Smaller command decreases selected text one point in size.

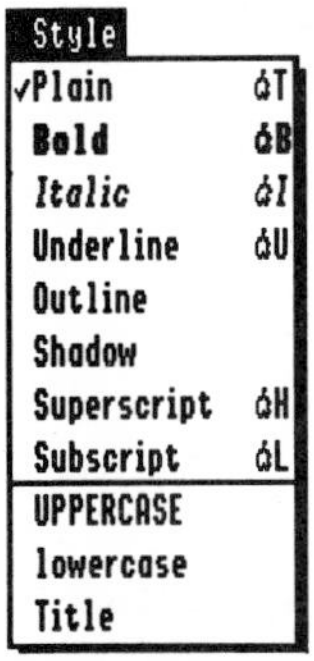

Figure 4-8
Style menu

Figure 4-9
Color menu

Style menu

The Style menu lets you select the style to be used for selected text in your document. (See Figure 4-8.) The styles that are available include

Plain: Plain style removes all other text styles.

Bold Text is printed boldface.

Italic Text is printed in italics

Underline: Text is printed underlined.

Outline: Each letter is outlined.

Shadow: A shadow is printed behind each letter.

Superscript: Text is printed ^above the line^.

Subscript: Text is printed ₍below₎ the line.

UPPERCASE: ALL TEXT IS PRINTED UPPERCASE.

lowercase: all text is printed lowercase.

Title: The First Letter Of Each Word Is Printed Uppercase.

Color menu

The Color menu lets you select the color to be used for selected text in your document. (See Figure 4-9.) The Edit Colors command can be used to create additional color options for your text. See Appendix D, Using the Edit Colors Command.

Window menu

The Window menu lists all document windows that are open and lets you quickly view any other open window or the contents of the Clipboard.

Using this menu is discussed in Chapter 3, AppleWorks GS Common Commands.

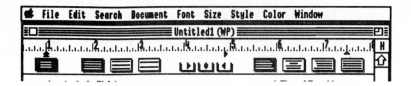

Figure 4-10   The word processing ruler

The word processing ruler

At the top of the document is a ruler, which controls the margin settings, tab settings, spacing, and alignment of text in your document. (See Figure 4-10.)

Margin settings mark the left edge and right edge of your document. Text cannot be typed to the left of your left margin setting or to the right of your right margin setting. The left margin is controlled by two markers: an indent marker that sets the left margin for the first line of a paragraph, and the left margin marker that sets the left margin for the remaining lines of a paragraph.

Tab settings mark the location on a line where the cursor advances when you press the Tab key. When you press the Tab key, the cursor advances to the next location where you have placed a tab setting on the ruler. Tab settings are useful for creating columns of information.

Three kinds of tab settings are provided:

- Left tabs: When you press the Tab key and advance to a left tab, letters that you type begin at the tab setting and flow to the right. The left edge of the text is even with the tab setting.
- Right tab: When you press the Tab key and advance to a right tab, letters that you type begin at the tab setting; as you continue to type, the text is moved backwards (to the left), so that the right edge of the text is even with the tab settings.
- Decimal tab: When you press the Tab key and advance to a decimal tab, any numbers that you type are handled in a special way. If the number contains a decimal point, the decimal point is aligned with the decimal tab setting. This makes it easy to produce columns of numbers that have the decimal points aligned.

Note: *A number with no decimal point is aligned as though the decimal point is at the end of the number:*

2.5

3.68

12

14.3

The spacing adjustments determine how much space should be left between lines of text. Double spacing prints one blank line between each line of your text, 1 1/2 spacing prints one-half blank line between each line of your text, and single spacing prints no blank lines between lines of text.

Four alignment settings are available:

- Left-justified: A line of your text begins at the left margin and flows to the right.
- Centered: The contents of a line are centered on the line.
- Right-justified: The contents of a line are aligned so that the line ends at the right margin.
- Full-justified: The contents of a line are adjusted so that the line begins at the left margin and ends at the right margin. Spaces are placed between words to adjust the length of the line.

The Lock Paragraph icon is used to avoid breaking a paragraph over two pages. When you click on this icon, it is selected, and the current paragraph will not be split over two pages when it is printed. If the paragraph does not fit at the bottom of one page, the entire paragraph is printed at the top of the next page.

What does the ruler control?

AppleWorks GS uses paragraph-based formatting. That means that each paragraph may have its own ruler settings. This provides great power and flexibility in formatting. You can use different ruler settings for different parts of your document, different margin settings for different paragraphs, different tab settings in different paragraphs.

But don't panic: that doesn't mean that you absolutely must adjust the settings for each paragraph. The setting on a ruler automatically are transferred from one paragraph to the next, unless you choose to change the settings.

That means that it's easy to create simple formatting for a new document. If you adjust the margin settings and tab settings at the beginning of a new document, those settings are effective throughout the document. The general rule is that ruler settings remain in effect until you change them.

(You can always return to a paragraph later and change the ruler for any selected paragraph. This is described in Chapter 5 under Changing Ruler Settings.)

The point is that you can adjust the rulers for each paragraph, thus giving you great power for formatting. However, for simple documents, you can set the ruler at the beginning of the document and just enter your text without further bother.

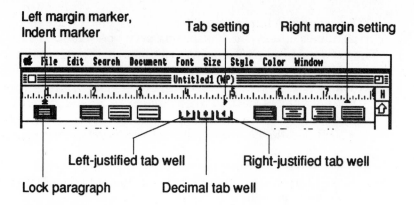

Figure 4-11 Margins and tabs

Setting the ruler

How do you adjust the margin settings, tab settings, spacing, or alignment?

The following sections describe how to adjust these settings at the beginning of a document. When you make these adjustments at the beginning of a document, they will be in effect for the rest of your document.

Margins and tabs

The margin and tab settings are displayed as triangles below the inch markings on the ruler. (See Figure 4-11.)

Two markers are used to control the left margin of your document: the indentation marker is used to set indentation for the first line of a paragraph, and the left margin marker is used to set the margin for the remaining lines of a paragraph.

Adjusting the right margin

1 Move the arrow pointer to the right margin icon.

2 Hold down the mouse button and drag the right margin icon to the desired location.

3 Release the mouse button.

Now as you type your text, it will not pass beyond the right margin setting.

Adjusting the left margin

1   **Move the arrow pointer to the left margin markers.**

Notice that the left margin is marked by two triangles, stacked on top of each other. The lower triangle, the indent marker, sets the indentation for the first line of the paragraph, and the upper triangle, the left margin marker, sets the left margin for the remaining lines of the paragraph.

2   **Drag the upper triangle (the left margin setting) to the location that you want to use as the left edge for the body of the paragraph.**

3   **Drag the lower triangle (the indent setting) to the location where you want the first line of the paragraph to begin.**

Note: *You can place the indent marker to the left or to the right of the left margin setting. This lets you indent or outdent the first line of the paragraph. If the indent marker is placed to the right of the left margin settings, the first line of the paragraph will be indented. If the indent marker is placed to the left of the left margin setting, the first line will be outdented. This second format is sometimes called a "hanging" paragraph, with the first line flush left and all following lines indented.*

Setting a new tab

1   **Move the arrow pointer to the tab well that you want to use.**

Remember that you can use left-justified tabs, decimal tabs, or right-justified tabs.

2   **Hold down the mouse button and drag a tab icon from the well.**

3   **Drag the tab to the position on the ruler scale where you want the tab.**

4   **Release the mouse button, and the tab is placed at that location.**

Adjusting tabs on the ruler

1   **Move the arrow pointer to the tab icon.**

2   **Hold down the mouse button and drag the tab icon to a new location.**

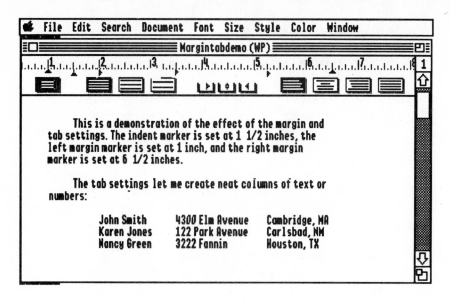

This is a demonstration of the effect of the margin and tab settings. The indent marker is set at 1 1/2 inches, the left margin marker is set at 1 inch, and the right margin marker is set at 6 1/2 inches.

The tab settings let me create neat columns of text or numbers:

John Smith	4300 Elm Avenue	Cambridge, MA
Karen Jones	122 Park Avenue	Carlsbad, NM
Nancy Green	3222 Fannin	Houston, TX

Figure 4-12   Sample showing margins and tabs

3 | **Release the mouse button, and the tab is placed at the new location.**

To completely remove a tab setting, drag the tab marker down off the ruler, and it will disappear.

After you have set the left and right margins and adjusted tabs on the ruler, your text will be controlled by these settings as you enter it (see Figure 4-12).

Spacing and alignment

You can also control the amount of spacing used in your document and the alignment of text. (See Figure 4-13.)

Adjusting the spacing

To adjust the spacing of your text, click on the icon representing your choice:

- single spacing
- 1 1/2 spacing
- double spacing

After you click on the icon, the icon is highlighted and the selected spacing is in effect.

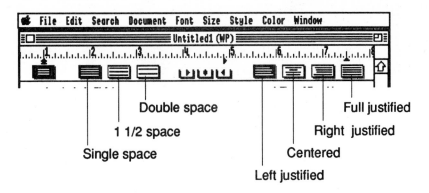

Figure 4-13   Spacing and alignment

Adjusting the alignment

To adjust the alignment, click on the icon that represents your choice:

- left-justified
- centered
- right-justified
- full-justified

Now as you type your text, your text is displayed with the selected alignment. (See Figure 4-14.)

Locking paragraphs

The Lock Paragraphs icon is used to lock together the lines in a paragraph. When you select the Lock Paragraph icon, the lines of the paragraph are not separated at the end of a page. If the entire paragraph does not fit at the end of a page, the entire paragraph is moved to the next page.

Entering your text

When the margin settings, tab settings, spacing, and alignment on the ruler are correct, you are ready to begin entering your text.

The I-beam and the insertion point

When you open a new document, a vertical line is blinking in the upper-left corner of the document. This is the I-beam cursor. (See Figure 4-15.)

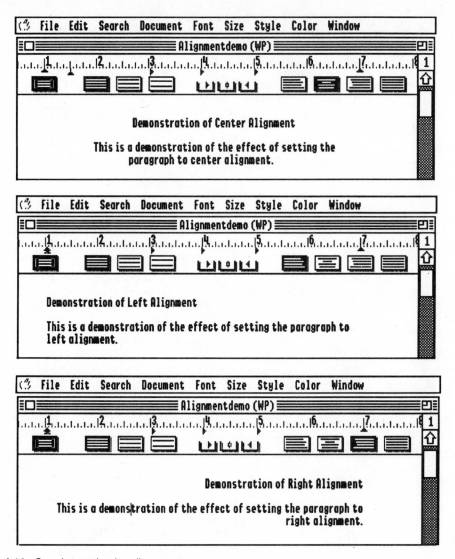

Figure 4-14 Sample text showing alignments

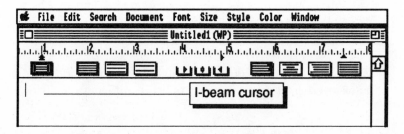

Figure 4-15 The I-beam and insertion point

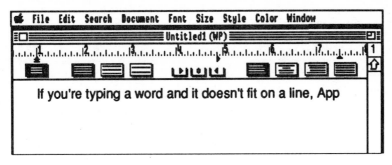

Figure 4-16 Word wrap

This cursor marks the insertion point, which is the location in your text where the next typed character will appear. You will see the I-beam cursor in other AppleWorks GS applications when you work with text.

As you type in text, the I-beam automatically moves ahead of your typing. It always marks the location where the next character will be located.

Entering text and correcting mistakes

Now you can enter the text of your document, using the Apple IIGS keyboard as a standard typewriter keyboard.

As you type, you may make a mistake. You can use the Delete key to correct simple mistakes. The Delete key erases one character each time that you press the key.

To correct a mistake, press the Delete key to remove the mistake, and then retype the text correctly.

Word-wrap and the Return key

If you are an experienced typist, you will be tempted to tap the Return key as you near the end of a line. However, this is not necessary. When you reach the right margin, just keep typing.

If you are in the middle of a word when you reach the right margin, AppleWorks GS automatically moves the entire word to the beginning of the next line. This feature is called word-wrap. (See Figures 4-16 and 4-17.)

The word-wrap feature means that you seldom need to press the Return key.

Note: *Sometimes you may want to keep two or more words together on the same line. For instance, you usually want to keep someone's first and last name on the same line, rather than printing the first name at the end of one line and the last name at the beginning of the following line.*

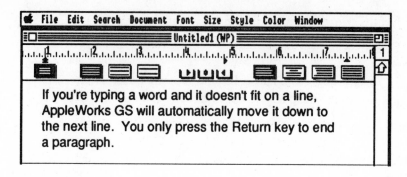

Figure 4-17 Word wrap

To keep two or more words together on the same line, type a sticky-space between the words. If you type a sticky-space between words, the two words are not separated at the end of a line; rather, they are treated as if they were a single word.

To type a sticky-space, hold down the Open Apple key and press the space bar.

When should you press Return?

When you press the Return key, AppleWorks GS ends the current paragraph and moves the cursor to the beginning of the next line. There are really only a few times when you should press the Return key.

Press the Return key:

- to end the current paragraph and begin a new paragraph.
- to place one or more blank lines in your document. When you press the Return key, the cursor moves to the beginning of the next line. If you press the Return key several times, a blank line is inserted into your document each time that you press the key.

Using the scroll bar

If you are typing a short letter or note, it may fit entirely within the document window. However, most documents will not fit entirely within the window.

If you approach the bottom of the window and continue to type, the text at the top of the window moves off the top of the window and temporarily disappears. Don't worry — AppleWorks GS still remembers that text; it was moved off the screen to make room for new text at the bottom of the screen.

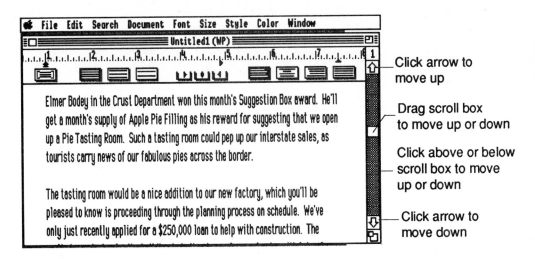

Figure 4-18 Using the scroll bar

You can think of the document window as being a window into a larger document. It shows as much of the larger document as possible, but much of the larger document is usually off the screen.

The scroll bars at the right side of the window let you browse through the contents of your document. (See Figure 4-18.)

Click on the scroll arrows at the top of the scroll bar to move up in your document, or click on the scroll arrow at the bottom of the scroll bar to move down in the document.

To move more quickly, drag the scroll box up or down in the scroll bar. Drag the scroll box to the top of the scroll bar to move to the top of the document, or drag the scroll box to the bottom of the bar to move to the bottom of the document. If you drag the scroll box to the middle of the scroll bar, the middle of the document is shown; the page number of the page showing in the window is displayed above the scroll bar.

Shortcut: *You can quickly replace the current text in the window with the window of text immediately above or below the current text. To move up one window in the document, click in the gray area of the scroll bar above the scroll box. To move down one window in the document, click in the gray area of the scroll bar below the scroll box.*

Editing your text

As you create your document, you may need to make simple changes in the text. Editing the text in your document usually involves

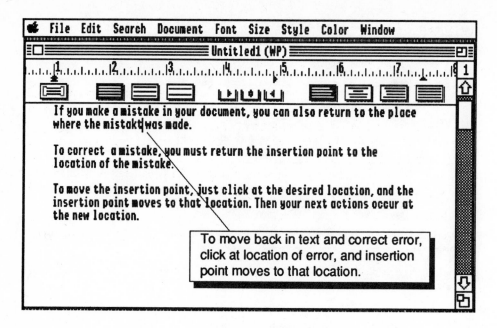

Figure 4-19   Moving the insertion point

1. moving the insertion point to the location of the change that you want to make,
2. making the change, and
3. returning to the location where you started.

Moving the insertion point

The I-beam cursor (blinking vertical line) always marks the insertion point, your current location in the document. To make a change in the document, you must first move the insertion point to the location where a change is necessary:

1. Bring the desired location into view in the document window. Use the scroll bar if necessary.

2. Move the cursor into the document window. As you enter the window, the cursor takes the form of the I-beam pointer.

3. Move the I-beam to the exact location where a change is needed.

4. Click the mouse button.

The insertion point is now located at that position. (See Figure 4-19.)

Using the keyboard to move the insertion point

The arrow keys can be used to move the insertion point to the left, right, up, and down in your text:

- Press the up-arrow key to move the insertion point up one line.
- Press the down-arrow key to move the insertion point down one line.
- Press the left-arrow key to move the insertion point left one character. Hold down the Option key and press the left-arrow key to move left one word.
- Press the right-arrow key to move the insertion point right one character. Hold down the Option key and press the right-arrow key to move right one word.

You can also make larger jumps in your document by combining the Open Apple key with other keys.
Hold down the Open Apple key, and press

- the up-arrow key to move to the top of the window.
- the down-arrow key to move to the bottom of the window.
- the left-arrow key to move to the left margin.
- the right-arrow key to move to the right margin.
- the number 1 to move to the top of the document.
- the number 9 to move to the end of the document.
- a number between 1 and 9 to move to a proportional location in the document. For example, press 5 to move to the middle of the document.

Erasing part of your text

1. Move the insertion point to the location immediately after the text that you want to delete.

2. Press the Delete key on the keyboard.

Each time you press the Delete key, one character is erased from the document.

3. Continue pressing the Delete key until the desired text is erased.

4. Move the insertion point, if necessary, to another location and continue working on your text.

To erase a word:

1. Move the I-beam cursor to a word that you want to erase.

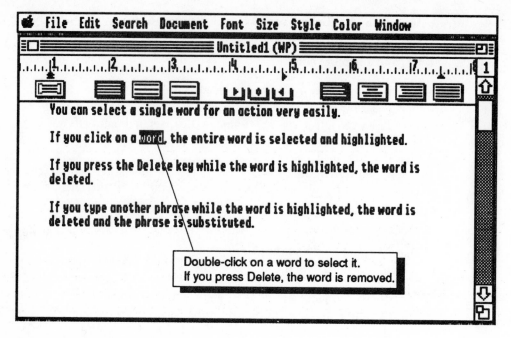

Figure 4-20 Word to delete is highlighted

| 2 | **Double-click on the word.**

The word is highlighted and selected. (See Figure 4-20.)

| 3 | **Press the Delete key.**

The selected word disappears.

Shortcut: *To replace a word with another word or phrase, select the word to replace.*
While the word is highlighted, type a new word or phrase and it replaces
the highlighted word.

Inserting text into the document

You might want to insert new text into the middle of existing text. To insert new text:

| 1 | **Move the insertion point to the location where you want to insert the new text.**

| 2 | **Type the new text on the keyboard.**

The new text is inserted into the old text, squeezed into the text at the location of the insertion point.

After you have inserted the desired text, move the insertion point to a new location and continue to work on the document.

Saving your text

As you enter your document, it's extremely important to save your document periodically on a disk!

As you are typing, your document is kept temporarily in the Apple IIGS memory. However, this memory is erased whenever the power to the computer is turned off.

For example, if you turn off your computer before saving your work, all of the work done at this session is erased and forgotten! If lightning strikes nearby and your lights flicker, a document that you haven't saved is lost. If your cat or dog accidentally unplugs your power cord, your work would be lost.

It's easy to avoid this problem . . . save your work on a storage disk often! Some people only save work at the end of a session. This is certainly better than not saving your work at all, but it's much better to save your work often.

Refer to Chapter 3 for a discussion of the Save and Save As commands.

When you save your document with Save As command, pay special attention to the formatting buttons at the bottom of the dialog box (see Figure 4-21). Unless you have a special reason to save your work as ASCII text, always click the With Formatting button. If you save your work as ASCII text, the text of your document is saved, but any special AppleWorks GS formatting is lost. If a document is saved as ASCII text, it is easier to trasfer to other computers and other programs, but it loses special AppleWorks GS features.

Printing your word processing document

After you've created and saved a word processing document, you can easily print out a copy. You must use three commands to print your document: Choose Printer, Page Setup, and Print.

1. Select the Choose Printer command on the File menu to select the printer to use. The Choose Printer dialog box is displayed, and you

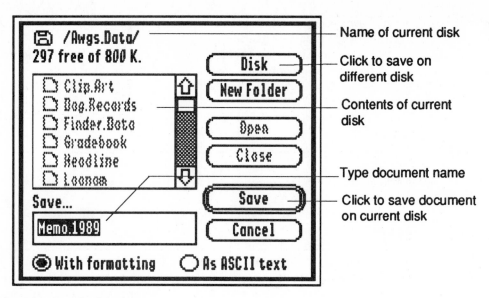

Figure 4-21 Save As dialog box

The following labels point to parts of the dialog box:
- Name of current disk
- Click to save on different disk
- Contents of current disk
- Type document name
- Click to save document on current disk

should enter the information about your printer. When the settings are correct, click the OK button to return to your document. For more information, see the Choose Printer command in Chapter 3, AppleWorks GS Common Commands.

2. Select the Page Setup command on the File menu to specify the type of paper, vertical sizing, printer effects, and orientation that you want to use. When you select this command, the Page Setup dialog box is displayed and you should enter your desired information. When the settings are correct, click the OK button to return to your document. For more information, see the Page Setup command in Chapter 3, AppleWorks GS Common Commands.

3. Select the Print command on the File menu to select the print quality, page range, and number of copies that you want to use. After the Print dialog box is displayed and you have entered your information, click the OK button to begin printing. For more information, see the Page Setup command in Chapter 3, AppleWorks GS Common Commands.

You only need to select the Choose Printer command and the Page Setup command once during an AppleWorks GS session. If you don't need to change the settings later in the session, you don't need to select these commands again.

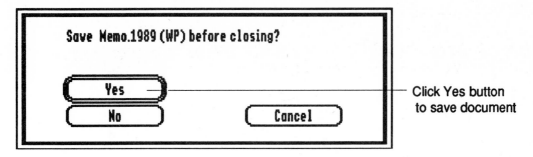

Click Yes button
to save document

Figure 4-22   Save before closing box

The next step

After you have created, saved, and printed a word processing document, you can

- Continue to work on the document. This chapter has introduced basic word processing operations, but the next chapter demonstrates special AppleWorks GS features. For example, you will learn to change fonts and styles to produce distinctive word processing documents.
- Close the current document window. If you are finished with the document, you can close the current window by selecting the Close command from the File menu, or by clicking in the Close box in the upper-left corner of the window.

If the document has not been saved, a dialog box appears and warns you that the document has not been saved. (See Figure 4-22.)

- Create another new word processing document, by selecting the New or Open command on the File menu and opening a new word processing document.
- Create a new document for one of the other AppleWorks GS applications. Select the New or Open command from the File menu, and open a new document.
- Quit AppleWorks GS by selecting the Quit command from the File menu.

Chapter 5

Working with Word Processing Documents

About this chapter

After you have created a basic word processing document, you are ready to explore some of the special AppleWorks GS word processing features. This chapter explores these features:

- Opening a saved document
- Making changes in your text
- Selecting text in your document
- Using different fonts in your document
- Using different font sizes in your document
- Using different font styles in your document
- Using different colors in your document
- Combining fonts, sizes, styles, and colors
- Setting rulers for different paragraphs
- Using headers and footers in your document
- Finding and replacing phrases
- Checking your spelling
- Finding synonyms for your words
- Checking the statistics on your document

Opening a saved document

After you have saved a word processing document, you can safely close the document window and leave the word processing application. You can even turn off your Apple IIGS — the document is safely saved on a disk for storage.

You can always retrieve a document that is saved on a disk and revise it later.

To open a saved document:

1   **Select the Open command on the File menu.**

2   **Click on the name of the document that you want to open.**

3   **Click on the Open button in the dialog box.**

A new document window is opened and the selected document appears in the window.

Making changes in your text

AppleWorks GS provides many special features to produce an exciting, professional document. You can use different fonts, sizes, and styles for your text, and you can even make different parts of your text different colors.

To use these features, you must

1   **Select the text that you want to change.**

2   **Choose the change that you want to make.**

After you choose a change, it is made to the selected text.

Selecting and changing text lets you change your text from plain (Figure 5-1) to a style that better reflects your own personal style and taste (Figure 5-2).

Selecting text in your document

Before you can make a change in your text, you must select the text to change. The term **selected** has a special meaning in AppleWorks GS.

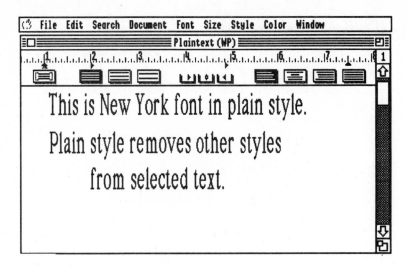

Figure 5-1   Plain text

When text is selected in AppleWorks GS, it is highlighted on the screen. (See Figure 5-3.)
You can select text in several ways, including

- dragging the mouse
- shift-clicking
- double-clicking
- using special commands on the Edit menu

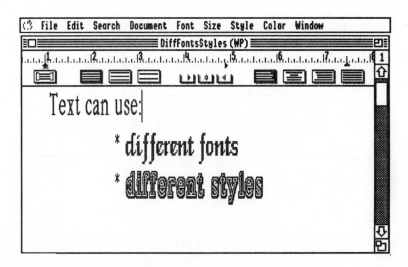

Figure 5-2   Different fonts, sizes, and styles

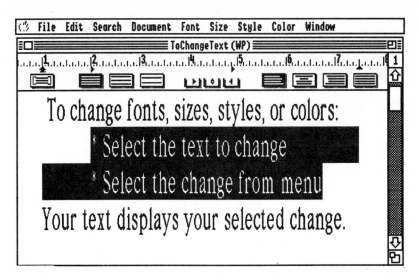

Figure 5-3   Selected text

Selecting text by dragging

Dragging is a special term, which means moving the mouse while the mouse button is held down.

To select text by dragging:

1. **Move the I-beam cursor to the beginning of the text that you want to select.**

2. **Hold down the mouse button and move the mouse with the button held down.**

This is called dragging the mouse. As you drag the mouse, text is highlighted and selected.

3. **Release the mouse button when the desired text is selected.**

Selecting text by shift-clicking

You can select a block of text by shift-clicking.

1. **Move the I-beam cursor to the beginning of the text that you want to select.**

2. **Click the mouse button once.**

3 Move the I-beam to the end of the text that you want to select.

4 Hold down the Shift key, and click the mouse button again.

This is called shift-clicking,
All of the text between the first click and the shift-click is now selected and highlighted.

Selecting a word by double-clicking

You can quickly select a single word by double-clicking on the word.

1 Move the I-beam cursor to the word that you want to select.

2 Click the mouse button quickly two times.

This is called double-clicking.
The word is selected and highlighted.

Selecting a line by triple-clicking

You can quickly select an entire line by triple-clicking.

1 Move the I-beam cursor to the line that you want to select.

2 Click the mouse button quickly three times.

The entire line is selected and highlighted.

Using special Edit menu commands

You can also select a block of text using special commands on the Edit menu.

1 Move the I-beam into a sentence or paragraph that you want to select, and click the mouse button.

2 Choose one of the special Select commands on the Edit menu.

Choose the Select Sentence command to highlight the current sentence. Choose the Select Paragraph command to highlight the current paragraph. Choose the Select All command to highlight the entire document.

3 The desired block of your document is selected and highlighted.

Changing text fonts

A font is a set of particular shapes for each character including letters, numbers, and symbols on the keyboard.

For example, here are characters in three of the fonts that are available in AppleWorks GS:

Geneva font: ABCDEFGHIJKLMNOPQRSTUVWXYZ

Times font: ABCDEFGHIJKLMNOPQRSTUVWXYZ

Venice font: *ABCDEFGHIJKLMNOPQRSTUVWXYZ*

When you begin an AppleWorks GS word processing document, text is displayed on the screen using Geneva font. You can easily change some or all of the text in your document to one of the other fonts.

Using the Font menu

The fonts that are available are listed in the Font menu. A checkmark appears to the left of the font that is currently selected.

Choosing the font of the next text

The I-beam cursor always marks the insertion point, which is your current location in the document. Any text that you type appears at the current location of the insertion point. You can always change the font used for the next text that you will type.

To change the font of the next characters that you type:

1.   Move the arrow pointer to the Font menu at the top of the screen.

2.   Hold down the mouse button, and select the font that you want to use for the next characters.

3.   When the desired font is highlighted, release the mouse button.

A checkmark appears on the menu next to the selected style, and the next characters that you type will appear in the selected font.

If you have not used a selected font before, there may be a slight delay while the font is loaded from your disk.

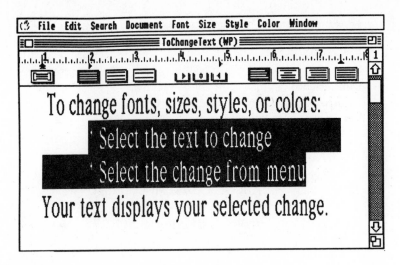

Figure 5-4 Selected text

Changing the font of existing text

You can also change the font of any text that you've already typed into a document. (See Figures 5-4, 5-5, and 5-6.)

1 **Select the text that you want to change.**

2 **Choose the desired font for the selected text from the Font menu.**

The selected text is displayed in the selected font.

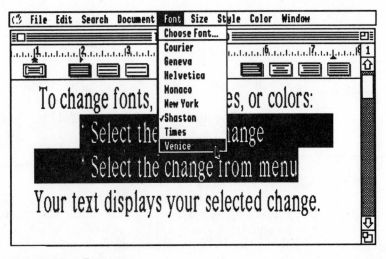

Figure 5-5 Choosing a font from Font menu

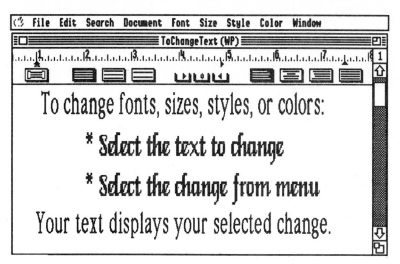

Figure 5-6 Changing the fonts of selected text

Changing font sizes

The characters in your text can appear in different sizes. The different sizes are defined in terms of points, such as 10 points, 12 points, or 18 points. Each font that is available can be displayed in many different sizes.

For example, Figure 5-7 shows characters displayed in several different combinations of fonts and sizes.

When you begin an AppleWorks GS word processing document, text is displayed on the screen using Geneva 12-point font. You can easily change some or all of the text in your document to one of the other sizes.

The Size Menu

When you choose a font for your text, the sizes available for that font are listed on the Size menu. A checkmark appears to the left of the currently selected size.

The Larger and Smaller commands can be used to select sizes that are not listed on the Size menu.

Changing the size of the font in the next text

When you type text at the insertion point, it continues to use the font and size to the left of the insertion point.

To change the size of the next characters:

1 **Move the arrow pointer to the Size menu at the top of the screen.**

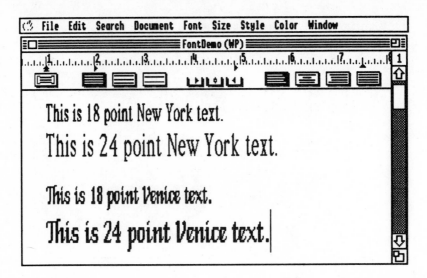

Figure 5-7 Different font sizes

> **2** Choose the font size that you want to use for the next characters.

A checkmark appears on the menu next to the selected size, and the next characters that you type will appear in the selected size.

Changing the size of the font in text you've already typed

You can change the size of the font in any text that you've already typed into a document.

> **1** Select the text that you want to change.

> **2** Move the arrow pointer to the Size menu at the top of the screen.

> **3** Choose the font size that you want to use for the selected text.

When the desired size is highlighted, a checkmark appears on the menu next to the chosen size, and the selected text is displayed in the selected font.

Using the Larger and Smaller commands

You may want to change the size of font to a size that is not listed on the Size menu. The Larger and Smaller commands let you use font sizes that are not listed on the menu.

|1| Select the text that you want to change.

|2| Move the arrow pointer to the Size menu at the top of the screen.

|3| Hold down the mouse button, and select the Larger command or the Smaller command.

If you choose the Larger command, the selected text increases in size by one point. If you choose the Smaller command, the size of selected text decreases by one point.

|4| Repeat until the text is displayed in the desired font size.

Shortcut: |1| Select the desired text.

|2| Hold down the Open Apple key and press the less-than (<) key or greater-than (>) key.

The right-arrow key increases the size of the text by one point, and the left-arrow key decreases the size of selected text by one point.

Changing font styles

The previous sections showed you how to set the font and size used for text in your document. You can also specify the style used for all or part of your text.

The Style menu

The font styles that are available are listed on the Style menu. The styles include plain, bold, italic, underline, outline, shadow, super-script, subscript, uppercase, lowercase, and title.
A checkmark appears to the left of the currently selected style.
Figure 5-8 shows a sample of text that demonstrates these styles.

Changing the style of the next text

To change the style of the next characters typed at the insertion point:

|1| Move the arrow pointer to the Style menu at the top of the screen.

|2| Choose the font style that you want to use for the next characters.

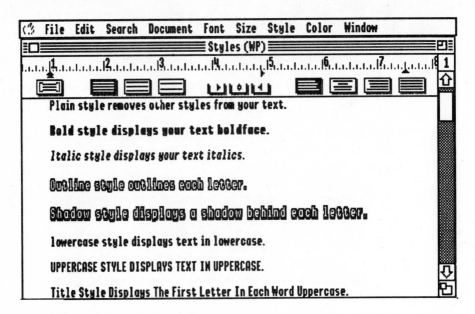

Figure 5-8 Different styles

The next characters that you type will appear in the selected style.

Changing the style of text you've already typed

You can change the style of any text that you've already typed into a document.

|1| **Select the text that you want to change.**

|2| **Choose the style that you want to use for the selected text.**

A checkmark appears on the menu next to the selected style, and the selected text is displayed in the selected style.

Using multiple styles

You can select more than one style for your selected text. For example, you can select both bold and underline style for selected text, and the text is displayed both bold and underlined. Remember that a checkmark is displayed to the left of selected styles. If you select more than one style, a checkmark appears to the left of each style that you select.

Selecting multiple styles

1   **Select the text that you want to change.**

2   **Move the arrow pointer to the Style menu and select the first style.**

A checkmark appears to the left of the selected style, and the selected text is displayed with that style.

3   **Move the arrow pointer back to the Style menu and select the next style to be applied to the text.**

A checkmark appears to the left of this style, and this style is added to the selected text.

4   **Continue to add any desired styles to the selected text.**

A few style combinations are not possible, since the styles are mutually exclusive. For example, plain text can't be combined with bold, italic, underline, outline, or shadow. You can also only select one of the case styles for selected text: uppercase, lowercase, or title.

Removing styles

Suppose that you have displayed some of your text in a style, and then later decide to use a different style. You can always return to the text and remove some or all of the styles.

To remove one style:

1   **Select the text that is displayed in a style that you want to change.**

2   **Pull down the Style menu.**

A checkmark is shown to the left of each style that is used in the selected text. If the text is displayed in Bold style, a checkmark is displayed to the left of the Bold command.

3   **Select the style that you want to remove.**

For example, if the text were displayed in Bold, and you wanted to remove that style, select the Bold command again.

The checkmark is removed from the Bold command, and the Bold style is removed from the selected text.

To remove all styles, select the Plain style from the menu.

Changing text colors

Part or all of your text can be displayed in a selected color. The colors that are available for use in the document appear on the Color menu.

The Color menu

Sixteen colors are available on the Color menu. A checkmark appears to the left of the currently selected color.

If the 16 colors do not include a specific color that you want to use, you can create your own colors by selecting the Edit Colors command on the Color menu. (See Appendix D, Using the Edit Colors Command.)

Changing the color of the next text

To change the color of the next characters typed at the insertion point:

1. **Move the arrow pointer to the Color menu at the top of the screen.**

2. **Choose the color that you want to use for the next characters.**

The next characters that you type will appear in the selected color.

Changing the color of existing text

You can change the color of any text that you've already typed into a document.

1. **Select the text that you want to change.**

2. **Choose the color that you want to use for the selected text.**

The selected text is displayed in the selected color.

Combining fonts, sizes, styles, and colors

You can use the Font, Size, Style, or Color menu to change the display of text in your document.

When you change one of these characteristics, you can often combine your selection with one or more additional selections to change more than one characteristic at the same time.

Making multiple selections

You can make selections from more than one menu, continuing to make changes until the text is displayed with the desired appearance.

For example, if text in your document is displayed in Geneva 12-point plain text, you can adjust the appearance of the text by making more than one change to selected text:

1   **Select the text in your document to change.**

2   **While the text is selected, you can select a new font from the Font menu. Then you can select a new size from the Size menu. a new style from the Style menu, and a new color from the Color menu.**

After making each selection, the text remains selected, and you can continue to make changes until the text is displayed the way that you want it displayed.

Using the Choose Font command

The Choose Font command on the Font menu lets you choose the font, size, and style of your text with a single command. Not all styles are available with this command, but it provides a quick way to handle font selection for most situations.

1   **Select the text that you want to change, or place the insertion point at the location where new text will be entered.**

2   **Select the Choose Font command from the Font menu. (See Figure 5-9.)**

3   **Click on the font that you want to use.**

4   **Click on the check box next to the styles that you want to use.**

5   **Click on the size of the font that you want to use. If the font size does not appear in the list, type the size that you want to use in the Other Size box.**

6   **Click on the OK button.**

If you selected text, that text is now displayed with your selections. If you clicked to establish a new insertion point, new text typed at the insertion point will be displayed with this selection.

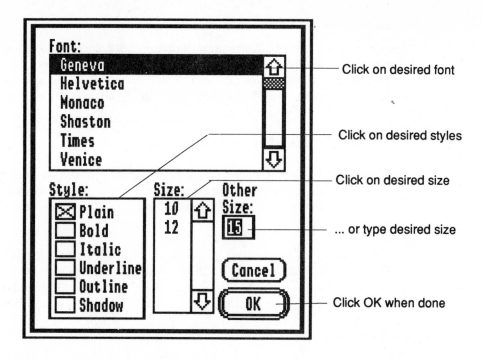

Figure 5-9 Choose Font dialog box

Changing formats of paragraphs

When you begin a word processing document, a ruler is displayed at the top of the document. The settings on the ruler control the margin, tab, spacing, and alignment settings for the first paragraph in the document.

When you press the Return key, the first paragraph is ended. When you continue to type, the next paragraph begins, and the same settings on the ruler continue to control the format of the second paragraph.

As you continue to type, a new paragraph begins each time that you press the Return key. The ruler settings in effect for the previous paragraph continue to control the format of the current paragraph.

If you wish, you can use the same ruler settings for the entire document.

However, you can change the ruler settings for any paragraph. Each paragraph can have its own ruler settings. This is called **paragraph-based formatting**.

For example, a paragraph can have different left margin settings, making it easy for you to indent an entire paragraph. You can also have different tab settings, spacing, or alignment for each paragraph.

Changing the ruler for a new paragraph

Each time you press the Return key, a new paragraph begins. The ruler settings for the paragraph that was just completed continue in effect, unless you wish to change the settings for the new paragraph.

To change the ruler settings for a new paragraph:

1. **When you begin the new paragraph, move the arrow pointer into the ruler at the top of the screen.**

2. **Use the arrow pointer to adjust the margin settings, tab settings, spacing, and alignment on the ruler.**

The new settings take effect for the new paragraph.

Changing the ruler of an existing paragraph

As you enter the text in a document, you might review the text entered earlier in the document and want to change the ruler settings of earlier text.

For example, you might want to change the left or right margins of a paragraph earlier in your text.

To change the ruler settings of existing paragraphs:

1. **Click the mouse button anywhere in the paragraph, so that the insertion point appears anywhere in the paragraph.**

When the insertion point is placed anywhere in a paragraph, the ruler settings automatically display the settings for that paragraph. (See Figure 5-10.)

2. **Use the arrow pointer to adjust the ruler settings. Move the margin settings, tab settings, spacing, and alignment.**

As you make the changes in the ruler, the text in the paragraph is automatically adjusted to reflect the new settings. (See Figure 5-11.)

Changing the ruler of multiple paragraphs

You might want to adjust the ruler settings on more than one paragraph at once. For example, you might want to change the margins of the first three paragraphs of your document.

To adjust the settings on multiple paragraphs, you must select the desired paragraphs and then change the ruler settings for the selected paragraphs.

1. **Select the paragraphs where you want to change the ruler settings.**

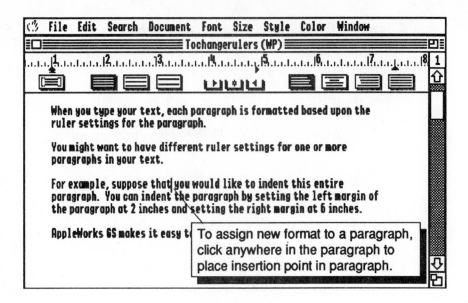

Figure 5-10 Click inside a paragraph to select it for a new format

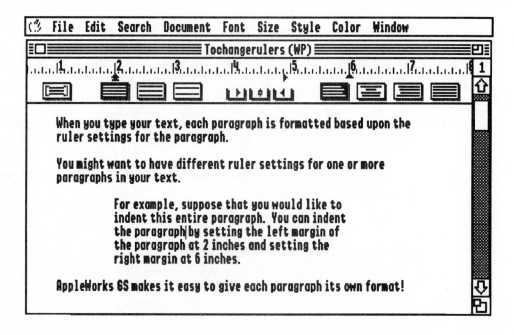

Figure 5-11 When you change ruler settings, the current paragraph reflects the new settings

The easiest way to select multiple paragraphs is to drag the mouse over multiple paragraphs or use the Shift-click method to select several paragraphs. If any of the text in a paragraph is selected, changes in the ruler will affect the entire paragraph.

After you select the paragraphs to adjust, the ruler displays the settings of the first selected paragraph.

2. Use the arrow pointer to adjust the ruler settings. Move the margin settings, tab settings, spacing, and alignment.

As you make the changes in the ruler, the text in all of the selected paragraphs is automatically adjusted to reflect the new settings.

3. When the ruler settings are correct, move the insertion point to the point in the text where you want to continue working.

Copying and pasting ruler formats

If you use a ruler in one paragraph that you would like to use for another paragraph later in your document, you can easily copy the ruler format for use later in the document.

1. Move the I-beam cursor anywhere into the paragraph that contains the format that you want to copy.

2. Click the mouse button, and the insertion point is inserted into the paragraph.

The ruler displays the settings for that paragraph.

3. Select the Copy Ruler command from the Edit menu.

4. Move the I-beam cursor into the paragraph that you would like to format like the first paragraph.

5. Click the mouse button, and the insertion point appears in the paragraph.

The ruler settings reflect the current paragraph settings.

6. Select the Paste Ruler command from the Edit menu.

The ruler settings from the first paragraph are copied to this paragraph and replace the old paragraph settings.

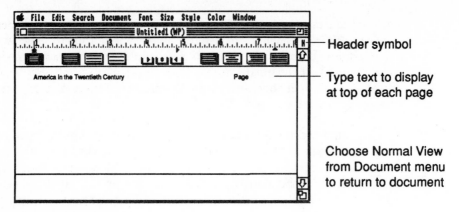

Figure 5-12 Header window

Adding headers and footers

A header is text that appears at the top of each page in your document, and a footer is text that appears at the bottom of each page of your document.

AppleWorks GS lets you easily add headers and footers to your document. These headers and footers can contain not only text, but also page numbers, the current date, and the current time. AppleWorks GS can automatically calculate and display the page number of each page, and your Apple IIGS contains a built-in clock to automatically provide the current date and time.

Adding a header to your document

To add a header to the document:

1 **Select View Header from the Document menu.**

A special header window opens, with its own ruler settings. (See Figure 5-12.)

2 **Type into the header window any text that you want to appear at the top of each page in your document.**

To add the page number to the header, place the insertion point where you would like the page number to appear. Then select the Insert Page # command from the Document menu. The correct page number will automatically appear at this location in the header.

To add the current date to the header, place the insertion point where you would like the date to appear. Then select the Insert Date command from the Document menu. The correct date will appear at this location in the header.

To add the current time to the header, place the insertion point where you would like the time to appear. Then select the Insert Time command from the Document menu. The current time will automatically appear at this location in the text.

3   **Adjust the ruler settings to format the text in the header.**

4   **To return to the main body of your document, select Normal View from the Document menu.**

Note: *Do not click the Close box to leave the Header window. This will close the entire document. If you accidentally click the Close box, the Save Before Closing dialog box appears. You can return to your document by clicking the Cancel button in this dialog box.*

Now as you type text into your document, the header text appears at the top of each page.

Adding a footer to your document

A footer is text that is automatically displayed at the bottom of each page.

To add a footer to the document, select View Footer from the Document menu. Complete the footer by following the steps described previously for headers.

Which pages have headers, footers?

You may not want the header or footer information to appear on each page. For example, you may not want the header or footer on the first page of the document.

To control which pages display the header or footer:

1   **Select the Pages command from the Document menu.**

The Pages dialog box appears. (See Figure 5-13.)

2   **Click on the pages where you want the header or footer to appear.**

3   **If you would like the pages to begin numbering with some number other than 1, type in the new first page number.**

4   **When the settings are correct, click on the OK button.**

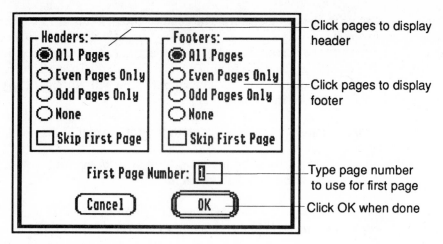

Figure 5-13   Pages dialog box

Finding and replacing text

As you enter text into your document, you might want to move quickly to one particular word or phrase in your document. You might want to move to the location simply to inspect the text, or you might want to edit the text at that location. AppleWorks GS provides the Find/Replace command to let you move quickly to a word or phrase in your text.

You may want to quickly find a word or phrase in your text and replace it with another word or phrase. For example, you might want to find the word "college" and replace it everywhere in the document with the word "university." The Find/Replace command lets you find one phrase and replace it with another phrase quickly.

Finding text in your document

To quickly move to the location of some specific text in your document, you can use the Find/Replace command:

1   **Select the Find/Replace command on the Search menu.**

The Find/Replace dialog box appears (see Figure 5-14):

2   **Type into the Search For input bar the phrase to search for.**

3   **Click on the Ignore Case and Whole Word box if you wish.**

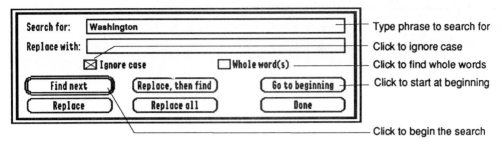

Search for: **Washington**	Type phrase to search for
Replace with:	Click to ignore case
☒ Ignore case ☐ Whole word(s)	Click to find whole words
Find next	Replace, then find	Go to beginning	Click to start at beginning
Replace	Replace all	Done	
	Click to begin the search

Figure 5-14 Find dialog box

If you check Ignore Case, AppleWorks GS searches for the phrase, regardless of uppercase or lowercase differences. If you check the Whole Word box, AppleWorks GS ignores the phrase if it is found in the middle of a larger word.

4 **Click on the Find Next button to begin the search.**

AppleWorks GS begins to search for your phrase , beginning at the current insertion point. If the phrase is found, it is highlighted in the document. If you want to stop the search, click the Done button.

If you want to continue to search for another occurrence of the phrase, click on the Find Next button.

The Find operation begins at the current location of the insertion point and continues until the end of the document is reached. When the end of the document is found, a dialog box reports no further occurrences.

If you would like to search again beginning at the top of the document, click on the Go To Beginning button.

5 **When you have completed the search, click the Done button to return to your document.**

Find and Replace command

AppleWorks GS lets you quickly move to the location of some specific text in your document and replace the phrase with another phrase.

1 **Select the Find/Replace command on the Search menu.**

The Find/Replace dialog box appears (see Figure 5-15).

2 **Type into the Search For input bar the phrase to search for. Type into the Replace With input bar the phrase to use as a replacement.**

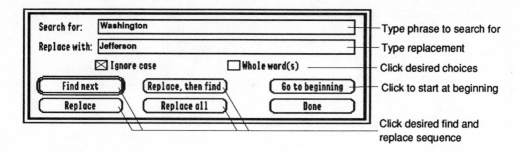

Figure 5-15   Find/Replace dialog box

3   **Click on the Ignore Case and Whole Word box if you wish.**

4   **Click on the Find Next button to begin the search.**

AppleWorks GS begins to search for your phrase , beginning at the
current insertion point. If the phrase is found, it is highlighted in the
document.

Click the Replace button to replace the current highlighted phrase.
The replacement phrase is substituted for the highlighted phrase, and
AppleWorks GS remains at the same location.

Click the Replace button, then the Find button to replace the current
highlighted phrase and automatically move to the next occurrence.

Click the Replace All button to automatically replace all occurrences
of the search phrase with the replacement text. The replacement text is
substituted for the search phrase from the current insertion point to the
end of the document.

5   **When you want to stop the search, click on the Done button,
and you return to the document.**

Note: *You can use the Find and Replace command to search for tab and return
characters in your document. To enter a tab character into the Find input
bar or Replace input bar, hold down the Option key and press the Tab key.
To enter a return character, hold down the Option key and press the Return
key.*

Find Again

You might want to quickly search again for the last search text that you
specified. To quickly search for the last search text, select the Find Again
command from the Search menu. The next occurrence of the search text
is highlighted. If the text does not occur between the current insertion

point and the end of the document, an alert box responds that no occurrences were found.

Shortcut: *Hold down the Open Apple key and press the F key to quickly search for*
                   the next occurrence of the last search text.

Using the Clipboard to move text

The AppleWorks GS Clipboard can be used to move one part of your text
to another location in your document. The Clipboard uses the Cut and
Copy commands on the Edit menu to create a temporary copy of selected
text. The Paste command is used to place this copy in a new location.

Using the Cut and Copy commands

The Cut and Copy commands on the Edit menu are similar, but they have
one important difference. The Copy command makes a temporary copy
of selected text, but leaves the original copy in its current location. The
Cut command makes a temporary copy of selected text and removes the
original text from the document.

1 **Select the text that you want to move to another location in your
   document. (See Figure 5-16.)**

2 **Choose the Copy or Cut command on the Edit menu. (See
   Figure 5-17.)**

Choose the Copy command if you want to leave one copy of the text in
its original location. Choose the Cut command if you want to remove the
original copy from its current location.
    A copy of the selected text is placed on the Clipboard. If you want to
verify the contents of the Clipboard, choose the Show Clipboard command on the Windows menu. A window is opened and displays the contents of the Clipboard.

Using the Paste command

You can now place the contents of the Clipboard anywhere else in your
document.

1 **Move the I-beam cursor to the location in the text where you
   want to place the contents of the Clipboard.**

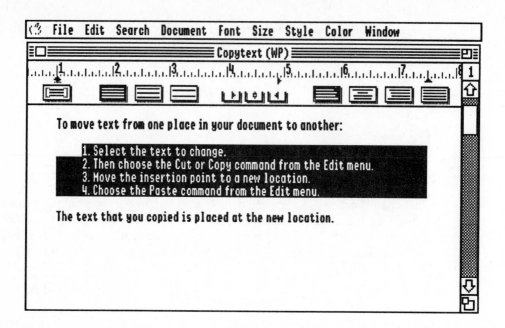

Figure 5-16   Select text to copy

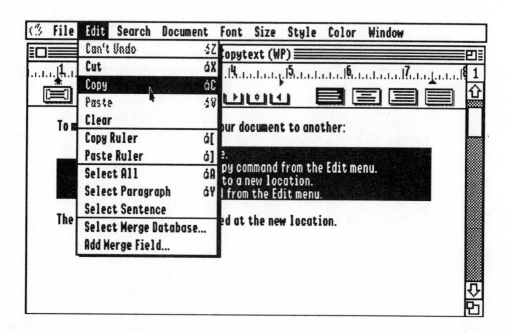

Figure 5-17   Select Copy command

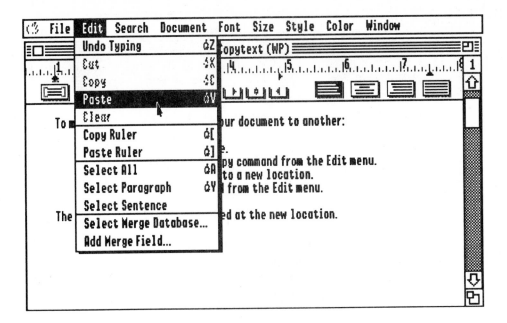

Figure 5-18 Select Paste command

2 **Click the mouse button to place the insertion point at the new location.**

3 **Select the Paste command from the Edit menu. (See Figure 5-18.)**

The contents of the Clipboard are pasted into your document at the insertion point. (See Figure 5-19.)

If you used the Copy command to place the text on the Clipboard, the text has been duplicated. You now have two copies of the text in your document, one copy at the original location and one copy in the new location.

If you used the Cut command to place the text on the Clipboard, the text has been moved from the original location to the new location.

Checking your spelling

You can check the spelling of words in your document using the Check Spelling command on the Search menu. AppleWorks GS checks your spelling by using a built-in dictionary. To find misspelled words in your document, AppleWorks GS:

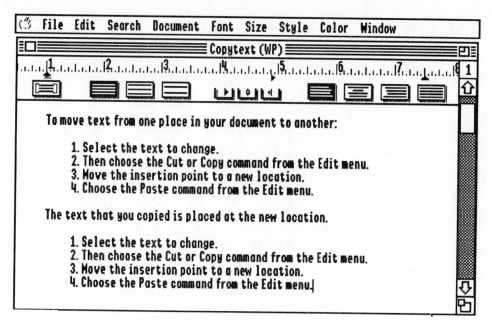

Figure 5-19 Text is copied in new location

- looks at each word in your document,
- compares each word with the words in the AppleWorks GS dictionary,
- looks in a special User Dictionary that contains additional words that you have added, and
- flags each word that is not in the dictionaries as a possible misspelled word.

Can you really find misspelled words?

It's important to realize what AppleWorks GS cannot do: AppleWorks GS can't really tell if each word is misspelled. All that it can do is find words that are not in the dictionary and tell you that those words may be misspelled.

Some of the words that the spelling checker finds may be spelled correctly, but may not be in the dictionary. Specialized medical terms, for instance, may not be in the dictionary These words are not really misspelled, but the AppleWorks GS spelling checker will present these words as possibly misspelled because they are not in the dictionary.

You can add these specialized terms to the User Dictionary. Once a word is added to the User Dictionary, that word will be in the dictionary in the future and will not be identified as possibly misspelled in the future.

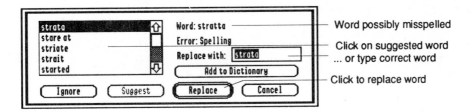

Figure 5-20 Check Spelling dialog box

It's important to realize that the spelling checker cannot tell you which words are spelled correctly but are used incorrectly. For instance, if you use the word "there" in your text where the word "their" should be used, the spelling checker will not identify this mistake.

Checking your spelling

To check the spelling in your document:

1. **Move the insertion point to the place in your document where you want to begin checking the spelling.**

2. **Select the Check Spelling command from the Search menu.**

The Check Spelling dialog box appears (see Figure 5-20).

3. **The first word that is not in the dictionary appears in the dialog box.**

To replace the word with an alternative word, type in the replacement word and click the Replace button.

Click the Suggest button to see suggested alternatives. Alternative spellings appear in the list box. To use one of the suggested alternatives, click on the alternative, and then click on the Replace button.

Click the Add to Dictionary button to add the current word to the dictionary. The word will not be seen as misspelled later.

To ignore the word and go to the next word, click the Ignore button.

4. **When you reach the end of the document, you are returned to your document to continue your work. You can also end the checking at any time by clicking on the Cancel button.**

Remember: the spelling checker begins to check your spelling at the current insertion point and continues to the end of the document. If you want to check the entire document, click the Go to Beginning button in the dialog box.

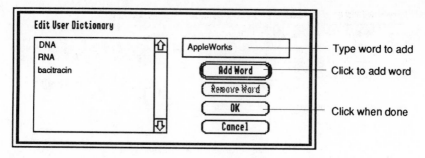

Figure 5-21 Edit Dictionary dialog box

Adding words to the User Dictionary

As you check the spelling of words in your document, you can add words to the User Dictionary one by one. These words will not be identified as possibly misspelled in future documents.

If you have many words to add to the AppleWorks GS User Dictionary, you can add those words quickly with the Edit Dictionary command:

1 Select the Edit Dictionary command from the Search menu.

The Edit Dictionary dialog box appears (see Figure 5-21).

2 Type a new word to add to the dictionary in the input bar, and click on the Add Word button to add the word to the User Dictionary.

3 To remove a word from the User Dictionary, click on the word in the list box. Then click the Remove Word button, and the word is removed from the dictionary.

4 Continue to add words to the list until you are finished. Click on the OK button to return to your document.

Looking for synonyms

AppleWorks GS can suggest possible synonyms for a selected word in your document.

1 Select the word in your document that you want to replace with a synonym.

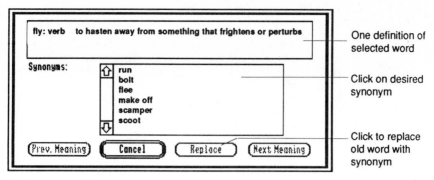

Figure 5-22   Synonyms dialog box

The following labels appear to the right of the figure:

One definition of selected word

Click on desired synonym

Click to replace old word with synonym

The dialog box contains:

fly: verb   to hasten away from something that frightens or perturbs

Synonyms:
run
bolt
flee
make off
scamper
scoot

Buttons: Prev. Meaning   Cancel   Replace   Next Meaning

---

2 **Select the Synonyms command from the Search menu.**

The Synonyms dialog box appears (see Figure 5-22).

3 **A suggested list of synonyms is displayed.**

The first list of synonyms appears, based on the first meaning of the word.

To replace the selected word with a suggested synonym, select the synonym and click the Replace button.

You can also see other suggested synonyms. Click the Next Meaning button to go on to the next suggested list of synonyms, based on the next meaning of the word. Click the Prev. Meaning button to go back to the last suggested synonym. When you want to use one of these synonyms, click the Replace button.

4 **Click on the Cancel button to return to the document without making a change.**

Checking the statistics on your document

As you work on your document, you might want to check the current length of the text, as well as other statistics.

To check the statistics on your document:

1 **Choose the Statistics command from the Document menu.**

The Statistics dialog box appears (see Figure 5-23).

This box displays the number of characters, words, lines, paragraphs, and pages in the document.

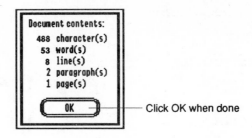

Document contents:
    488 character(s)
    53 word(s)
    8 line(s)
    2 paragraph(s)
    1 page(s)

    OK ———— Click OK when done

Figure 5-23 Statistics dialog box

[2] **Click OK to return to your document.**

Saving your revised document

After you revise your document, don't forget to save the current version of your work.

Use the Save command to save the current version of your document with the same name and on the same disk as it was last saved.

Use the Save As command to save the current version with a different name or on a different disk from previous versions.

Refer to Chapter 3 for a discussion of the Save and Save As commands.

The next step

Chapters 4 and 5 have discussed AppleWorks GS word processing. This is an important application, but AppleWorks GS provides far more than just word processing. Chapters 6 and 7 show you how to organize and retrieve information using the AppleWorks GS database application. Chapter 8 will show you how to combine word processing and database information to generate form letters, or mail-merge documents.

Chapter 6

Creating a Database Document

About this chapter

This chapter introduces the AppleWorks GS database application, which lets you save and work with information. Topics in the chapter include

- Introduction to database concepts
- Planning the database
- Creating a new database
- The new database document window
- The database menu bar
- Defining a new database form
- Setting field formats
- Using calculated fields
- Entering information in Form view
- Moving between Form view and List view
- Entering information in List view
- Saving the database
- Printing the database

Introduction to database concepts

Overview

What is a database? A database is just a collection of information. You've probably been using databases for years, even if the term isn't familiar to you. For instance, a good example of a database is your telephone book, that familiar collection of names, addresses, and telephone numbers.

An AppleWorks GS database is a similar collection of information, but the information is stored electronically.

An electronic database offers many advantages over a printed database:

- You can find information in the database quickly. It is much easier to retrieve your information from an electronic database than from a printed database.
- You can rearrange information in the database quickly. When you type information into a database, you don't need to worry about the order of the information, since you can rearrange it easily. For instance, you can quickly rearrange names in your database in alphabetical order, regardless of the order that you entered them.
- You can print out reports that summarize the information. For instance, if you'd like a list that contains some of the information in the database, you can print a summary report containing this information quickly.

Electronic index cards

Many computer applications provide the electronic equivalents of older paper-and-pencil methods. Word processing, for example, provides the electronic equivalent of the older typewriter technology.

You can think of a database as the electronic equivalent of a collection of index cards. If you store information on index cards, each index card might contain information on one particular item, and your "database" would consist of the collection of cards.

For example, suppose that you store the names and addresses of friends on index cards. You might use one index card for each friend, storing on each index card the name, address, and telephone number of one particular person.

The AppleWorks GS database works in a similar way. Your electronic database consists of a series of electronic "cards," with each "card" storing specific pieces of information about one individual, organization, or other entity.

Records and fields

Each of the "cards" in a database is called a record, and each AppleWorks GS database consists of a collection of records.

Each record contains one or more pieces of information, arranged in categories. For example, the categories in a record might be the name, address, and telephone number of an individual. Each category is called a field.

For example, if your database stores names, addresses, and telephone numbers of friends, each record would contain the information on each friend. Each record would contain fields that stored the name, address, and telephone number.

When you create a database, it's important to carefully plan the fields, or categories of information, that you want to store in each record. You can always change these fields later, but it's a good idea to think about these fields a bit in advance.

What information can you store?

Each field in a record stores one piece of information. For example, a field might store a name, a telephone number, a test score, or some other item of information.

What kinds of information can you store? AppleWorks GS can store these kinds of information in a field

- **Text.** Text information must be less than 255 characters in length. You can edit and format this text, just as you would in the word processing application.
- **Numeric data**, or numbers.
- **Date.** The date can be displayed in several formats, and the current date can be automatically entered from your Apple IIGS.
- **Time.** The time can be displayed in 12-hour or 24-hour format, and the current time can be automatically entered from your Apple IIGS.
- **Picture.** A field can display a graphic image created with Apple-Works GS or other graphic applications.
- **Static text.** Static text is text that is imported from another application. Static text can be longer than 255 characters in length, but this text cannot be changed or edited within the database. You can create and format lengthy text in the word processor, and then import the formatted text as static text.

Steps toward a database

When you are ready to use the database application, these steps are involved:

1. Planning the design of the database. This includes thinking about the fields that you need and the arrangement of the fields on the screen.
2. Creating a new database document. Once you've planned the fields needed for your database, you will define a blank database form on the screen. You will create each of the fields that you need and arrange them logically on the screen.
3. Entering information into the database. After you define a blank database form that contains the required fields, you will enter information into the database by filling out a series of these blank forms. Each form represents a record in the database, storing information on one individual, organization, or other entity.

   As you complete each form, a new blank form is presented. You can continue to fill out as many forms as you wish. You need not enter all of the information at one time; you can continue to add to the database over days, weeks, or years.

4. Using the database to organize your information. After you have entered information into the database, you can:

   • Retrieve information from the database. For example, if your database contains a list of names and telephone numbers, you can retrieve a specific number quickly.
   • Rearrange the contents of the database. You can quickly rearrange the database alphabetically or numerically.
   • Print out a report that contains some or all of the information in the database.

These operations are much faster and easier with an AppleWorks GS database than with a collection of index cards!

Planning the database

Overview

The first step in any database is planning the database, thinking about how the database should be organized.

• Think about the fields, or kinds of information, that you want to store in each record. Typical fields might include names, addresses, salaries, telephone numbers, or test scores. Each field should contain one piece of information.

If you wish, you can add or delete fields later, but it is easier to plan the fields carefully in advance.

- Think about the arrangement of the fields on the screen. When you create the database, you will create a form on the screen that will be used to enter your information; this form is the electronic equivalent of a blank index card. Before you create this form, think about a logical arrangement of the fields on the screen. You can always change the arrangement of fields on the screen later, but it's easier to begin with a logical arrangement.

Three kinds of fields

As you plan your database, you should know that each form can use three different kinds of fields:

1. Data-entry fields. A data-entry field is a field where you enter information on the form. For example, in a database that stores names and addresses, the Last Name field, First Name field, and Address field are all data-entry fields. Most of the fields in your databases will be data-entry fields.
2. Calculated fields. You can create a field that calculates and displays a value automatically, based on the values in other fields. For example, if a record in your database stores test scores on a student, one of the fields can be a calculated field that automatically displays the average of the test scores. After you enter the test scores into the appropriate data-entry fields, the calculated field uses those values to calculate and display the average.
3. Label fields. A label field is a special kind of field. When you create a label field, it displays the same information in every record. A label field is used to provide a label for the data-entry field or a calculated field, so that you remember what kind of value is being displayed.

Planning label fields

It's very important to include label fields as you plan your database. Practically speaking, you need to create a label field for every data-entry field or calculated field in the database.

For example, suppose that your first database stores names and addresses and contains these typical fields: Last name, First name, Street address, City, State, ZIP code, and Telephone number.

Your database form would contain seven fields to let you enter these seven pieces of information. These seven fields would be **data-entry fields**, where you would enter the actual information for each person included in your database.

When you create your database, these seven fields will appear as blank boxes on the screen where the seven pieces of information will be typed (see Figure 6-1).

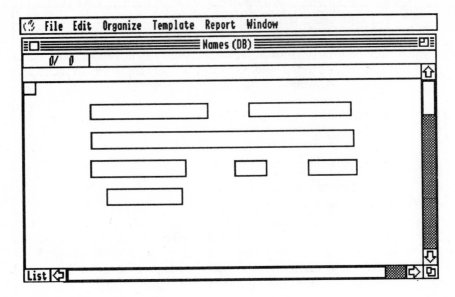

Figure 6-1   Blank form with data-entry fields

If you tried to use your database in this format, you would probably forget which piece of information should be entered in each blank field. This database form needs labels before each of these fields, to help you remember which information belongs in each data field.

A label field is a special kind of field. It contains information that does not change from one record to another. A label field might contain text like Name:, Address:, or other information to described the type of information to be added to a nearby data-entry field. After adding label fields to the sample database, the database form is much easier to understand (see Figure 6-2).

Creating a new database document

When you are ready to begin a new database document, there are two ways that you can create the new document:

- You can create a new document with the New command on the File menu.
- You can create a new document with the Open command on the File menu.

Opening a new database document with the New or Open command is discussed in Chapter 3, AppleWorks GS Common Commands,

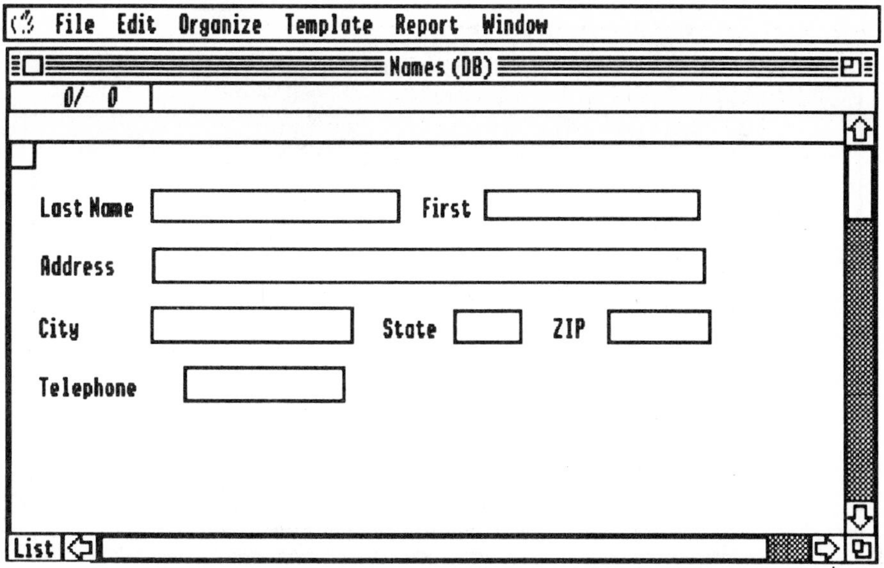

Figure 6-2   Add label fields

The new database document window

When you open a new database document, a document window appears on the screen. (See Figure 6-3.)

The first screen that is displayed in the new document is the database definition form. You will use this definition form to specify your database fields and place them in a desired arrangement on the screen. After you've defined your database form, you will use it to enter your actual information later.

The definition form includes a blank area where you will define and arrange your fields. The form also includes

- the database ruler, which helps you place specific fields at specific locations on the blank form.
- the header tab, which is the small box marked with the letter H. This tab can be pulled down to create a space for header information. Header information appears at the top of each page when you print the contents of the database. (If you use the scroll bar to view the part of the definition form that is off-screen, you will see two other tabs: the body tab marked with the letter B, and the footer tab marked with the letter F.)
- the Form/List box. This box lets you display your database in two ways. You can display one record on the screen at a time (Form view),

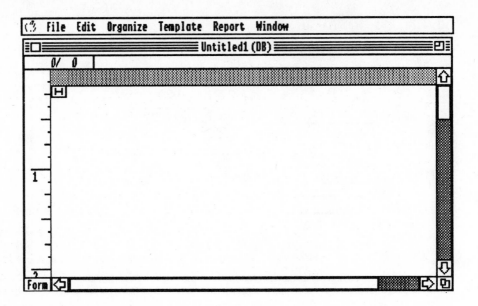

Figure 6-3 New database document

or you can see the information in many records displayed as a table (List view).

- the number of active records. AppleWorks GS lets you select some of your records and work with them as a temporary subset of the original database. For example, you might select 15 records with some special information, out of an original collection of 100 records. While you are working with this subset, the number of active records is displayed as 15/100.

The database menu bar

Figure 6-4
File menu

The database menu bar displayed at the top of the screen includes some commands that are common to all AppleWorks GS documents and some commands that are specific to the database.

The File menu

The commands on the File menu (Figure 6-4) include New, Open, Close, Save, Save As, Delete File, Import File, Choose Printer, Page Setup, Print, and Quit. The Print Merge command is dimmed on the File menu, since it is only available in the word processing application. The use of these commands is discussed in Chapter 3, AppleWorks GS Common Commands.

The Edit menu

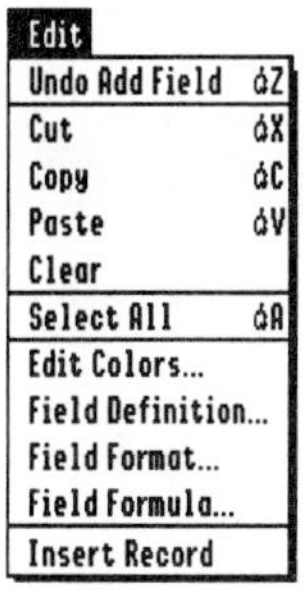

Figure 6-5
Edit menu

The commands on the Edit menu include Undo, Cut, Copy, Paste, Clear, and Select All. (See Figure 6-5.) These commands are discussed in Chapter 3, AppleWorks GS Common Commands.

The remaining commands on the database Edit menu control the type of data stored in a field and the format used to display the data. You can even control the colors displayed on the screen, using the Edit Colors command; the use of this specialized command is discussed in Appendix D, Using the Edit Colors command.

Field Definition: This command lets you specify a name for a field and define the type of data that will be entered into the field.

Field Format: This command lets you specify the styles to be used with the field, as well as other formats that vary with the type of data in the field.

Field Formula: This command lets you create a field that displays a value calculated from the values in other fields. For example, you could create a field that displays the sum or average of other fields in a record.

Insert Record: This command lets you create a new blank record between existing records in the database.

The Organize menu

Figure 6-6
Organize menu

The Organize menu contains commands that let you find specific records, display specific records and fields, and rearrange your records in a desired order. (See Figure 6-6.)

Find: This command lets you find any record that contains a specified value.

Find Next: This command repeats the last previous Find command.

Replace: This command lets you quickly find specified text and replace it with replacement text.

Match Records: This command selects and highlights any records that contain specified values.

Show All Records: This command lets you return to your original database after working with a subset of the database.

Hide Selected Records: This command temporarily removes selected records from display and lets you work with the remaining subset of the database.

Hide Unselected Records: This command temporarily removes unselected records from display and lets you work with the remaining subset of the database.

Mark Fields: This command places a special "mark" on selected fields. You can then control the display of these fields using the Display Marked Fields command.

Unmark Fields: This command removes the special "mark" from selected fields, and they are no longer controlled by the Display Marked Fields command.

Display Marked Fields: This command lets you control the display of the marked fields. If you choose this command, a check mark appears to the left of the command and marked fields are displayed. If you choose the command again, the checkmark is removed and marked fields are hidden.

Sort: This command rearranges the contents of the database into alphabetical or numeric order.

Figure 6-7
Template menu

The Template menu

In the database environment, a template describes the current working environment. This menu controls that environment. (See Figure 6-7.)

Show Definition: This command lets you return to the definition form to add, delete, or rearrange fields on the form.

Show Form: This displays your database in Form view, with each record displayed in the arrangement specified on the definition form.

Show List: This displays your database in List view, with the information from several records summarized in a table.

Open Template: This command opens a template that contains a previously-saved database environment.

Save Template: This command saves the current database environment, including current selection criteria and definition form.

Grid: This command controls an invisible grid of horizontal and vertical lines on the definition form. This grid makes it easier for you to align the left and top edges of your fields. When you select the Grid command, the grid is active and a checkmark appears next to the command; on the definition form, a field is automatically placed next to the nearest horizontal and vertical grid lines.

Grid Size: This command controls the spacing of the invisible horizontal and vertical lines on the grid.

Display Preferences: This command lets you display more than one form per page in Form view, print lines between forms, or hide the horizontal and vertical lines in the List view of your database.

Return Key Preferences: This command lets you control the action taken when you press the Return key: go to the beginning of the next record, go to the same field in the next record, or go to the next field in the current record.

Choose Font: This command lets you select the font name, style, and size for selected text.

The Report menu

The Report menu controls the format of your reports. The commands on the Report menu include Header, Footer, Format, Summary Only, and Create Report. (See Figure 6-8.)

Header: This command lets you create a header for your report.

Footer: This command creates footers for the report.

Figure 6-8
Report menu

Format: This command lets you specify column headings, subtotal, and total information for the reports. Reporting options include the number of records in the report, sum, average value, maximum value, minimum value, and standard deviation.

Summary Only: This command lets you generate a summary of the data, with subtotals and totals, but the database information itself is not printed.

Create Report: This command creates a new word processing document containing the specified report.

The Window menu

This menu lists the currently open windows and the Clipboard. The use of this menu is discussed in Chapter 3, AppleWorks GS Common Commands.

Defining a new database form

Defining a field on the definition form

After you've thought about your database fields, you're ready to work with the database definition form:

1   **Move the arrow pointer into the database definition form and place the arrow at the location where you want the first field.**

2   **Hold down the mouse button, and drag the mouse diagonally.**

As you drag the mouse, a rectangle appears on the screen. (See Figure 6-9.) This marks the location of the first field. This rectangle can be moved and resized later, so the precise size and location are not critically important.

3   **When the desired rectangle is drawn on the screen, release the mouse button.**

The rectangle remains at the location, and a Field Definition dialog box appears. (See Figure 6-10.) The Field Definition box lets you name the field and specify the kind of information that it will contain.

4   **If the field is a label, check the Label box. Remember that a label field will show the same information on each record.**

5   **Type a name for the field, and click on the type of data that will be entered in the field later.**

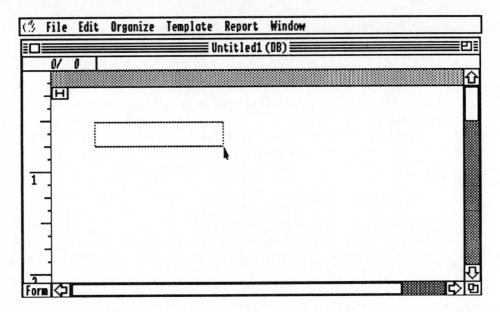

Figure 6-9   Field being drawn on definition form

Types of data include text, numeric, picture, date, static text, or time. These types are discussed later in the chapter with the Field Format command.

| 6 | **Click on the OK button when the dialog box is completed.** |

You are returned to the definition form, and the field remains selected. The name of the field appears in the input bar above the form. You can edit the name of the field in the input bar. Click in the input bar and edit the name using the Delete key or any of the methods used to edit text in the word processing application.

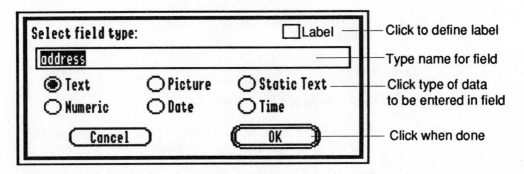

Figure 6-10   Field Definition dialog box

Moving and stretching the field box

After you define the field, the field box is selected. The field appears highlighted, and small boxes (called handles) appear at each corner. You can move the box and stretch it to make it larger or smaller.

To move the field:

[1] Move the arrow pointer into the box.

[2] Hold down the mouse button.

[3] Drag the box to another location on the form.

To resize the field:

[1] Move the tip of the arrow pointer until it touches one of the handles.

[2] Hold down the mouse button, and drag the handle.

As you drag the handle, the box stretches in the direction that you are dragging. (See Figure 6-11.)

[3] When the box is the desired size, release the button.

Defining other fields on the definition form

After the first field has been defined, repeat the same process for the other fields on the form.

[1] For each field, drag a rectangle on the form where you would like to enter information later.

[2] Complete the Field Definition dialog box defining the type of data that will be entered into the field.

[3] Adjust the position and size of the field as required.

After you have entered several fields on the definition form, the definition form might look like the form in Figure 6-12.

This definition form has seven fields where data will be entered: Last Name, First Name, Address, City, State, Zip Code, and Telephone. All of these fields are defined as text fields. (Even the Zip Code field is defined as a text field. If it were defined as a numeric field, zip codes like 01867 would be displayed as 1867.)

A separate label field has been created in front of each of the data-entry fields. The label fields provide a category name for each location

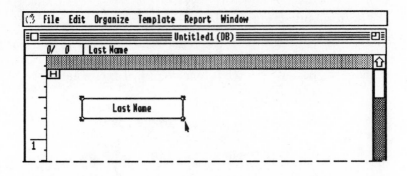

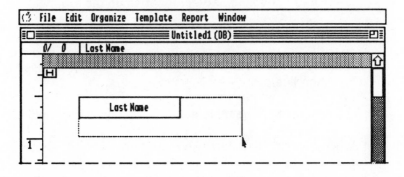

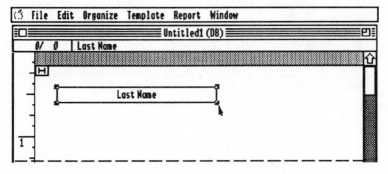

Figure 6-11 Field being resized

where you will enter data later. Most of the data-entry fields on a database form require additional label fields like these.

Enlarging the definition form

You may find that the definition form is too small for the number of fields that you are creating. You can easily enlarge the working area on the definition form.

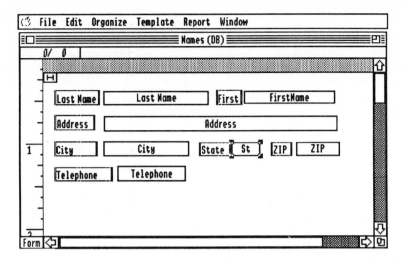

Figure 6-12 Sample definition form

1️⃣ **Move the arrow pointer to the body tab (the box labeled with letter B) located at the bottom of the definition form.**

2️⃣ **Place the arrow pointer on the body tab, and drag the tab up or down.**

This resizes the body of the form. You can adjust it to any desired size.

Revising the definition form

You may want to make changes in the database definition form later. For example, you may want to return to the definition form to add new fields, delete fields, move fields on the form, or make other changes.

You can easily return to the definition form to make these changes:

1️⃣ **Choose the Show Definition command on the Template menu.**

The definition form returns to the screen.

2️⃣ **Make the desired changes.**

You can select a field by clicking on the field, and then make desired changes to the field. You can add more fields to the form, delete forms, or change existing fields. These changes are discussed in more detail in Chapter 7.

Setting field formats

After you have defined the fields for your database and arranged them on the form, you can control the format that is used to display the information in each field. (If you are impatient, you can skip this section and begin to enter information without setting field formats. You can return to this section later and adjust the field formats any time that you wish!)

To set the format for a field, you must:

1. **Select the field to change.**

2. **Choose the desired changes from the menu and from dialog boxes.**

Selecting a field

When you create a field by dragging a rectangle on the definition form, the field is selected and four handles appear at each corner of the field.

When you create another field, the first field is deselected and the handles disappear. However, you can always go back to a field later and select it for action.

To select a field later, click on the field, and the handles appear at each corner of the field.

When no field on the definition form is selected, the Field Format and Field Formula commands are dimmed on the Edit menu and not available for use. After you select a field, those two commands are available to control the display of the selected field.

Using the Field Format command

The Field Format command controls the styles and other format used to display the contents of a field. To use the Field Format command:

1. **Select the field that you want to control.**

2. **Choose the Field Format command from the Edit menu.**

One of the Field Format dialog boxes appears.

Each of the six data types (text, numeric, date, time, picture, and static text) has a Field Format dialog box, since each type has different needs.

Shortcut: *To display the Field Format dialog box for a specific field, double-click on the field box on the definition form.*

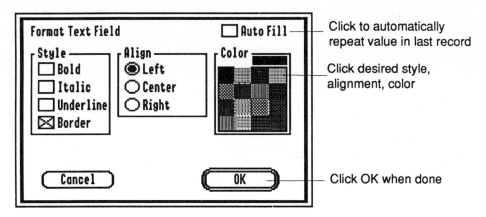

Figure 6-13   Text Field Format dialog

Text Field Format dialog

If a field is defined as a text field, you can enter up to 255 characters into the field. The Text Field Format dialog lets you control how the text is displayed in the field (see Figure 6-13).

1   **Choose the style, alignment, and color desired for the text in the field.**

2   **Click the Autofill box if you wish to use this feature.**

The Autofill feature is a time-saving convenience that helps you avoid unnecessary typing. If you check Autofill, this field will automatically display in each record the same value that you entered in the last record.

For example, if your database stores student information, one of the fields in each record may be Grade Level. Many students will have the same entry for the Grade Level field, and Autofill can be used to automatically begin each record with the same entry in the Grade Level field as was entered in the previous record. This prevents repetitive typing of the same information.

3   **Click OK when the settings are correct.**

You are returned to the definition form and the field remains selected.

Numeric Field Format dialog

If a field is defined as a numeric field, the Numeric Field Format dialog lets you control how numeric values are displayed (see Figure 6-14).

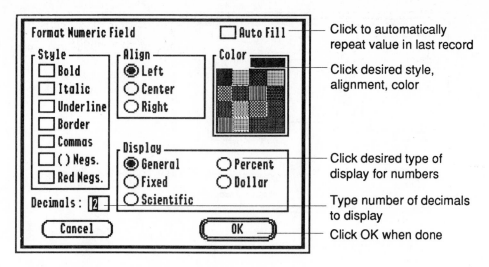

Figure 6-14   Numeric Field Format dialog

1. **Click the style, alignment, and color desired for the numbers in this field.**

You can also select the Autofill feature, described above.

2. **Click the numeric format used for the data.**

You can display the values in

- General format. AppleWorks GS will fit the number into the field provided, showing as many significant figures as possible.
- Fixed format. If you select this option, the number is displayed with the number of decimal places that you specify.
- Scientific notation. The number is displayed in scientific notation. For example, the number 345 would be displayed as 3.45e2, and the number .00567 would be displayed as 5.67e-3.
- Percent. The number is displayed as a percentage. For example, the number .106 would be displayed as 10.6%.
- Dollar. The number is displayed with two decimal places and preceded with a dollar sign. For example, the number 98.3 would be displayed as $98.30.

3. **Click OK when the settings are correct.**

You are returned to the definition form and the field remains selected.

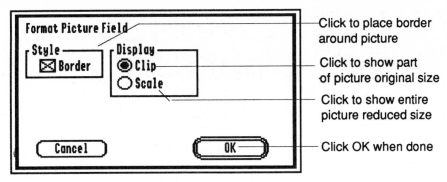

Figure 6-15 Picture Field Format dialog

Picture Field Format dialog

You can include picture fields in the database. A picture field can contain graphics created with AppleWorks GS graphics applications or graphics imported from other sources. The Picture Field Format dialog lets you control how a graphic is displayed in the field (see Figure 6-15).

1. **Click the style and type of display that you want to use.**

If you check Clip, the picture is displayed in the field in its original size. The upper left corner of the graphic is displayed in the upper left corner of the field, and the rest of the field is filled from that corner. If the picture is too large to fit in the field, only the area that fits into the field is displayed.

If you check Scale, the picture is scaled down until the entire picture can fit into the field area.

2. **Click OK when the settings are correct.**

You are returned to the definition form and the field remains selected.

Date Field Format dialog

When you define a date field, you can enter dates into the field using any of these formats: June 1, 1989, 06/01/89, 6-1-89, or 6.1.89. The Date Field format box sets the format used to display the dates in the field (see Figure 6-16).

1. **Select the style, alignment, and color desired for the numbers in this field.**

You can also select the Autofill feature, described previously.

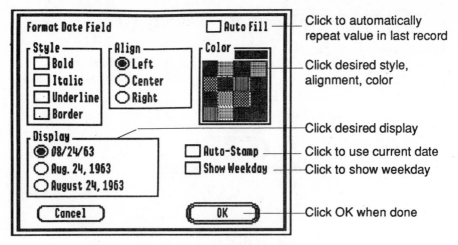

Format Date Field   ☐ Auto Fill ——— Click to automatically
                                           repeat value in last record
┌Style──┐ ┌Align──┐ ┌Color─────┐
☐ Bold   ⊙ Left   ——— Click desired style,
☐ Italic   ○ Center   alignment, color
☐ Underline ○ Right
☐ Border

┌Display────┐   ——— Click desired display
⊙ 08/24/63   ☐ Auto-Stamp ——— Click to use current date
○ Aug. 24, 1963   ☐ Show Weekday ——— Click to show weekday
○ August 24, 1963

(Cancel)   (OK)   ——— Click OK when done

Figure 6-16   Date Field Format dialog

☐2☐   **Click the format used to display the date.**

When you enter a date in this field, it will be displayed using the format that you select here.

☐3☐   **Select Auto-Stamp if you want AppleWorks GS to automatically enter today's date into the field.**

☐4☐   **Click Show Weekday if you want the day of the week automatically included as part of the date.**

☐5☐   **Click OK when the settings are correct.**

You are returned to the definition form and the field remains selected.

Static Text Field Format dialog

Static text is formatted text that is imported from another application. It can be longer than the 255 characters permitted in an ordinary text field, but it cannot be edited or changed.

You can create and format lengthy text in the AppleWorks GS word processing application and then copy the text into a static text field using the Clipboard. You can also import an entire file of formatted text into a static text field with the Import File command on the File menu.

The Static Text Field Format dialog lets you control the display of static text (see Figure 6-17).

☐1☐   **Click the Border box if you want to display a border around the static text.**

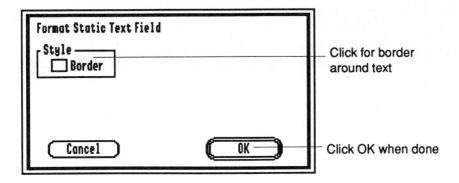

Figure 6-17   Static Text Field Format dialog

Click for border
around text

Click OK when done

---

2   **Click the OK button to return to the definition form.**

You are returned to the definition form and the field remains selected.

Time Field Format dialog

When you define a time field, you can enter times into the field using any of these formats: 1:30 pm (to indicate 1:30 in the afternoon), 1:30 (to indicate 1:30 am), or 13:30 (to indicate 1:30 in the afternoon). The Time Field format box sets the format used to display the times in the field (see Figure 6-18).

1   **Choose the style, alignment, and color desired for the numbers in this field.**

You can also select the Autofill feature, described above.

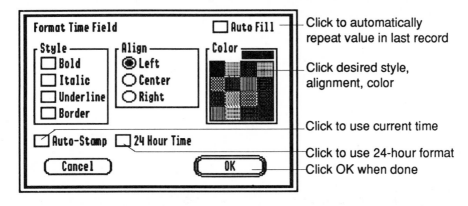

Click to automatically
repeat value in last record

Click desired style,
alignment, color

Click to use current time

Click to use 24-hour format
Click OK when done

Figure 6-18   Time Field Format dialog

2 **Click Auto-Stamp if you want AppleWorks GS to automatically enter the current time into this field.**

3 **Click 24-hour Time to display the time in 24-hour format.**

For example, 6:00 p.m. is displayed as 18:00 in 24-hour format.

4 **Click OK when the settings are correct.**

You are returned to the definition form and the field remains selected.

Using calculated fields

A calculated field is a special kind of field. It displays a value that is calculated from the other values found in the record.

For example, a calculated field might display the total of other fields contained in a record, or the average of values found in other fields.

AppleWorks GS lets you easily create calculated fields that can show the sum or average of other fields. In fact, it lets you create calculated fields that will display the results of virtually any formula that you can construct.

Creating a calculated field

To create a calculated field:

1 **Create the field by dragging a rectangle on the definition form in the usual way.**

When the Field Definition dialog box is displayed, click the type of data that will be displayed in the field.

2 **Select the field by clicking on the field.**

When the field is selected, handles appear at each corner of the field.

3 **Choose the Field Formula command on the Edit menu.**

The Field Formula dialog box appears (see Figure 6-19). The dialog box includes three list boxes that list

- all of the available fields in the database,
- operations that can be performed, and
- AppleWorks GS built-in functions that can be used in the formula.

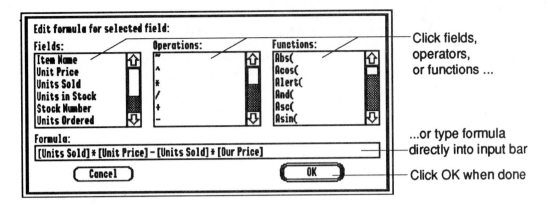

Edit formula for selected field:

Fields:	Operations:	Functions:
Item Name	^	Abs(
Unit Price	*	Acos(
Units Sold	/	Alert(
Units in Stock	+	And(
Stock Number	-	Asc(
Units Ordered		Asin(

Formula:

[Units Sold] * [Unit Price] - [Units Sold] * [Our Price]

Cancel   OK

— Click fields, operators, or functions ...

...or type formula
directly into input bar

Click OK when done

Figure 6-19   Field Formula dialog

---

4   **Enter the formula to use to calculate the value for the field.**

You can enter the formula by double-clicking on the elements of the formula that are provided in the three list boxes.

For instance, if you want the field to display the sum of the values in Field1 and Field2, double-click on the name Field1 in the first list box, double-click on the plus sign in the middle list box, and double-click on the name Field2 in the first list box.

This formula appears in the input bar:

[Field1] + [Field2]

5   **Click the OK button when the formula is correct.**

In this example the current field will now display the sum of the values in Field1 and Field2.

You can also enter the formula by typing any desired formula directly into the input bar. Any field names that you enter into the formula must be surrounded by square brackets.

Using a calculated field

It's very simple to use a calculated field. As you enter information into the database, you never enter information into a calculated field. As you enter values into the fields that are needed for the calculation, the calculated field automatically performs the required calculations and displays the calculated value.

For more information

For more information on AppleWorks GS formulas and functions, see Appendix B, AppleWorks GS Formulas and Appendix C, AppleWorks GS Functions.

Entering information in Form view

After you have defined your database form, you can enter information into the database.

AppleWorks GS lets you view your database in two ways: Form view, which displays your database as forms on the screen, or List view, which displays the information in table format. You can enter information in either view, but Form view is the easiest way to begin.

In Form view, you are presented with a blank data-entry form on the screen that corresponds to the form that you just defined. You enter information into the database by completing the form.

After that first form has been completed, another blank form is displayed, and you enter the next set of information. You can continue to add information as long as you wish.

You can stop entering information at any point, save your work, and leave the application. You can return at any time (next week, next month, or next year), open the database, and add to or retrieve the information stored in the database.

Entering information into forms

1 **Choose the Show Form command from the Template menu.**

A blank data-entry form appears.

Shortcut: *Click on the Form box in the lower-left corner of the document window, and a data-entry form appears.*

The blank data-entry form displays labels and data-entry fields (see Figure 6-20).

2 **Click on the first field where you want to enter a value.**

The field is selected and highlighted.

3 **Enter the type of data expected for that field.**

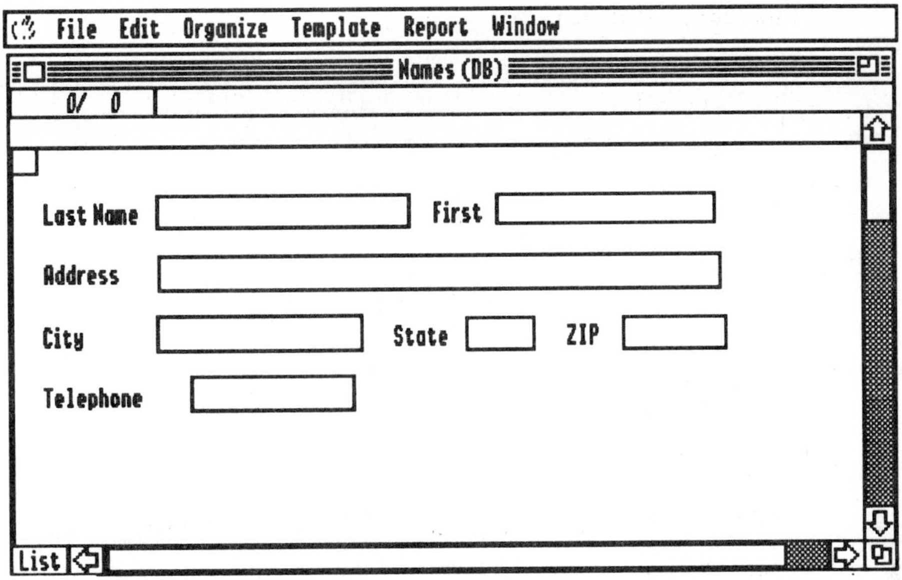

Figure 6-20 Blank data-entry form

If the type of data is text, numeric, date, or time, you can type the information at the keyboard. As you type in the data, the data appears in the input bar at the top of the screen. You can edit the data in the input bar using the Delete key or any other method used to edit text in the word processing application. You can also copy text, numeric, date, or time data into a field from the Clipboard.

If the field is defined as a picture field, enter the picture into the field by copying the picture from the Clipboard or by importing a graphics file using the Import File command on the File menu.

If the field is static text, enter the static text into the field by copying the text from the Clipboard or by importing a formatted text file using the Import File command on the File menu.

4 **When the data for the first field is complete, press the Tab key.**

The data is entered into the first field, and the second field in the form is highlighted.

5 **Enter the data for the second field, and press the Tab key.**

Continue to complete each field on the first form. (See Figure 6-21.)

6 **When you complete the first form, press the Return key.**

```
 File   Edit   Organize   Template   Report   Window
┌─────────────────────────────── Names (DB) ───────────────────────────────┐
│  1/ 1                                                                      │
│  ┌──────────────────────────────────────────────────────────────────┐  ⇧ │
│  │                                                                    │    │
│  │  Last Name  ┌Smith──────────┐     First  ┌Susan─────────┐          │    │
│  │                                                                    │    │
│  │  Address    ┌1122 Pine Oak Lane──────────────────────┐             │    │
│  │                                                                    │    │
│  │  City       ┌Louisville─────┐   State ┌KY┐   ZIP ┌  40205┐         │    │
│  │                                                                    │    │
│  │  Telephone  ┌555-1234───┐                                          │    │
│  │                                                                    │  ⇩ │
│  │                                                                    │    │
│  └───────────────────────────────────────────────────────────────────   │
│ ┌List┐◁─┤                                                    ⇨ ┐         │
└───────────────────────────────────────────────────────────────────────────┘
```

Figure 6-21   Completed first form

The next blank form is presented, with the first field on the form highlighted. Continue to enter data into this form and subsequent forms until
you have entered the desired information into the database.

Blank fields

What about fields where you do not have the required information? You
can always leave a field blank. Just press the tab key — the current field
is left blank, and the next field is highlighted. You can return to the form
later in the session (or at a later date) to enter information into any field
in the database, so you can leave any field blank for now.

Return Key Preferences

When you press the Return key, the next form is displayed with the first
field highlighted. You may want to change this action. For instance, you
might like to move to the next field in the current record when you press
the Return key.

To change the action of the Return key, choose the Return Key
Preferences command from the Template menu and click on the action
that you want to occur when you press the Return key.

To return to previous forms

Once you've entered information into several blank forms, you might
want to return to a previous form to review the information on the form.

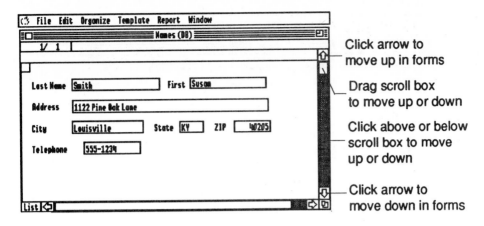

Figure 6-22 Document window, callouts to scroll bar operations

To return to an earlier form:

1 **Move the arrow pointer to the scroll bar at the right of the window.**

2 **Click on the up-arrow at the top of the scroll bar to move up to previous records in the database.**

You can also click in the gray area above the scroll box to move up one form in the database, or drag the scroll box upwards to move to earlier forms in the database. (See Figure 6-22.)

Click on the down-arrow at the bottom of the scroll bar to move to the next form in the database, or drag the scroll box down in the scroll bar to move to later forms.

Changing information on previous forms

When you return to an earlier form, you can correct or update the information in a field:

1 **Use the scroll bar to move the desired form to the screen.**

2 **Click on the field that you want to change.**

The field is selected and highlighted. (See Figure 6-23.)

3 **Type the corrected or updated information, and press the tab or Return key.**

The new or revised information is displayed in the field.

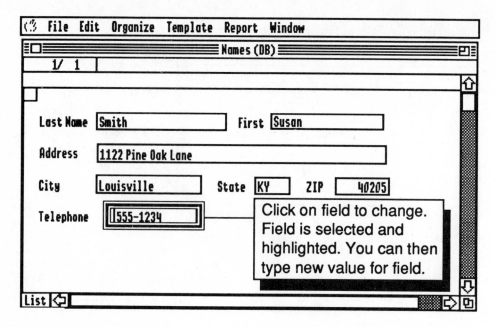

Figure 6-23 Revise information in form

Finding the next blank form

The next blank form can be found at the end of the current forms. To find the next blank form, drag the scroll box to the bottom of the scroll bar.

Form view and List view

AppleWorks GS lets you view and work with your database in Form view or in List view.

In Form view, each record is shown on the screen with the fields arranged in the same way that you defined them. When you work with your database using Form view, it is similar to working with index cards. Form view is similar to Single-Record Format in the classic AppleWorks database, where you can work with the contents of one record on the screen at one time.

AppleWorks GS also lets you enter and work with your database a second way, using List view. In List view, your database information is displayed as a table. List view is similar to Multiple-Record format in the classic AppleWorks database, where you can see the contents of several records on the screen at once.

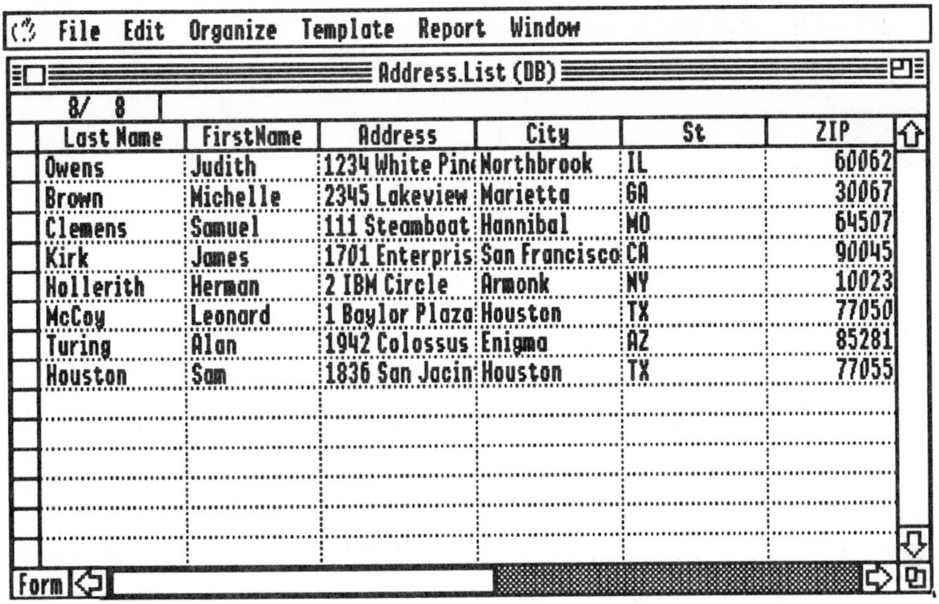

Figure 6-24 List view

Entering List view from Form view

When you are viewing your data in Form view, you can easily move to List view:

1. **Select the Show List command from the Template menu.**

The database is now displayed on the screen as a table. (See Figure 6-24.)

The field names are provided at the top of the table, and each record is displayed as a row in the table. The first record in the database is displayed in the first row in the table, the second record is displayed in the second row, and so forth.

Some fields are not displayed in List view. Label fields, picture fields, and static text fields are not displayed in List view.

Each piece of information is contained in a cell on the screen. If you click on a cell, it is selected for some action; the selected cell is called the active cell.

Some of the information may not fit on the screen, since each record may contain more fields than can fit on the screen. Use the scroll bar at the bottom of the window to view fields on each record that are not initially visible on the screen.

The database may contain more records than can be viewed on the screen at one time. Use the scroll bar at the right side of the document window to view records not initially visible on the screen.

Shortcut: *You can enter List view from Form view by clicking on the word List in the lower-left corner of the document window.*

To enter Form view from List view

When you are viewing your data in List view, you can easily move back to Form view:

1   **Select the Show Form command from the Template menu.**

The database is again displayed in Form view.

Shortcut: *You can enter Form view from List view by clicking on the word Form in the lower-left corner of the document window.*

Entering information in List view

Adjusting field widths in List view

When you view your information in List view, some fields may be too narrow to display all of the information in the field. Other fields may be wider than necessary, and you can view more fields on the screen if you narrow the width of these fields.

To adjust the width of the fields in List view:

1   **Move the arrow pointer into the field names at the top of the table.**

2   **Adjust the tip of the arrow until it touches the line to the right of one of the field names.**

This is the field boundary. As you touch the field boundary, the arrow pointer turns into a double-arrow cursor. (See Figure 6-25.)

3   **Hold down the mouse button, and drag the field boundary left or right.**

As you move the double-arrow, the border between the two adjacent fields is adjusted, and the field to the left of the field boundary is widened or narrowed. (See Figure 6-26.)

Figure 6-25 Adjusting the width of a field

You can expand the area allowed for the field to display more information, or you can shrink the area used for the field to permit more fields
to be displayed on the screen.

When you adjust the width of each field in List view, these changes have
no effect on the fields in Form view. The fields in Form view are displayed
with the widths and shapes that you defined on the definition form.

Moving fields in List view

Since you may not be able to view all of the fields in the window at once
in List view, you may want to rearrange the order of fields in the table.
You can move fields to the left or right by moving entire columns of data.

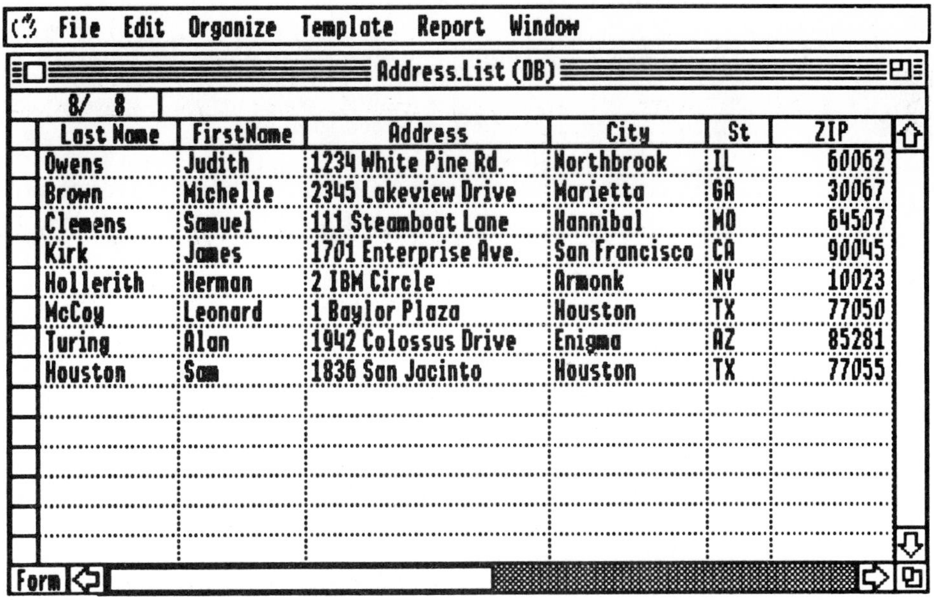

Figure 6-26 List view with adjusted field widths

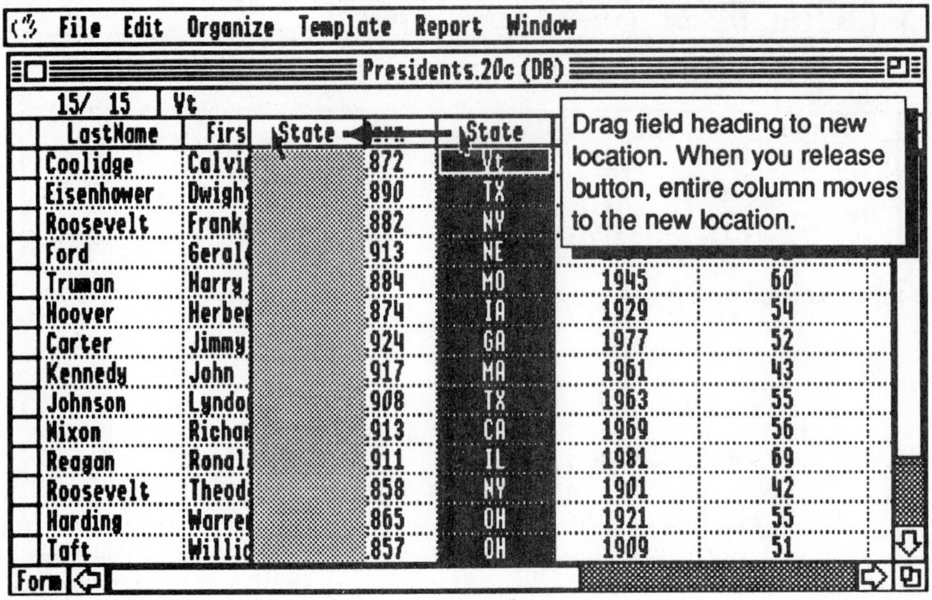

Figure 6-27 Field being moved

To move a field:

1 **Move the arrow pointer into the field name at the top of the column.**

2 **Hold down the Option key, and press down the mouse button.**

The entire column of data is selected to move.

3 **Continue to hold down the Option key and the mouse button, and drag the column to the left or right.**

As you drag the column, a marker representing the column moves across the window. (See Figure 6-27.)

4 **When the marker is located where you want to move the column, release the mouse button and Option key.**

The entire field is moved to the new location.

Entering data in List view

Both Form view and List view offer distinct advantages. Form view lets you see more fields at one time, but List view lets you add information quickly using the table format.

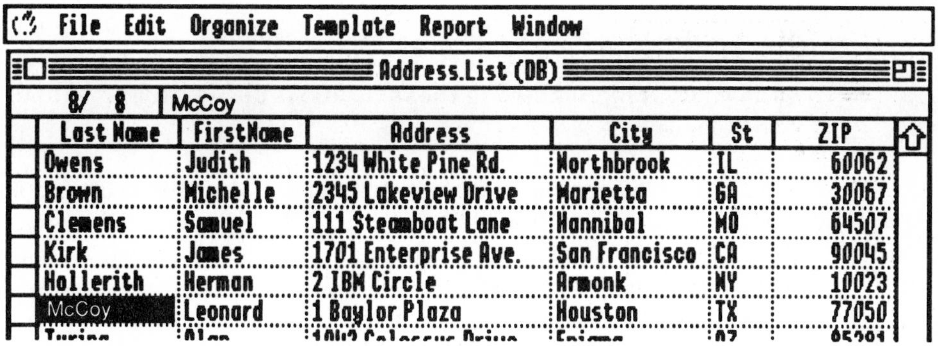

	File	Edit	Organize	Template	Report	Window

Address.List (DB)

| 8/ 8 | McCoy |

Last Name	FirstName	Address	City	St	ZIP	
Owens	Judith	1234 White Pine Rd.	Northbrook	IL	60062	
Brown	Michelle	2345 Lakeview Drive	Marietta	GA	30067	
Clemens	Samuel	111 Steamboat Lane	Hannibal	MO	64507	
Kirk	James	1701 Enterprise Ave.	San Francisco	CA	90045	
Hollerith	Herman	2 IBM Circle	Armonk	NY	10023	
McCoy	Leonard	1 Baylor Plaza	Houston	TX	77050	
Turing	Alan	1002 Colossus Drive	Enigma	AZ	85301	

Figure 6-28   Selected cell

To enter data in List view:

1   **Click on the first cell where you want to enter a value.**

You might want to begin by entering a value into the first data-entry field of a new record, or you may want to begin with another cell. Click on the cell where you want to enter a data value.

After you click on the cell, it is selected and highlighted. (See Figure 6-28.)

2   **Type the information that you want to enter into the cell, and press the Tab key.**

The next field in the current record is highlighted and ready for new information. Continue to enter information into each cell. Press the Return key to move to the first field in the next record.

Remember that you can use the Return Key Preferences command on the Template menu to change the action that occurs when you press the Return key.

Shortcut: *You can quickly enter the same value in a record's field that was contained in that field in the previous record.*

1   **Highlight the cell where you want to enter a value.**

2   **Hold down the Option key and press the quote key.**

The value in the cell immediately above this cell is copied to the selected cell.

Changing data in List view

To change a value that is displayed in a field:

1   **Click on the value that you want to change.**

The value is highlighted in the table and is displayed in the input bar at the top of the screen.

2   **Type in a replacement value or edit the old value in the input bar.**

3   **Press the Tab key.**

The new value replaces the old value in the database.

Finding the next blank record in List view

The next blank record in List view is always found immediately beneath the last record in the table. To enter information into the next blank record, move to the row beneath the last record in the table.

Saving the database

After you've entered information into your database, you can use the data in many ways. You can retrieve the information in a record, you can rearrange the records in a desired numeric or alphabetic order, and you can print out summary reports containing some or all of the information.

Before using the data in the database, however, you should always save your information to your storage disk. Remember to save your work often.

Refer to Chapter 3 for a discussion of the Save and Save As commands.

When you save your database using the Save As command, pay special attention to the formatting buttons at the bottom of the dialog box (see Figure 6-29). The Save As dialog box lets you save your work in database format or as ASCII text. The ASCII text format saves a simplified version of your database that can be transferred to other computers and program more easily. The ASCII version does not retain special AppleWorks GS information, including picture information, styles, and other AppleWorks GS features.

Printing your database document

Printing the entire database

After you have entered information into your database, you will probably want to print a copy of the information on your printer. You can print a copy of the definition form, or you can print a copy of the database information in Form view or in List view.

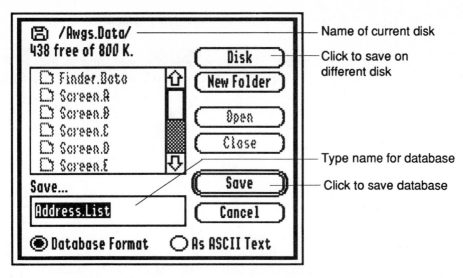

Figure 6-29   Save As dialog box

To print the database:

1 **Select the definition form, Form view, or List view.**

You can choose the Show Definition, Show Form, or Show List command on the Template menu to move to the desired view. If you select Form view, choose the Display Preferences command on the Template menu and check Multiple Forms Per Page to print more than one form per page.

2 **Use the Choose Printer command on the File menu to select the printer to use.**

3 **Use the Page Setup command on the File menu to specify the type of paper, vertical sizing, printer effects, and orientation that you want to use.**

4 **Select the Print command on the File menu; select the print quality, page range, and number of copies that you want to use. (You can also specify automatic or manual paper feed, as well as color printing.) When you have made your selections, click the OK button in the Print dialog box to begin printing.**

(For more information about printing, see the Choose Printer command, Page Setup command, and Print command in Chapter 3: Apple-Works GS Common Commands.)

Printing summary reports from your database

The Print command prints your entire database, but you have many more printing options. You can print specialized reports that include part or all of the database information, and you can include summary information, including field totals, average values, minimum and maximum values. You can even print the standard deviation of field values in your reports. The next chapter describes how to produce these specialized reports.

The next step

Now that the basic information has been entered into your database, you can use the database to retrieve and organize the information. In the next chapter, you will learn how to find information in the database, how to rearrange the information in any desired order, and how to print reports that summarize the information in the database.

Chapter 7

Working with Database Documents

About this chapter

After you have created a database document, you can find specific items of information quickly, rearrange the information easily, and print summary reports that contain some or all of the information.

This chapter surveys how to use an AppleWorks GS database. The topics in this chapter include

- Opening a saved database document
- Adding to or changing information in the database
- Sorting or rearranging information in the database
- Finding or retrieving information in the database
- Selecting part of the database for further action
- Printing specialized reports of database information
- Using templates to save database environments

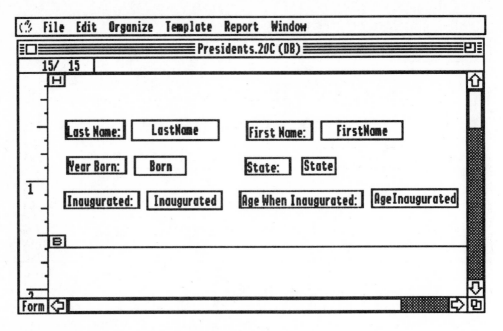

Figure 7-1   Display definition form of Presidents database

Opening a saved database document

If you have used the database application to create a database in an earlier session, you might want to return to the document later to add to the document, retrieve information, revise part of the information, or print out a summary report.

To open a saved database document:

1 **Select Open from the File menu.**

2 **Click on the name of the database document that you want to open, and click on the Open button.**

Shortcut: *Double-click on the name of the database document that you want to open.*

The saved database document is opened into a document window, and the definition form is displayed.

For example, the database in Figure 7-1 stores simple information on 20th century American presidents.

Note: *If you open a classic AppleWorks database file, the database categories are converted to AppleWorks GS fields, and the fields are placed on the definition form aligned with the left edge of the form. You can move and resize these fields or add any desired fields to the definition form.*

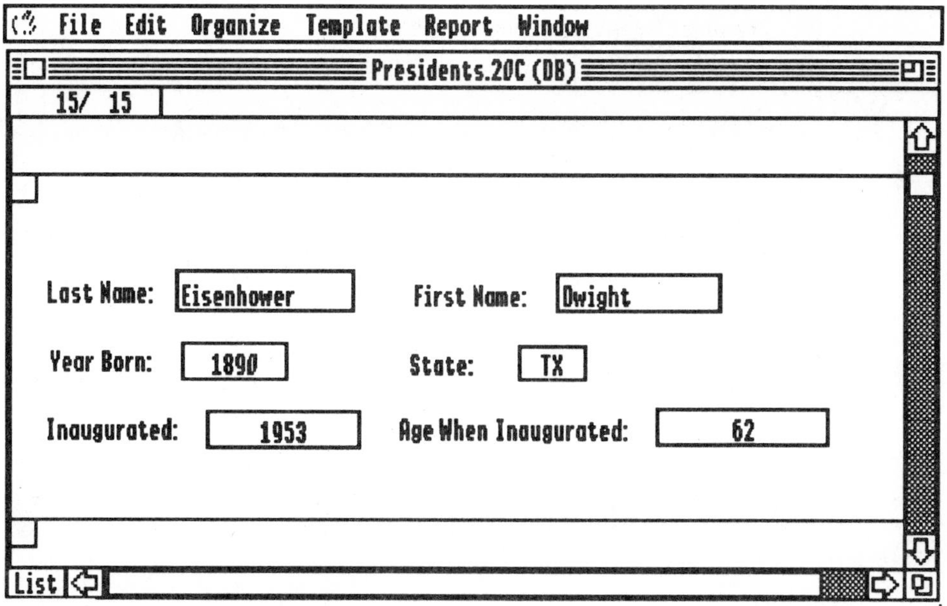

```
 ( *  File   Edit   Organize   Template   Report   Window
 ▤□ ═══════════════════ Presidents.20C (DB) ════════════════ 回▤
   15/  15

                                                            ⇧
 ┌─┐                                                        ▓
 └─┘                                                        ▓

     Last Name:  │Eisenhower    │    First Name:  │Dwight       │

     Year Born:  │   1890  │         State:    │  TX  │

     Inaugurated:   │    1953  │    Age When Inaugurated:   │      62      │



 ┌─┐                                                        ⇩
 └─┘
 │List│◁▏▔▔▔▔▔▔▔▔▔▔▔▔▔▔▔▔▔▔▔▔▔▔▔▔▔▔▔▔▔▔▔▔▔▔▔▔▓▓▷│回│
```

Figure 7-2 Display Presidents database in Form view

Click on the Form box to display the first record in the database (see Figure 7-2). You can then click on the List box to display the database in List view (see Figure 7-3).

Now you can continue to work with the information in the database.

Adding records to the database

You can easily add new information to a database, using either Form view or List view.

Adding new records in Form view

1   **Drag the scroll box to the bottom of the scroll bar.**

The last form in the document is displayed, which is always a blank data-entry form. If necessary, use the scroll arrows to adjust the form so that the first field in the form is visible on the screen. (See Figure 7-4.)

2   **Click on the first field in the database.**

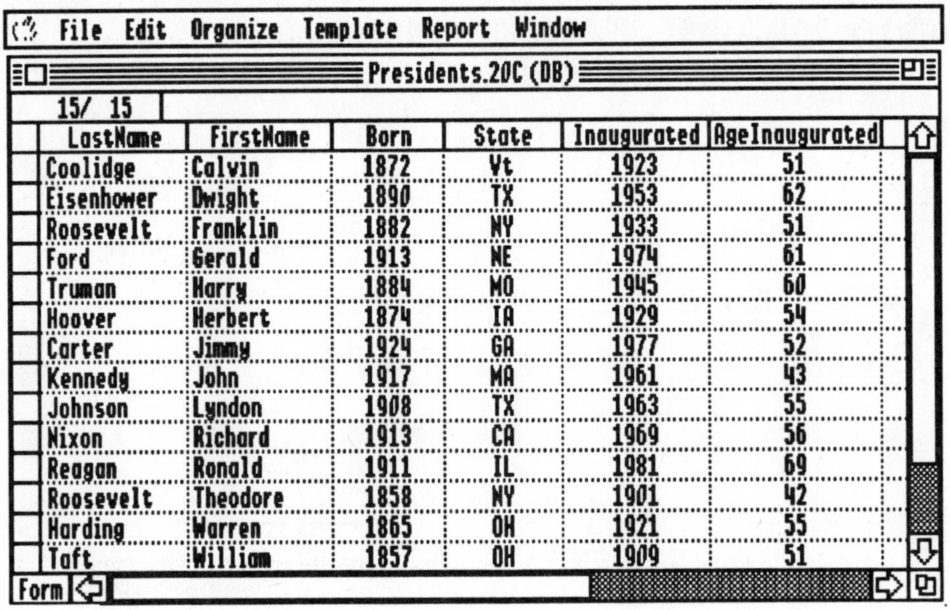

Presidents.20C (DB)

15/ 15

LastName	FirstName	Born	State	Inaugurated	AgeInaugurated
Coolidge	Calvin	1872	Vt	1923	51
Eisenhower	Dwight	1890	TX	1953	62
Roosevelt	Franklin	1882	NY	1933	51
Ford	Gerald	1913	NE	1974	61
Truman	Harry	1884	MO	1945	60
Hoover	Herbert	1874	IA	1929	54
Carter	Jimmy	1924	GA	1977	52
Kennedy	John	1917	MA	1961	43
Johnson	Lyndon	1908	TX	1963	55
Nixon	Richard	1913	CA	1969	56
Reagan	Ronald	1911	IL	1981	69
Roosevelt	Theodore	1858	NY	1901	42
Harding	Warren	1865	OH	1921	55
Taft	William	1857	OH	1909	51

Form

Figure 7-3   Display Presidents database in List view

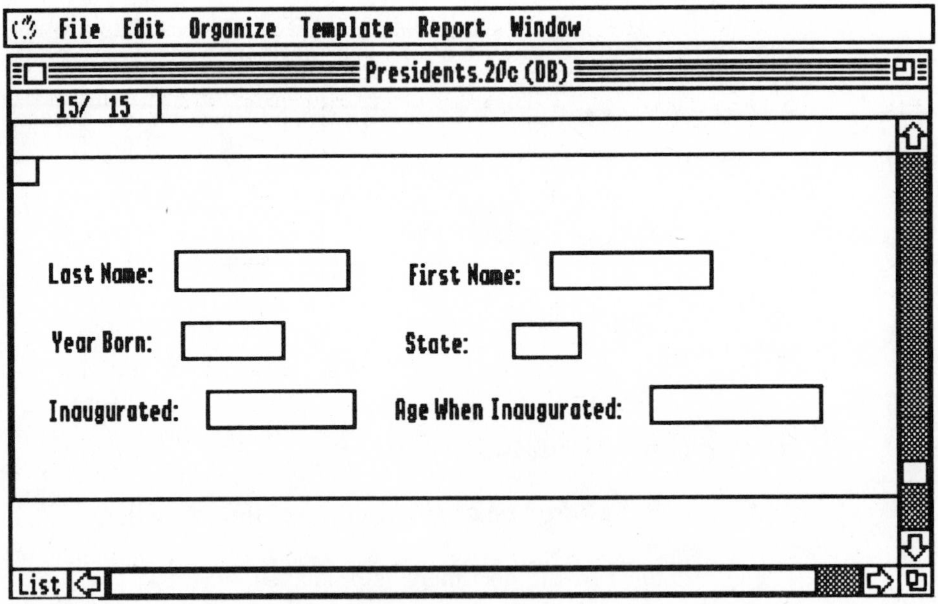

Presidents.20c (DB)

15/ 15

Last Name: First Name:

Year Born: State:

Inaugurated: Age When Inaugurated:

List

Figure 7-4   Display blank form in Presidents database

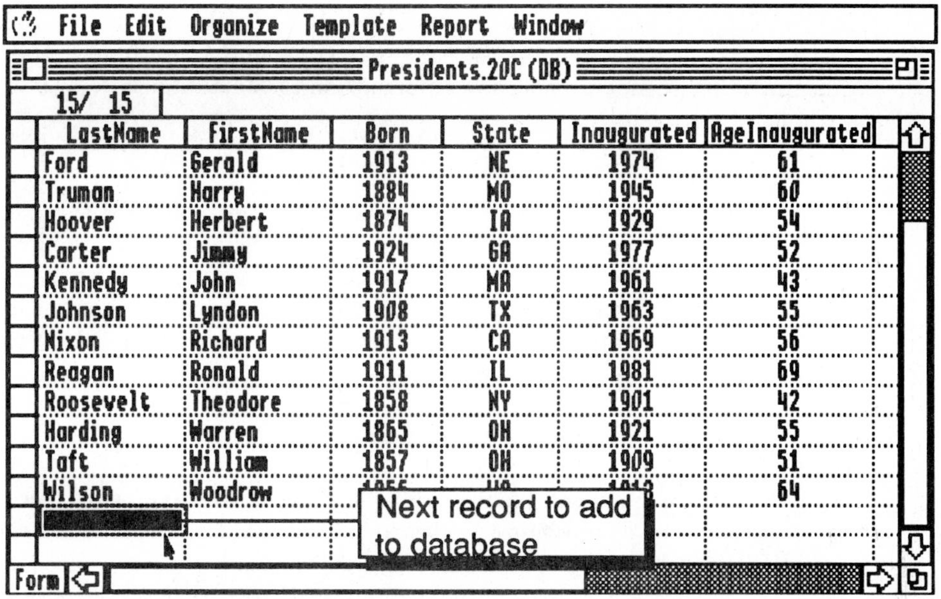

```
 File   Edit   Organize   Template   Report   Window
```

	Presidents.20C (DB)				
15/ 15					

	LastName	FirstName	Born	State	Inaugurated	AgeInaugurated	
	Ford	Gerald	1913	NE	1974	61	
	Truman	Harry	1884	MO	1945	60	
	Hoover	Herbert	1874	IA	1929	54	
	Carter	Jimmy	1924	GA	1977	52	
	Kennedy	John	1917	MA	1961	43	
	Johnson	Lyndon	1908	TX	1963	55	
	Nixon	Richard	1913	CA	1969	56	
	Reagan	Ronald	1911	IL	1981	69	
	Roosevelt	Theodore	1858	NY	1901	42	
	Harding	Warren	1865	OH	1921	55	
	Taft	William	1857	OH	1909	51	
	Wilson	Woodrow				64	

Next record to add
to database

`Form`

Figure 7-5   Display blank record in List view

After the field is highlighted, enter data into the field. Press the Tab key to move to the next field, and complete the form in the usual way.

3   **When the new record is completed, press the Return key to move to the next record.**

Continue to add as many records as desired.

Adding new records in List view

1   **Drag the scroll box to the bottom of the scroll bar.**

The last records in the document are displayed, and a blank row is displayed beneath your last record. Enter your new record into this blank row. (See Figure 7-5.)

2   **Click on the first field in the blank row, and the field is selected.**

3   **Type data into the first field, and then press the Tab key to move to the next field.**

Complete the record in the usual way. When the new record is completed, you can press the Return key to move to the first field in the next row and continue to add new information to the database.

Inserting records into the database

You may want to insert a new record into the middle of the current records. This usually isn't required, since it is easy to rearrange your database into any desired order; you can enter new records at the end of the database, and then rearrange the database records in a desired order.

If you do want to insert a new record into a specific location in the database:

1 **Select the record where you want to insert a new blank record.**

The new record will be inserted just above a selected record. A record is selected by clicking on the record selection box to the left of a record in Form view or List view.

2 **Choose the Insert Record command from the Edit menu.**

A new blank record is inserted above the selected record. You can enter information into this new record in the usual way.

Revising the definition form

You may want to revise the definition form for the database, or you may want to change some of the information that is stored in the database. Some of the information may have changed, some of the fields may have been left blank earlier, or some of the information may have been entered incorrectly. It's easy to revise your definition form or your information.

Revising fields on the definition form

1 **Select the Show Definition command on the Template menu.**

The definition form is displayed.

2 **Add any desired fields to the definition.**

You can add fields in the same way that you originally created fields on the form. Drag a rectangle, define the type of data stored in the field, and use the Field Format command to select how to display the data in the field.

3   **Delete any desired fields from the definition form.**

Click a field to select it, and then press the Delete key.

4   **Move or resize any desired field.**

Click a field to select it, and then drag the field to a new location or drag the handles to resize the field.

After you have changed the definition form, select the Show Form command on the Template menu or click the Form box to display the database in Form view.

The changes that you made to the definition form are immediately visible on the data-entry form.

Adding headers to the form

A header is information displayed at the top of each page of forms in Form view and printed at the top of each page when you print the database.

To create a header:

1   **Choose the Show Definition command on the Template menu to display the definition form.**

2   **Drag down the header tab on the definition form.**

As you drag the header tag, a space opens for the header information. (See Figure 7-6.)

3   **Drag a rectangle to define the area where you will display header information. (See Figure 7-7.)**

After you create the header field, the Header Field Definition dialog appears (see Figure 7-8).

4   **Specify the type of information that the header field will display.**

5   **If the data type is text, type the text into the input bar.**

6   **Click the OK button to return to the definition form. (See Figure 7-9.)**

To enter or change the information in the header field, click the field to select it. If the data type is text, the text appears in the input bar at the top of the form, and you can edit the text in the input bar.

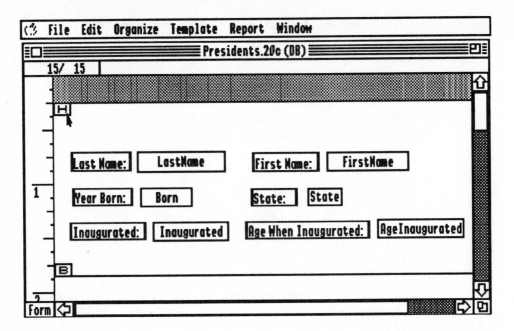

Figure 7-6 Header tab

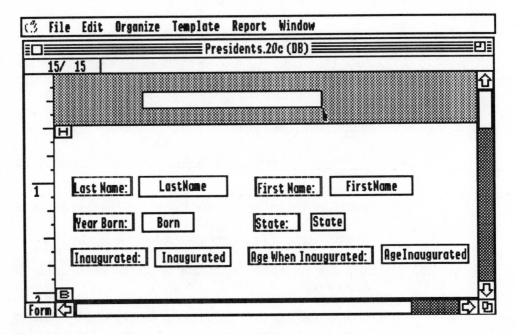

Figure 7-7 Create header field

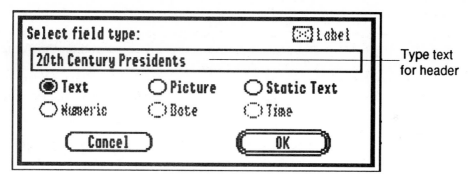

Figure 7-8   Header field definition dialog

If the data type is picture or static text, select the field and enter data into the field by copying the information from the Clipboard or by importing the information using the Import File command on the File menu.

Adding footers to the form

A footer is information that is displayed at the bottom of each page of forms in Form view and printed at the bottom of each page when you print the database.

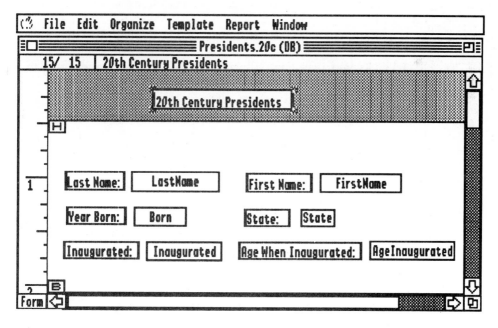

Figure 7-9   Header in place

To create a footer for each form:

☐1 **Choose the Show Definition command on the Template menu to display the definition form.**

☐2 **Move the arrow pointer to the bottom of the definition form to the footer tab (box labeled F).**

☐3 **Drag the footer tab up to create an area for the footer information.**

☐4 **Drag a rectangle in the footer area for a footer field, complete the Field Definition dialog box, and enter your desired information into the footer field.**

The footer information will be displayed at the bottom of each form.

Revising information in Form or List view

☐1 **Use the scroll bar to display in the window the record that you want to change.**

☐2 **Click on the field that you want to change.**

The field will be highlighted, selected for action.

☐3 **Enter the revised information into the field, and press the Tab key.**

The revised information is displayed in the field.

Erasing a field or record

You might want to erase all of the contents of a field or record.
To erase a field:

☐1 **Click on the field to select the field.**

☐2 **Choose the Clear command from the Edit menu or press the Delete key.**

The contents of the selected field are erased.
To erase a record:

☐1 **Click on the record selection box.**

The record selection box is the small box to the left of a record in List view or in the upper-left corner of a form in Form view. All of the fields in the record are highlighted and selected.

2 **Choose the Clear command from the Edit menu.**

All of the fields in the record are erased.

Sorting information in the database

You may want to arrange the information in your database in a specific order. For example, if you created a database containing a list of names and addresses, you might want to rearrange the database so that the entries are displayed in alphabetical order by name.

AppleWorks GS can easily rearrange your database in this way. That means that you need not enter your database information in any particular order. You can always rearrange it in any desired order later.

You can sort the records in your database in either Form view or List view, but it is usually more convenient to sort the records in List view. List view displays more than one record on the screen and you can see the effect of each rearrangement more easily.

To rearrange your records, you must:

1. Select the Sort command from the Organize menu.
2. Specify the first field to use as a basis for rearrangement for sorting. This field is called the primary key used for sorting the database.
3. Specify the order of the sort. For example, you may want to sort text information in alphabetical (A..Z) or reverse alphabetical (Z..A) order.
4. Specify any other fields to use for sorting. These other fields are used as "tie-breakers" when two or more records contain the same information in the primary key field.

Selecting the Sort command

1 **Select the Sort command from the Organize menu.**

The Sort dialog box is displayed (see Figure 7-10).

This dialog box is used to select the fields used as a basis for the sort. For example, if you want to display your records alphabetically by the information in the Last Name field, this dialog box is used to specify that order.

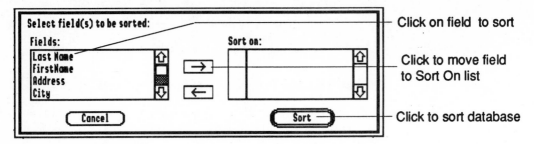

Figure 7-10 Sort dialog box

Selecting a field to use as basis for the sort

The Fields list box displays the fields in your database that can be used as the basis of the rearrangement. If the field that you want to use is not visible, use the scroll box to move the field into the list box.

1 **Click on the first field that you would like to use as the basis for rearrangement.**

For example, if you want to sort the records in the database based on the entries in a field called "Inaugurated," click on that field in the dialog box.

This first field is called the primary sort key, since it is the primary piece of information used to rearrange the records.

2 **Click on the right-arrow box.**

This moves your selected field into the Sort On list box. (See Figure 7-11.)

Shortcut: *Double-click on the field that you want to move to the Sort On box, and the field is moved into the Sort On list box.*

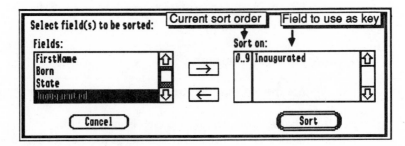

Figure 7-11 Sort dialog box — Inaugurated example

Specifying the sort order

When a field is moved into the Sort On box, the sort order is displayed to the left of the field.

If the field is text, the sort order is A..Z; this means that the field will be sorted in increasing alphabetic order. If the field is numeric, time, or date, the sort order is 0..9; that means that the field will be sorted in increasing numeric order.

You might want to reverse the sort order. For example, you might want a text field sorted in reverse alphabetic order, or you might want a numeric field sorted in decreasing numeric order.

To reverse the order of the sort: click on the current sort order, and the reverse sort order is displayed.

To return to the alternative sort order, click on the sort order again.

Adding other fields to the sort list

After you have specified the first field to be used for sorting, you can add other fields to the list.

The other fields are called secondary sort keys, and they are used as tie-breakers if some records contain identical information in the primary key field.

For example, if you specify that the Last Name field is used as the primary field to sort your records, you might want to specify that the First Name field is used as the second sort field. If two records have the same information in the Last Name field, they will be arranged based on the information stored in the First Name field.

You can add as many fields as you wish to the Sort On box. Each field that you add is used only to settle ties in the fields listed above it. For example, a third field in the Sort On box would be used only if two records have the same value in both the primary sort key field and the secondary sort key field.

Removing fields from the Sort On box

You might change your mind and decide that you want to remove one or more fields from the Sort On box.

To remove a field from the Sort On box:

1. **Click on the field in the Sort On list box that you want to remove.**

2. **Click on the left-arrow box.**

The field is removed from the Sort On box and moved back to the Fields box.

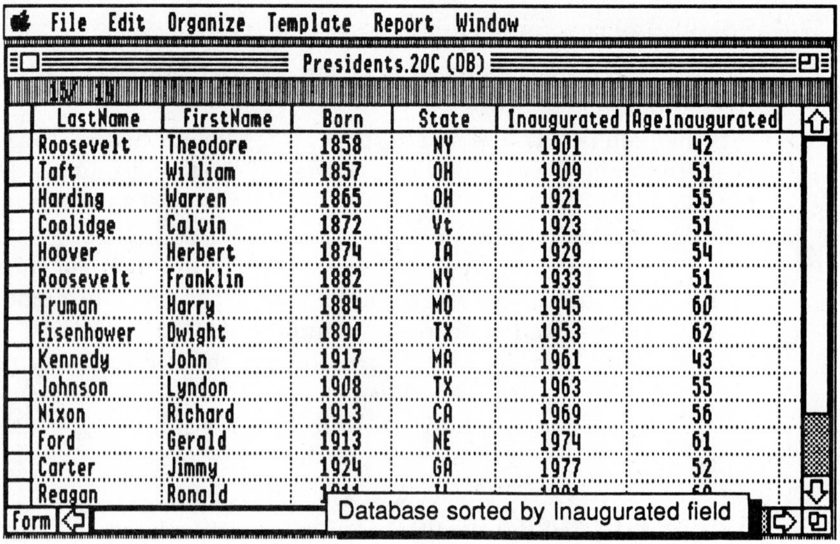

Figure 7-12 Database sorted on values in Inaugurated field

Shortcut: *To remove a field from the Sort On box, double-click on the field, and it is removed from the Sort On box and moved back to the Fields box.*

Sorting the records

When you have selected your sort fields and sort orders, click the Sort button in the dialog box.

Your records are rearranged, based on your selections. If you are using List view, the new arrangement of the records is displayed on the screen. (See Figure 7-12.)

To save the new arrangement of the database, select the Save command from the File menu. The new arrangement of your database replaces the previous saved version of the database.

If you want to keep a copy of the original arrangement of the database, you can use the Save As command to save this new arrangement of your database with a different name. Since it is easy to rearrange your database in different orders, it isn't often necessary to save different arrangements as independent documents.

After you have sorted the database using one field as the basis for the sort, you might rearrange the database using another field. For example, we could rearrange our database based on the Age Inaugurated field (see Figure 7-13).

Note: *You can also save any specific arrangement of the database as a template. The advantage of a template is that your disk contains only a single copy*

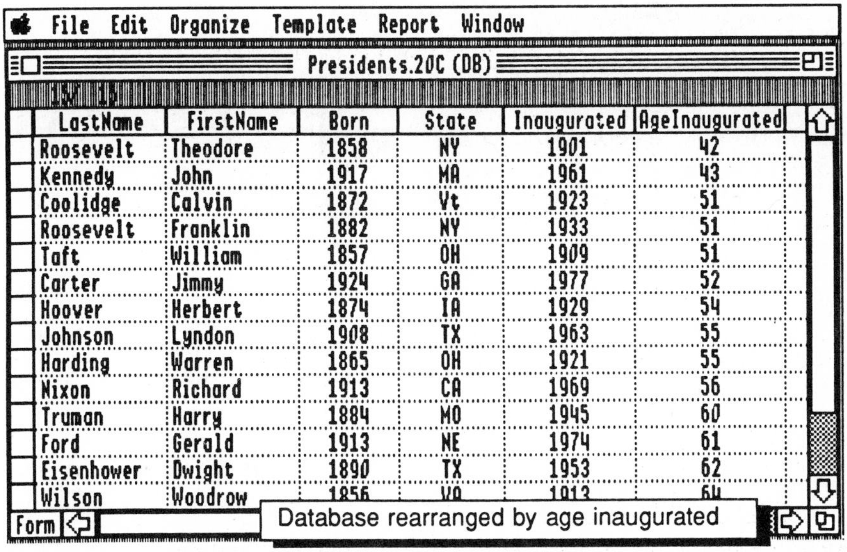

```
 🍎  File  Edit  Organize  Template  Report  Window
```

```
                         Presidents.20C (DB)
```

LastName	FirstName	Born	State	Inaugurated	AgeInaugurated
Roosevelt	Theodore	1858	NY	1901	42
Kennedy	John	1917	MA	1961	43
Coolidge	Calvin	1872	Vt	1923	51
Roosevelt	Franklin	1882	NY	1933	51
Taft	William	1857	OH	1909	51
Carter	Jimmy	1924	GA	1977	52
Hoover	Herbert	1874	IA	1929	54
Johnson	Lyndon	1908	TX	1963	55
Harding	Warren	1865	OH	1921	55
Nixon	Richard	1913	CA	1969	56
Truman	Harry	1884	MO	1945	60
Ford	Gerald	1913	NE	1974	61
Eisenhower	Dwight	1890	TX	1953	62
Wilson	Woodrow	1856	VA	1913	64

Form   Database rearranged by age inaugurated

Figure 7-13   Database sorted by values in Age Inaugurated field

of the database, rather than multiple copies. For more information on templates, see "Using Templates" later in this chapter.

Finding information in the database

Another important way to use your database is to find a specific record in the database. As your database grows to hundreds or thousands of records, it is increasingly useful to find specific records.

AppleWorks GS provides several commands to find and work with specific information:

- The Find command lets you find records that contain specific values in a field.
- The Find Again command lets you quickly repeat the last search operation.
- The Replace command lets you search for specific information and replace it with substitute information.

Finding specific values in the database

You can quickly find fields that contain specific values.

To retrieve the records that contain specific values:

1   **Select the Find command from the Organize menu.**

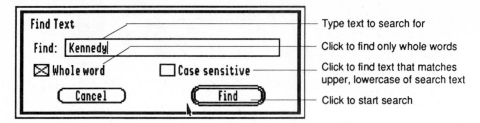

Find Text	
Find:	Kennedy	——— Type text to search for
☒ Whole word	☐ Case sensitive	——— Click to find only whole words
	——— Click to find text that matches upper, lowercase of search text
(Cancel)	(Find)	——— Click to start search

Figure 7-14 Find dialog

After you select the command, the Find dialog box appears (see Figure 7-14).

2 **Type the value that you want to search for into the Find input bar.**

If the value is a whole word, click the Whole Word button. If you want to search for the value exactly as typed (including uppercase and lowercase letters), click on Case Sensitive button.

3 **Click the Find button in the dialog box.**

The first record containing the value is displayed on the screen, with the field containing the value selected. (See Figure 7-15.)

 File Edit Organize Template Report Window

≡ Presidents.20C(DB) ≡

LastName	FirstName	Born	State	Inaugurated	AgeInaugurated
Roosevelt	Theodore	1858	NY	1901	42
Kennedy	John	1917	MA	1961	43
Coolidge	Calvin	1872	Vt	1923	51
Roosevelt	Franklin	1882	NY	1933	51
Taft	William	1857	OH	1909	51
Carter	Jimmy	1924	GA	1977	52
Hoover	Herbert	1874	IA	1929	54
Johnson	Lyndon	1908	TX	1963	55
Harding	Warren	1865	OH	1921	55
Nixon	Richard	1913	CA	1969	56
Truman	Harry	1884	MO	1945	60
Ford	Gerald	1913	NE	1974	61
Eisenhower	Dwight	1890	TX	1953	62
Wilson	Woodrow	1856	VA	1913	64

Form

Figure 7-15 Find Kennedy in database

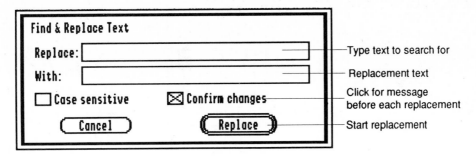

Figure 7-16 Find/Replace dialog

Finding the next record with the value

To move to the next record that contains your search value, select the Find Next command from the Organize menu.

The next occurrence of the search value is highlighted on the screen. This occurrence may be in another field in the same record, or in another record.

Finding and replacing a value

You can search for a value in the database and replace it with a different value with the Replace command:

1 **Select the Replace command on the Organize menu.**

The Replace dialog box appears (Figure 7-16).

2 **Type into the Find input bar the value to search for, and type into the Replace input bar the value to use as a replacement.**

AppleWorks GS searches for each occurrence of your search text, and replaces it with the replacement text.

Click the Case Sensitive button if you want to search for the value exactly as you typed it (including uppercase and lowercase characters).

Click the Confirm Changes button if you want a warning message before each change is made.

3 **When all of the entries are correct, click the Replace button, and the changes are made.**

If you clicked the Confirm Changes button, a warning message is displayed before each change is made. When the message is displayed, type Y to replace the current value found, type N to cancel the change, and Q to quit the replacement procedure and return to the database.

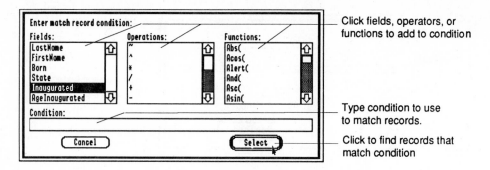

Figure 7-17   Match records dialog

Selecting part of a database

As you use your database more, you may want to work with part of the database. For example, you might want to work with the records that contain one specific value in a specific field. You might want to identify and work with:

- part of a database of names and addresses that contain one specific zip code
- part of a student database that contains students in one particular grade
- part of an employee database that contains employees earning more than a specific pay level

You can easily select part of your original database and create a mini-database containing some of the original records. From this mini-database you can print reports, find and replace values, rearrange records, or perform any other database operations.

Selecting records in a database

☐1 **Select the Match Records command from the Organize menu.**

The Match Records dialog box appears (see Figure 7-17).

☐2 **Enter a formula to use to identify the records that you want to select.**

The formula is the rule that is used to find certain records. Usually the formula asks AppleWorks GS to search the records and find all the records where some field contains some value. You can specify that the field is equal to a value, less than a value, greater than a value, or has some other relationship to the value.

The formula that you enter will usually be in this form:

[field name] [relational operator] [value]

For example, typical formulas might be

[LastName] = 'Smith'

This formula finds all records where the Last Name field contains the value Smith.

[Year]>1980

This formula finds all records where the Year field contains a value greater than 1980.

[Salary]<20000

This formula finds all records where the Salary field is less than 20000.

To enter field names, double-click on one of the field names listed in the Fields list box. You can also type in the field name directly, surrounding the name with square braces.

To enter operators, double-click on one of the operators in the Operations list box, or type in the operator.

To use one of the functions, double-click on one of the functions in the Functions list box and complete the function by supplying the necessary information required by the function. (For more information on functions, see Appendix B, AppleWorks GS Functions.)

To enter a value, type in the value at the keyboard. Text values must be surrounded by quotation marks.

3̲ **When the selection formula is complete, click on the OK button**

AppleWorks GS searches for all records that match your formula. When the search is completed, all of the records that match your criteria are highlighted and selected for further action.

For example, if the Match Records formula is [Inaugurated] > 1950 (see Figure 7-18), the Presidents database would show highlighted all records where the Inaugurated field is greater than 1950.

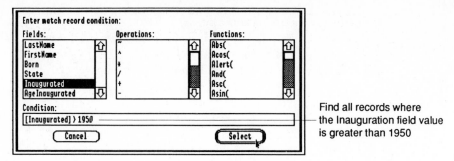

Find all records where
the Inauguration field value
is greater than 1950

Figure 7-18 Find records where Inaugurated field is greater than 1950

Working with selected records

After you have used the Match Records command to select some of the records from the original database, you can work with those selected records.

- If you wish, you can display only the selected records. This temporarily removes the rest of the database records from the screen and creates a temporary mini-database consisting of the selected records. These selected records become the active records, ready for further action.
- If you wish, you can remove the selected records from view. The remaining records become the active records.
- You can print reports summarizing the information from the active records,
- You could use the Match Records command again to further limit the number of active records based on some new criteria.

Displaying only selected records

You can display only the selected records and temporarily remove the unselected records from the screen.

To display only selected records:

1. **Select the desired records with the Match Records commands.**

The selected records are highlighted in the database.

2. **Choose the Hide Unselected Records command from the Organize menu. (See Figure 7-19.)**

The unselected records are temporarily removed from the screen. (See Figure 7-20.)

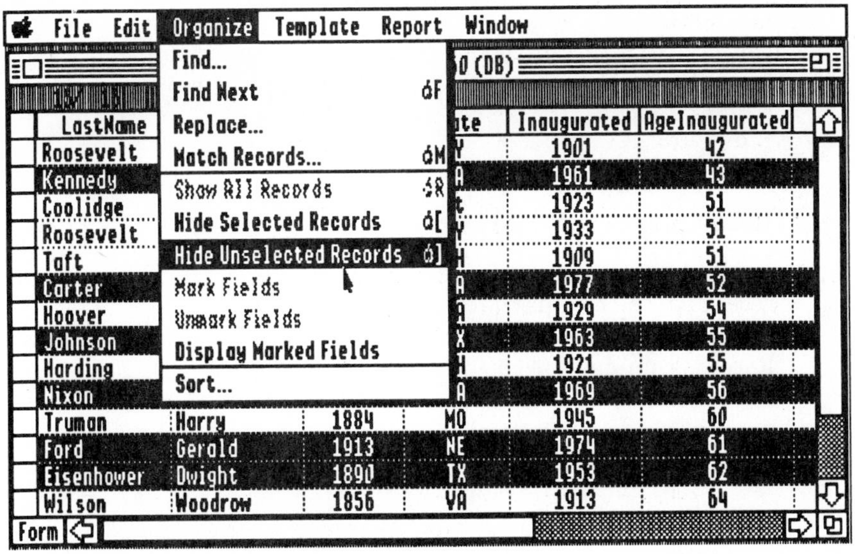

Figure 7-19 Choose Hide Unselected Records

The records that remain on the screen are now the active records in the database, and any further commands refer to these active records.

The number of active records and the number of records in the original database are displayed in the upper left corner of the database document.

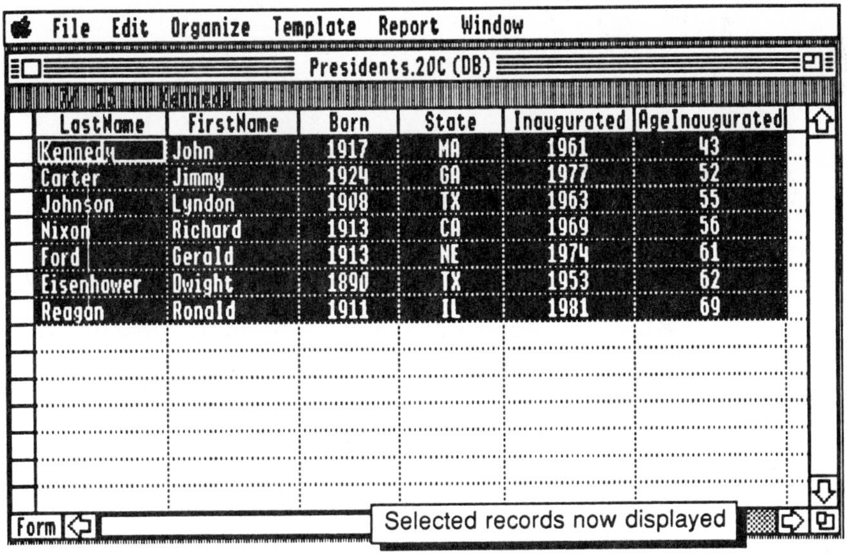

Figure 7-20 Only selected records remain

Note: *If you wish, you could remove the selected records from the screen and leave the unselected records as the active records. To remove the selected records from the screen, use the Hide Selected Records command on the Organize menu.*

Returning to original database

Later in the session, you may want to return from the current active records to the original database.

You can return to the original database by selecting the Show All Records command from the Organize menu.

All hidden records are returned to the screen, and the original database is restored to view.

Removing fields from view

You may want to temporarily hide specific fields from view in the database. For example, you may want to remove one or more fields from view before creating a report, or you may want to temporarily remove from view fields that contain sensitive information.

To control the visibility of fields in the database:

1. Use the Mark Fields command on the Organize menu to tag the fields that you want to hide.
2. Use the Display Marked Fields command on the Organize menu to display or hide the marked fields.

Marking fields

To mark a field so that you can control its visibility:

1. **Return to the definition form by choosing the Show Definition command on the Template menu.**

2. **Click the field that you want to mark.**

The field is selected and highlighted. You can shift-click on several fields to select a group of fields at the same time. (See Figure 7-21.)

3. **Choose the Mark Fields command from the Organize menu. (See Figure 7-22.)**

The selected fields are marked and tagged for further action.

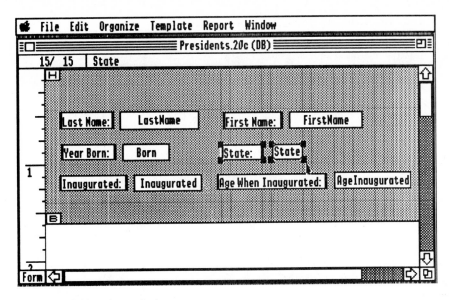

Figure 7-21 Select fields to be marked

Temporarily hiding fields

After a field has been marked, it can be temporarily removed from view.

1 **Use the Mark Fields command to mark the fields that you want to hide.**

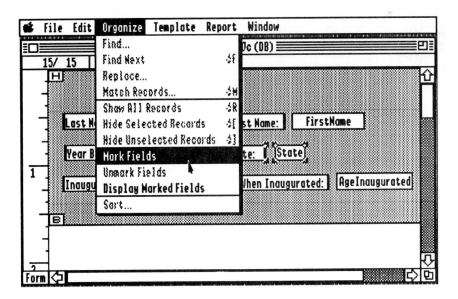

Figure 7-22 Choose Mark Fields command

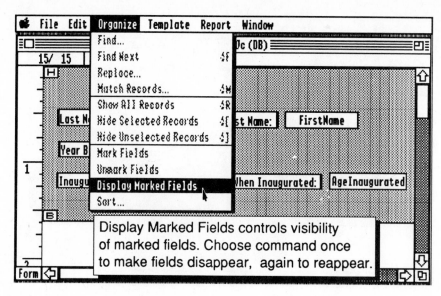

Figure 7-23 Choose Display Marked Fields

> **2** **Choose the Display Marked Fields command on the Organize menu to hide or display marked fields. (See Figure 7-23.)**

If a checkmark does not appear next to the command, marked fields are removed from view. When you view the database in List view or Form view, the marked fields are not displayed. (See Figure 7-24.)

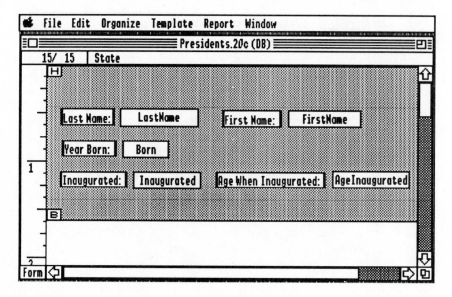

Figure 7-24 Hiding marked fields

To return the hidden fields to view, select the Display Marked Fields command again. The checkmark is added to the command and marked fields are displayed again.

Printing database reports

If you select the Print command from the File menu, the entire contents of the current database are printed.

Many times, however, you will want to print a report that contains information from part of the database, or that summarizes the information in the database.

For example, you may want to print a report:

- from a database of names and addresses that prints a list of names from one specific zip code
- from a student database that contains information on students in one specific grade
- from an employee database that lists all employees above a specific pay level

AppleWorks GS lets you print reports that contain all or part of the information in the database. You can also print reports that contain summary information, including the total number of records, average of values in a field, and other summary information.

Steps to a database report

To produce a database report:

1 **Select the records that you want to include in the report.**

2 **Sort the database in the order that you want to print the report.**

3 **Select the fields that you want to include in the report.**

4 **Create any desired header or footer information for the report.**

5 **Select the format that you want to use for the format.**

This includes selecting the type of summary information that you want to display, such as totals or averages.

6 **Decide if you want a summary report or a full report.**

A **summary report** prints only the field names and summary information (totals, averages) that you have requested. A **full report** prints this information, as well as the actual data contained in the selected records.

> ### 7   Create the report.

When you create the report, it is not printed directly. Rather, the report is created as a word processing document, so that you can change fonts or edit the report before printing it.

Selecting records for report

Before creating a report, select the records that you want to include in the report. A report summarizes the information from the current active records. You can produce a report that includes all of the records in the database, or you can produce a report using only some of the records.

To produce a report using only some of the records:

> ### 1   Use the Match Records command to select a specific set of records.

> ### 2   Use the Hide Unselected Records command to display only the selected records or use the Hide Selected Records to remove the selected records from view.

The desired records appear on the screen as the current active records, and the information in those records is used for the report.

Sorting records

The records in the summary report will be printed in the order that they occur in the active records. Examine the records and make certain that they are in the desired order.

If you want to print a report that lists the records alphabetically by last name, be sure that the records have been arranged alphabetically by information in the Last Name field in your database. If you want to print a report listing addresses by ZIP code, be sure that the records are arranged by the information stored in the ZIP code field.

If the order is not correct, use the Sort command on the Organize menu as described earlier in this chapter to rearrange them in the desired order.

Selecting fields for report

You may not want to include all of the fields in each record in a report.

To temporarily remove fields from display:

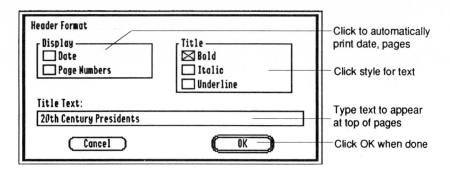

Header Format

Display
☐ Date
☐ Page Numbers

Title
☒ Bold
☐ Italic
☐ Underline

Title Text:
20th Century Presidents

Cancel   OK

— Click to automatically print date, pages

— Click style for text

— Type text to appear at top of pages

— Click OK when done

Figure 7-25   Report Header dialog

1 Use the Mark Field command to mark selected fields that you want to remove.

2 Use the Display Marked Fields command to remove the selected fields from view.

While the marked fields are temporarily removed from view, the reports that you print do not include those fields.

Creating a header for your report

Your database report can contain a header, which is specified text printed at the top of each page of the report:

1 Select the Header command on the Report menu.

The Header dialog box is displayed (see Figure 7-25).

2 Click the appropriate boxes to automatically display the date or time at the top of each page.

3 Click the style boxes to set the text style for your header text.

4 Type the text into the input bar that you want to appear at the top of the page.

5 When the box is completed, click the OK box to return to the database.

Creating a footer for your report

Your database report can also display a footer, which is specified text that is printed at the bottom of each page of the report:

To create a footer, select the Footer command on the Report Menu. Complete the dialog box as described above for report headers.

Defining the report format

Finally, you must specify the format of the report. This is the most important task that you must perform before printing your report.

Your report can include different summary information, including the number of records in the report, the total of values in a field, the average of values in a field, the maximum value in a field, the minimum value in a field, and the standard deviation of values in a field.

You can display this information at the bottom of the report, where the information summarizes the data found in all records.

You can also specify that the report should be broken periodically to report subtotal information. The report can be broken to report subtotals whenever the value in a sorted field changes from one record to the next.

When you specify a format for the report:

- You must specify where you want to break the report for subtotals. If you wish, you can print the report with summary information at the bottom of the report and no subtotals.
- You must specify which summary information you want to display. You must specify which kinds of information you want reported for each field.

Defining a report with no subtotals

The simplest report format prints summary information at the bottom of a report, without breaking the report to report subtotal information.

To define a report with only summary totals at the bottom of the report:

1. **Select the Format command on the Report menu.**

The Format dialog box appears (see Figure 7-26).
The Field list box lists the fields in the database.
The Subtotal Break After box displays the entry Totals Only. If you do not change this entry, summary information will be printed at the bottom of the report, and no subtotal breaks will be included.

2. **Click on one of the fields in the Field list box.**

The field is highlighted and the name of the field appears in the Column Heading box.

3. **If you want to print a different name at the top of this field in the report, enter the different name in the Column Heading input bar.**

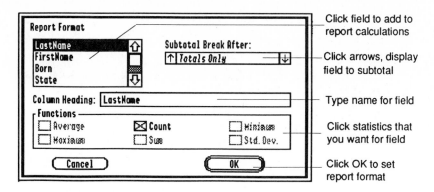

Report Format

LastName	Subtotal Break After:
FirstName	⬆
Born	⬆ Totals Only ⬇
State	⬇

Column Heading: LastName

Functions
☐ Average   ☒ Count   ☐ Minimum
☐ Maximum   ☐ Sum   ☐ Std. Dev.

(Cancel)   (OK)

Click field to add to
report calculations

Click arrows, display
field to subtotal

Type name for field

Click statistics that
you want for field

Click OK to set
report format

Figure 7-26 Report Format dialog

4 **Click on the summary information that you want to print at the bottom of the report for this field.**

If the subtotal field is numeric, you can display the count, sum, average, maximum, minimum, or standard deviation of values in the field. (For other data types, some of the calculated information is not available.)

For example, the report format shown in Figure 7-26 prints a simple count of the Last Name entries in the database:

5 **Repeat this process for any other desired fields in the report.**

For example, the format in Figure 7-27 prints at the bottom of the report a calculation of the average value found in the Age Inaugurated field.

After you have made your desired selections, click the OK button to return to the database. Then generate the report using the Summary Only command or Create Report command on the Report menu.

Figure 7-28 shows a report that prints the data from selected records and the average of one field (the Age Inagaurated field) at the bottom of the report.

Defining a report with subtotals

The report can break and report subtotal information when the value in a sorted field changes from one record to the next.

To define a report that includes subtotals:

1 **Select the Format command on the Report menu.**

The Format dialog box appears (see Figure 7-29).

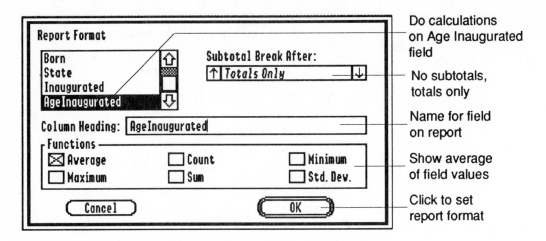

Figure 7-27　Example: Print the average of Age Inaugurated values

You can define the place where you want subtotals to appear by adding fields to the Subtotal Break After box.

When you click on one of the fields in the Field list box, it is added to the Subtotal Break After box. When the report is printed, the report will be broken every time that the value in this field changes, and subtotal information will be printed.

In addition, the report is also broken when the value changes in any field that was higher than this field on the Sort On list when you used the Sort command.

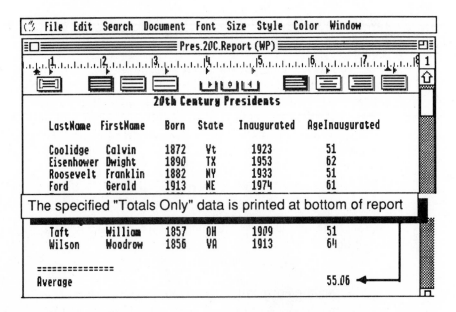

Figure 7-28　Report — Totals Only format, with no subtotal in information included

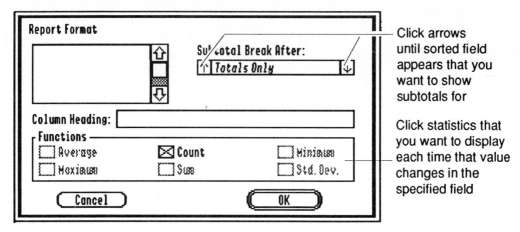

Figure 7-29   Report Format dialog — defining subtotal breaks

The Subtotal Break After box can display the order of fields in the Sort On list. By clicking on the up arrow and down arrow, you can scroll through the list of fields used in the sort operation.

For example, suppose that you sorted a database with State as the primary key and ZIP code as the secondary key. If you now enter ZIP code into the Subtotal Break After box, the report will break and display subtotals whenever the value in the ZIP code field changes and whenever the value in the State field changes.

2   **Click on the field in the list box where you want to break the report and display subtotals.**

Remember: The field that you select must have been sorted. If it is not displayed in the Field list box, it has not been sorted. When the value in the field that you select changes, the report will break and report subtotal information.

Don't forget: The report will also break whenever the value changes in any field that was higher than your selected field in the Sort On box when you used the Sort command. Click on the arrow keys in the Subtotal Break After box to review fields that have higher priority.

3   **Click on the summary information that you would like to include in the report.**

If the subtotal field is numeric, you can display the count, sum, average, maximum, minimum, or standard deviation of values in the field. (For other data types, some of the calculated information is not available.)

The summary information that you select will be provided on the report at each point where the specified field changes in value, or where any field that was higher in priority changes.

You can report different information for different fields. Click on arrows on the Subtotal Break After box, and display each field for which summary information can be printed. When a given field is displayed in the box, click on the summary information that you want to print for that field.

4 **When the information in the Format dialog box is correct, click the OK button.**

After you have defined the format for the report, you can generate the report with the Create Report command on the Report menu.

Example of subtotals

The Report Format command is powerful, but not particularly easy to understand. Suppose that your database includes name and addresses, including a ZIP code field.

Suppose that you

- sort the database based on ZIP code,
- select ZIP code as the subtotal field, and
- select count as the function desired.

The report breaks each time that the ZIP code value changes and prints the total number of records with the previous ZIP code value. (See Figure 7-30.)

The report breaks each time that the specified field (the ZIP code field) changes in value and reports subtotal information. At the bottom of the report, grand total information will be printed.

Summary Only

You may not want to generate a complete report that prints all of the information in the database. You might want to see only the summary information from the report, without printing all of the actual data in the database.

To generate this simple summary format, select the Summary Only command from the Report menu.

Figure 7-31 shows a typical summary report. Note that header (and footer) information is printed, field names are printed, and the specified summary information is printed. The actual data in the records, however, is not printed.

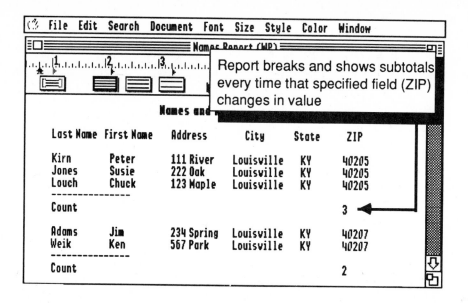

Figure 7-30 Subtotal report

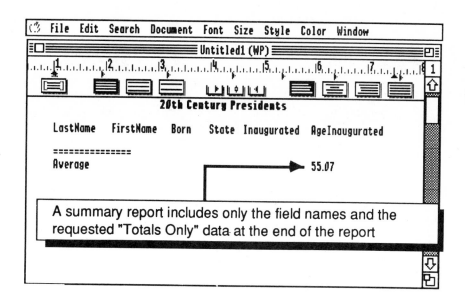

Figure 7-31 Summary Only report

Create Report

In most cases you want to generate a more complete report than provided by a summary report.

To generate a complete report that includes both the database records and summary information, select the Create Report command on the Report menu.

After you select the Create Report command, a new word processing document window is automatically opened, and the database report is displayed in the word processing window.

The report can now be treated as any other word processing document. You can use any of the usual word processing commands to change the format of the report, change the font or styles used in the document, or make any other desired changes.

When the report is displayed in final form, you can use the Save command on the File menu to save the document to disk.

Finally, when you are ready to print a copy of the report on your printer, you can use the Print command on the File menu in the usual way to print the report.

Using Templates

What is a template?

A template provides a way to let you save the current working environment in the database and return to this environment at a later time.

The current environment in a database includes

- the current definition form, including the fields that you specified, which fields are marked, and which fields are currently displayed
- the current format used in List view
- the current selection criteria of records
- the current report format

The current environment that can be saved in a template does not include the actual information stored in the database.

What can you do with templates?

AppleWorks GS provides two commands to work with a database environment:

- The Save Template command lets you save the current database environment.

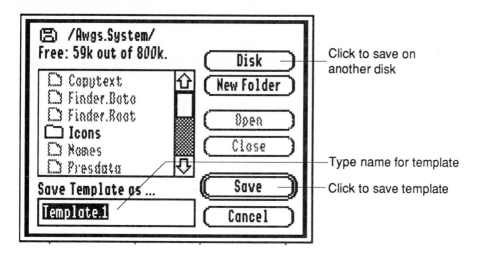

Figure 7-32 Save Template dialog

When you use the Save Template command, you save the current definition form, the selection criteria, and report format on your storage disk. When you save a template, you do not save any of the information stored in the database records; only the format used to display the information is saved.

For example, after you have used the Match Records command to select a specific set of records and then specified a report format for the database, you can use the Save Template command to save this current environment. You can use this template at a later time to return to this particular set of records and report format.

- The Open Template command lets you retrieve an environment that you previously used and saved as a template. This command loads a previously-saved template back into the database, and the format of the saved template takes effect on the current database.

Saving templates

To save the current database environment:

1   **Select the Save Template command from the Template menu.**

The Save Template As dialog box is displayed (see Figure 7-32).

2   **If the desired storage disk is not displayed, click the Disk button until the name is shown.**

3   **Type in a name for the template, and click the OK button.**

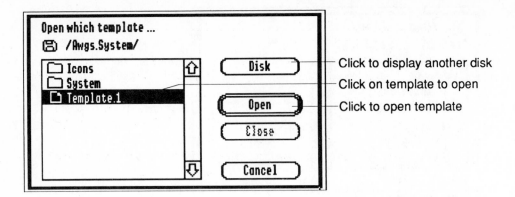

Figure 7-33 Open Template dialog

The current database environment is saved on the specified disk with the specified name.

The template saves the current database environment, including the fields that you have defined, which fields are marked, which fields are displayed, and the current report format.

Remember: The actual data in the database is not saved in the template; only the format of the information is saved in the template.

Using a template environment later

To use a previously-saved database template at a later point:

1 **Select the Open Template command from the Template menu.**

The Open Template dialog box is displayed, with available templates listed in the list box. (See Figure 7-33.)

2 **Double-click the name of the template that you want to open.**

The previously-saved database template is loaded and the format saved in the template becomes active again in the database.

You can only open a template for use in a database that contains all of the fields recorded in the template. You cannot open a template for use with a database that does not contain those fields.

The next step

The previous chapters have shown you how to create text documents with the word processing application and how to store and work with information using the database application. Each of these two applications can be used independently, but you can also combine them to produce personalized form letters, one of the most powerful uses of AppleWorks GS.

The next chapter will introduce you to form letters and will show you how to combine information stored in a database document with special word processing documents (called merge documents) to print personalized form letters. The chapter will also show you how to use the database application to produce mailing labels for these letters.

Chapter 8

Merge Documents and Mailing Labels

About this chapter

The AppleWorks GS word processing application lets you create text documents, and the database lets you store and retrieve information. But some important computer uses combine information from more than one application or document.

This chapter discusses one of these important computer uses: the production of form letters and mailing labels.

AppleWorks GS lets you create special word processing documents called **merge documents**. When a merge document is printed, the text in the document is combined with information from a database to produce a personalized version of the letter. You can print many personalized versions of the merge document. The production of form letters like these are an important use for AppleWorks GS.

You can also produce **mailing labels** from a database document. The combination of personalized form letters and matching mailing labels is a powerful computer application. The AppleWorks GS database application is particularly well-suited to help you lay out and print mailing labels on your printer, since you can visually design the mailing labels by rearranging database fields on the screen.

This chapter describes how to produce form letters and mailing labels with AppleWorks GS. The topics in this chapter include

- Merge document concepts
- Creating a merge document
- Saving a merge document
- Printing a merge document
- Creating mailing labels
- Printing mailing labels

Merge document concepts

We've all received form letters in the mail at some point. Virtually everyone has received a letter that begins with a message like this: "Dear Mr. Brown: You may have already won $16 million in the Discount Clearing House sweepstakes!" Many form letters have similar inviting messages, but form letters can be used for many different purposes.

Form letters are known in AppleWorks GS as **merge documents** or **mail-merge documents**. In general, a merge document is a special word processing document that lets you produce multiple copies that include certain individualized information in each copy. AppleWorks GS lets you produce a merge document relatively easily.

Why would you print a form letter?

A form letter has a useful purpose. A form letter lets you produce many copies of a document that includes personalized information. In most settings, form letters are an efficient way to convey specialized information to many different people.

For example, a teacher might produce a form letter to the parents of each student in a class that includes the parents' names and the latest test scores for their child. In a small business, a form letter could be printed for each employee that includes sales and salary information for that employee. In a home setting, a form letter could be used to produce a personalized holiday letter sent to friends.

How is a form letter produced?

Form letters are generally produced using the same basic technique. A typical form letter that includes the name and address of each individual might be created in this way:

- A database is created that contains all of the names, addresses, and other specific information that is required in the letter.
- A special word processing document (a merge document) is created, with blank spaces reserved for individualized names, addresses, and other specific information.
- Then many copies of the letter are printed, with each copy slightly different.
- When the first copy is printed, it incorporates the first name and address from the database. When the second copy is printed, it uses the second name and address from the database. Copy after copy of the document is printed, until a personalized letter is printed for each name and address in the database.

Planning for a merge document

This same general technique is used to create and print merge documents in AppleWorks GS.

To create a merge document in AppleWorks:

1 **Create a database that contains all of the personalized information that will be required in the form letters.**

For example, a typical form letter might require a database that contains the names and addresses of all the people who will receive a copy of the form letter. You can create the database at any time, and then open the database later when you are ready to generate the merge document.

2 **Create the basic document in the word processing application, with merge fields placed where personalized information should be inserted.**

A **merge field** is a placeholder in the word processing document. It reserves a space in the document for the personalized information that will be inserted when the document is printed.

Wherever personalized information should be printed in each copy of the document, place a merge field by choosing the Add Merge Field command on the Edit menu.

3 **Print copies of the document with the Print Merge command on the File menu.**

The appropriate information is retrieved from the database for each personalized copy of the document. The information from the database is substituted wherever you placed merge fields as placeholders in the merge document.

Creating the database for the merge document

Before producing a merge document, you must create or open a database that contains the personalized information that you want to include in the form letter.

Creating a new database

If you have not previously created a database that contains the required information, you must create a database with the information before you can

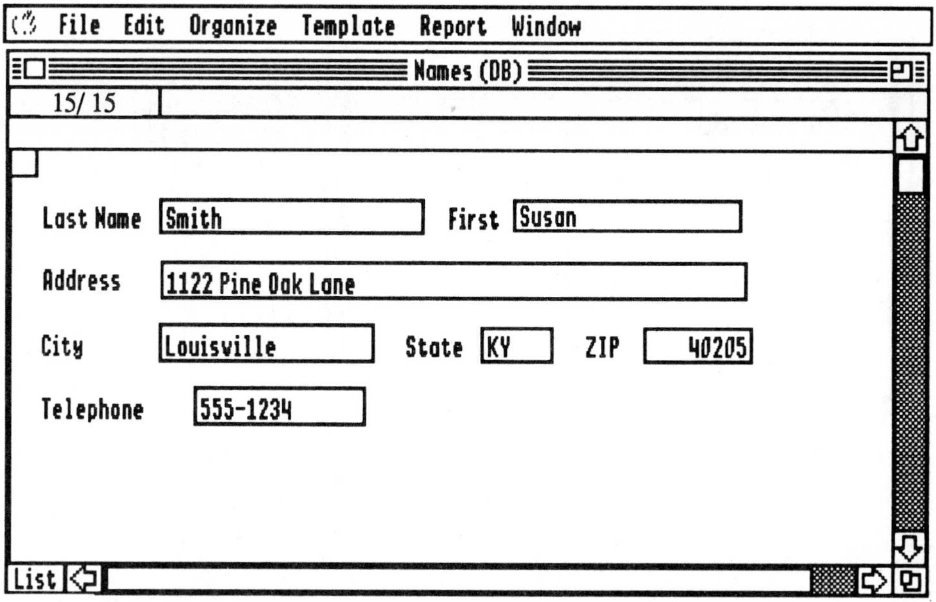

Figure 8-1 Sample database

produce the merge document. Think about the personalized information that you would like to include in each copy of the document, and create a database document that includes fields for the required information.

For example, a simple merge document might include the first name, last name, street address, city, state, and zip code of specific individuals.

Opening an existing database

You may have already created and saved a database that contains the required information. If you created such a database earlier, open the database when you are ready to create the merge document. The database can contain extra fields, beyond those that are required for the merge document.

When you are ready to create the merge document, open the database that contains the required information (see Figure 8-1).

Creating the merge document

After you open the database that contains the personalized information to be included in the merge documents, you can create the merge document.

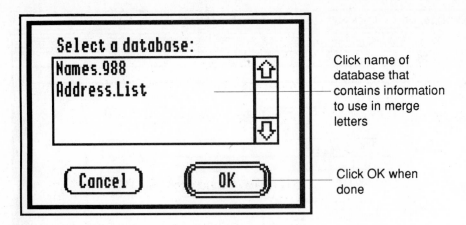

Figure 8-2 Select Merge Database dialog box

A merge document is a special kind of word processing document. It contains the basic text that you want to print on every copy of the form letter, along with placeholders (merge fields) that reserve space for the personalized information that will be printed in each copy.

To create the merge document:

1 **Open a new word processing document.**

2 **Type the basic text of the document that you want to print on every copy of the form letter, and stop at the first location where you want to print personalized information.**

3 **Choose the Select Merge Database command on the Edit menu.**

A dialog box appears that displays the current open databases (see Figure 8-2).

Click the name of the database that contains the information to be printed in the merge document, and click the OK button.

4 **Choose the Add Merge Field command from the Edit menu.**

The Add Merge Field command is used to insert the first placeholder, or merge field, in the document. This is the location where the first personalized information will be placed in the document.

The Add Merge Field dialog box appears (see Figure 8-3).

The dialog box lists the fields that are used in the database that you selected with the Select Merge Database command.

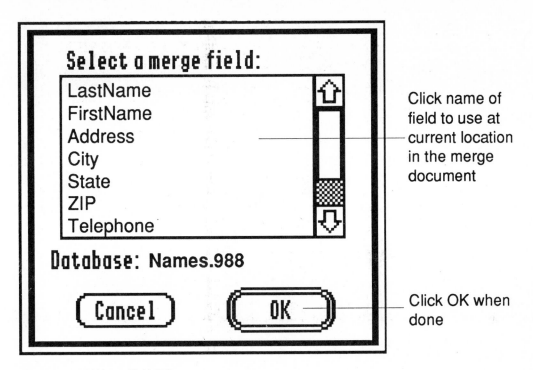

Select a merge field:

LastName
FirstName
Address
City
State
ZIP
Telephone

Database: Names.988

Cancel   OK

Click name of
field to use at
current location
in the merge
document

Click OK when
done

Figure 8-3 Add Merge Field dialog

5 | **Click on the name of the field that contains the information that you want to place at this location in the merge document.**

The field name is selected and highlighted.

6 | **Click the OK button in the dialog box.**

A placeholder is inserted into your document, with the field name surrounded by angle brackets (see Figure 8-4).

When you print the document, the information stored in that field will be printed at this location in the document.

7 | **Continue to type text into the merge document. When you reach the next location where personalized information should be printed, choose the Add Merge Field command again and insert another placeholder into the merge document.**

Continue to add placeholders into the merge document until you have placed all of the desired placeholders into the document (see Figure 8-5).

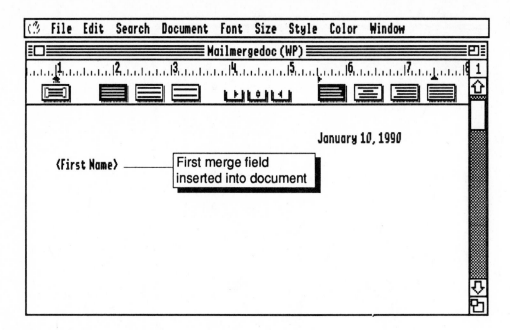

Figure 8-4 Sample document with first merge field

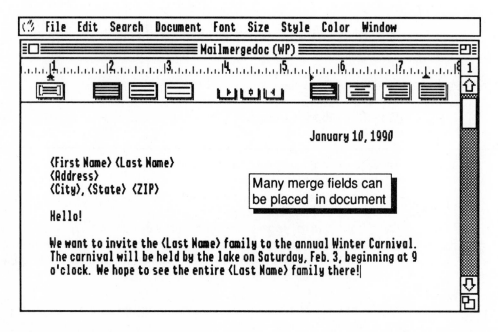

Figure 8-5 Sample document with many fields

Printing the merge document

After you have created the merge document, you are ready to print the actual form letters. You can save the merge document and return to print the document later, but remember that both the word processing merge document and the database that contains the personalized information must be open when the documents are printed.

When you are ready to print the merge document:

1 **Choose the Print Merge command from the File menu.**

The usual Print dialog box appears.

2 **Complete the Print dialog box and click the OK button.**

Complete the Print dialog box in the usual way. For more information, see the Print command in Chapter 3, AppleWorks GS Common Commands.

After you click OK, the first copy of the merge document is printed. Each placeholder in the document is replaced by the information stored in those fields in the first record of the database.

The second copy is printed, and each placeholder is replaced by the information stored in the second record in the database.

Copy after copy is printed, with each copy containing information from the next record in the database. When the copy containing information from the final record in the database has been printed, printing is completed and you are returned to the merge document.

Saving and using the merge document later

You can use the Save As command to save the merge document for later use.

1 **Select the Save As command on the File menu.**

2 **Complete the dialog box, specifying the name of the document and the desired storage disk.**

After the merge document is saved, you can return to this merge document at a later time and print more form letters.

To use this merge document again:

1 **Open the merge document.**

2 **Open the database that contains the desired information.**

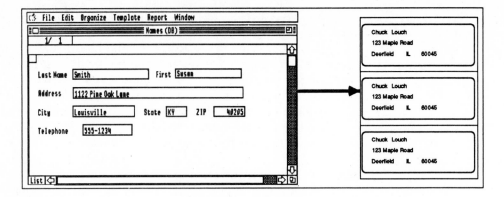

Figure 8-6 You can print mailing labels from an AppleWorks GS database

The database does not need to be the same database used previously, but the database must contain the same field names that are used as placeholders in the merge document.

3   **Select the Print Merge command from the File menu.**

Thinking about mailing labels

One of the most powerful combinations of computer applications is the production of form letters and matching mailing labels to address the form letters.

In the previous sections, you saw that AppleWorks GS can produce form letters using the special Add Merge Field and Print Merge commands in the word processing application.

You can easily produce mailing labels from an AppleWorks GS database that contains a list of names and addresses. Mailing labels would print selected information from the database, arranged in an appropriate order for mailing purposes (see Figure 8-6).

How can this be accomplished? A good general plan for producing mailing labels includes these steps:

- Plan the mailing labels. You need to consider the information to include on each mailing label and the arrangement of the informaton on the label. What information do you want to print on each label? How should the information be arranged on each label? AppleWorks GS is flexible about these matters. You can change your mind later, but it's generally useful to think about these issues in advance.

- Open the database that contains the information to print on the mailing labels. Usually this database will contain more information than will be included on the mailing labels. For instance, the database might store telephone numbers with each record, in addition to names and addresses.
- Change the definition form for the database to reflect the desired format of the mailing label. Mark and hide any fields that you don't want to print on the mailing labels. Rearrange the remaining fields so that they are displayed in an appropriate arrangement on the form. Change the size of the form so that it matches the size of the mailing labels.
- Select the records from which to print the mailing labels. You might want to print mailing labels for the entire database, but often you would want to print labels from only selected records from the database.
- Print the labels. Information from the selected records will be printed in the format that you have defined.
- Save current environment as a template to use again later.

Setting up the database for mailing labels

Before you produce mailing labels from a database, it's important to use the page setup commands to display the database correctly, so that the printed form matches the display as closely as possible. When you are ready to print mailing labels, open the database that contains the necessary information. After the database is open, you can check that the display is set up correctly.

Follow this setup procedure:

1 **Select the Choose Printer command on the File menu.**

When the dialog box appears, select the ImageWriter printer or one of the other dot-matrix printers. Although it is possible to print labels on a LaserWriter, it is far more common to use a dot-matrix printer like the ImageWriter.

2 **Choose the Page Setup command on the File menu.**

When the Imagewriter Page Setup dialog box appears (see Figure 8-7), check the boxes for Condensed Sizing and for No Gaps Between Pages.

3 **Choose the Display Preferences command on the Template menu.**

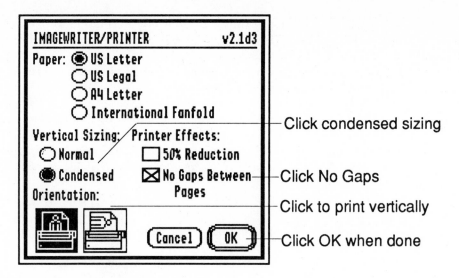

IMAGEWRITER/PRINTER   v2.1d3
Paper: ⦿ US Letter
       ◯ US Legal
       ◯ A4 Letter
       ◯ International Fanfold

Vertical Sizing: Printer Effects:
◯ Normal   ☐ 50% Reduction   ── Click condensed sizing
⦿ Condensed   ☒ No Gaps Between ───────── Click No Gaps
Orientation: Pages
                                              ── Click to print vertically
                    [Cancel] [OK] ──────── Click OK when done

Figure 8-7   Imagewriter Page Setup dialog box

When the Display Preferences dialog box appears, check the box for Multiple Records Per Page. It's important to check this box; otherwise, only one will be printed per page of labels.

Now you can move to the definition form and create the form to use for the mailing labels.

Changing the definition form

You usually begin with a database that contains more information than you want to include on the mailing labels.

For example, a typical database from which you might want to print mailing labels might begin with the form seen in Figure 8-8.

On the other hand, a typical mailing label that you might want to print from this database might need to be in the format seen in Figure 8-9.

To produce the desired mailing label from the database:

- You must hide any fields that you don't want to include on the mailing label.
- You must rearrange the remaining fields on the form until they resemble the mailing label.
- You must change the size of the form to match your mailing labels.

Hiding fields

AppleWorks GS lets you temporarily remove fields from view in the database.

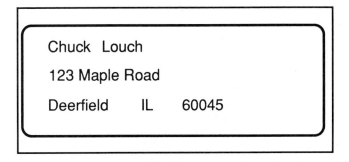

Figure 8-8 A database might contain more information than required for the mailing label

To hide a field:

1 **Select the field.**

2 **Select the Mark Field command on the Organize menu.**

3 **Select the Display Marked Fields command.**

When a checkmark is shown to the left of this command, marked fields are visible on the form. When the checkmark is not displayed to the left of the Display Marked Fields command, marked fields are temporarily

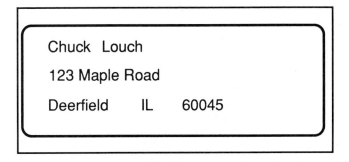

```
Chuck  Louch
123 Maple Road
Deerfield     IL     60045
```

Figure 8-9 Typical mailing label

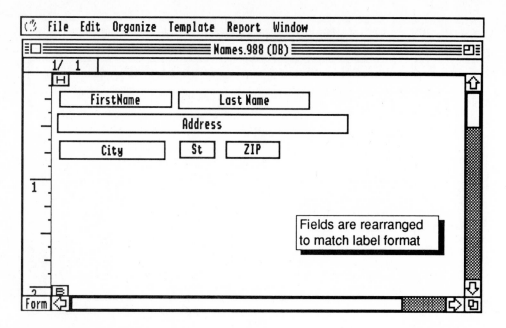

Figure 8-10 Definition form layout

removed from the screen. When you select the command, the current status of the command is reversed.

You may need to repeat Steps 1 and 2 for many of the fields on the definition form to remove all necessary fields from view.

Shortcut:

[1] **Shift-click on all of the fields that you want to remove.**

[2] **Select the Mark Fields command to mark all of the fields.**

[3] **Choose the Display Marked Fields command to remove all of the fields from view.**

Rearranging fields

After you have marked and removed from view all of the fields that you don't want to include in the mailing label, rearrange the remaining fields to match the desired layout for the labels (see Figure 8-10).

To move a field, move the arrow pointer into the field, hold down the mouse button, and drag the field to a new position.

Checking the format of fields

Each of the remaining fields will appear on the mailing labels. However, you may need to adjust the format of those fields. For example, when you first defined each field on the definition form, you used the Field Format command to determine the alignment of information in the field. You may want to change this display on the mailing labels.

☐1   **Click on a field to select the field.**

☐2   **Select the Field Format command on the Edit menu.**

If you double-click on a field, the Field Format command is automatically selected.

☐3   **Change any of the selections for this field.**

In many cases, the field was originally defined to display a border around the field. You would usually deselect the Border box at this point when you are printing mailing labels. You would usually select left-alignment for the display as well.

Resizing the form

Finally, you need to readjust the size of the definition form so that it matches the actual size of your mailing labels.

Measure the height of your mailing labels from the top of one label to the top of the following label. You need to adjust the size of the definition form to match that size.

☐1   **Remove any headers or footers from the definition form.**

If the form contains a header, remove any header fields and drag the header tab up to remove the header area from the form. If the form contains a footer, remove any footer fields and drag the footer tab down to remove the footer area from the form.

☐2   **Drag the body tab up or down until the size of the form matches the measured size of your mailing labels.**

The ruler to the left of the form lets you match the form size to your label size (see Figure 8-11).

Selecting records

After the definition form has been changed to match the desired format of your mailing labels, select the records that you want to print on the mailing labels.

☐1   **Use the Match Records command on the Organize menu to select the desired records.**

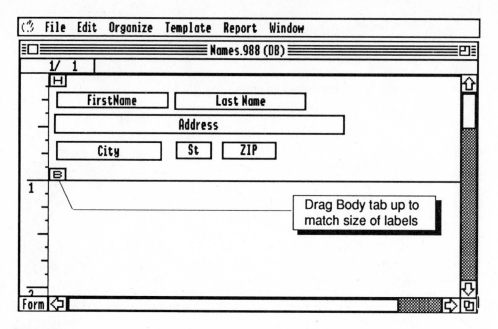

Figure 8-11 Resized form

2 **Use the Hide Selected Records or Hide Unselected Records command to display the records that you want to print.**

The information on the records that remain as the active records will be printed on the mailing labels.

Previewing and adjusting the mailing labels

Before printing the labels, you can preview the appearance of the labels, by selecting the Show Form command on the Template menu.

The database should appear on the screen in the mailing label format that you have defined. If only a single record is displayed, be sure that you have selected Multiple Records Per Form Page with the Display Preferences command. (See Figure 8-12.)

If the information inside a field is not displayed in an appropriate way, you can change the display by returning to the definition form, selecting the field, and selecting the Field Format command to change.

Creating new fields that combine information

You can generally improve the appearance of your mailing labels. For example, if you used a field named FirstName to store the first names of individuals and a field called LastName to store last names, you probably arranged these two fields next to one another on the mailing label.

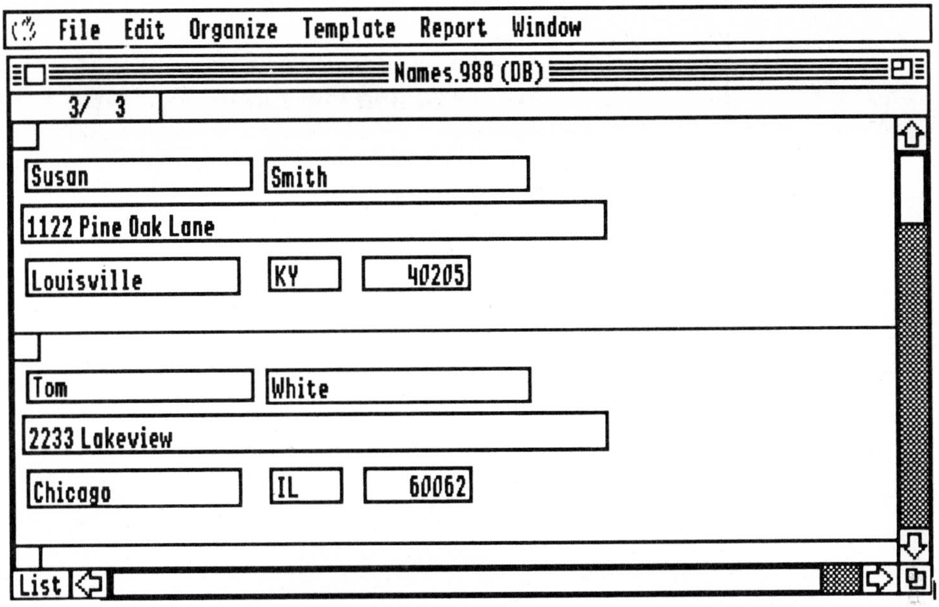

File Edit Organize Template Report Window
Names.988 (DB)
3/ 3
Susan
Smith
1122 Pine Oak Lane
Louisville
KY
40205
Tom
White
2233 Lakeview
Chicago
IL
60062
List

Figure 8-12 Review appearance of database before printing labels

However, when you display the mailing label in Form view, the appearance isn't perfect: spaces are seen between the first name and the last name, since a space is reserved for the entire width of the FirstName field on the form (see Figure 8-13).

How can you improve this appearance? You can create a new third field, FullName, on the definition form that combines the information

Peter Kirn
111 River Road
Louisville KY 40205
Susie Jones
222 Oak Drive
Louisville KY 40205
Too much space between first and last name

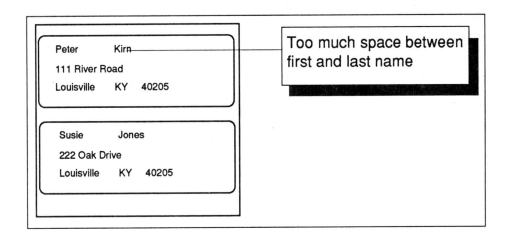

Figure 8-13 Mailing labels with intervening spaces

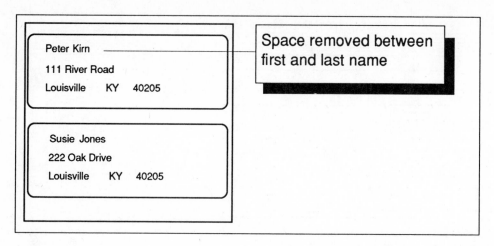

Figure 8-14 Mailing labels without intervening spaces

stored in the FirstName field and the LastName field. This new field could store the full name of the individual; when you use this new field for your mailing label, the intervening blank spaces seen previously are eliminated (see Figure 8-14).

To create a new field that combines information:

| 1 | **Create the new field by dragging a rectangle on the definition form.** |

| 2 | **Give the field a name and define the field as a text field.** |

For example, you might give the field a name like FullName.

| 3 | **Select the field by clicking on it, and then choose the Field Formula command on the Edit menu.** |

This will let us enter a formula into the field that combines other information.

| 4 | **Enter a formula that combines the desired information.** |

The CONCAT function lets you combine the text in two (or more) fields. This function **concatenates** or joins together the text that is supplied to the function. (For more information on functions, see Appendix C, AppleWorks GS Functions.)

To place in the new field the text that is contained in the field called FirstName and the field called LastName, this formula can be used:

CONCAT([FirstName], " ", [LastName])

This places in the new field the text stored in the FirstName field, followed by a blank space, followed by the text stored in the LastName field.

Now you can use this new field on the mailing label definition form, and the names will be printed with only one space between first names and last names.

Printing mailing labels

When you are ready to print the actual mailing labels, you don't need to select the Choose Printer or Page Setup commands, since you made those selections earlier in the session.

1   **Turn on your printer and insert the mailing labels into the printer.**

2   **Select the Print command from the File menu.**

If you are printing more than one page of labels, be sure to click the Automatic button in the dialog box, so that the printer does not stop at the end of each page.

The labels will be printed from the selected records in the format that you defined.

Caution

When you place your labels in your printer, be sure to align the top of the first label to be printed with the top-of-page mark on the printer. It is very important that the labels be aligned correctly in the printer. If the labels are slightly too high or too low in the printer, every label will be too high or too low.

If you have many labels to print, it is a good idea to select a few records for a test-print to check the alignment before printing all of the labels.

Saving the mailing label format

Creating a mailing label format for the database is a bit of work, but fortunately you can save this format and use it again later. Remember that the Save Template command on the Template menu can save the current database environment, which includes the current definition form, List format, and report format. In this case, the definition form is the crucial information that needs to be saved.

To save the mailing label format:

1 **Create the mailing label on the definition form.**

2 **Select the Save Template command on the Template menu.**

When the Save Template dialog box appears, give the current environment an appropriate name (like MailingLabels).

After the template is saved, you can retrieve the saved environment later with the Open Template command. When you choose the Open Template command, you can load the mailing label format back into any database that contains the same fields.

The next step

The previous chapters have shown you how to create text documents in the word processing application, store and work with information using the database application, and combine these two applications to produce form letters. But AppleWorks GS provides many more features beyond these two applications.

The next chapter introduces the third application: the AppleWorks GS spreadsheet. Using the spreadsheet application, you can work with text and numbers to perform simple (or complicated) calculations and produce presentation graphics from your data. Chapter 9 will show you how to create and add information to a new spreadsheet document. Chapter 10 will show you how to format your spreadsheet entries and how to generate pie charts, bar graphs, and line graphs from your data.

Creating a Spreadsheet Document

About this chapter

This chapter introduces the AppleWorks GS spreadsheet. A spreadsheet lets you organize information into rows and columns, perform calculations using the information, and display the information in a graph.

This chapter introduces the spreadsheet application and includes these topics:

- Spreadsheet concepts
- Creating a new spreadsheet document
- The spreadsheet document window
- The spreadsheet menu bar
- Moving around the spreadsheet
- Selecting cells in the spreadsheet
- Entering information into the spreadsheet
- Entering formulas into the spreadsheet
- Using functions in the spreadsheet
- Asking "what if?" questions
- Saving the spreadsheet
- Printing the spreadsheet

Spreadsheet concepts

What is a spreadsheet?

A spreadsheet is simply a collection of information that is arranged in rows and columns. In many ways a spreadsheet is similar to an Apple-Works GS database viewed in List view. Although you can arrange information in rows and columns in both the spreadsheet and the database, the spreadsheet offers one important advantage: the power of calculation.

A database can perform very limited calculations: a calculated field in a database can display a value that is based on other values in a record. The spreadsheet, on the other hand, lets you use any value in any row and column to calculate new values.

Remember: a computer is basically a powerful calculating tool. The spreadsheet gives you access to this calculating power.

When would you use a spreadsheet?

One of the important choices that you must make when you use Apple-Works GS is the selection of the right application for the current job. When should you choose the spreadsheet?

Generally you should choose the spreadsheet to handle information that is naturally arranged in rows and columns, and where you want to perform calculations based on that information.

AppleWorks GS also provides a special spreadsheet feature: it can produce charts and graphs from your data. You should use the spreadsheet application if you want to produce pie charts, bar graphs, or line graphs of your information.

Some typical spreadsheet examples are

- financial budget
- loan payments
- tax information
- student gradebook information
- employee personnel information
- scientific laboratory data

In each of these situations, the information is naturally arranged in rows and columns, and calculations would be performed on the data. For instance, a typical spreadsheet might track projected and actual office expenses (see Figure 9-1).

Since AppleWorks GS can produce graphs of your spreadsheet data, you can also view your information as a pie chart, bar graph, or line graph (see Figure 9-2).

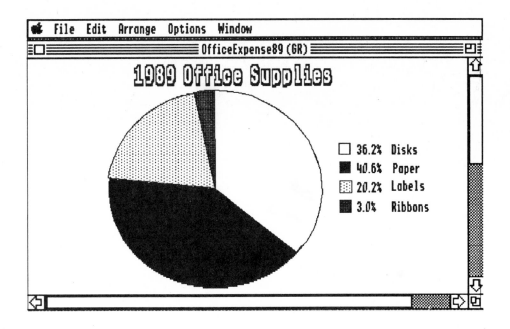

Figure 9-1   Sample spreadsheet

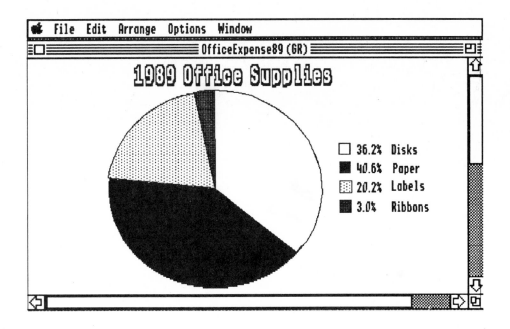

Figure 9-2   Sample spreadsheet chart

Spreadsheet cells and values

When you use the AppleWorks GS spreadsheet, the screen is divided into a series of rectangles called cells, with the cells arranged in rows and columns.

What kinds of information can you enter in each cell? There are three kinds of information that you place in a cell:

- Numeric values, such as integers, real values, dollar values, and percentage values.
- Text values (also called labels). A text value is any entry that begins with a letter of the alphabet.
- Formulas. A formula calculates a value for the cell, using the values in other cells or other values that you may provide.

The power of formulas

Entering numeric and text values lets you arrange your information neatly in rows and columns, but it is the use of formulas that gives the spreadsheet great calculating power. In fact, the power of your calculations is almost unlimited; the only real limit is your ability to create a formula to express your desired calculation.

When you enter a formula into a cell, the cell displays the value of that formula. For example, you can place a formula in one cell that displays the total of other cells in the spreadsheet.

What happens to that total value if you replace one of the values in the spreadsheet? One of the most powerful features of formulas is that the value of the formula changes whenever the value of other cells change. For example, if a formula displays the total of other cells, the value of the formula automatically changes whenever the values of the other cells change.

Asking "what-if" questions

The value of a formula is dynamic; it changes whenever the value of other cells in the spreadsheet change. This lets you ask "what if?" questions with a spreadsheet.

Suppose that you create a spreadsheet with information on your family budget that contains a list of your monthly income and expenses. You might enter a formula in this spreadsheet to calculate the monthly budget balance, calculated by subtracting expenses from income.

Then you can ask "what if?" questions about your budget. You could change the value of your family income and ask "what if the family income increased to . . . ." The formula that calculates the budget balance automatically calculates a revised value and displays the new value in the spreadsheet.

Advantages of electronic spreadsheets

The AppleWorks GS spreadsheet resembles an electronic version of a paper ledger. You could enter your information manually into a paper ledger sheet, and produce a neat summary of your information in rows and columns. However, the AppleWorks GS spreadsheet offers many advantages over a manual ledger:

You can easily edit or correct your information at a later time.

You can quickly rearrange information in the spreadsheet. For instance, you can quickly sort your numeric values in increasing or decreasing order.

You can ask "what-if" questions. You can change one or more values in a spreadsheet, and the formulas that use those values in calculations are automatically updated and display new values.

Historical note

Interestingly enough, this last advantage led to the creation of the first popular spreadsheet, VisiCalc. One of the creators watched a business professor draw a spreadsheet on a blackboard, change one value, and then laboriously recalculate the effects of the change on the blackboard. It occurred to him that this was a natural application for microcomputers, which were just being introduced at the time. The rest is history. VisiCalc was created to run on the Apple II computer; it contributed greatly to the early success of the computer.

Creating a new spreadsheet document

When you are ready to begin a new spreadsheet document, there are two ways that you can create the new document:

- You can create a new document with the New command on the File menu.
- You can create a new document with the Open command on the File menu.

Using the New or Open command to create a new document is discussed in Chapter 3, AppleWorks GS Common Commands.

The spreadsheet document window

When you open a spreadsheet document, a document window appears on the screen (see Figure 9-3).

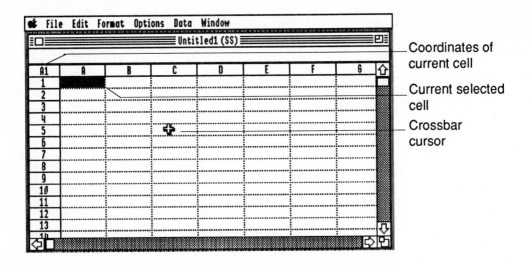

Coordinates of current cell

Current selected cell

Crossbar cursor

Figure 9-3 New spreadsheet document

The new spreadsheet document window has features found on all windows, including the title bar, scroll bars, close box, zoom box, and size box.

The document also includes features that are specific to this application:

- At the top of the screen is the **spreadsheet menu bar**, which contains the commands that are available in this application.
- Most of the window is occupied by the spreadsheet **cells** (or small rectangles) where you will enter your information. One cell is highlighted; this is the active cell, where the next piece of information will be entered.
- The cells are arranged in **rows and columns**. At the top of each column is a letter that identifies the column, and at the left of each row is a number that identifies the row. Each cell is identified by a cell coordinate that includes the row and column; for example, the cell in the upper-left corner of the spreadsheet has the cell coordinate A1, meaning that it is located in column A and row 1.
- The **crossbar cursor** appears; it is used to select the next active cell.

The spreadsheet menu bar

The spreadsheet menu bar includes the File, Edit, Format, Options, Data, and Window menu.

The File menu

Figure 9-4
File menu

The commands on the File menu include New, Open, Close, Save, Save As, Delete File, Import File, Choose Printer, Page Setup, Print, and Quit (see Figure 9-4). The use of these commands was discussed in Chapter 3, Apple-Works GS Common Commands. The Print Merge command is dimmed on the File menu, since it is only available in the Word Processing application.

The Edit menu

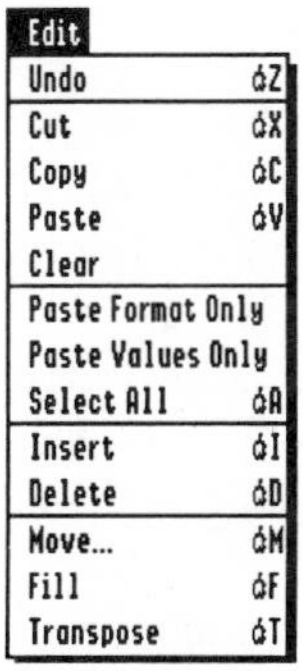

The commands on the Edit menu include Undo, Cut, Copy, Paste, Clear, and Select All (see Figure 9-5). The use of these commands has been described in Chapter 3, AppleWorks GS Common Commands. In addition, the spreadsheet Edit menu includes

Paste Format Only: Lets you copy a cell to the Clipboard in the usual way, and then paste the format of that cell to another cell or range of cells. This is a convenient way to transfer one format to a range of new cells.

Paste Values Only: Lets you copy a cell or range of cells in one location and then paste the values of those cells in a new location. This is a convenient way to transfer the value(s) displayed in cells by a formula to a new location, without transferring the actual formula.

Insert: Lets you insert one or more rows or columns into the spreadsheet.

Delete: Removes one or more rows or columns from the spreadsheet.

Move: Lets you move a range of cells (including formulas) from one location to another.

Fill: Lets you quickly fill a range of cells with a value.

Transpose: Lets you convert rows of values to columns of values, and vice-versa.

Figure 9-5
Edit menu

The Format menu

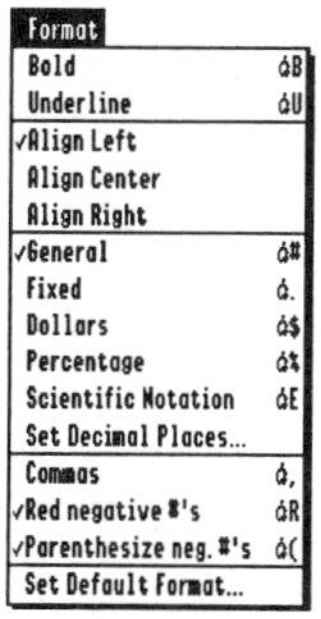

The commands on the Format Menu include Bold, Underline, Align Left, Align Center, Align Right, General, Fixed, Dollars, Percentage, Scientific Notation, Set Decimal Places, Commas, Red Negative #, Parenthesize Neg. #, Set Default Format (see Figure 9-6).

Bold, Underline: These commands display the value of the selected cell in boldface or underline, or they can be used together to display values in boldface and underlined.

Align Left, Align Center, Align Right: These commands display text values of selected cells aligned with the left edge of the cell, centered in the cell, or aligned with the right edge of the cell.

General: This command displays the numeric value of the selected cell in general format. In general format, AppleWorks GS ignores other formatting to fit the number into the cell. If a value is too large to fit in the cell, it is displayed in scientific notation.

Figure 9-6
Format menu

Fixed: This command displays in selected cells a fixed number of places to the right of the decimal point. The number of places is set with the Set Decimal Places command.

Dollars: This command displays the values in selected cells as dollar values. A dollar sign is placed in front of the value, and the number of places last specified with the Set Decimal Places command are displayed to the right of the decimal point.

Percentage: This command displays the values in selected cells as percentages. The numeric value is multiplied by 100 and a percent sign is placed to the right of the value. The number of places last specified with the Set Decimal Places command are displayed to the right of the decimal point. For example, .105 would be displayed as 10.5%.

Scientific Notation: This command displays the values in selected cells in scientific notation. The value is expressed as a real value multiplied by a power of ten. For example, 105.6 would be displayed as 1.056e2, and .0098 would be displayed as 9.8e-3. The number of places last specified with the Set Decimal Places command are displayed to the right of the decimal point.

Set Decimal Places: This command lets you specify the number of places to display to the right of a decimal point. Choose this command to select the number of decimal places, and then choose the Fixed, Dollar, Percentage, or Scientific Notation format to control selected cells.

Commas: This command displays the values in selected cells with commas placed in appropriate places. When you initially enter a numeric value, commas are not displayed. Use this command to display commas if they are desired.

Red Negative #: This command displays negative values in selected cells in red.

Parenthesize Neg. #: This command displays negative values in selected cells surrounded by parentheses.

Set Default Format: The default format automatically controls the format of new values that you enter. This command lets you set or change the default format, including styles, alignment, and decimal places.

The Options menu

The commands on the Options menu are shown in Figure 9-7.

Figure 9-7
Options menu

Manual Calculation/Automatic Calculation: This command lets you control when recalculation occurs in the spreadsheet. Initially, all formula cells are recalculated every time that the value in a cell is changed; this may slow the spreadsheet's operation as the size of the spreadsheet grows. If you choose Manual Calculation, the spreadsheet only calculates new values when you select the Recalculate command.

Recalculate: When you select this command, all formula cells in the spreadsheet are updated to reflect any changes in the spreadsheet.

View Formulas/View Data: Initially, any cell that contains a formula displays the value expressed by the formula. If you choose View formulas, the spreadsheet displays the actual formula in formula cells.

List Functions: This command displays a list of the functions available for use and helps you build a formula using the functions.

Change Default Width: Each column begins with a default width, which you can manually change for each column. This command lets you change the default width for all columns that you have not manually changed.

Restore Width to Default: This command changes the width of selected columns back to the default width, even if you have manually changed the column width.

Set Titles: This command lets you freeze selected rows and columns in place as you scroll the rest of the spreadsheet.

Hide Cell Lines/Show Cell Lines: Initially the spreadsheet displays rows and columns separated by lines on the screen. If you choose Hide Cell Lines, the spreadsheet temporarily removes the row and column lines from the screen.

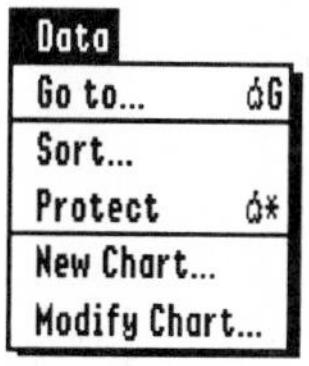

Figure 9-8
Data menu

The Data menu

The commands on the Data menu are shown in Figure 9-8.

Go To: This command lets you quickly move to any cell coordinate on the spreadsheet.

Sort: This command lets you rearrange selected cells into numeric or alphabetic order.

Protect: This command lets you lock the values in selected cells. The values in protected cells cannot be changed until you unprotect the cells.

New Chart: This command lets you display the values in selected cells as a pie chart, bar graph, or line graph.

Modify Chart: This command lets you change the format or type of an existing chart to another format or type.

The Window menu

This menu lists the currently open windows and the Clipboard. The use of this menu is discussed in Chapter 3, AppleWorks GS Common Commands.

Moving around the spreadsheet

When you open a spreadsheet, only a small part of the document is visible on the screen. You can see only the first few columns and the first few rows of the spreadsheet. However, the total spreadsheet may be quite large.

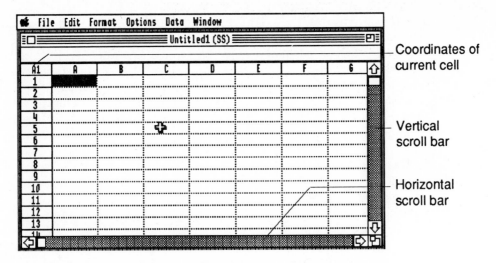

Figure 9-9   Scroll bars, cell coordinates

Using the scroll bars

If a specific cell is not visible on the screen, use the scroll bars at the right of the screen or at the bottom of the screen to bring the cell into view. Refer to Figure 9-9.

If you scroll to the very bottom of the spreadsheet or to the right edge of the spreadsheet, you will find that the number of columns and rows that are available is quite large:

- Each column is labeled with a letter. The first column is labeled A, the second column is labeled B, and so forth. There are many more than 26 columns; after column Z, the next columns are labeled AA, AB, AC, and so forth. After column AZ, the next columns are labeled BA, BB, BC, and so forth. The last column in the spreadsheet is labeled ZZ.
- The rows are each labeled with a number, beginning with 1 and continuing to 9999.

Cell coordinates

Each cell has its own "address," specified by a column letter and row number. The "address" of a cell is called the cell coordinate. For example, the address of the first cell in the upper left corner is A1 (column A, row 1), and the address of the cell to the right of A1 is B1 (column B, row 1), and so forth.

You can use the AppleWorks GS spreadsheet without using cell coordinates, but it is important to understand coordinates for some spreadsheet operations.

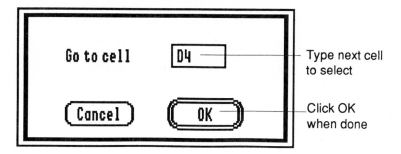

Figure 9-10 Go to dialog

As you use the spreadsheet, the coordinates of the current selected cell are always shown in the box at the upper left of the document.

Using the arrow keys to navigate

When you begin a new spreadsheet, the cell in the upper-left corner of the spreadsheet is selected and highlighted. This is cell A1; it is the current active cell.

To use the spreadsheet, you will select a cell, and then enter a value for the cell. The value that you enter is always displayed in the current active cell.

How can you change the current active cell from cell A1 to another cell? Here are two ways:

- You can use the mouse to move the crossbar pointer to the next cell where you want to enter a value, and click the mouse button. The new cell is highlighted and becomes the current active cell.
- You can use the arrow keys to select a cell that is adjacent to the current active cell. If you press the right-arrow key, the cell to the right is selected. If you press the left-arrow key, the cell to the left is selected. If you press the up-arrow key, the cell above the current cell is selected. If you press the down-arrow key, the cell below the current cell is selected.

The arrow keys are a quick and easy way to move from one location to another when the two locations are near one another.

Moving to a specific cell

You can also move quickly to a specific cell, even if the cell is distant from the current cell:

1 **Select the Go To command on the Data menu.**

The Go To dialog box is shown on the screen (see Figure 9-10).

2 | Type in the cell coordinate of the desired cell and click the OK button.

The desired cell is displayed on the screen and selected for action.

Plan for using the spreadsheet

After you create a new spreadsheet document, you are ready to begin entering information. As you enter information into the spreadsheet, you will find yourself repeating this pattern:

1 | Select and highlight the cell where you want to enter the next piece of information.

This becomes the current active cell.

2 | Type the entry for the cell.

As you type, the entry appears in the input line at the top of the document.

3 | Enter the value by pressing the Return key, Tab key, Enter key, or one of the arrow keys.

The value appears in the selected cell.

Data-entry keys

The Return key, Tab key, Enter key, and the arrow keys are the **data-entry keys**. When you press any of these keys, the value from the input line at the top of the document moves into the selected cell.

Depending on the key that you press, different cells are selected for the next action:

- Pressing the Return key displays your value in the current cell, and then highlights the cell below the current cell.
- Pressing the Tab key displays your value in the current cell, and then highlights the cell to the right of the current cell.
- Pressing the up-arrow or down-arrow key displays your value in the current cell, and then highlights the cell above or below the current cell.
- Pressing the Enter key displays your value in the current cell, and leaves the current cell highlighted for further action.

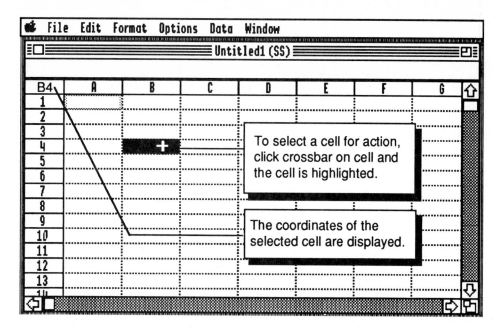

Figure 9-11 Select a cell

Note: *In some other spreadsheet programs, the left-arrow key and right-arrow key can be used for data entry. In AppleWorks GS, pressing these keys moves the cursor left or right in the input box.*

Selecting spreadsheet cells

Selecting a single cell

Before you can enter a piece of information into a cell, you must select and highlight the cell.

To select a cell, move the crossbar cursor to the cell and click the mouse button. The selected cell is highlighted and ready for you to enter a value (see Figure 9-11).

You can also use the keyboard to select a cell:

- Press the Return key to select the cell below the current cell.
- Press the Tab key to select the key to the right of the current cell.
- Press one of the four arrow keys to highlight the cell above, below, to the right, or to the left of the current cell.

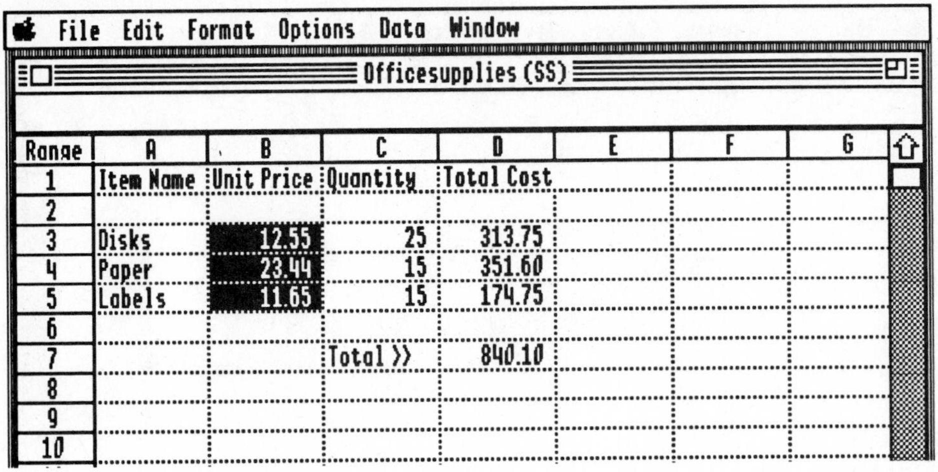

Figure 9-12 Select a range in column

Selecting a range of cells in a column

A range of cells is a series of adjacent cells. A range of cells could be a series of adjacent cells in the same column, a series of adjacent cells in the same row, or a rectangular block of cells in adjacent rows and columns.

To select a range of cells in the same column:

1 **Move the cursor to the top cell in the range.**

2 **Hold down the mouse button, and drag the cursor downward.**

As you move the cursor, the adjacent cells are highlighted (see Figure 9-12).

3 **When the desired range has been selected, release the mouse button.**

Selecting a range of cells in the same row

1 **Move the cursor to the leftmost cell in the range.**

2 **Hold down the mouse button, and drag the cursor to the right.**

As you move the cursor, the adjacent cells are highlighted.

3 **When the desired range has been selected, release the mouse button.**

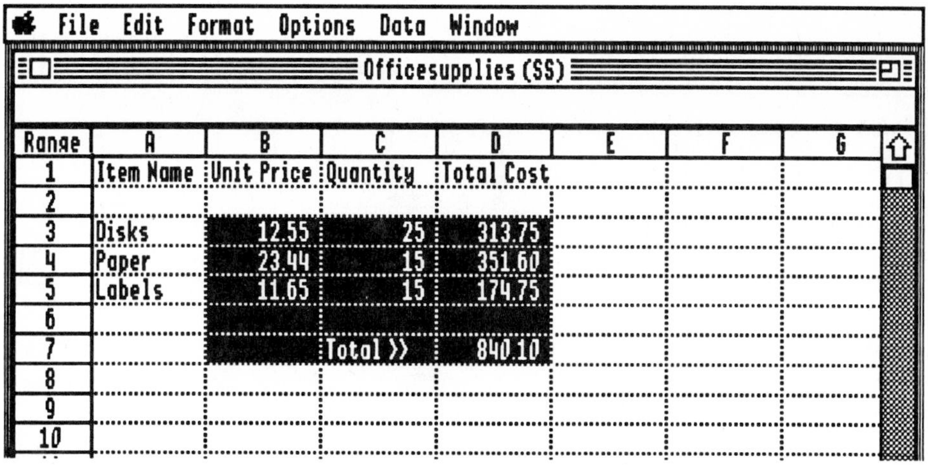

Figure 9-13 Select rectangular range

To select a rectangular range of cells

| 1 | Move the cursor to the cell in the upper left corner of the range that you want to select. |

| 2 | Hold down the mouse button, and drag the cursor toward the cell in the lower right corner of the block. |

As you move the pointer, the adjacent cells in the rectangular block are highlighted (see Figure 9-13).

| 3 | When the desired range has been selected, release the mouse button. |

Shortcut: *You can shift-click to select a range of cells:*

| 1 | Move the pointer to the first cell in a desired range and click the mouse button. |

| 2 | Release the mouse button, and move the pointer to the last cell in the range. |

| 3 | Hold down the shift key, and click on the last cell in the range. |

All of the cells between the first and last cells are selected.

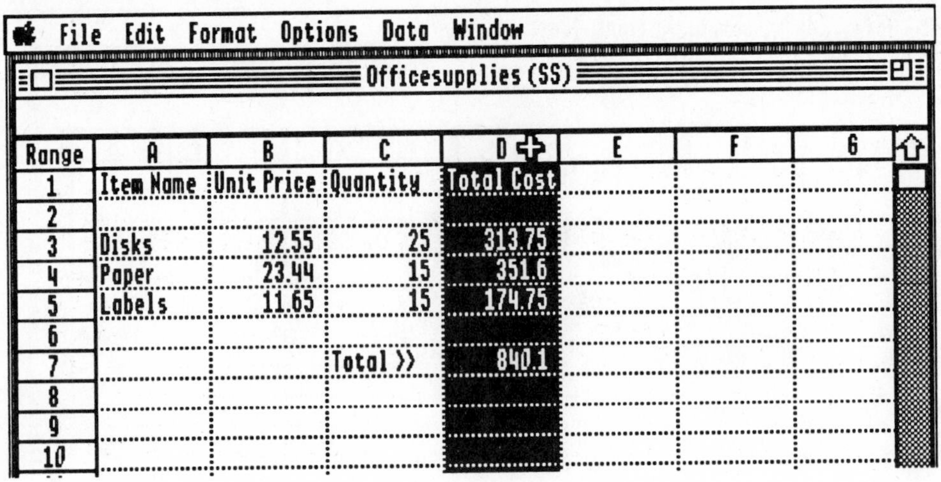

Figure 9-14   Select column

Selecting an entire column of cells

Some spreadsheet operations can affect an entire column of cells. To select an entire column:

1️⃣ **Move the pointer into the column label at the top of the document.**

2️⃣ **Click on the column label.**

The entire column is highlighted and selected (see Figure 9-14).
A range of columns is a set of adjacent columns. To select a range of columns, click on the column label of the first column, and then shift-click on the column label of the last column.

Selecting an entire row of cells

You can also select an entire row of cells. To select an entire row:

1️⃣ **Move the pointer into the row labels at the left of the document.**

2️⃣ **Click on the row label, and the entire row is highlighted and selected.**

The entire row is highlighted and selected (see Figure 9-15).
A range of rows is a set of adjacent rows. To select a range of rows, click on the row label of the first row, and shift-click on the row label of the final row.

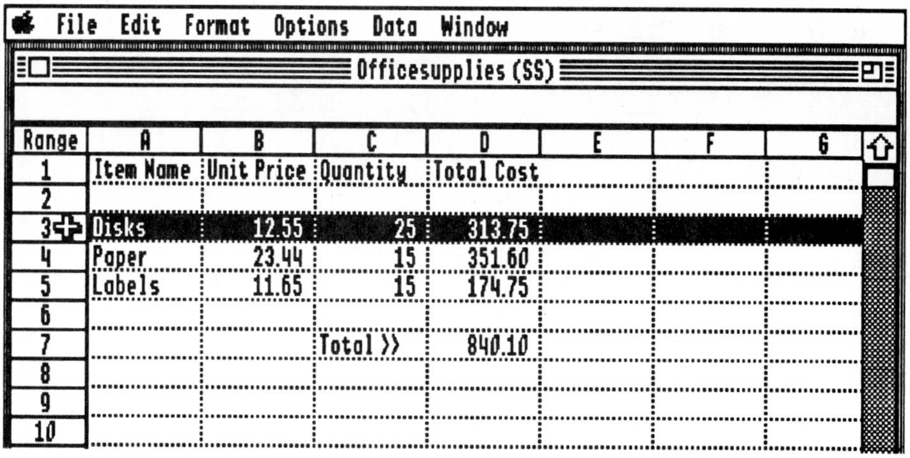

Figure 9-15 Select row

Entering text and numbers into the spreadsheet

The first values that you enter into your spreadsheet are usually text and numbers. After you have entered text and numeric values, you are usually ready to enter formulas into cells to perform calculations based on those values.

Entering text into a cell

1   Select the cell where you want to place the value.

2   Type the text that you want to enter.

As you type the text, it appears in the input line at the top of the document (see Figure 9-16).

3   When the text is correct, press one of the data-entry keys.

Your text is displayed in the selected cell (see Figure 9-17).

The text is displayed aligned with the left edge of the cell. To change this alignment, select the cell and choose the desired alignment from the Format menu.

You might continue to enter text values into the spreadsheet, creating column headings for your data and entering other text values (see Figure 9-18).

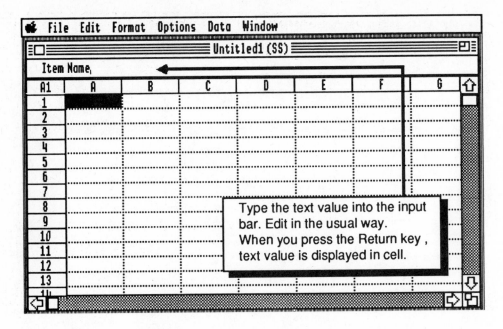

Figure 9-16 Entering text into input bar

Entering a number into a cell

| 1 | Select the cell where you want to place the value.

| 2 | Type the number that you want to enter.

As you type the number, it appears in the input line at the top of the document (see Figure 9-19).

| 3 | When the number is correct, press one of the data-entry keys.

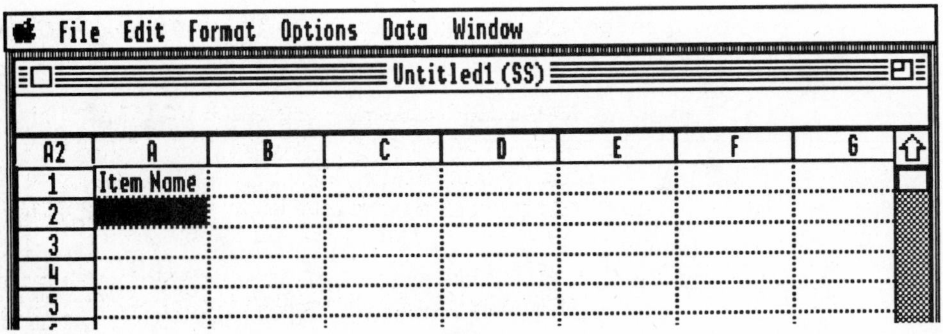

Figure 9-17 After you press data-entry key, text appears in cell

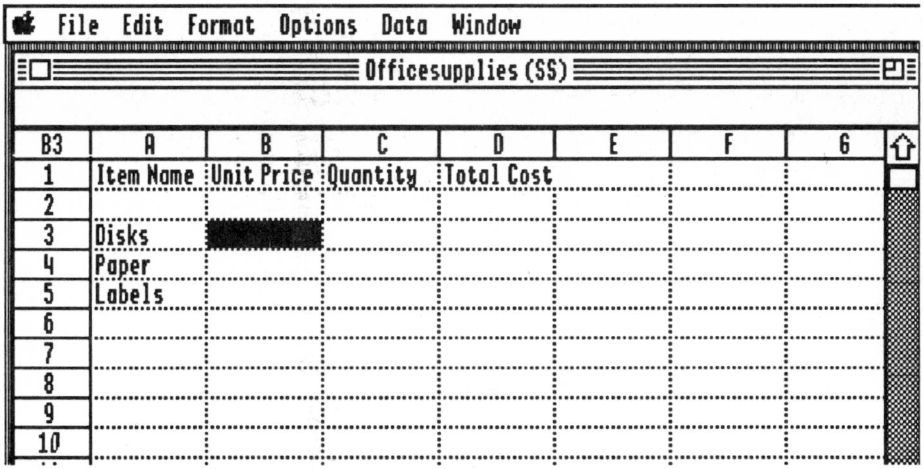

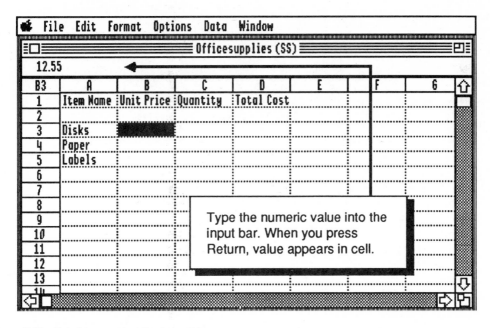

Figure 9-18　Text is used for column headings, item names

Your number is displayed in the selected cell (see Figure 9-20).

If the symbol "##" appears, the value is too wide to fit in the cell. Chapter 10 describes how to adjust column width.

Figure 9-21 shows a typical spreadsheet containing both text and numeric values.

> Type the numeric value into the input bar. When you press Return, value appears in cell.

Figure 9-19　Entering numeric value in input bar

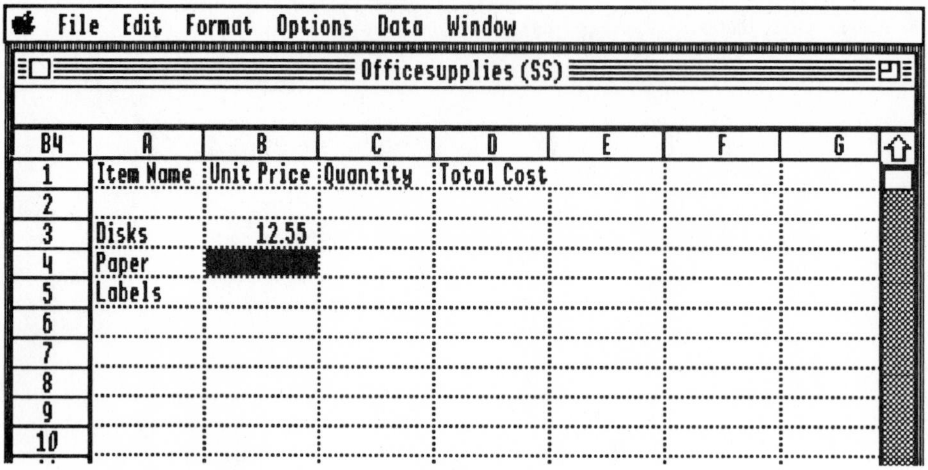

◆ File Edit Format Options Data Window

≡□≡═══════════════════ Officesupplies (SS) ═══════════════════⊡≡

B4	A	B	C	D	E	F	G	
1	Item Name	Unit Price	Quantity	Total Cost				
2								
3	Disks	12.55						
4	Paper	▓▓▓▓▓						
5	Labels							
6								
7								
8								
9								
10								

Figure 9-20   After you press data-entry key, value appears in cell

Alert

Numbers are not initially displayed with commas included. To display commas, select the desired cells and then choose the Commas command on the Format menu.

To enter a number in scientific notation, substitute the character "e" for the characters "x10"; for example, enter 7.4×10^{2} as 7.4e2.

◆ File Edit Format Options Data Window

≡□≡═══════════════════ Officesupplies (SS) ═══════════════════⊡≡

D3	A	B	C	D	E	F	G	
1	Item Name	Unit Price	Quantity	Total Cost				
2								
3	Disks	12.55	25	▓▓▓▓▓				
4	Paper	23.44	15					
5	Labels	11.65	15					
6								
7								
8								
9								
10								

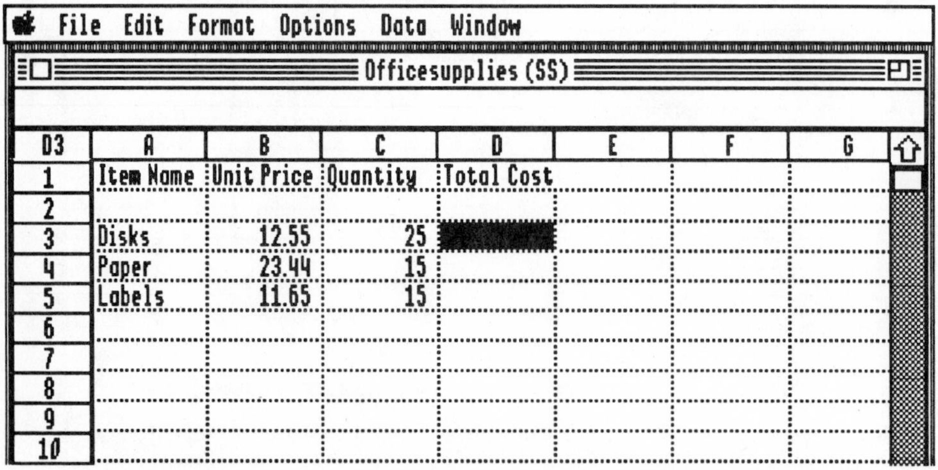

Figure 9-21   Typical spreadsheet contains both text and numeric values

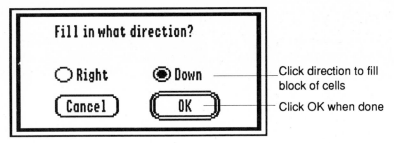

Figure 9-22   Fill dialog

Filling a cell range with the same value

Sometimes you might want to fill one or more adjacent cells with the same value. This can be done easily:

1 **Enter the desired value in a cell.**

2 **Select the range of cells that you want to fill with this value. The cell that contains the desired value must be the first cell in the range.**

3 **Select the Fill command from the Edit menu.**

If you have selected adjacent cells in the same column, all of the selected cells are filled downward with the top value. If you have selected adjacent cells in the same row, all of the selected cells are filled to the right with the leftmost value.

If you have selected a rectangular block of cells, a dialog box is displayed (see Figure 9-22).

You must specify whether you want to copy the values in the top row downwards in the block, or whether you want to copy the values in the leftmost column to the right in the block.

Click the appropriate button, and then click the OK button. The block of cells is filled with your specified values.

Erasing the information in a cell

As you enter information, you may want to erase one or more values entered previously:

1 **Select the cell or range of cells to erase.**

2 **Select the Clear command on the Edit menu, or press the Delete key.**

The values in the selected cells are erased.

Changing information in a cell

If you made a mistake in a cell or if the information has changed, you can return to a cell at any time and correct or update the information in the cell:

[1] **Select the cell that contains the value that you want to change.**

[2] **Type in the new value for the cell.**

[3] **Press one of the data-entry keys, and the new value is shown in the cell.**

Protecting information in a cell

Some of the cells in your spreadsheet might contain values that you want to protect against accidental changes. You can protect any cell or range of cells against change:

[1] **Select the cell or range that you want to protect.**

[2] **Select the Protect command from the Data menu.**

The selected cells are now protected against accidental change. While a cell is protected, you cannot replace the value in the cell. If a change is attempted, an alert box is displayed that warns you against the attempt.

How do you know if a cell is protected? Select a cell and then look at the Protect command on the Data menu. If the cell is protected, a checkmark is shown to the left of the Protect command. If a cell is not protected, no checkmark is displayed.

Removing protection from a protected cell

If you need to change the value in a protected cell, you must first remove the protection from the cell:

[1] **Select the protected cell.**

[2] **Select the Protect command again.**

The checkmark disappears from the menu, and the cell value can now be changed.

Entering formulas into the spreadsheet

After you have entered text and numeric values, you may want to place formulas in some of the spreadsheet cells. The correct use of formulas is the most powerful feature of a spreadsheet.

A formula is a set of instructions that tells the spreadsheet how to calculate the value to display in the cell. For example, a cell might contain a formula to total the values found in certain other cells, and the cell will display the totals in those cells.

It is very important to realize that a cell that contains a formula may display a current value, but it doesn't really contain any specific value. Instead, it contains instructions on how to **calculate** a current value.

Typing a formula directly into a cell

You can enter a simple formula by simply typing it into the input line, just as you entered numbers and text values.

[1] **Select the cell where you want to place a formula.**

[2] **When the cell is highlighted, type in the formula:**

- **Type an equal sign (=). Every formula must begin with this symbol.**
- **Type the remaining elements of the formula.**

[3] **When the formula is complete, press the Return key, Tab key, Enter key, or one of the arrow keys.**

The formula is evaluated, and the value of the formula is shown in the cell.

Example: Showing the product of cells

The sample spreadsheet in Figure 9-23 has numeric values in cells B3 and C3. Cell B3 stores the unit price of a box of disks, and cell C3 stores the number of boxes that will be purchased. Cell D3 should display the product, the total cost of the disks.

To display the product of cells B3 and C3 in cell D3:

[1] **Select cell D3.**

[2] **Type an equal sign. (Remember, every formula begins with the equal sign.)**

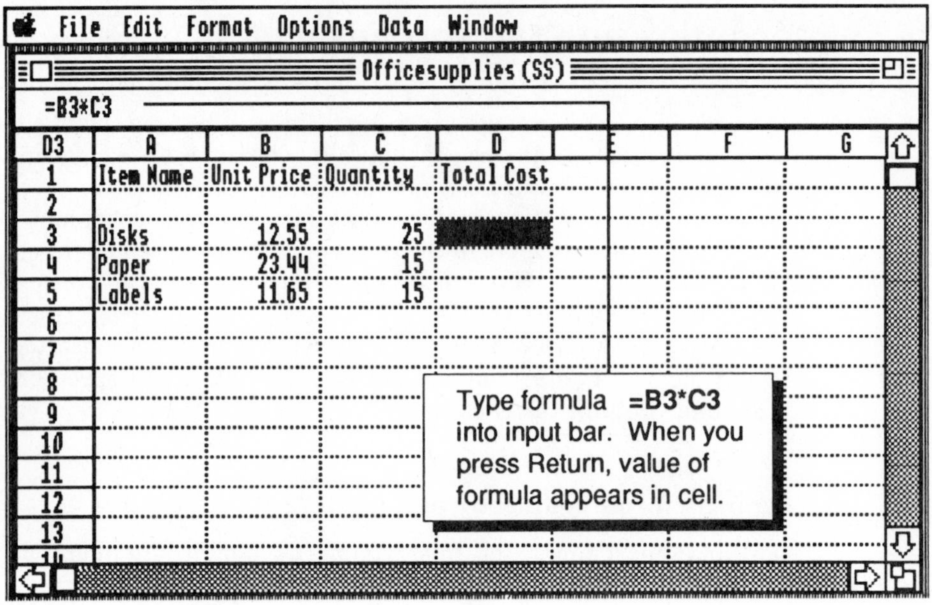

Figure 9-23 Entering a formula into the input bar

[3] **Type a formula that displays the product of the cells. One example of this formula might be**

=B3*C3

The asterisk is used to indicate multiplication.

Press one of the data-entry keys, and the correct value is displayed in cell D3 (see Figure 9-24).

This is a very simple example of a formula, but it demonstrates the concept.

Notice that this formula uses the asterisk to indicate multiplication. You can use any of the usual arithmetic operators in a formula:

- The plus sign (+) indicates addition. For example, =A1+A2 adds the values in A1 and A2.
- The minus sign (-) indicates subtraction. The formula =A1-A2 subtracts the value in A2 from the value in A1.
- The asterisk (*) indicates multiplication. The formula =A1*A2 multiplies the value in A1 times the value in A2.
- The slash (/) indicates division. The formula =A1/A2 divides the value in A1 by the value in A2.

There are many other operators that can be used in a formula. (See Appendix B, AppleWorks GS Formulas).

```
 🍎  File   Edit   Format   Options   Data   Window
═╪═══════════════════════════ Officesupplies (SS) ═══════════════════════════╪═
┌──────┬──────────┬──────────┬──────────┬──────────┬──────┬──────┬──────┬───┐
│  D4  │    A     │    B     │    C     │    D     │  E   │  F   │  G   │ ⬆ │
├──────┼──────────┼──────────┼──────────┼──────────┼──────┼──────┼──────┼───┤
│  1   │Item Name │Unit Price│Quantity  │Total Cost│      │      │      │   │
│  2   │          │          │          │          │      │      │      │   │
│  3   │Disks     │   12.55  │    25    │  313.75  │      │      │      │   │
│  4   │Paper     │   23.44  │    15    │ ████████ │      │      │      │   │
│  5   │Labels    │   11.65  │    15    │          │      │      │      │   │
│  6   │          │          │          │          │      │      │      │   │
│  7   │          │          │          │          │      │      │      │   │
│  8   │          │          │          │          │      │      │      │   │
│  9   │          │          │          │          │      │      │      │   │
│  10  │          │          │          │          │      │      │      │   │
└──────┴──────────┴──────────┴──────────┴──────────┴──────┴──────┴──────┴───┘
```

Figure 9-24 When you press data-entry key, the results of formula are displayed in cell

Clicking to enter cell coordinates

When you enter a formula, you can type in the cell coordinates of the cells in the formula, or you can use a shortcut. When you need to enter a cell coordinate into a formula, just click on the cell that you need to use in the formula. When you click on a cell, its coordinates are automatically typed into the formula.

If you accidentally click on the wrong cell, press the Delete key to remove the wrong coordinates from the formula.

Relative and absolute references

When you enter a formula into a cell, the formula refers to the values found in other cells.

There are two ways that the formula can refer to the other cells: in relative terms, or in absolute terms.

Most cell references in formulas are **relative references**. For example, suppose the formula in cell C1 is

=A1+B1

The meaning of this formula is "add the value found in the cell located two cells to the left and the value found in the cell located one cell to the left." The formula doesn't know or care about the cell coordinates A1 and B1: it looks at the values located two cells to the left and one cell to the left. The references in this formula refer to cells located at a certain position **relative** to the location of the formula cell.

Relative references are useful, because we can copy this formula anywhere in the spreadsheet where we would like to display the sum of the values found in the two cells to the left of a specific cell.

On the other hand, sometimes you want a formula to refer to a certain, specific cell, regardless of where we choose to move the formula later. Suppose that critical values are found in cells A1 and B1, and we want to place a formula in cell C1 that refers to these values — and if we ever move the formula anywhere else in the spreadsheet we want the formula to continue to refer to cells A1 and B1.

This kind of a reference is called an **absolute reference**. To specify an absolute reference in a formula, we add the $ character before the element of the formula that we want to make absolute. To create a formula that always adds the values of cell A1 and B1, no matter where we copy the formula later, we would enter

= $A$1+$B$1

This formula now means "add the value found absolutely in cell A1 to the value found absolutely in B1." This is very different from the meaning of the formula when it included relative references.

To enter an absolute reference in a formula, add the $ character before the column or row coordinate that you want to always remain unchanged in the formula's calculations.

For more information about absolute and relative references, see Appendix B, AppleWorks GS Formulas.

Copying formulas into other cells

Once you enter a formula into a cell, you may want to copy the formula into other cells. If you want to copy a formula into a cell that is adjacent to the formula cell, you can use the Fill command on the Edit menu. If you want to copy the formula to a cell that is not adjacent to the formula cell, you can use the Copy and Paste commands on the Edit menu and transfer the formula using the Clipboard.

What happens when you copy a formula? Remember: A formula is a set of instructions that tells AppleWorks GS what value to display in the formula cell. The cell itself doesn't contain any specific value; it contains instructions on how to calculate a value.

For example, in the sample spreadsheet, the cell D3 contains instructions: display the product of the cell two columns to the left (cell B3) and the cell one column to the left (cell C3).

If you copy this formula to another cell, it will display in the new cell the product of the cell that is two columns to the left and and the cell that is one column to the left of the new formula cell.

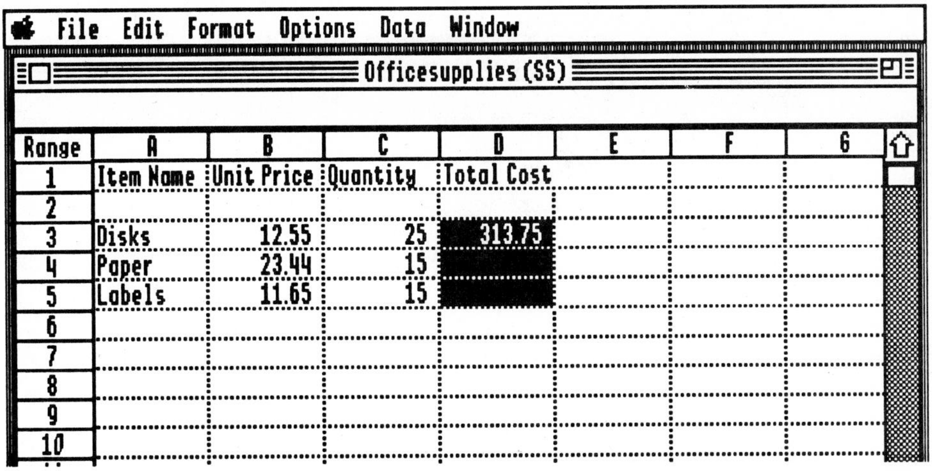

Figure 9-25 Highlighted range of cells

Copying formulas with the Fill command

You can enter a specific formula into each cell that requires one, but you can often copy a formula from one cell into other cells that can use the same formula.

For example, the formula in cell D3 in Figure 9-25 displays the product of the two cells to the left of cell D3.

Cell D4 should display a similar value, the product of the two cells to the left, and cell D5 should also display a similar value. Since cell D3 already contains a formula that calculates and displays the product of the two cells to the left, that formula can be copied down into cells D4 and D5.

The Fill command can copy the formula from cell D3 into cells D4 and D5. The Fill command fills a range of cells with the entry found in the first cell in the range. This value can be a text or numeric value, or it can be a formula.

To use the Fill command:

1 **Select the range of cells to fill with the same entry.**

A range of cells can be selected by dragging over the range, or by shift-clicking on the first and last cells in the range (see Figure 9-25).

2 **Select the Fill command from the Edit menu (see Figure 9-26).**

3 **The entry in the first cell in the range is copied to the other cells in the range (see Figure 9-27).**

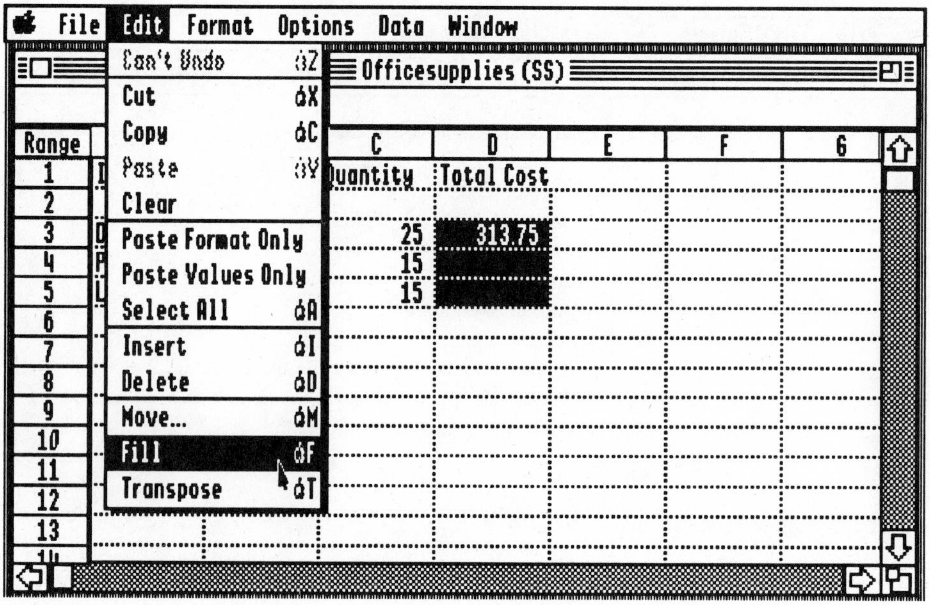

Figure 9-26   Select Fill command

Cells D4 and D5 now contain the same formula found in cell D3 and display the product of the two cells to the left of the formula cell.

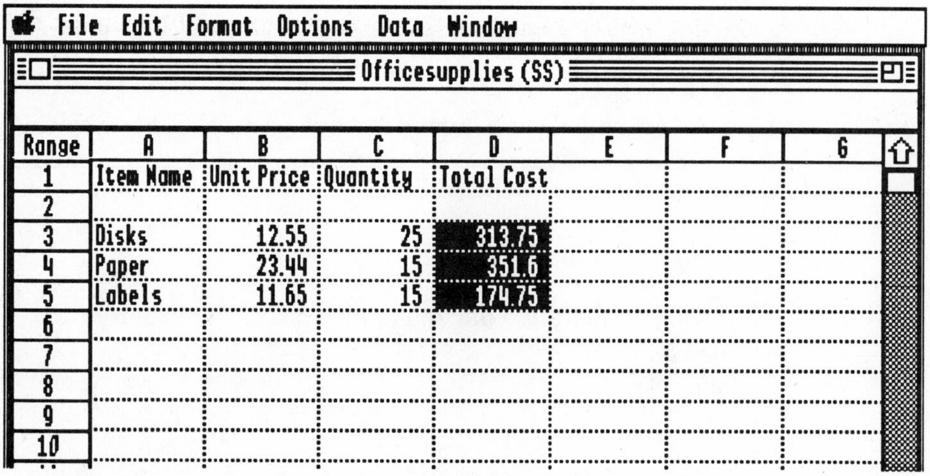

Figure 9-27   Formula in top cell is copied down into other cells

Using functions in a formula

You can type a simple formula into a cell using simple arithmetic operators like the plus or minus signs to indicate operations.

However, if the formula is complicated or involves a large number of cells, it is inconvenient to type all of the elements of a formula.

- For example, if you want to display the standard deviation of a large number of cells, it would be inconvenient to type all of the operations for the calculation.
- For example, if you want to display the total of a large number of cells, it would be inconvenient to sum all of the individual cells, one by one in a formula.

Fortunately, AppleWorks GS provides over 70 built-in functions to automatically calculate many common math operations. It is also easy to indicate a range of cells in a calculation, letting you perform calculations over a range of cells without typing each of the individual cell coordinates.

What is a function?

A function is simply the name of an operation that performs some calculation. After you specify the cells to be used in the calculation, the function returns the appropriate value based on those cells.

For example, one function is the sum function. After you specify the cells that you would like to total, the sum function displays the total of the values in those cells.

Another AppleWorks GS function is the avg function, which displays the average of the values in the specified cells.

Using a function

To use an AppleWorks GS function you must

- Enter the name of the function into the formula.
- Provide any information required for the functions calculations, surrounded by parentheses. This information, called the function parameters, usually includes the cells that you want the calculations based on.

For example, a formula that calculates the sum of the values in cells A1 through A10 would be

= sum(A1..A10)

Notice that the formula uses the function name **sum**, followed by the cells that should be used for the calculation. The characters ".." indicate the range of cells between A1 and A10.

Specifying a range of cells in a function

Most spreadsheet functions perform calculations on cells that are located adjacent to one another. For example, you might want to display the total or average of a column of numbers. The most common functions perform calculations based on

- a series of cells in the same column,
- a series of cells in the same row, or
- a rectangular block of cells in adjacent rows and columns.

To indicate a range of cells to a function:

- Type the cell coordinates of the first cell in the range. If the range is a rectangular block of cells, type the coordinates of the upper-left cell in the block.
- Type two period-symbols (..), with no spaces between the periods, These two dots stand for the word "through."
- Type the cell coordinates of the last cell in the range. If the range is a block of cells, type the coordinates of the lower-right cell in the block.

For example, the range A1..A10 means all of the cells between A1 and A10, including A1 and A10. The range A1..B5 means the cells in the rectangle defined by A1 and B5.

Example: Using the sum function

The sum function displays the total of specified cells.

| 1 | Select the cell where you want to place the formula. |

| 2 | Begin the formula by typing the equal sign. |

| 3 | Type the function name, sum. |

| 4 | Type in the cells that should be totalled, surrounded by parentheses. (See Figure 9-28 on page 241.) |

When you press the data-entry key, the formula cell displays the sum of the specified cells (see Figure 9-29 on page 241).

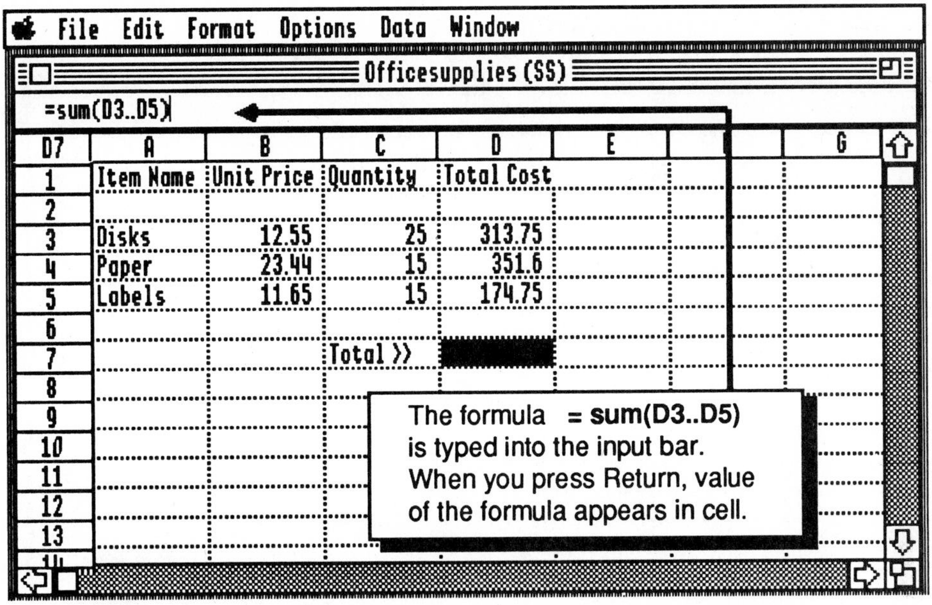

```
 File  Edit  Format  Options  Data  Window
═══════════════════════ Officesupplies (SS) ═══════════════════════
=sum(D3..D5)  ◄─────────────────────────────────────────────────┐
D7 │    A     │    B     │    C     │     D      │  E  │      │  G │
 1 │Item Name │Unit Price│Quantity  │Total Cost  │     │      │    │
 2 │          │          │          │            │     │      │    │
 3 │Disks     │   12.55  │    25    │   313.75   │     │      │    │
 4 │Paper     │   23.44  │    15    │   351.6    │     │      │    │
 5 │Labels    │   11.65  │    15    │   174.75   │     │      │    │
 6 │          │          │          │            │     │      │    │
 7 │          │          │ Total >> │ ██████████ │     │      │    │
 8 │          │          │          │            │     │      │    │
 9 │          │          │ ┌──────────────────────────────────┐   │
10 │          │          │ │ The formula  = sum(D3..D5)       │   │
11 │          │          │ │ is typed into the input bar.     │   │
12 │          │          │ │ When you press Return, value     │   │
13 │          │          │ │ of the formula appears in cell.  │   │
14 │          │          │ └──────────────────────────────────┘   │
```

Figure 9-28 Entering a formula with a function into input bar

Note: *You can use the sum function to total individual cells located at separate locations in the spreadsheet. If the cells to be totaled are not a range of cells, enter the cell coordinates, separated by commas. For example, =sum(A1,C4,D10) produces the sum of cells A1, C4, and D10.*

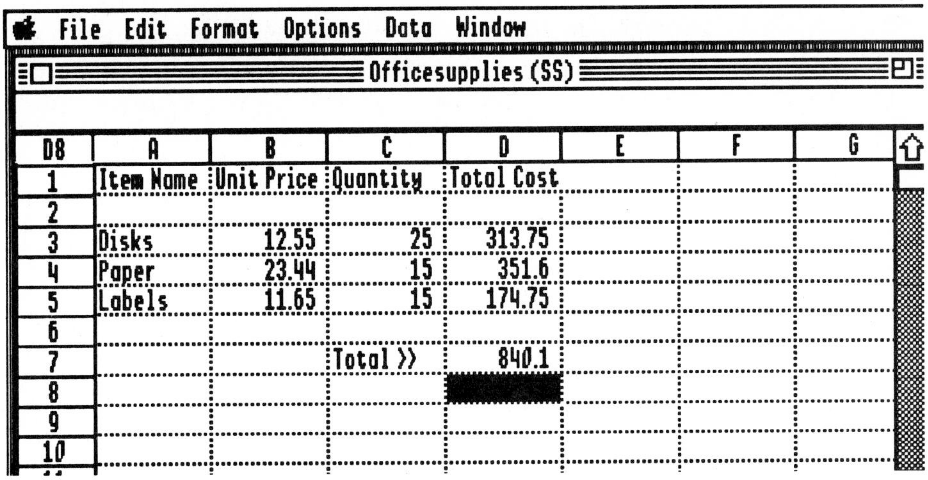

```
 File  Edit  Format  Options  Data  Window
═══════════════════════ Officesupplies (SS) ═══════════════════════
D8 │    A     │    B     │    C     │     D      │  E  │  F   │  G │
 1 │Item Name │Unit Price│Quantity  │Total Cost  │     │      │    │
 2 │          │          │          │            │     │      │    │
 3 │Disks     │   12.55  │    25    │   313.75   │     │      │    │
 4 │Paper     │   23.44  │    15    │   351.6    │     │      │    │
 5 │Labels    │   11.65  │    15    │   174.75   │     │      │    │
 6 │          │          │          │            │     │      │    │
 7 │          │          │ Total >> │   840.1    │     │      │    │
 8 │          │          │          │ ██████████ │     │      │    │
 9 │          │          │          │            │     │      │    │
10 │          │          │          │            │     │      │    │
```

Figure 9-29 After you press data-entry key, results of formula are displayed in cell

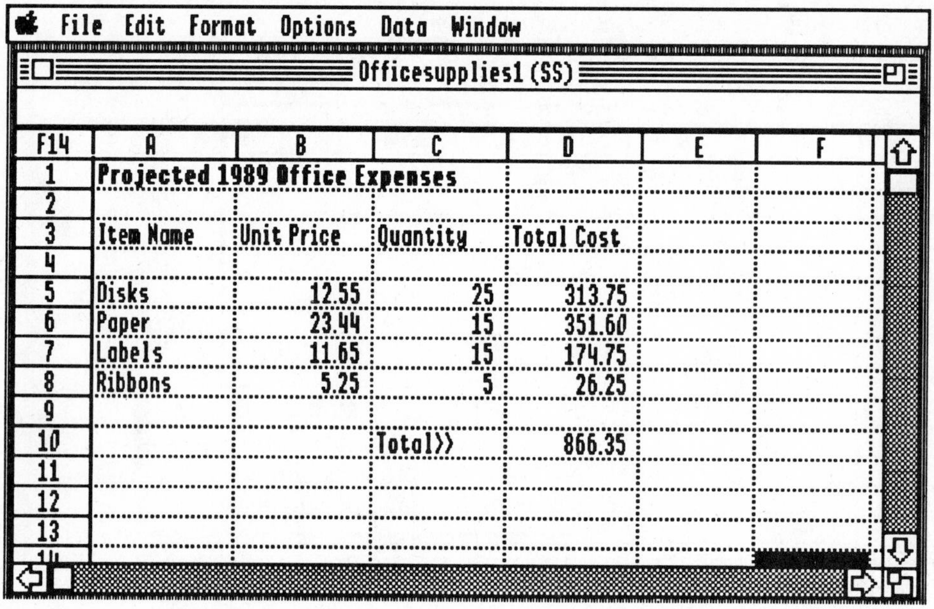

Figure 9-30 Formatted spreadsheet, with cells in column B and D displayed with two decimal places

Formatting values

Notice that the numeric values in the spreadsheet do not display trailing zeroes, or zeroes that are not necessary to convey the value of the number. Since the values in this spreadsheet are dollar values, the values should be displayed with two decimal places.

AppleWorks GS provides many formatting options. These will be discussed in Chapter 10, Working with Spreadsheet Documents. To display the values with two decimal places, select the cells that you want to format, set the number of decimal places to 2 with the Set Decimal Places command, and then select the Fixed command on the Format menu (see Figure 9-30).

You could also select Dollars format, which displays 2 decimal places by default.

Using the List Functions command

AppleWorks GS provides more than 70 built-in functions, ranging from simple math functions like sum and avg to financial functions that can calculate payments on a loan to statistical functions that can calculate the standard deviation of cell values.

The List Functions command lets you see a list of these built-in functions and include them easily in your formulas:

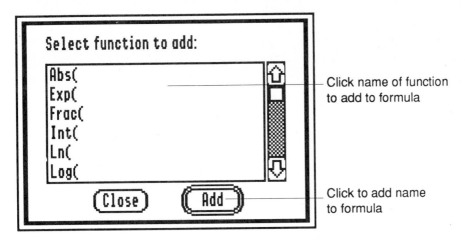

Select function to add:

Abs(
Exp(
Frac(
Int(
Ln(
Log(

(Close)   (Add)

— Click name of function to add to formula

— Click to add name to formula

Figure 9-31   List Functions dialog

1   Select a cell where you want to enter a formula.

2   Type an equal sign into the input bar to begin the formula.

3   Type any desired elements into the formula, until you reach the point where you want to use a function.

4   Choose the List Functions command on the Options menu.

A dialog box appears (see Figure 9-31).

5   Click on the name of the function that you want to add, and then click on the Add button.

The name of the function and left parenthesis (if required) is added to your formula. You can simply double-click on the function name to add the function to your formula.

6   Provide the function parameters that are required for the function and then continue to enter your formula.

7   To remove the List Functions box from the screen, click the Close button.

8   When the formula is complete, press a data-entry key, and the value of the formula is displayed in the cell.

Function parameters

You must supply some values to most AppleWorks GS functions before they can calculate and return the desired value. These required function parameters might be cell coordinates, numeric values, text values, or logical values, depending on the specific function.

How do you know what information is required for each function? Some function parameters are obvious ; the sum or avg functions obviously require a list of cells or values to total or average. However, the parameters for the financial functions or statistical functions are not as obvious. The parameters for each AppleWorks GS function are summarized in Appendix C, AppleWorks GS Functions.

Asking "what if?" questions

Using formulas in a spreadsheet lets you explore the effects of changing values in the spreadsheet. A formula cell contains instructions rather than any specific value. It displays a value that is calculated based on the value in other cells.

What happens if the value in one of the other cells is changed? When you change one of the values in a cell, all of the formulas that use the value are recalculated, and new values are displayed in the formula cells.

This lets you explore the effects of changing values. You can ask "what if?" questions, changing one or more values in your spreadsheet and observing the effects.

Changing the value in a cell

To change the value in a cell:

1   **Select the cell to change.**

2   **Type a new value for the cell, and press one of the data-entry keys.**

The new value is displayed in the cell, and any formulas that depend on that cell are updated with new values.

Seeing the effects of a change

For example, suppose that one of the values in the sample spreadsheet are changed.

What if the number of disks planned for purchase (displayed in cell C3) is increased from 25 to 35? What other cells in the spreadsheet depend upon the value of C3? Cell D3 displays the product of cell B3 and

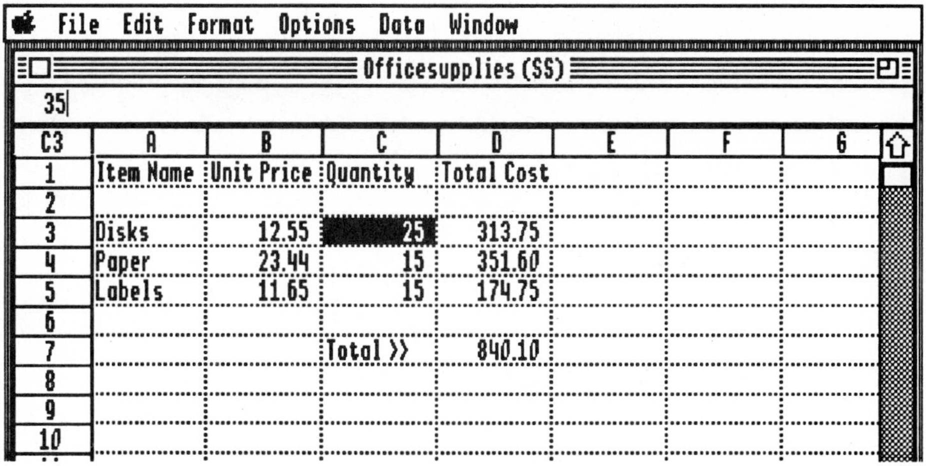

Figure 9-32 To ask "what if?" question, select a cell and type a new value

C3, so that value will change, and so will the value in cell D7, which displays the total of cells D3 through D5.

To change the value and see the effect:

1 **Select cell C3, and type a new value. (Refer to Figure 9-32.)**

2 **Press a data-entry key, and the effects of the change are seen in cells D3 and D7. (Refer to Figure 9-33.)**

The effects of the change are displayed in the spreadsheet.

The power of "what if?" questions

"What if?" questions are one of the reasons that spreadsheets are so popular. Once you have created a basic spreadsheet that contains your basic information and the necessary formulas, you can change the data values endlessly and explore the effects of various changes.

An employer who stores sales records in a spreadsheet might explore the effects of different prices on sales or the total cost of incentive payments.

A classroom teacher who stores student records in a spreadsheet could show a student the effect of the final exam grade on the final average.

A homeowner could explore the effects of different interest rates on the cost of a home loan.

The possibilities are literally endless and limited only by your imagination.

File   Edit   Format   Options   Data   Window

Officesupplies (SS)

D8	A	B	C	D	E	F	G
1	Item Name	Unit Price	Quantity	Total Cost			
2							
3	Disks	12.55	35	439.25			
4	Paper	23.44	15	351.60			
5	Labels	11.65	15	174.75			
6							
7			Total >>	965.60			
8							
9							
10							

Figure 9-33   After new value for C3 is entered, formulas in cells D3 and D7 show updated values

Using manual calculation

When you begin a spreadsheet, AppleWorks GS automatically recalculates formulas whenever you change a cell value. While this is usually desirable, this recalculation can slow down the response of your spreadsheet as it grows in size and includes many more formulas. If the delay in response becomes unacceptable, you can turn off automatic recalculation and perform manual calculations at convenient times.

To set the spreadsheet for manual calculation, select Manual Calculation from the menu.

After you select Manual Calculation, the Recalculate command is available on the Options menu. Manual Calculation is replaced by Auto Calculation on the Options menu.

Now as you enter your data, spreadsheet formulas are not automatically updated as you change cell values. At convenient times, select the Recalculate command on the Options menu, and the entire spreadsheet is updated to show current values.

Caution

When your spreadsheet is set for manual calculation, it's very important to remember that formulas are not being updated automatically. Do not be misled by the values displayed on the screen, since these values may include formula cells that have not been updated yet. Be very careful to recalculate your spreadsheet before using the spreadsheet for any decisions!

Returning to automatic calculation

You can return to automatic calculation whenever you wish.

Select the Auto Calculation command from the Options menu, and spreadsheet formulas are automatically revised again as cell values are changed.

After you select the Auto Calculation command, it is replaced by Manual Calculation on the Options menu.

Checking the formulas in a spreadsheet

Formulas give spreadsheets great power, but they also can make spreadsheets very dangerous. When you look at a spreadsheet and use it for a decision, an error in a formula can lead to very wrong conclusions. That makes it very important to locate and check your formulas carefully before using your spreadsheet for any decisions.

But when you look at a spreadsheet, how can you tell which cells have formulas in them? It isn't always easy to look at a spreadsheet and find the formulas. A cell that contains a formula displays the value calculated from the formula, and not the formula instructions themselves. The result of the formula is shown in the cell, not the formula itself.

Fortunately, you can display the formulas when you wish.

Viewing all the formulas in a spreadsheet

To see all the spreadsheet formulas:

1. **Select the View Formulas command on the Options menu.**

All the cells in the spreadsheet that contain formulas now display their formulas, rather than the values of the formulas (see Figure 9-34). The View Formulas command is replaced by the View Data command on the menu.

2. **After you have checked your formulas, you can display the values in the formula cells again, by selecting the View Data command on the Options menu. After you select the command, it is replaced by View Formulas on the menu again.**

Viewing and revising the formula in a cell

You can also see the formula in any single cell:

1. **Select the cell that contains the formula that you want to see.**

The formula is displayed in the input line at the top of the document. The value of the formula is still displayed in the cell.

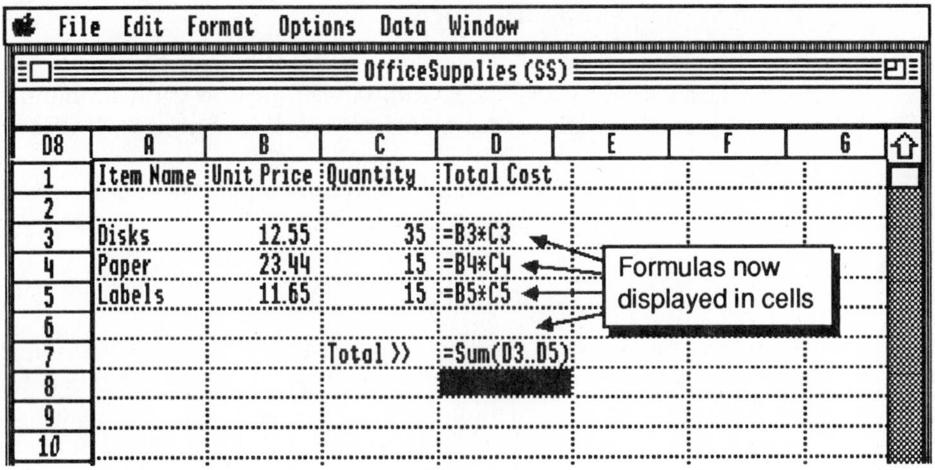

Figure 9-34 View formulas

2 You can now edit the formula in the input line and make any desired changes. After you have made any desired changes, press a data-entry key, and the revised formula is entered into the cell.

Saving the spreadsheet

After you've entered information into your spreadsheet, you can use the data in many ways. You can rearrange the cell values in a desired numeric or alphabetic order, you can print out reports containing some or all of the information, or you can generate graphs from the cell values.

Before using the data in the spreadsheet, however, you should always save your information to your storage disk. Remember to save your work often!

Refer to Chapter 3 for a discussion of the Save and Save As commands.

When you save your spreadsheet with the Save As command, pay special attention to the formatting buttons at the bottom of the dialog box (see Figure 9-35). ASCII text is a standard storage format used by many computers and programs. If you save the spreadsheet as ASCII text, you could send the spreadsheet to another computer via a modem, or you could import the information into applications other than AppleWorks GS. The ASCII text format, however, is not able to store information on special AppleWorks GS features.

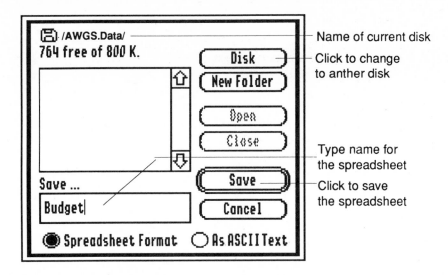

Figure 9-35 Save As dialog box

Printing your spreadsheet

After you have entered information into your spreadsheet, you will probably want to print a copy of the information on your printer. Printing out a copy of your spreadsheet involves four steps:

1. Use the mouse to select and highlight the area of the spreadsheet that you want to print.

If you do not select a range in the spreadsheet, the entire spreadsheet is printed.

2. Use the Choose Printer command on the File menu to select the printer to use.

3. Use the Page Setup command on the File menu to specify the type of paper, vertical sizing, printer effects, and orientation that you want to use.

4. Select the Print command on the File menu to select the print quality, page range, and number of copies that you want.

For more information about printing, see the Choose Printer command, Page Setup command, and Print command in Chapter 3, Apple-Works GS Common Commands.

The next step

Once you've entered your basic information into the spreadsheet, you can format the values to control how they are displayed, move values around in the spreadsheet, and rearrange values in a desired order. You can also produce bar charts or pie charts from the values in the spreadsheet. Chapter 10, "Working with Spreadsheet Documents" discusses these and other spreadsheet operations.

Working with Spreadsheet Documents

About this chapter

After you have created a spreadsheet, you can change the format of the spreadsheet, change column widths, rearrange your data, and continue to work with the numbers in the spreadsheet. You can even produce graphs that summarize the numbers as pie charts, bar charts, or line graphs.

This chapter discusses these spreadsheet operations:

- Opening a saved spreadsheet
- Formatting spreadsheet cells
- Changing spreadsheet rows and columns
- Moving spreadsheet values
- Sorting spreadsheet values
- Producing new charts from the spreadsheet
- Modifying charts that were previously produced

Opening a saved spreadsheet

To open a saved AppleWorks GS spreadsheet document:

1   **Select Open from the File menu.**

2   **Click on the document to open, and click the Open box.**

Formatting spreadsheet cells

After you've entered some or all of your information into your spreadsheet document, you may want to change the appearance of the spreadsheet. AppleWorks GS provides many different possible formats for each cell. You can control the format used for each cell in two ways:

- You can change the default settings that AppleWorks GS uses. Then as you type new entries, the cells are automatically formatted with your default settings.
- If you change default settings later in a session, the new default settings control the format of new entries but do not change previous entries.
- After you have entered values into cells, you can select a cell or a range of cells and assign special formats for that range.

Setting the default format

When you begin to use the spreadsheet, AppleWorks GS displays values automatically formatted with the program's default settings:

- Numeric values are aligned with the right edge of each cell.
- Text values are aligned with the left edge of each cell.
- Text and numeric values are not bold or underlined.
- Numeric values are displayed in general format. Real numbers are displayed with as many decimal values as you enter. Trailing zeroes are not displayed. If a value does not fit into the current width of a cell, the value is displayed in scientific notation.
- Negative values are displayed in red and surrounded by parentheses.

You can easily change the default settings:

1   **Select Set Default Format command from the Format menu.**

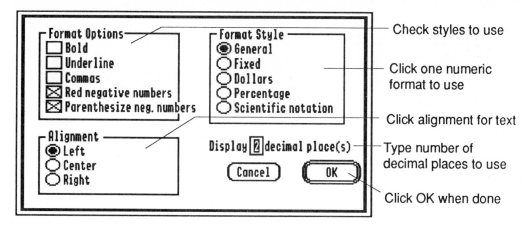

Figure 10-1 Set Format box

The Set Format dialog box appears on the screen (see Figure 10-1).

2 **Click the desired settings, and then click the OK button to set the new default preferences.**

Now when you enter new values, they are displayed with your new default settings.

Bold display of the values in specific cells

The default format settings control the display of cells as you enter them. If you want a specific cell or range of cells to have a different format, you can always set the format of specific cells.

To display the values in selected cells in bold style:

1 **Select the cell or range of cells.**

2 **Select the Bold command from the Format menu.**

The selected cell values are displayed in bold style. When any of the cells are selected later, a checkmark appears to the left of the Bold command on the menu.

Underlining the values in selected cells

1 **Select the cell or range of cells.**

2 **Select the Underline command from the Format menu.**

```
  🍎  File  Edit  Format  Options  Data  Window
 ┌──────────────────────────── Formatdemo (SS) ────────────────────────────┐
 │ ▢                                                                        │
 ├────┬──────────┬─────────┬─────────┬─────────┬─────────┬─────────┬────────┤
 │ A8 │    A     │    B    │    C    │    D    │    E    │    F    │   G   ⇧│
 ├────┼──────────┴─────────┴─────────┼─────────┼─────────┼─────────┼────────┤
 │  1 │                              │         │         │         │        │
 │  2 │ Value Displayed in General Format >> │ 123.4567 │       │ 0.1234567 │ │
 │  3 │ Displayed in Fixed Format >>          │   123.46 │       │    0.12   │ │
 │  4 │ Displayed in Dollar Format >>         │  $123.46 │       │   $0.12   │ │
 │  5 │ Displayed in Percentage Format >>     │ 12345.67%│       │   12.35%  │ │
 │  6 │ Displayed in Scientific Notation >>   │  1.23e+2 │       │  1.23e-1  │ │
 │  7 │                              │         │         │         │        │
 │  8 │ ████████                     │         │         │         │        │
 │  9 │                              │         │         │         │        │
 │ 10 │                              │         │         │         │        │
 └────┴──────────────────────────────┴─────────┴─────────┴─────────┴────────┘
```

Figure 10-2 Numeric value 123.4567 displayed in different formats

The selected cell values are displayed underlined. When any of the cells are selected later, a checkmark is displayed to the left of the Underline command.

Changing the alignment of text

1. **Select the cell or range of cells.**

2. **Select the Align Left, Align Center, or Align Right command from the Format menu to display cells aligned with the left edge, center, or right edge of the cell.**

When any of the cells are selected later, a checkmark appears to the left of the alignment command that you have chosen.

Numeric Formats

You can display numeric values in several formats: General, Fixed, Dollar, Percentage, or Scientific Notation. You can also control the number of digits displayed to the right of the decimal point.

To demonstrate the basic differences among these formats, the table in Figure 10-2 shows two values displayed in each of the available formats. The number of decimal places has been set to 2 in each case.

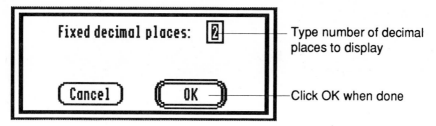

Figure 10-3   Set Decimal Places dialog

Setting the number of decimal places

1️⃣ Select the Set Decimal Places command from the Format menu.

The dialog box shown in Figure 10-3 appears.

2️⃣ Type the number of digits that you want to display to the right of the decimal in selected numeric values.

3️⃣ Select the cells that you want to format.

4️⃣ Choose one of the following numeric format commands: Fixed, Dollar, Percentage, or Scientific Notation.

The selected numeric values are displayed in your chosen format with the specified number of decimal places.

If you choose Fixed, the selected numeric values are displayed with the specified number of decimal places. If you choose Dollar, Percentage, or Scientific Notation, the values are displayed in those formats, which are discussed below.

Displaying dollar amounts

1️⃣ Select the range of cells that you want to format.

2️⃣ Select the Dollar command from the Format menu.

A dollar sign is displayed to the left of the selected values, and the numbers are displayed with the number of decimal places last specified with the Set Decimal Places command.

Displaying percentage values

1️⃣ Select the range of cells that you want to format.

2   **Select the Percentage command from the Format menu.**

The selected cell values are multiplied by 100 and displayed with a trailing percent sign. The numbers are displayed with the number of decimal places last specified with the Set Decimal Places command.

Displaying values in scientific notation

Scientific notation expresses numbers as a decimal value, multiplied by some power of 10. For example, the number 1024 is expressed in scientific notation as 1.024×10^3, and the decimal value .00032 is expressed in scientific notation as 3.2×10^{-4}.

For convenience AppleWorks GS uses a common scientific shorthand for this notation; the characters "x10" are replaced by the character "e." Thus 1024 is expressed in AppleWorks GS as 1.024e3 and .00032 is expressed as 3.2e-4.

To display selected numeric values in scientific notation:

1   **Select the range of cells that you want to format.**

2   **Select the Scientific Notation command from the Format menu.**

The selected cell values are displayed in scientific notation.

If a number is entered in General format, integer or real values are automatically displayed in scientific notation when the values are too large to fit into the current cell width.

Displaying selected values with commas

To display commas in selected numeric values:

1   **Select the range of cells to format.**

2   **Select the Commas command from the Format menu.**

The selected cell values are displayed with appropriate commas separating groups of three digits.

Displaying negative values in selected cells

The default setting displays negative values in red, surrounded by parentheses. This is convenient for financial spreadsheets, where it is important to notice negative values.

To control the display of negative values:

1   **Select the range of cells to format.**

2   Select the Red Negative #s command from the Format menu.

A checkmark appears to the left of the command, and negative numbers in the selected cells are displayed in red.

To display negative numbers in black, select the command again. The checkmark is removed, and negative numbers are displayed in black.

3   Select the Parenthesize Negative #s command from the Format menu.

A checkmark appears to the left of the command, and negative numbers in the selected cells are displayed in parentheses.

To display negative numbers without parentheses, select the command again. The checkmark is removed, and negative numbers are displayed without parentheses.

Either or both of these commands may be selected, so that you can display negative numbers four different ways.

Pasting a format to selected cells

If you have defined a format in one cell, you can quickly apply it to other cells:

1   Select a cell that is formatted in the desired way.

2   Select the Copy command from the Edit menu.

This copies the cell's contents to the Clipboard, including the format of the cell.

3   Select another cell or range of cells where you would like to use the same format.

4   Select the Paste Format Only command from the Edit menu.

The format of the first cell is copied to the selected range and those cells are displayed with that format.

Changing column widths

Default width

When you begin a new spreadsheet, AppleWorks GS displays each column as about one inch in width. Each cell is wide enough to display

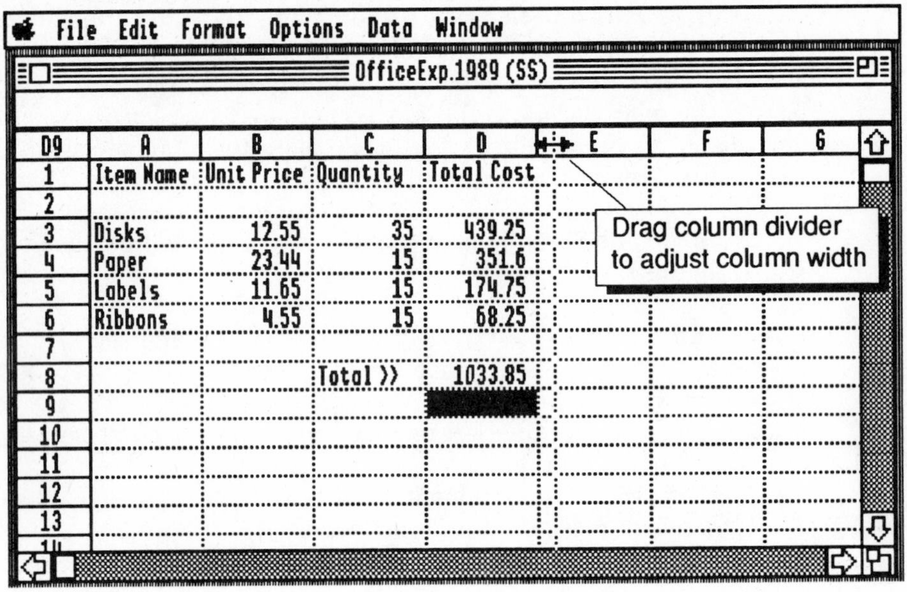

Figure 10-4 Adjusting width of column

about 10 characters in 10-pt Geneva font. The exact number of characters depends on exactly which characters you type; for example, more "i" characters fit into a cell than "m" characters.

You may want to adjust the width of the cells. You can do this two ways:

- You can adjust the size of specific columns
- You can adjust the default width, changing the size of all the cells in the spreadsheet except those columns that you have specifically set.

Adjusting the width of specific columns

1   **Find the column whose width you want to adjust.**

2   **Move the pointer into the row of column labels and position the pointer directly on the column boundary to the right of the label that you want to adjust.**

The pointer turns into the double-arrow cursor (see Figure 10-4).

3   **Hold down the mouse button, and drag the column divider line to the left or right.**

If you drag the column divider to the right, the column becomes wider. If you drag the column divider to the left, the column becomes narrower.

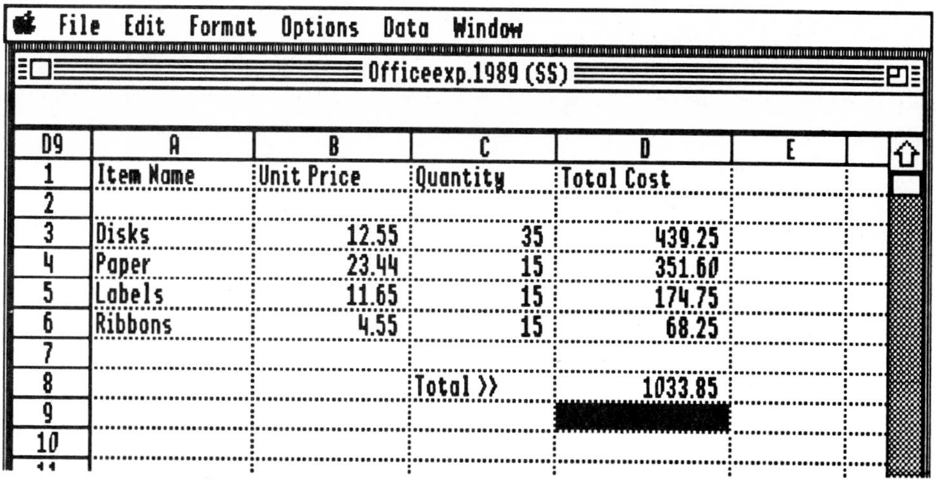

Figure 10-5   Spreadsheet after column widths are adjusted

4 **Release the mouse button when the width is appropriate, and the column is displayed with the adjusted width.**

Each of the columns can be widened until desired column widths are displayed (see Figure 10-5).

Resetting column width to the default width

You can easily change the column width of a specific column. At a later time, you might want to adjust the column width back to the default width.
To adjust the column width back to default setting:

1 **Select the entire column by clicking in the column label at the top of the spreadsheet.**

The entire column is highlighted and selected. You can also select a range of columns by dragging across the column labels or by shift-clicking on the first and last column label in the range.

2 **Select the Restore Width to Default command from the Options menu.**

The selected column or columns are restored to the default width.

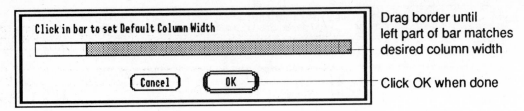

Figure 10-6 Column Width dialog box

Changing the default width

You can easily adjust the width of a specific column. You can also change the default width easily; this adjusts the size of all columns that you have not specifically adjusted.

1 | **Select the Change Default Width command from the Options menu.**

The Column Width dialog box is shown on the screen (see Figure 10-6).

The dialog box contains a control bar; the yellow area to the left of the bar indicates the current default cell width.

2 | **Move the arrow pointer to the control bar and place the tip of the arrow on the divider line. Hold down the mouse button, and drag the divider line to the left or right until the yellow area shows the desired default width.**

3 | **Release the mouse button, and click the OK button.**

All cells that you did not independently adjust are now displayed with the new default width.

Inserting and deleting cells

As you enter values in the spreadsheet, you may find that you need to add one or more blank rows or columns in the middle of the current spreadsheet. The Insert command lets you add these blank rows, moving existing rows or columns to adjust for the new ones. You can also insert one or more blank cells in the middle of a spreadsheet, moving existing cell values to adjust for the new cells.

You may also want to remove existing rows or columns from the spreadsheet. The Delete command lets you remove one or more rows or columns from the spreadsheet, and it shifts the remaining rows or columns to adjust for the removal. You can also delete one or more cells from the spreadsheet, with remaining cell values adjusted for the deleted cells.

Note: *It's easy to confuse inserting or deleting cells in a spreadsheet with clearing cells.*

- *When you clear cells in a spreadsheet, you erase the values in the existing cells. No new cells are added to the spreadsheet, and no cells are removed from the spreadsheet; only cell values are erased.*
- *When you insert cells into a spreadsheet, new cells are added to the spreadsheet. Any existing values are shifted and moved to make room for the new blank cells; no values are erased from any cells.*
- *When you delete cells from the spreadsheet, the selected cells are completely removed from the spreadsheet. Any remaining cells are shifted and moved to take the place of the deleted cells.*

If you were working with paper and pencil, deleting cells would be similar to cutting cells out with scissors, rearranging the remaining cells to cover up the hole, and then taping the rearranged cells together again.

Inserting one new column

1. **Move the pointer into the row of column labels and click on the column label where you want a new column to be added.**

The entire column is highlighted and selected.

2. **Select the Insert command from the Edit menu.**

A new blank column is added at the location of the selected column, and the existing columns are moved to the right to make room for the new column.

Inserting one new row

1. **Move the pointer into the column of row labels and click on the row label where you want a new row to be added.**

The entire row is highlighted and selected.

2. **Select the Insert command from the Edit menu.**

A new blank row is added at the location of the selected row, and the existing rows are moved down to make room for the new row.

Inserting multiple columns or rows

1.   **Move to the column labels or row labels.**

2.   **Click on the label where you want the first new column or row to be added, and drag across the labels to select the number of new columns or rows to add.**

As you drag, entire columns or rows are highlighted. This marks the location where the new columns or rows will be inserted.

3.   **After the desired number of new columns or rows are highlighted, select the Insert command from the Edit menu.**

The desired number of new blank columns or rows are inserted.

Inserting one or more blank cells

You may want to insert one or more blank cells into the middle of a spreadsheet. Remember: Inserting blank cells is different from clearing cells. When you clear a cell, the current contents of the specified cells are erased. When you insert new cells, existing cell values are shifted and moved to make room for the new cells.

1.   **Select the range on the spreadsheet where you need to insert new blank cells.**

This may involve highlighting existing cell values; don't worry... these values will be moved, not erased.

2.   **Select the Insert command from the Edit menu.**

A dialog box appears (see Figure 10-7).

3.   **Click on the direction that you want to move existing cell values.**

4.   **Click on the OK button.**

The existing cell values are moved, leaving new blank cells for new values.

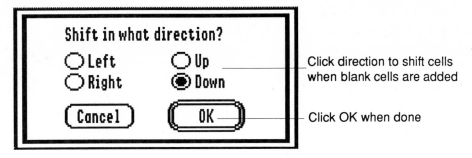

Figure 10-7 Insert dialog box

Deleting one or more columns

You may want to remove one or more columns from the spreadsheet, and the Delete command lets you perform that operation. When you delete one or more columns, the remaining columns are shifted to the left to take the place of the deleted columns.

[1] **Move the pointer into the row of column labels and click on the label of the column to delete.**

You can select multiple columns by dragging the pointer over multiple column labels, or you can click on the first column label and shift-click on the last column label in a range.
The selected columns are highlighted.

[2] **Select the Delete command from the Edit menu.**

The selected columns are deleted, and the remaining columns to the right of the deleted columns are moved to the left to take their place.

Deleting one or more rows

[1] **Move the pointer into the row labels and click on the label of the row to delete.**

You can select multiple rows by dragging the pointer over multiple row labels, or you can click on the first column label in a range and shift-click on the final column in a range.
The selected rows are highlighted.

[2] **Select the Delete command from the Edit menu.**

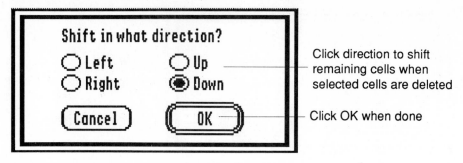

Figure 10-8 Delete dialog box

The selected rows are deleted, and the remaining rows are moved up to take their place.

Deleting one or more cells

Remember: Deleting blank cells is different from clearing cells. When you clear a cell, the current contents of the specified cells are erased. When you delete a range of cells, the cells are removed from the spreadsheet, and remaining cell values are shifted and moved to take the place of the deleted cells.

1 **Select the range on the spreadsheet that you want to delete.**

2 **Select the Delete command from the Edit menu.**

A dialog box appears (see Figure 10-8).

3 **Click on the appropriate direction that you want to move the cell values remaining after the deletion.**

4 **Click on the OK button.**

The selected cell values are deleted, and the remaining cells are moved to take the place of the deleted cells.

Rearranging cell values

After you have entered a number of cell values, you might want to rearrange the contents of the spreadsheet. You can move cell contents with the Move command, interchange rows and columns with the Transpose

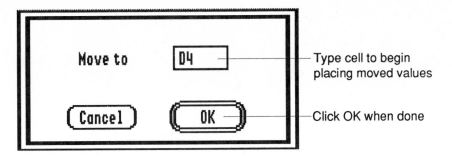

Move to   D4   — Type cell to begin placing moved values

Cancel   OK   — Click OK when done

Figure 10-9   Move dialog box

command, and rearrange values in alphabetic or numeric order with the Sort command.

Using the Move command

|1| **Select the range of cells that you want to move.**

|2| **Choose the Move command from the Edit menu.**

The Move dialog box appears (see Figure 10-9).

|3| **Type the cell coordinates where you want to move the cell.**

If the selected cells are a range of cells in a single column, type the coordinates of the topmost cell in the new location. If the selected cells are a range of cells in a single row, type the coordinates of the leftmost cell in the new location. If the selected cells are a block of cells, type the coordinates of the upper-left cell in the new desired location.

|4| **Click the OK button and the cell values are moved to the new location.**

The moved values overwrite and replace any existing values in the new location.

Formulas and the Move command

The Move command has a special effect on cells that contain formulas. If one of the moved cells contains a formula, that cell displays the same value after it is moved as before. This is true even if one or more of the cells referred to in the formula were not moved at the same time.

If one of the moved cells contains a formula and all the cells referred to by the formula are moved, the formula is adjusted to refer to the new locations of the referred cells.

If one of the moved cells contains a formula, and one or more cells referred to by the formula is not moved along with the formula, the formula still refers to the original location of those cells after it is moved.

The end result is that the formula cell still displays the same result after it is moved. However, the actual cell references in the formula may have been changed. If you examine the actual formula contained in the cell before and after the move, the cell references in the formula may be different.

Note: *How is this accomplished? More technically, all relative references in a formula that are being moved are temporarily considered absolute references, moved, and then converted back to relative references. For more information on absolute and relative references, see Appendix B, AppleWorks GS Formulas.*

Moving cell values with Cut and Paste

You can also move cell values using the Clipboard.

1 **Select the cells that you want to move.**

2 **Select the Cut or Copy command from the Edit menu.**

If you select the Cut command, the cell contents are copied to the Clipboard, and the cells are cleared. If you select the Copy command, the cell contents are copied to the Clipboard, but the selected cells retain their values.

3 **Move the pointer to the first cell in the new location where you want to copy the cell values, and click to select the cell.**

If the selected cells are a range of cells in a single column, click the topmost cell in the new location. If the selected cells are a range of cells in a single row, click the leftmost cell in the new location. If the selected cells are a block of cells, click the upper-left cell in the new desired location.

4 **Select the Paste command from the Edit menu.**

The cell values stored on the Clipboard are copied to the new location.

Shortcut: *You can quickly perform a Copy and Paste operation using the control-drag feature. Select the cells to copy and release the mouse button. Hold down the control key. Move the pointer into the highlighted range, and hold down the mouse button. Drag the selected range to a new location and release the mouse button. A copy of the selected range appears at the new location.*

Formulas and the Clipboard

When you copy formulas using Copy, Paste, or control-drag, the formulas are handled differently than when you use the Move command. This difference is particularly important in one situation: when you copy a formula cell to a new location and all of the cells referred to by the formula are not moved at the same time.

If you copy a formula cell with the Move command and one or more of the cells referred to by the formula are not moved at the same time, the formula is adjusted to continue to refer to those cells. This may change the actual cell references in the formula.

If you copy a formula cell with the Clipboard, the formula keeps its same relative cell references, regardless of whether or not all of the cells have been moved with the formula cell. That means the moved cell may not display the same results as previously, since some of the referred cells aren't in the same relative locations.

After you move a formula cell with the Move command, it will continue to display the same result, but the original entries in the formula may be changed greatly. After you move a formula cell with the Clipboard, it may not show the same result (if you did not move all referred cells along with the formula cell), but the original entries in the formula have not been changed.

These differences will produce very different effects if you move the formulas to new locations later.

Note: *More technically, the Clipboard does not change any relative references in a formula. When you paste a formula in a new location, any relative references now refer to different cells than the original cells referenced. If you move a formula with the Move command, the Move command adjusts any relative references in a formula so that they still refer to the original cells, even after the formula is moved. For more information, see Appendix B, AppleWorks GS Formulas.*

Interchanging rows and columns

After you have entered a number of cell values, you might wish you had entered your row values as column values, and vice-versa. The Transpose command lets you interchange rows and columns.

1   Select the cells that you want to interchange. (See Figure 10-10.)

2   Select the Transpose command from the Edit menu.

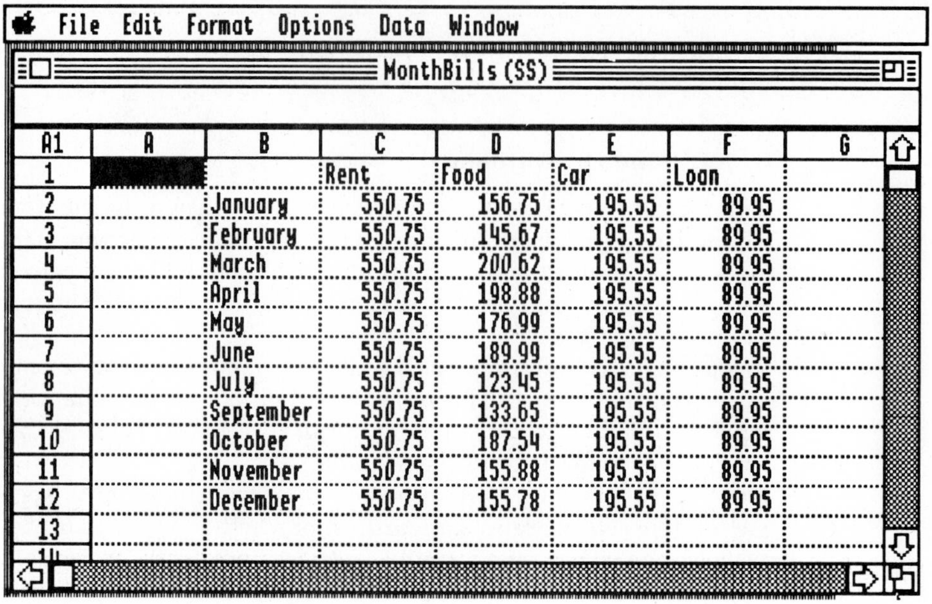

File Edit Format Options Data Window

MonthBills (SS)

A1	A	B	C	D	E	F	G
1			Rent	Food	Car	Loan	
2		January	550.75	156.75	195.55	89.95	
3		February	550.75	145.67	195.55	89.95	
4		March	550.75	200.62	195.55	89.95	
5		April	550.75	198.88	195.55	89.95	
6		May	550.75	176.99	195.55	89.95	
7		June	550.75	189.99	195.55	89.95	
8		July	550.75	123.45	195.55	89.95	
9		September	550.75	133.65	195.55	89.95	
10		October	550.75	187.54	195.55	89.95	
11		November	550.75	155.88	195.55	89.95	
12		December	550.75	155.78	195.55	89.95	
13							
14							

Figure 10-10 Typical spreadsheet before transpose operation

The values in the first column are placed in the first row, the values in the second column are placed in the second row, and so forth. (See Figure 10-11.)

Alert

If the selected area contains the same number of rows and columns, the row and column values can be interchanged without replacing any other values.

However, if there are more rows than columns in the selected range of cells, the additional rows will replace values in cells to the right of the original columns. Similarly, if there are more columns than rows, the additional columns will replace values below the original rows.

If you select the Transpose command under these conditions, a dialog box will ask you to confirm that you want to complete the operation before the replacement is made.

Sorting cell values

You may want to arrange selected cell values in numeric order or alphabetic order. The Sort command performs this operation:

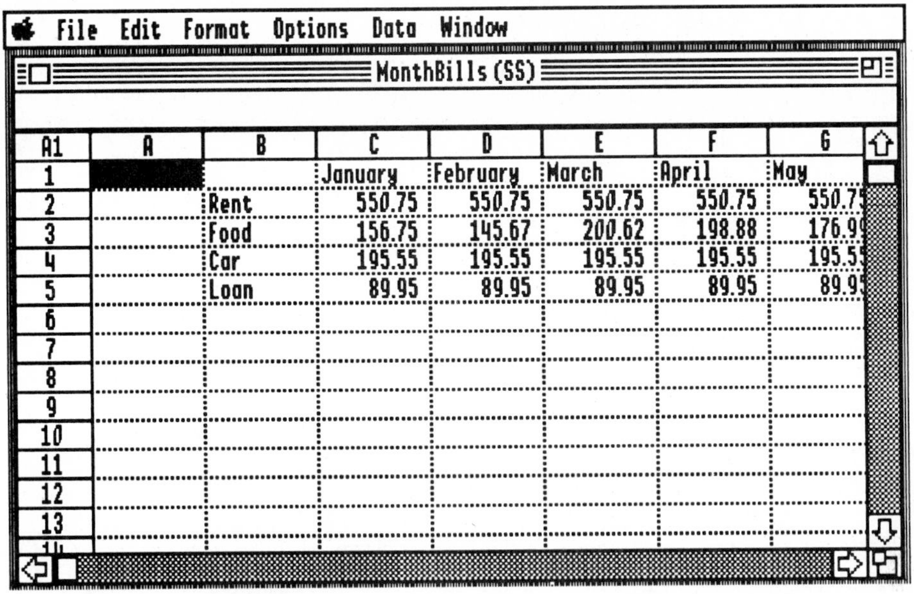

Figure 10-11 Transposed spreadsheet

1. Select the range of cells to be sorted. (See Figure 10-12.)

2. Select the Sort command on the Options menu.

The Sort dialog box appears (see Figure 10-13).

3. Click the Rows button if you want to rearrange rows of cells; click the Columns button if you want to rearrange columns of cells.

The selected cells will be rearranged by shuffling entire rows or columns of data. Click on the button that describes which kind of rearrangement you want to perform.

4. Click the Ascending button to sort entries in increasing order, or click the Descending button to sort entries in decreasing order.

5. Enter the cell coordinate of any cell in the row or column that you want to use as the basis of the sort.

The row or column where this cell is located is the primary key used as the basis for the sort. The values in this row or column will be sorted; all of the other values are rearranged based on those values.

In the AppleWorks GS database, you could specify several fields as the basis of a sort: a primary key to use as the basis of the sort, and other

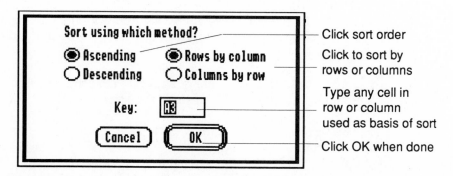

```
 File  Edit  Format  Options  Data  Window
─────────────────── Officeexp.1989 (SS) ───────────────────
```

Range	A	B	C	D	E	F	G
1	Item Name	Unit Price	Quantity	Total Cost			
2							
3	Disks	12.55	35	439.25			
4	Paper	23.44	15	351.6			
5	Labels	11.65	15	174.75			
6	Ribbons	4.55	15	68.25			
7							
8			Total >>	1033.85			
9							
10							
11							
12							
13							

Figure 10-12   Select the range of cells to sort

keys to use as "tie-breakers" if two or more records have the same value. In the spreadsheet, you can only specify which row or column should be used as the primary key; in the case of ties, the remaining cells are left in their original order.

6   **Click the OK button, and the selected range of cells are rearranged. (See Figure 10-14.)**

If you selected to sort by rows, the cells in each row are considered to be grouped as a unit. The cells in the same column as the sort key are

Sort using which method?
- ● Ascending   ● Rows by column
- ○ Descending   ○ Columns by row

Key: [A3]

(Cancel)   (OK)

— Click sort order

Click to sort by rows or columns

Type any cell in row or column used as basis of sort

— Click OK when done

Figure 10-13   Sort dialog box

```
 File  Edit  Format  Options  Data  Window
```

```
≡▤▢≡══════════════Officeexp.1989 (SS)═══════════════▤□≡

┌──────┬──────────┬──────────┬──────────┬──────────┬────────┬────────┬────────┬─┐
│Range │    A     │    B     │    C     │    D     │   E    │   F    │   G    │⇧│
├──────┼──────────┼──────────┼──────────┼──────────┼────────┼────────┼────────┤ │
│  1   │Item Name │Unit Price│Quantity  │Total Cost│        │        │        │ │
│  2   │          │          │          │          │        │        │        │ │
│  3   │Disks     │   12.55  │      35  │  439.25  │        │        │        │ │
│  4   │Labels    │   11.65  │      15  │  174.75  │        │        │        │ │
│  5   │Paper     │   23.44  │      15  │  351.6   │        │        │        │ │
│  6   │Ribbons   │    4.55  │      15  │   68.25  │        │        │        │ │
│  7   │          │          │          │          │        │        │        │ │
│  8   │          │          │Total >>  │ 1033.85  │        │        │        │ │
│  9   │          │          │          │          │        │        │        │ │
│ 10   │          │          │          │          │        │        │        │ │
│ 11   │    Rows sorted in ascending     │          │        │        │        │ │
│ 12   │    order, based on this column  │          │        │        │        │⇩│
│ 13   │          │          │          │          │        │        │        │ │
└──────┴──────────┴──────────┴──────────┴──────────┴────────┴────────┴────────┴─┘
```

Figure 10-14 Range of cells after sort operation

rearranged and moved up or down; as a cell is moved up or down, all of the cells in the same row move along with it.

If you selected to sort by columns, the cells in each column are considered to be grouped as a unit. The cells in the same row as the sort key are rearranged and moved left or right; as a cell is moved left or right, all of the cells in the same column move along with it.

Producing charts from your spreadsheet

A powerful feature of AppleWorks GS is the ability to produce charts from the data in your spreadsheets. AppleWorks GS provides five kinds of charts:

- pie charts
- bar charts
- shadowed bar charts
- line charts
- scatterplot charts

Producing a new chart

1 Select the range of values that you want to chart.

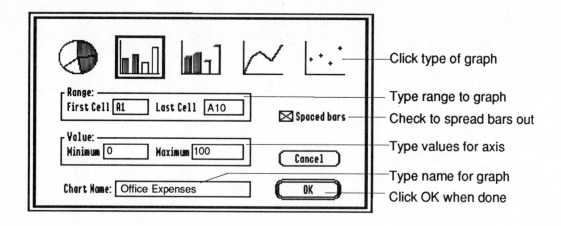

Click type of graph

Type range to graph

Check to spread bars out

Type values for axis

Type name for graph

Click OK when done

Figure 10-15 New Chart dialog

The values can be a range of cells in a single column, a range of cells in a single row, or a rectangular block of cells. If you select a rectangular block of cells, values in the cells in the top row are plotted by default.

☐2 **Select the New Chart command from the Data menu.**

The Chart dialog box appears on the screen (see Figure 10-15).

☐3 **Enter the appropriate information, and click the OK button.**

If you enter the coordinates for a rectangular block of cells in the range of boxes, the values in the range are plotted.

The AppleWorks GS graphics application is opened, and the new chart is drawn within the window (see Figure 10-16). This chart is actually a graphics document; you can modify it using any of the graphics tools or commands. (See Chapters 11 and 12 for information on the graphics application.)

This provides great flexibility and permits you to change any of the colors in the chart, add text or graphics, or use any of the other graphics capabilities. (See Figure 10-17.)

You can save the chart as an independent document, saving it on your storage disk for future use.

You can copy the final version of your chart into a page layout document with additional text, producing a professional report incorporating both text and charts.

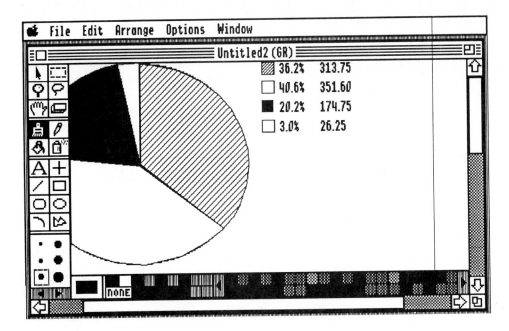

Figure 10-16 New Chart Window

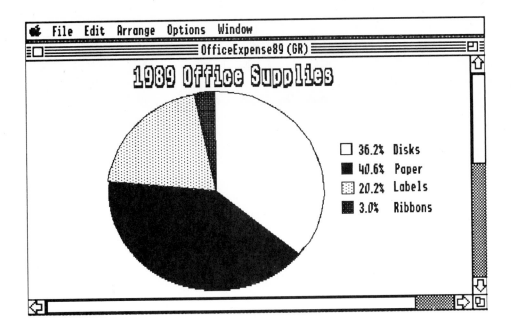

Figure 10-17 Chart with text added, colors changed

Alert

After you generate a chart, don't be confused about the location of the spreadsheet. AppleWorks GS can display up to 14 windows at once, and you now have at least two windows open: the spreadsheet document in its window, and the graphics document in its window.

The graphics document is currently displayed on top of the spreadsheet window, similar to having one sheet of paper on top of another.

To move the spreadsheet back into view, move the pointer to the Windows menu and select the spreadsheet document. The selected spreadsheet document is moved back to the top of the stack of windows.

Modifying your charts

After you have produced one version of a chart, you may want to modify the chart later:

- You may want to change the chart settings. For example, you might want to change from the current type of chart to another, or you might want to adjust the minimum or maximum values displayed.
- You may have changed the values in one or more of the cells displayed in the chart, and the chart needs to be updated.

Changing the chart settings

To change any of the settings for the current chart:

1 | **Select the Modify Chart command on the Data menu.**

The Modify Chart dialog box appears (see Figure 10-18).

2 | **Click the Change button.**

The New Chart dialog box appears. You can change any of the settings in the dialog box, including type of chart, minimum or maximum values, cell range, or chart title.

3 | **When the new settings are correct, click the OK button, and the modified chart is displayed.**

Updating the values on a chart

After you change the value of one or more of the cells that were charted, you can easily update the chart to reflect the new information:

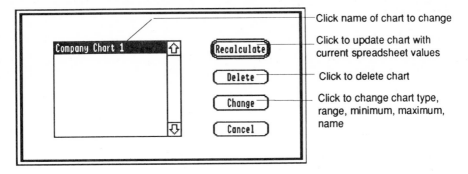

Click name of chart to change

Click to update chart with current spreadsheet values

Click to delete chart

Click to change chart type, range, minimum, maximum, name

Figure 10-18 Modify Chart dialog

1 **Select the Modify Chart command on the Data menu.**

2 **When the Modify Chart dialog box appears, click the Recalculate button.**

The Recalculate command leaves all of the chart settings unchanged, but replaces the old cell values with the new cell values.

The updated chart is displayed in its graphics window.

The next step

The previous two chapters have shown you how to create a spreadsheet document and work with the information stored in a spreadsheet. You have seen that an important feature lets you easily generate pie charts, bar graphs, or line graphs from your numeric information; these charts are automatically produced in an AppleWorks GS graphics document, and you can use the powerful tools in the graphics application to add or change information in the chart.

The next two chapters introduce the features of the AppleWorks GS graphics application. Chapter 11 describes how to create a new graphics document and use the powerful paint and draw tools to create full-color graphics. Chapter 12 shows you how to use the edit tools and menu commands to make changes in your graphics document. Later chapters will then show you how to combine graphics with text in a completed page layout document.

Creating a New Graphics Document

About this chapter

This chapter introduces the AppleWorks GS graphics application. The graphics application lets you create color graphics on the screen, and these graphics can be printed on your printer or incorporated into other AppleWorks GS documents.

The AppleWorks GS graphics application combines the best features of paint programs or draw programs into a single powerful environment. This chapter explains how to open a new graphics document and use the graphics tools to create a color image.

The topics in this chapter include

- Graphics concepts
- Creating a new graphics document
- The graphics document window
- The graphics menu bar
- Using the paint tools
- Using the draw tools
- Erasing parts of your graphic
- Saving a graphics document
- Printing a graphics document

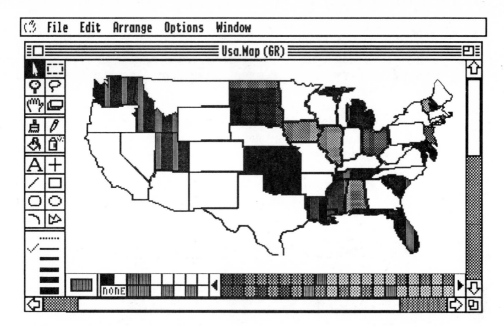

Figure 11-1 Sample graphic

Graphics concepts

What is a graphic? A graphic is simply a picture, and the AppleWorks GS graphics application lets you create professional, full-color graphic images.

The AppleWorks GS word processing application lets you create text documents, and the graphics application lets you create interesting graphic images. You can combine these two kinds of information in other AppleWorks GS applications: the AppleWorks GS database lets you store and organize both text and graphic information, and the page layout application lets you join text and graphics into a single document.

Just as the word processing application lets you create a text document by typing on the keyboard, the graphics application lets you create a graphics image on the screen using the graphics tools.

You can also import graphics created by other graphics programs and modify them with the powerful graphics tools (see Figure 11-1).

Painting and drawing on the computer

In the computer world, two kinds of graphics programs are common: paint programs and draw programs.

A **paint** program lets you sketch freehand on the screen using electronic versions of common artist tools like a pencil or paintbrush.

A graphic produced by a paint program consists of a finely-detailed image made up of many small colored dots on the screen. (This kind of image is called a **bit-mapped image**, since it is created by lighting up individual dots on the screen controlled by small memory locations called bits in your Apple IIGS's memory.)

A paint program lets you edit or change each dot on the screen, and this gives you fine control over the details in your graphic. However, it can be difficult to manipulate parts of the graphic independently of other parts.

A **draw** program lets you create an image on the screen composed of geometric shapes, such as straight lines, rectangles, or ovals. The shapes that you create are called objects, and these objects can easily be grouped, moved, or rearranged on the screen. A draw program doesn't let you edit the individual dots that make up the image, so it doesn't provide the fine control of detail found in paint programs. However, it is easy to manipulate one or more objects in the graphic independent of other objects. For instance, if you draw a rectangle as part of your graphic, it's easy to move or resize the rectangle at any point.

Paint objects: the best of both worlds

AppleWorks GS provides the best of both worlds. The graphic application provides the painting tools provided by most paint programs, as well as the drawing tools provided by draw programs. The graphics that you create also combine the best features of both kinds of graphics programs.

The graphics that you create with AppleWorks GS are composed of paint objects drawn on the screen. A paint object combines the best characteristics of graphics created with paint programs and draw programs. A paint object can be manipulated easily like the objects created by draw programs, but the fine details of each object can also be edited like the images produced by paint programs.

Three kinds of tools

The AppleWorks GS graphics application provides three kinds of tools to create and edit your images:

- **Paint tools**, which let you sketch freehand on the screen. The paint tools include a paintbrush to sketch broad strokes, a pencil to sketch fine lines, a paintbucket to fill areas with a color, and a spraycan to spray colors.
- **Draw tools**, which let you create precise geometric shapes like rectangles and ovals. The draw tools include tools to draw straight lines, horizontal or vertical lines, rectangles, rounded rectangles, ovals, arcs, and polygons. A text tool lets you add desired text to your graphic.
- **Edit tools**, which let you make changes in your graphic. The edit tools include tools to select and move parts of your graphic, a mag-

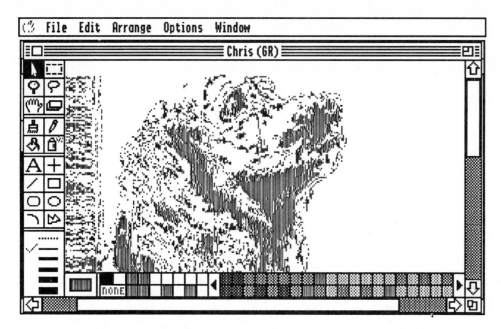

Figure 11-2 Imported digitized image

nifying tool to examine and modify your graphic at high magnification, and an eraser tool to erase parts of the graphic.

The graphics application also provides menu commands to rearrange, move, or duplicate parts of your graphic.

Importing graphics from other programs

The AppleWorks GS graphics application provides a powerful graphics environment, but you can also open or import images that were created with other programs and stored in most popular formats.

For example, you could import images digitized from an external video source (Figure 11-2) or images provided on clip art disks. After you import these images, you can modify them with the AppleWorks GS graphics tools and save them in AppleWorks GS format on a storage disk.

Steps toward a graphic

Using the AppleWorks GS graphics application involves these steps:

- Opening a new AppleWorks GS graphics document.
- Creating a graphic using the paint tools, draw tools, and edit tools.
- Rearranging, duplicating, and moving desired parts of the graphic using the menu commands.

- Saving the completed graphic on a storage disk.
- Printing a copy of the graphic on your printer.

After you've created a graphic, you can also copy the graphic into the page layout application, combine it with text from the word processor, and produce a completed document combining text and graphics. You could also copy the graphic into a graphic field in a database record.

Creating a new graphics document

When you are ready to begin a new graphics document, there are two ways that you can create the new document:

You can create a new document with the New command on the File menu.

You can create a new document with the Open command on the File menu.

Using the New Command or Open command to create a new document is discussed in Chapter 3, AppleWorks GS Common Commands.

The graphics document window

When you open a graphics document, a document window appears on the screen (see Figure 11-3).

The new graphics document window includes features found on all windows, including the title bar, scroll bars, close box, zoom box, and size box.

The document also includes features that are specific to this application:

- At the top of the screen is the **graphics menu bar**, which contains the commands that are available in this application.
- Most of the window is blank. This blank area corresponds to a blank paper where you can paint and draw your graphic.
- Three **tool palettes** along the left edge of the window. The **edit tool palette** contains tools used to change the graphic, the **draw tool palette** contains tools used to draw regular geometric shapes, and the **paint tool palette** contains tools used to sketch freehand on the screen. The paintbrush tool is selected when you begin a new document.
- The **brush palette** appears beneath the tool palettes. This is used to select the size and shape of brush used when you select the paintbrush. This palette is replaced by the **line width palette** when you choose any tool other than the paintbrush.

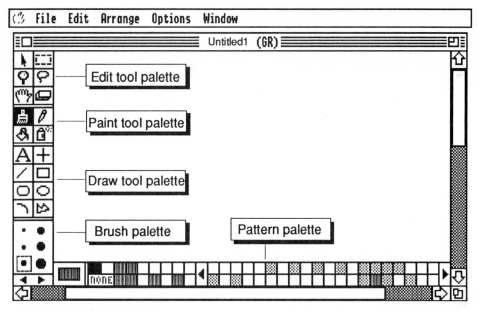

Figure 11-3   New graphics document

- The **pattern palette** at the bottom of the screen. This palette includes sixteen solid colors available to use, as well as patterns composed of mixtures of the solid colors. This palette also includes the **color selection box**, which displays the current selected color.
- A dark circle is displayed in the center of the new blank document. This is the cursor displayed when the paintbrush tool is selected.

The graphics menu bar

Figure 11-4
File menu

The graphics menu bar includes File, Edit, Arrange, Options, and Windows.

The File menu

The commands on the File menu (see Figure 11-4) include New, Open, Close, Save, Save As, Delete File, Import File, Choose Printer, Page Setup, Print, and Quit. The use of these commands was discussed in Chapter 3, AppleWorks GS Common Commands. The Print Merge command is dimmed on the File menu, since it is only available in the word processing application.

The Edit menu

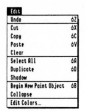

Figure 11-5
Edit menu

The commands on the Edit menu (see Figure 11-5) include Undo, Cut, Copy, Paste, Clear, and Select All. These commands have been described in Chapter 3, AppleWorks GS Common Commands. In addition to these commands, the graphics Edit menu includes

Duplicate: Produces a duplicate of the selected object.

Shadow: Produces a shadow beneath the selected object.

Begin New Paint Object: As you use the painting tools, the graphic elements that you sketch are automatically grouped into a single object that you can manipulate. This command lets you begin a new group of graphic elements.

Collapse: Groups all of the selected objects permanently into a single object.

Edit Colors: Lets you create a new set of colors for use in the color palette. The use of this command is discussed in Appendix D, Using the Edit Colors command.

The Arrange menu

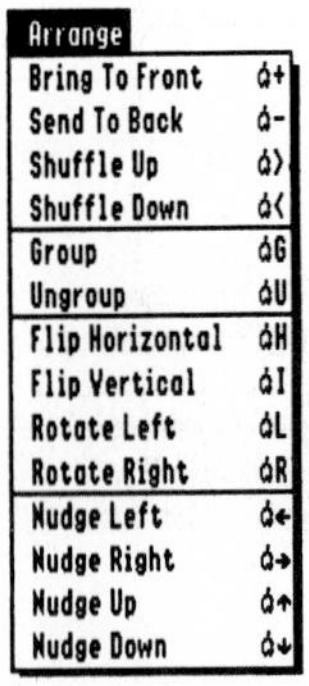

Figure 11-6
Arrange menu

The commands on the Arrange menu (see Figure 11-6) let you rearrange and move graphics objects on the screen.

Bring to Front: Moves a selected object to the top of any overlapping objects.

Send to Back: Moves a selected object behind any overlapping objects.

Shuffle Up: Moves a selected object up one level in a stack of overlapping objects.

Shuffle Down: Moves a selected object down one level in a stack of overlapping objects.

Group: Temporarily groups selected objects into a single object that you can manipulate.

Ungroup: Dissolves the group of objects created by the Group command back into individual graphic elements.

Flip Horizontal: Produces a mirror-image of a selected object by flipping it around its horizontal axis.

Flip Vertical: Flips a selected object around its vertical axis, flipping it upside-down.

Rotate Left: Rotates a selected object 90° to the left.

Rotate Right: Rotates a selected object 90° to the right.

Nudge Left: Moves a selected object slightly to the left.

Nudge Right: Moves a selected object slightly to the right.

Nudge Up: Moves a selected object slightly up.

Nudge Down: Moves a selected object slightly down.

Figure 11-7
Options menu

The Options menu

The commands on the Options menu (see Figure 11-7) lets you control the display of text in your graphic and the visibility of tools on the screen.

Choose Font: Lets you choose the font, style, and size of text in your graphic.

Tools: Controls the visibility of the tool palette at the left of the screen. When you begin, the tool palette is visible and a checkmark is displayed to the left of this command. When you choose this command, the palette disappears and the checkmark displayed to the left of the command is removed. To make the palette visible again, select the command again.

Patterns: Controls the visibility of the patterns palette at the bottom the screen. When you begin, the patterns palette is visible and a checkmark is displayed to the left of this command. When you choose this command, the palette disappears and the checkmark displayed to the left of the command is removed. To make the palette visible again, select the command again.

Grid: Lets you activate an invisible grid to the document to help you align objects. When you begin a new document, the grid is not active and you can place objects at any location. To activate the grid, select the Grid command. A checkmark is displayed to the left of the command, and the grid is active. An invisible grid of horizontal and vertical lines are drawn on the screen, and objects are automatically placed aligned with the nearest lines. To remove the grid, select the command again.

The Window menu

The Window menu lists the currently open windows and the Clipboard. The use of this menu is discussed in Chapter 3, AppleWorks GS Common Commands.

Using the paint tools

AppleWorks GS provides two kinds of graphics tools: **paint** tools and **draw** tools. The paint tools let you paint on the graphics area with freehand strokes and fill enclosed areas with a selected color or pattern. (See Figure 11-8.)

There are four paint tools:

- **Paintbrush** tool: Lets you paint in broad strokes in the graphics document. You can select the size and shape of the paintbrush that you use.
- **Pencil** tool: Lets you sketch fine lines in your document.

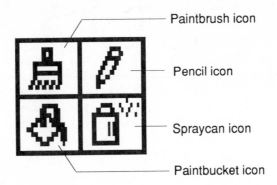

Paintbrush icon

Pencil icon

Spraycan icon

Paintbucket icon

Figure 11-8 Paint tool palette

- **Paintbucket** tool: Lets you fill an enclosed area with a selected color or pattern
- **Spraycan** tool: Lets you spray a selected color or pattern in the document.

Using one of the paint tools

To use one of the paint tools:

| 1 | **Click on the tool icon to select the tool.** |

| 2 | **If you select the paintbrush, click on the desired brush size in the brush palette.** |

| 3 | **Click on the color or pattern that you want to use.** |

| 4 | **Move the pointer into the graphics document.** |

The pointer changes into a cursor that is specific to the tool, and the tool is now ready to use.

Selecting a color or pattern

Each of the paint tools can use any of the colors or patterns that are shown in the pattern palette at the bottom of the document window. When you choose a paint tool, it will paint in the window with the currently selected color. You can select a new color to use at any time: you can select a color before you choose a paint tool, or you can select a tool and then choose the color to use.

To choose a color or pattern:

| 1 | **Move the cursor to the pattern palette. (See Figure 11-9.)** |

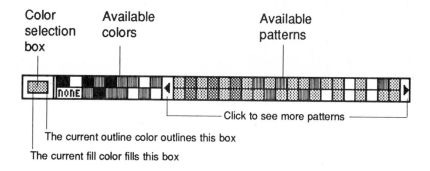

Figure 11-9   Pattern palette

The palette contains more patterns than can be displayed on the screen at one time. To see more patterns, click on the left or right arrow on the pattern palette.

[2]   **Click on the color or pattern that you want to use.**

The selected color or pattern is displayed in the color selection box at the left of the pattern palette. When you move the cursor back into the document window, the paint tool will paint with this color or pattern.

Using the paintbrush

The paintbrush lets you sketch freehand strokes in the document window. To use the paintbrush, you first select the paintbrush tool, the desired brush size and shape, and the desired color or pattern. Then you can paint with the desired color pattern in the document window.

[1]   **Position the arrow cursor on the paintbrush tool and click the mouse button to select the paintbrush tool. (See Figure 11-10.)**

[2]   **Click the desired brush size and shape from the brush palette.**

Figure 11-10
Paintbrush

When you choose the paintbrush tool, the brush palette appears beneath the tool palette (see Figure 11-11).

The brush palette provides a variety of brush sizes and shapes. Not all of the sizes and shapes are visible when you begin the application. To see other possible sizes and shapes, click the left or right arrow at the bottom of the brush palette.

Click on a shape that you want to use for the paintbrush. After you click on a shape, a selection rectangle is displayed around the shape.

[3]   **Click the desired color or pattern from the pattern palette.**

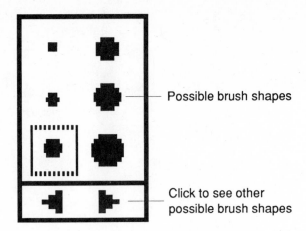

Possible brush shapes

Click to see other
possible brush shapes

Figure 11-11   Brush palette

The color selection box at the left of the pattern palette displays the selected color or pattern.

4   **Move the cursor into the document window.**

The arrow cursor turns into the paintbrush cursor. The size and shape of the paintbrush cursor depends on your selection from the brush palette.

5   **Move the paintbrush cursor to the location where you want to begin painting.**

6   **Hold down the mouse button and drag the mouse.**

As you drag the mouse, the paintbrush paints on the document window in the selected color or pattern with the selected brush shape and size. (See Figure 11-12.)

Changing the paintbrush

After you begin to use the paintbrush in the document, you may want to adjust the brush size or shape or change the color.

To adjust brush size and shape:

1   **Move to the brush palette.**

If the desired size and shape are not visible, click on the left or right arrow beneath the brush palette.

2   **Click on the brush size and shape that you desire.**

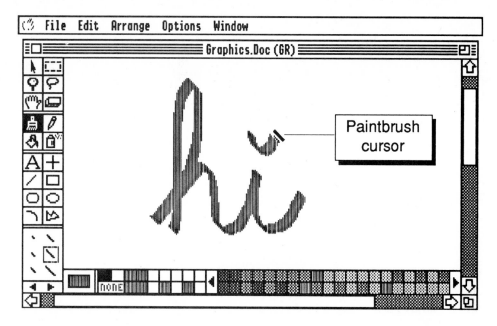

Figure 11-12 Paintbrush in use

A selection rectangle appears around your choice. When you move the cursor back into the document window, the paintbrush cursor reflects the brush that you selected.

To choose a different pattern or color:

1. **Move the cursor to the pattern palette.**

If the desired pattern is not visible, click on the left or right arrow beneath the brush palette.

2. **Click the color or pattern that you want to use.**

The selected color or pattern is displayed in the color selection box. When you move the cursor back into the document window, the paintbrush will paint with this color or pattern.

Using the pencil

The pencil lets you draw freehand lines in the document window. To use the pencil, you must select the pencil tool and the desired color or pattern. Then you can sketch lines with the desired color pattern in the document window.

Figure 11-13
Pencil icon

1 Position the arrow cursor on the pencil tool and click the mouse button to select the pencil tool. (See Figure 11-13.)

2 Select the desired color or pattern from the pattern palette.

The color selection box displays the selected color or pattern.

3 Move the cursor into the document window

When you move into the document window, the arrow cursor takes the shape of a small pencil.

4 Move the pencil cursor to the location where you want to begin drawing a line.

5 Hold down the mouse button and drag the mouse.

As you drag the mouse, the pencil paints a line on the document window in the selected color or pattern. (See Figure 11-14.)

Using the paintbucket

The paintbucket lets you fill graphics areas with a selected color or pattern. To use the paintbucket, you first select the paintbucket tool and

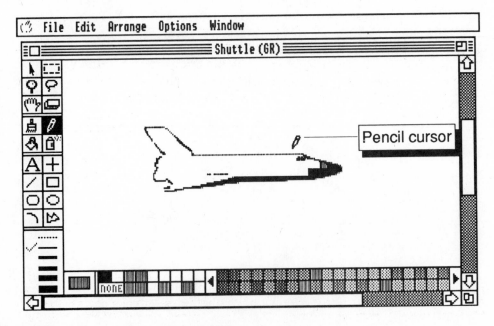

Figure 11-14   Using the pencil to create freehand lines

then select the desired color or pattern. Then you can fill any enclosed area in the document window with the selected color or pattern.

Figure 11-15
Paintbucket icon

1. Position the arrow cursor on the paintbucket tool and click the mouse button to select the paintbucket tool. (See Figure 11-15.)

2. Click the desired color or pattern from the pattern palette.

The color selection box displays the selected color or pattern.

3. Move the cursor into the document window

As you move into the document window, the arrow cursor turns into the paintbucket cursor.

4. Move the paintbucket cursor into the area that you want to fill with the selected color pattern.

5. Click the mouse button.

After you click the mouse button, the paintbucket fills the area with the selected color pattern. (See Figure 11-16.)

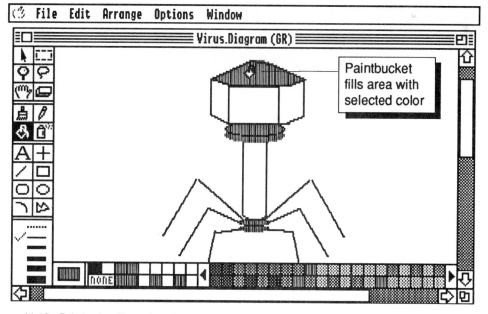

Figure 11-16   Paintbucket fills enclosed area with selected color

Alert

Be careful to use the paintbucket to fill only enclosed areas. If the graphic area that you fill is not completely enclosed, the color will "spill" from any holes in the object and fill areas outside the object. The color may even spill from the object and fill the entire screen!

If the fill color accidentally spills over into an area that you don't want to fill, don't panic. Select the Undo command on the Edit menu, and the screen will be restored to its previous condition. The Undo command can reverse the effects of the last command that you used.

Using the spraycan

The spraycan tool lets you spray a color or pattern in the graphics area. To use the spraycan, you must select the spraycan tool and the desired color or pattern.

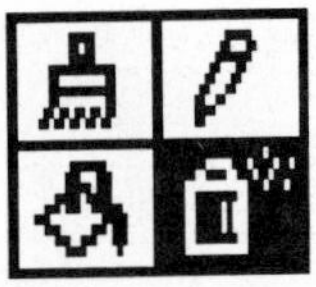

Figure 11-17
Spraycan icon

1. Position the arrow cursor on the spraycan tool and click the mouse button to select the spraycan tool. (See Figure 11-17.)

2. Select the desired color or pattern from the pattern palette.

The selected color or pattern is displayed in the color selection box at the left of the pattern palette.

3. Move the cursor into the document window.

When you move into the document window, the arrow cursor turns into the spraycan cursor.

4. Move the spraycan cursor to the location that you want to begin spraying.

5. Hold down the mouse button, and drag the mouse.

As you drag the mouse, the spraycan cursor sprays the selected color or pattern across the document window. (See Figure 11-18.)

Using paint objects

As you use the paint tools, the graphics that you create with those tools are automatically grouped into a paint object.

For example, if you use the paintbrush to paint on the screen, and then use the pencil to sketch a fine line, and then use the paintbrush again

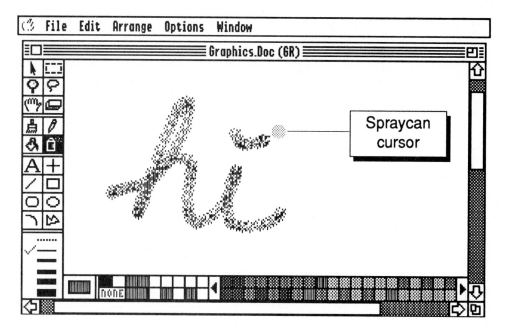

Figure 11-18 Using the spraycan tool

to paint another area, all of these elements are automatically combined into a single paint object.

In earlier paint programs, the graphics that you painted could not easily be moved or otherwise manipulated. AppleWorks GS paint objects have an important advantage over these older programs. The graphic elements that make up a paint object can be manipulated as a group.

You can select all of the elements in a paint object by clicking on any element in the object. After a paint object is selected, handles appear at each corner of the object (see Figure 11-19).

After a paint object is selected, the entire paint object can be modified as a group:

- You can move all the elements as a group.
- You can change all the colors used in the object.
- You can resize all the elements with a single command.
- You can duplicate all the elements in the paint object with a single command.

After you work with an object, you can deselect the object by clicking outside the document window and continue to work with your document.

Working with paint objects is discussed in detail in Chapter 12.

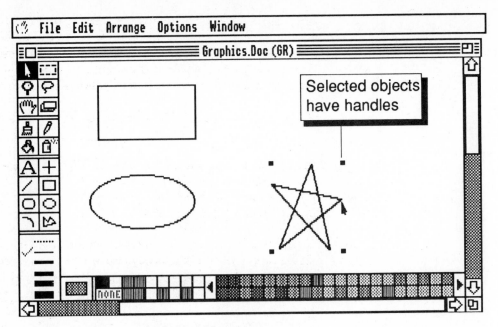

Figure 11-19 Selected paint object has handles at corners

Starting a new paint object

As you paint on the screen with the paint tools, the elements that you paint are all automatically grouped into a single paint object that you can manipulate as a group later.

A paint object is automatically ended when you select a draw tool. If you draw on the screen with one of the draw tools or use one of the edit tools and then select one of the paint tools again, the next graphic elements that you paint begin a new paint object.

You can also choose to begin a new paint object at any time. The graphics application includes a menu command that lets you begin a new paint object while you are using the paint tools:

- When you are ready to begin a new paint object, choose the Begin New Paint Object command from the Edit Menu.

When you use the next paint tool to create the next graphic element, the graphic that you create begins a new paint object. These next graphic elements are not members of the same object that you created before you chose the Begin New Paint Object command.

Using the draw tools

The paint tools let you paint freehand on the graphics area, but it's difficult to create precise geometric shapes with these freehand tools. The

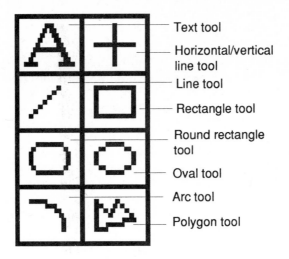

Text tool

Horizontal/vertical line tool

Line tool

Rectangle tool

Round rectangle tool

Oval tool

Arc tool

Polygon tool

Figure 11-20 Draw tool palette

draw tools let you create precise geometric shapes quickly and easily or add any desired text to the document. (See Figure 11-20.)

AppleWorks GS provides eight draw tools:

- **Text tool**: Lets you add formatted to the graphic. (The text is formatted with the Choose Font command on the Options menu.)
- **Horizontal/vertical line tool**: Lets you draw a straight line of any desired length, perfectly horizontal or vertical.
- **Line tool**: Lets you draw a straight line of any desired length.
- **Rectangle tool**: Lets you draw a rectangle of any desired size. This tool can also be used to draw a square, which is really a special kind of rectangle.
- **Round rectangle tool**: Lets you draw a rectangle or square of any desired size, and the rectangle is displayed with rounded corners.
- **Oval tool**: Lets you draw an oval of any desired size. This tool can also be used to draw a circle, which is really a special kind of oval.
- **Arc tool**: Lets you draw an arc of any desired size.
- **Polygon tool**: Lets you draw a polygon with any desired number of vertices.

You can select different widths to be used for the lines or for the borders of the geometric shapes. You can also fill each object with a selected color or pattern or draw the border of a shape with a selected color or pattern.

As you use the draw tools, each graphic that you create is a separate graphics object. If you wish, you can group selected objects together into larger objects.

Using one of the draw tools

To use one of the draw tools:

1. **Click the icon of the tool that you want to use.**

2. **Click the desired line width to use with the object.**

When you select a draw tool, the line width palette appears beneath the tool palette. When you click on one of the line widths, that width is used to draw the lines that define the object. The dotted line draws an invisible line to define the object.If you choose the rectangle, round rectangle, oval, or polygon tool, this width is used for the border of the object.

3. **Click on the color or pattern that you want to use to fill the object that you will draw.**

If a color or pattern is selected from the pattern palette, the shape that is drawn is automatically filled with the selected color. If "none" is selected on the pattern palette, the shape that is drawn will be hollow, or filled with no color. The selected color is displayed in the color selection box at the left of the pattern palette.

4. **If desired, select a separate color for the border of the object.**

You may want to draw the border of an object in a color different from the color used to fill the object. To select a different color or pattern for the border, hold down the Option key and click on the desired color. The selected border color is displayed as the border around the color selection box at the left of the pattern palette. If no border color is chosen, the border is drawn in the fill color.

5. **Move the pointer into the graphics document.**

The pointer turns into a cursor that is specific to the tool, and the tool is now ready to use.

Adding text to your graphic

The text tool is used to add text to your graphic. The text tool can only be used to enter one line of text at a time. You can use the text tool to create more than one text object, but each text object can only contain one line. You can use the AppleWorks GS page layout application to combine a graphic with multiple lines of formatted text.

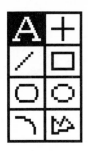

Figure 11-21
Text tool

To use the text tool:

| 1 | Position the arrow cursor on the text tool and click the mouse button to select the text tool. (See Figure 11-21.) |

| 2 | Select the Choose Font command on the Options menu. |

The Choose Font dialog appears (see Figure 11-22).
Select the text font, size, and style that you wish to use for your text. When you type your text, it will be displayed using these selections.

| 3 | Click the color that you want to use as a background for the text. |

As you type, your text will be displayed in a rectangular area on the screen. This rectangular area will be filled with a selected color. Click on the color or pattern in the pattern palette that you want to use as the background for your text. If you want to display the text on an invisible background, click the None box. The selected background color is displayed in the color selection box at the left of the palette.

| 4 | Select the color that you want to use to display your text. |

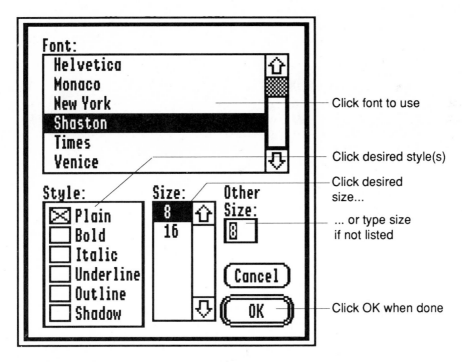

Figure 11-22   Choose Font dialog box

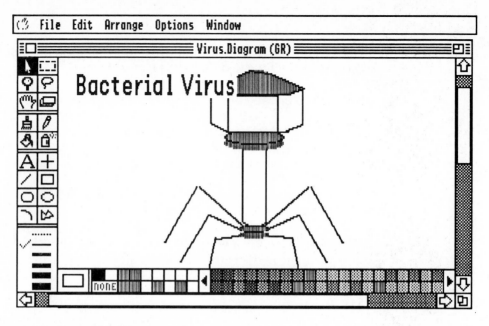

Figure 11-23 Text can be added to graphic

Hold down the Option key and click on the color to use to display your text. The selected text color is displayed as the border color in the color selection box.

5 **Move the cursor into the document window.**

The arrow pointer turns into the I-beam cursor as it enters the document.

6 **Click the I-beam cursor at the location where you want to enter text.**

7 **Type your text at the keyboard.**

As you type, the text appears displayed in black on a white background. When you press the Return key, the text is displayed in the selected color on the selected background color. (See Figure 11-23.)

Drawing horizontal and vertical lines

The horizontal/vertical line tool draws lines that are perfectly horizontal or vertical. To draw a line at any other angle, use the line tool described in the next section.

To draw a horizontal or vertical line:

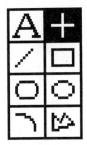

Figure 11-24
Horizontal/
Vertical tool

1   **Position the arrow cursor on the horizontal/vertical line tool, and click the mouse button to select the tool. (See Figure 11-24)**

2   **Click the desired line width to use with the object.**

The line width palette beneath the tool palette displays possible line widths. When you click on one of the line widths, a checkmark appears to the left of that width. The dotted line on the palette draws an invisible line. (See Figure 11-25.)

3   **Click on the color or pattern that you want to use.**

The selected color appears in the color selection box on the pattern palette.

4   **Move the cursor into the document window.**

When you move into the document window, the arrow cursor turns into the crossbar cursor.

5   **Move the crossbar cursor to the location where you want to begin drawing a horizontal or vertical line.**

This location will serve as the anchor point for the line.

6   **Hold down the mouse button and drag the mouse.**

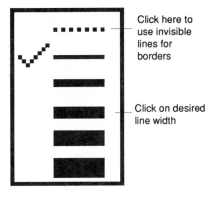

Figure 11-25   Line width palette

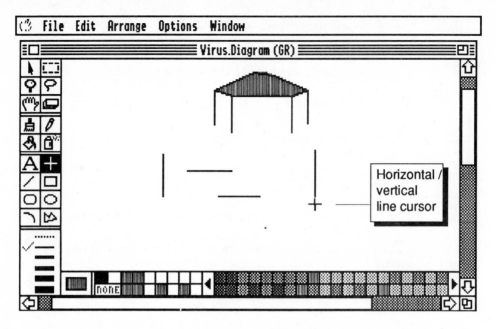

Figure 11-26 You can draw perfectly-straight horizontal or vertical lines

The location where you first began serves as an "anchor" for the line. As you drag the mouse, the tool draws a straight line to the current location of the cursor. As long as you hold down the mouse button, you can continue to adjust the cursor location until the desired line is drawn.

7 **Release the mouse button when the desired line is completed. (See Figure 11-26.)**

Drawing straight lines

The line tool lets you draw straight lines at any angle.

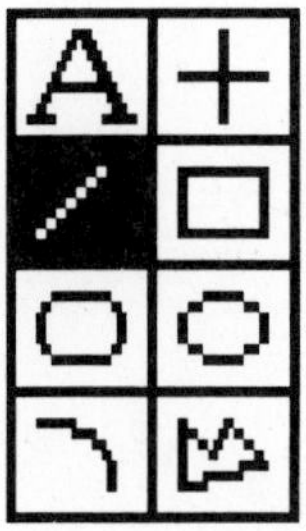

1 **Position the arrow cursor on the line tool and click the mouse button to select the line tool. (See Figure 11-27.)**

2 **Move the cursor to the line width palette and click on the line width that you want to draw.**

Figure 11-27
Line tool icon

A checkmark appears next to the selected line width. An invisible line is drawn if you select the dotted line.

3 **Click the color or pattern that you want to use.**

The selected color is displayed in the color selection box on the pattern palette.

4 **Move the cursor into the document window.**

When you move into the document window, the arrow cursor turns into the crossbar cursor. The appearance of the crossbar cursor reflects the width of the line that you selected.

5 **Move the crossbar cursor to the location where you want to begin drawing a line.**

6 **Hold down the mouse button and drag the mouse.**

The location where you first began serves as an "anchor" for the line. As you drag the mouse, the line tool draws a straight line to the current location of the cursor. As long as you hold down the mouse button, you can continue to adjust the cursor location until the desired line is drawn. (The effect is that of a "rubber band" line on the screen that you can stretch in any direction.)

7 **Release the mouse button when the line is completed. (See Figure 11-28.)**

Note: *If you hold down the Shift key as you draw a line, you can only draw a line that extends at 45° or 90° angles from the starting point. Holding down the Shift key constrains the line to certain angles.*

Drawing rectangles and squares

The rectangle tool lets you draw rectangles and squares.

1 **Position the arrow cursor on the rectangle tool and click the mouse button to select the rectangle tool. (See Figure 11-29.)**

2 **Click the desired line width that you want to use for the border of the rectangle.**

When you click on one of the line widths, a checkmark appears to the left of the width. The dotted line draws an invisible border around the object.

3 **Click the color or pattern that you want to use to fill the rectangle that you will draw.**

The selected color appears in the color selection box. If you click "none," the shape that is drawn will be hollow, or filled with no color.

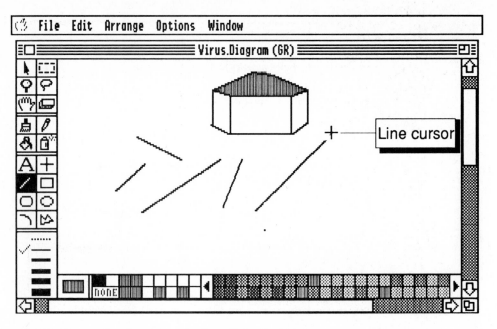

Figure 11-28 You can draw lines in any direction with the line tool

---

4 **If desired, select a separate color for the border of the rectangle.**

You may want to draw the border of an object in a color different from the color used to fill the object. To select a different color or pattern for the border, hold down the Option key and click on the desired color. The selected border color is displayed in the color selection box as a border around the box. If no border color is chosen, the border is drawn in the fill color.

5 **Move the cursor into the document window.**

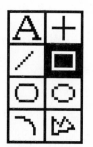

Figure 11-29
Rectangle tool
icon

When you move into the document window, the arrow cursor turns into the crossbar cursor. The size of the cursor reflects the line width that you chose: the wider the line, the larger the crossbar cursor.

6 **Move the crossbar cursor to one corner of a rectangle that you want to draw. Hold down the mouse button and drag the mouse to the opposite corner of the rectangle that you want to draw.**

As you drag the mouse, the rectangle tool draws your rectangle in the document window. The first corner of the rectangle serves as an "anchor" for the rectangle. As long as you hold down the mouse button, you can continue to adjust the opposite corner until the rectangle is the desired

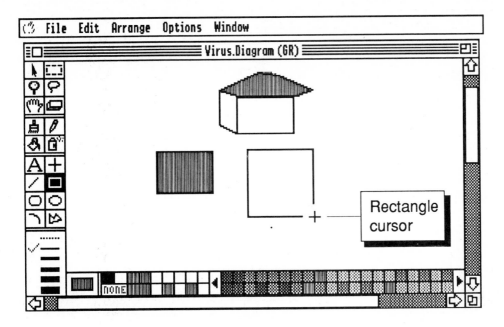

Figure 11-30 The rectangle tool draws rectangles of any size

size. (The effect is a "rubber-band" rectangle on the screen that you can stretch to any size or shape as long as the mouse button is held down.)

| 7 | When the rectangle is completed, release the mouse button. (See Figure 11-30.) |

To draw a square, hold down the Shift key as you draw the rectangle on the screen. The Shift key constrains the rectangle tool so that only squares can be drawn.

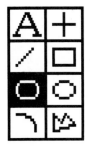

Drawing rounded rectangles

The round rectangle tool (Figure 11-31) lets you draw rectangles or squares with rounded corners. This tool is used in exactly the same way as the rectangle tool:

| 1 | Click the round rectangle tool to select the tool. |

| 2 | Click the desired line width that you want to use for the border of the rectangle. |

Figure 11-31
Round
rectangle tool

| 3 | Click the color or pattern that you want to use to fill the rectangle that you will draw. |

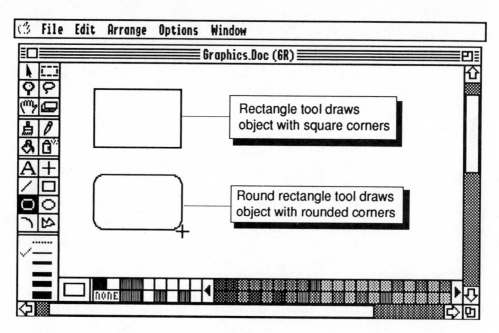

Figure 11-32 Rounded rectangle tool creates shapes with rounded edges

4 If desired, select a separate color for the border of the rectangle.

5 Move the cursor into the document window.

6 Move the crossbar cursor to one corner of a rectangle that you want to draw. Hold down the mouse button and drag the mouse to the opposite corner of the rectangle that you want to draw.

7 When the rectangle is completed, release the mouse button.

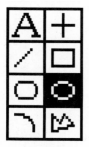

The completed rectangle is displayed with rounded corners (see Figure 11-32).

To draw a square with rounded corners, hold down the Shift key as you draw the rectangle in the window.

Drawing ovals and circles

The oval tool is used to draw ovals and circles in the document.

Figure 11-33
Oval tool icon

1 Position the arrow cursor on the oval tool, and click the mouse button to select the tool. (See Figure 11-33.)

2 | Move the cursor to the line width palette and click on the width that you want to use for the border of the oval.

3 | Move the cursor to the color pattern palette and click the color that you want to fill the oval. Click on "none" if you want the oval to be filled with no color.

The selected color is displayed in the color selection box.

4 | If desired, select a different color to use for the border of the oval.

Hold down the Option key and click the color to use for the border. The border color is displayed as a border around the color selection box.

5 | Move the cursor into the document window.

When you move into the window, the arrow cursor turns into the crossbar cursor.

6 | Move the crossbar cursor to one corner of the desired oval.

7 | Hold down the mouse button and drag the mouse to the opposite corner of the oval that you want to draw.

As you drag the mouse, the tool draws the oval in the document window. How is the shape of the oval determined? As you drag the crossbar cursor diagonally, imagine that you are drawing an invisible rectangle on the screen. The oval is drawn to fill that imaginary rectangle.

8 | When the oval is finished, release the mouse button. (See Figure 11-34.)

To draw a circle, hold down the Shift key as you draw the oval on the screen. The Shift key constrains the oval tool so that only circles can be drawn.

Drawing arcs

The arc tool lets you draw curved lines and partial circles on the screen. You can draw simple curved lines, or you can draw a curved line and fill the area defined by the arc with a selected color.

1 | Position the arrow cursor on the arc tool, and click the mouse button to select the tool. (See Figure 11-35.)

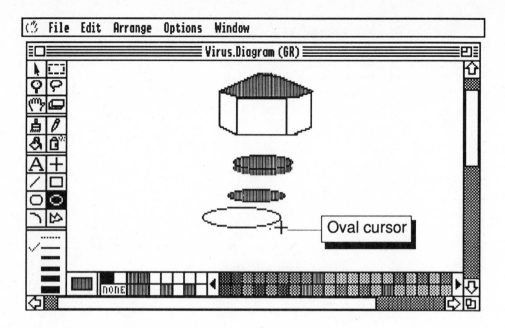

Figure 11-34 Oval tool creates ovals or circles

---

2   **Move the cursor to the line width palette and click on the width that you want to use for the border of the arc.**

When you click on one of the line widths, a checkmark appears to the left of the width. The dotted line draws an invisible line for the arc itself.

3   **Select the color to use to draw the arc.**

Hold down the Option key and click on the desired color. The selected color is displayed as a border around the color selection box. If no color is selected, the arc is drawn in the fill color selected below.

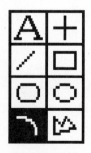

Figure 11-35
Arc tool

4   **Click the color or pattern that you want to use to fill the area defined by the arc.**

The arc tool draws a curved line on the screen and defines a curved wedge on the screen. When you draw an arc, you can automatically fill the curved wedge with a selected color. Click on the color to use to the fill the wedge. The selected color appears in the color selection box. If you click "none," the wedge will be hollow, or filled with no color.

5   **Move the cursor into the document window.**

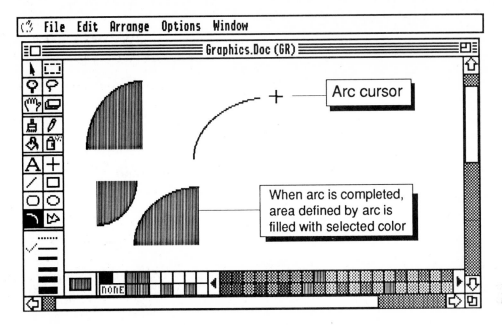

Figure 11-36 Arc tool creates arcs of any length

When you move into the document window, the arrow cursor turns into the crossbar cursor. The size of the cursor reflects the line width that you chose: the wider the line, the larger the crossbar cursor.

6   **Move the crossbar cursor to one end of the arc that you want to define. Hold down the mouse button and drag the mouse to the opposite end of the arc that you want to define.**

As you drag the mouse, the arc tool draws a curved line that begins at the first location of the cursor and passes through the current cursor location.

As long as you hold down the mouse button, you can continue to adjust the arc until it has the desired size and angle.

7   **When the arc is finished, release the mouse button.**

When you release the mouse button, the area defined by the arc is automatically filled with the selected fill color. (See Figure 11-36.)

If you hold down the Shift key while drawing an arc, the arc tool is constrained and can only draw quarter-circles. A quarter-circle is drawn that begins at the first location of the cursor and ends at the current cursor location.

Drawing polygons

A polygon is a geometric shape with many sides. (The word "polygon" means "many sides.") The polygon tool lets you easily create a shape with many sides by clicking on each corner of the shape.

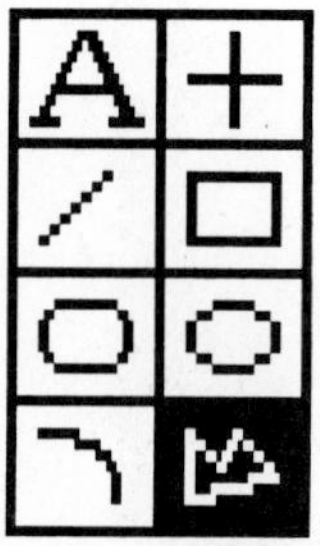

Figure 11-37
Polygon tool

1. Position the arrow cursor on the polygon tool, and click the mouse button to select the tool. (See Figure 11-37.)

2. Move the cursor to the line width palette and click on the width that you want to use for the border of the polygon.

When you click on one of the line widths, a checkmark appears to the left of that width. The dotted line draws the border as an invisible line.

3. Select the color that you want to use to fill the the polygon.

When you draw a polygon, it is automatically filled with a selected color. Click on the color that you want to fill the polygon. The selected color is displayed in the color selection box. If you click "none," the polygon will be hollow, or filled with no color.

4. Click the color or pattern that you want to use for the border of the polygon.

Hold down the Option key and click on the desired color. The selected color is displayed as a border around the color selection box. If no color is selected, the border is drawn in the color selected as the fill color.

5. Move the cursor into the document window.

When you move into the document window, the arrow cursor turns into the crossbar cursor. The size of the cursor reflects the line width that you chose: the wider the line, the larger the crossbar cursor.

6. Click the mouse button at the first corner of the polygon.

7. Move the crossbar cursor to the next corner of the polygon, and click the mouse button again.

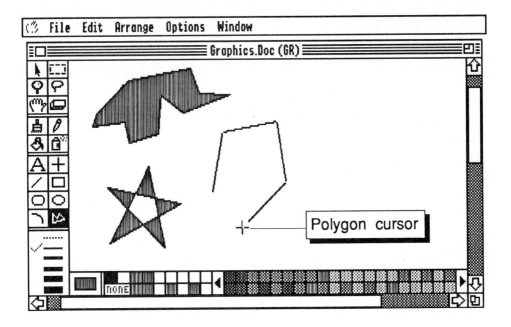

Figure 11-38 Polygon tool creates objects of any shape

As you move the cursor, a line is automatically drawn from the last corner to the current cursor location. When you click the mouse button, a line is automatically drawn that connects this corner with the previous corner.

8 **Move to the next corner of the polygon and click the mouse button again. Draw the rest of the polygon by clicking on each corner of the polygon.**

9 **When you reach the original corner of the polygon again, click on the original corner again to complete the polygon.**

You can also complete the polygon by clicking outside the document window; a line is automatically drawn between the last corner clicked and the first corner. You can also complete a polygon by double-clicking anywhere.

When the polygon is completed, it is filled with the selected fill color. (See Figure 11-38.)

If you hold down the Shift key while drawing a polygon, the polygon tool is constrained and can only draw lines at 45° or 90° angles from the last corner.

Using the eraser

Figure 11-39
Edit tool palette

The graphics application provides powerful edit tools and menu commands to make changes in your graphics. (See Figure 11-39.) The edit tools include

- the arrow pointer tool, used to select objects and commands
- the marquee tool, used to select rectangular areas
- the magnifying glass tool, used to examine and change fine details
- the lasso tool, used to select irregular-shaped areas
- the grabber tool, used to change the current viewing area
- the eraser tool, used to erase part of an object

These are discussed in detail in Chapter 12, but the following example shows how these tools can be used.

Erasing parts of your graphic

One of the edit tools is a small eraser that lets you erase parts of your graphic.

To use the eraser:

Figure 11-40
Eraser tool selected

| 1 | Click on the eraser tool to select that tool. (See Figure 11-40.)

| 2 | Move the cursor into the document window.

The cursor takes the shape of a small rectangle that represents an eraser.

| 3 | Move the eraser cursor to the part of the graphic that you want to erase. Hold down the mouse button and drag the eraser across the graphic that you want to erase.

As you drag the cursor across the cursor, the area touched by the eraser disappears. (See Figure 11-41.)

This is only one example of the edit tools. Chapter 12 explores the other tools in detail.

Saving a graphics document

After you've created a graphics document, you can use the graphic in many ways. You can print the graphic, you can combine the graphic with text in a page layout document, or you can copy the graphic into a picture field in a database record.

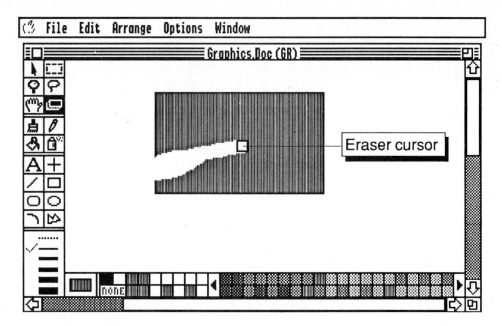

Figure 11-41 Eraser crossing graphic

Before using the graphic, however, you should always save your document to your storage disk. Don't forget to save your work often.

Refer to Chapter 3 for a discussion of the Save and Save As commands.

When you save your document with the Save As command, pay special attention to the formatting buttons at the bottom of the dialog box (see Figure 11-42). You can save your graphic in the AppleWorks GS graphics format or in Apple Preferred Format. In most cases, you should save the graphics in the AppleWorks GS format.

Apple Preferred Format is a storage format used by some Apple IIGS graphics application programs. If you store your graphic in Apple Preferred Format, your graphic document can be opened and modified by these other programs. If you want to use your graphics with those programs, click the Apple Preferred Format button, and the graphic is saved in that format.

Printing your graphics document

After you have created your graphics document, you will probably want to print a copy of the graphic on your printer. Printing out a copy of your graphic involves three steps:

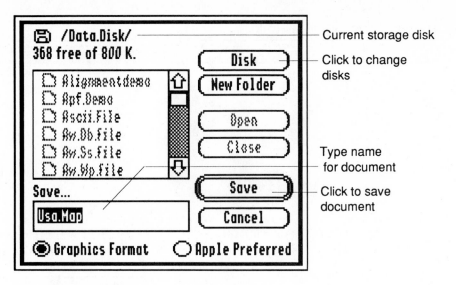

Current storage disk

Click to change disks

Type name for document

Click to save document

Figure 11-42 Save As dialog

1. Use the Choose Printer command on the File menu to select the printer to use.

2. Use the Page Setup command on the File menu to specify the type of paper, vertical sizing, printer effects, and orientation that you want to use.

3. Select the Print command on the File menu select the print quality, page range, and number of copies that you want to use.

You can also specify automatic or manual paper feed, as well as color printing. If you have a color printer like the Imagewriter II, you can print your graphics in full color. Be sure to check the Better Color button and COlor box in the Print dialog box.

4. When you have made your selections, click the OK button in the Print dialog box to begin printing.

For more information about printing, see the Choose Printer command, Page Setup command, and Print command in Chapter 3, Apple-Works GS Common Commands.

The next step

This chapter has shown you how to open a new graphics document and use the powerful paint and draw tools to create full color graphics. As you create a graphic, however, you might want to make changes in the graphic; you might want to move objects to a different location, change the color of objects, or even make changes in the individual dots that make up your graphics.

Chapter 12 will demonstrate the editing features that are available to change your graphics document. You will be shown how to use the edit tools to erase, move, or magnify parts of your graphics. You will also learn how to change the colors of objects and how to use menu commands to move, rotate, and flip objects on the screen. You will even learn how to use the graphics tools to produce stylized illustrations from existing artwork.

Chapter 12

Working with Graphics Documents

About this chapter

This chapter introduces the ways that you can make changes in your graphics. AppleWorks GS provides an edit tool palette that provides powerful editing features, and the graphics menu bar includes commands that let you move, rearrange, and modify your graphics.

The topics in this chapter include

- Opening a saved document
- Using the edit tools to
- Grouping and ungrouping objects
- Moving objects
- Changing colors and shapes of objects
- Rearranging objects on the screen
- Producing illustrations

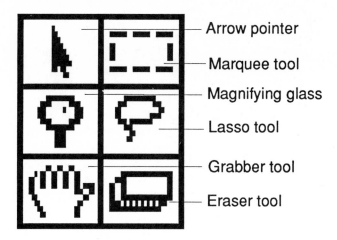

Figure 12-1   Edit Tool palette

Opening a saved graphics document

After you create and save a graphics document, you may want to return to the document later to make changes to the document. This chapter examines ways that you can make changes in your graphics document while you are creating it or at a later date.

To open a saved graphics document:

☐1   **Select Open from the File menu.**

All of the graphics documents that can be opened on the current disk are displayed in the list box. AppleWorks GS can open graphics created by its own graphics application, as well as graphics that were stored in Paint format, PICT format, Apple Preferred Format, or Screen format by other programs.

☐2   **Click on the name of the graphics document that you want to open, and then click on the Open button.**

Shortcut: *Double-click on the name of the graphics document that you want to open.*

Using the edit tools

AppleWorks GS provides many features that let you make changes in your graphics. These features include a powerful set of edit tools, provided on the edit tool palette at the left of the window (see Figure 12-1).

The edit tools include:

- The **arrow pointer** tool. This tool lets you select part of the graphic for action.
- The **marquee** tool. This tool lets you select a rectangular area on the graphic and move it to another location.
- The **magnifying glass** tool. This tool lets you magnify an area on the graphic, where you can use any of the other tools to make small changes in the image.
- The **lasso** tool. This tool lets you select an irregularly-shaped part of the graphic for use with other commands.
- The **grabber** tool. This tool lets you move the entire graphic on the screen.
- The **eraser** tool. This tool lets you erase part of the graphic.

Using one of the edit tools

To use one of the editing tools:

| 1 | Click on the desired editing tool icon to select the tool.

| 2 | Move the pointer into the graphics document.

The pointer takes the shape of a cursor that is specific to the tool. The tool is now ready to use.

Figure 12-2
Arrow tool

Using the arrow pointer

The arrow pointer tool is a selection tool. The arrow pointer is used to select the tool, color, line width, or brush that you want to use. It is also used to select one or more objects in a document for further action. (See Figure 12-2.)

- **To select the arrow pointer tool, click on the arrow pointer.**

Selecting a tool, color, line width, or brush with the arrow pointer

The arrow pointer can be used to select tools from the tool palettes, colors on the pattern palette, line widths on the line palette, and brush sizes on the brush palette.

To select a tool, color, line width, or brush, click the arrow pointer on the desired selection.

Selecting objects with the arrow pointer

The arrow pointer can be used to select an object for further action. You can also select multiple objects and take action on all of the selected objects.

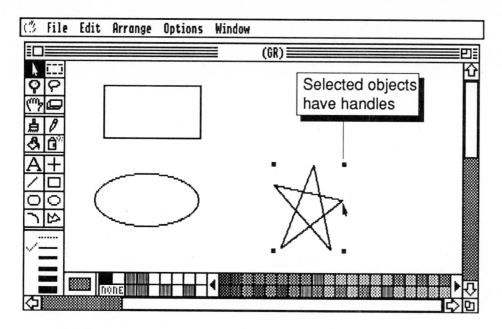

Figure 12-3   Window with object selected, handles visible

To select an object:

☐1   **Click on the arrow pointer tool.**

The current cursor turns into the arrow cursor.

☐2   **Click on the object in the document window that you want to select.**

Handles appear at the corners of the selected object. (See Figure 12-3.) These handles are used to stretch and resize the selected object. (See Resizing objects later in this chapter, under "Changing colors and sizes.") As you work with objects, be careful not to accidentally drag one of the handles; you might stretch and resize the object when you don't want to! If you accidentally drag one of the handles, select the Undo command on the Edit menu immediately.

Deselecting an object with the arrow pointer

To deselect an object, click on the object again. The handles disappear from the object. You can also deselect an object by clicking on any draw tool, or by clicking on the marquee, lasso, or eraser tools.

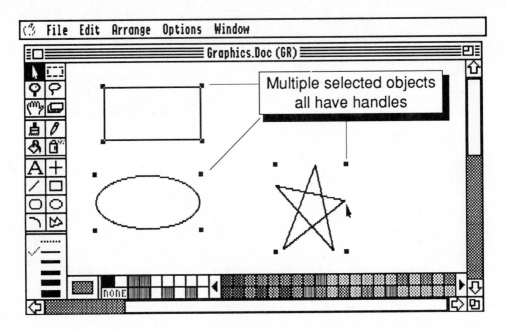

Figure 12-4 Window with multiple objects selected

Selecting multiple objects with the arrow

1 **Select the arrow pointer tool.**

2 **Move the arrow cursor into the document window and click on the first object to be selected.**

The selected object is surrounded by handles.

3 **Move the arrow cursor to the next object to be selected. Hold down the Shift key, and click the mouse button again.**

Both objects are now selected and shown with handles.

4 **Repeat with any other objects that you want to select with this group.**

As you continue to Shift-click on objects, all selected objects are shown with handles at each corner of each object. (See Figure 12-4.)

Using a selection rectangle to select objects

The arrow pointer can be used to quickly select one or more objects that are located in the same part of the graphic.

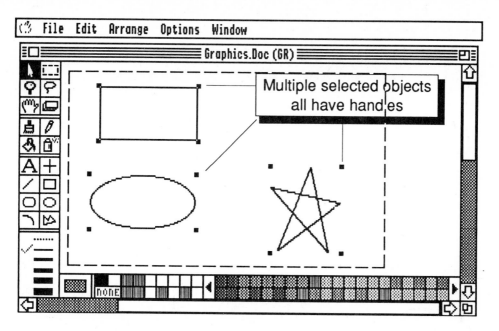

Figure 12-5 Window with multiple objects selected inside selection rectangle

1 **Select the arrow pointer tool.**

2 **Move the cursor to one corner of a rectangle that includes the objects to be selected.**

Imagine a rectangle on the screen that includes the objects that you want to select. Place the cursor at one corner of the imaginary rectangle.

3 **Hold down the mouse button and drag the mouse to the opposite corner of the rectangle that contains the objects to be selected.**

As you drag the mouse, a selection rectangle is temporarily drawn on the screen. Adjust the rectangle until all the objects that you want to select are completely included inside the rectangle.

4 **When all desired objects are included inside the selection rectangle, release the mouse button.**

When you release the mouse button, all objects completely included within the box are selected and shown with handles. (See Figure 12-5.)

Note: *If you hold down the Option key as you draw the selection rectangle, any object that is partially included inside the rectangle is selected when you release the mouse button.*

Deselecting one of multiple selected objects

After you have selected multiple objects, you can deselect any of the individual selected objects.

1. **Select the arrow pointer tool.**

2. **Hold down the Shift key.**

3. **Move the arrow cursor to the object that you want to deselect, and click the mouse button.**

The object is deselected and the handles around the object disappear.

Deselecting all objects

To deselect all selected objects on the screen, click on any draw tool, or click on the marquee, lasso, or eraser tools.

Shortcut: *You can always return quickly to the arrow pointer from any other tool. While you are using any other tool, you can return to the arrow pointer by pressing the space bar. The cursor takes the shape of the arrow pointer, and you can use it in the usual way. After you have finished using the arrow pointer, press the space bar to return to the previous tool.*

Using the marquee tool

The marquee tool is used to select a rectangular part of the graphic for further action.

Figure 12-6
Marquee tool

1. **Click the marquee icon to select the marquee tool. (See Figure 12-6.)**

2. **Move the cursor to one corner of a rectangular area that you want to select.**

3. **Hold down the mouse button and drag the mouse to the opposite corner of the rectangular area that you want to select.**

As you drag the mouse, a rectangle with a dotted-line border is temporarily drawn on the screen, and the area within the rectangle is temporarily selected.

4. **Adjust the rectangle until the desired area is included, and release the mouse button when the desired area is selected.**

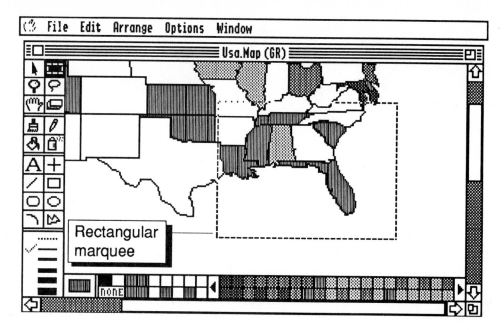

Figure 12-7 Marqueed area of a drawing

When you release the mouse button, the rectangular area is selected for further action. (See Figure 12-7.)

The marqueed area can be manipulated many ways:

- You can drag the rectangular area to another part of the document. Move the cursor into the marqueed area. The cursor takes the shape of the arrow pointer. Hold down the mouse button and drag the marqueed area to a new location. After the area is moved, the elements of the marqueed area become separate objects, distinct from the original objects. (See Figure 12-8.)
- You can move a copy of the selected area, while leaving the original graphic behind. Select an area with the marquee. Then hold down the Option key as you drag the selected area away. A copy of the selected area moves away, but the original area remains in place.
- You can select the Cut or Copy commands on the Edit menu to place a copy of the marqueed area on the Clipboard.
- You can select the Clear command to erase the marqueed area. You can also simply press the Delete key to erase the marqueed area.
- You can select the Flip Horizontal, Flip Vertical, Rotate Left, Rotate Right, Nudge Up, Nudge Down, Nudge Left, or Nudge Right commands on the Arrange menu to change the display of the marqueed area. These commands are discussed later in this chapter, under "Changing the arrangement and direction of objects."

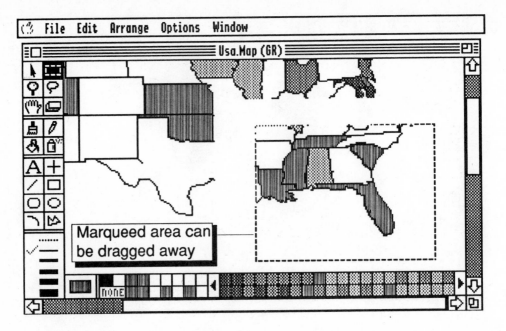

Figure 12-8 Marqueed area moved

Using the magnifying glass tool

The magnifying glass lets you examine your graphic in fine detail and use any of the other tools to make changes under the magnified view.

To use the magnifying glass:

Figure 12-9
Magnifying
glass icon

1 **Click the magnifying glass icon to select the magnifying glass tool. (See Figure 12-9.)**

2 **Move the cursor into the document window,**

When you enter the window, the cursor takes the shape of a small magnifying glass.

3 **Move the magnifying glass to the location that you want to examine under higher magnification.**

4 **Click the mouse button.**

The graphic at the selected location is displayed at higher magnification. This magnified view is often nicknamed "fatbits" mode, since each individual dot (or bit) that makes up your graphic is now visible. You can now use any of the other tools to make detailed changes in your graphic. (See Figure 12-10.)

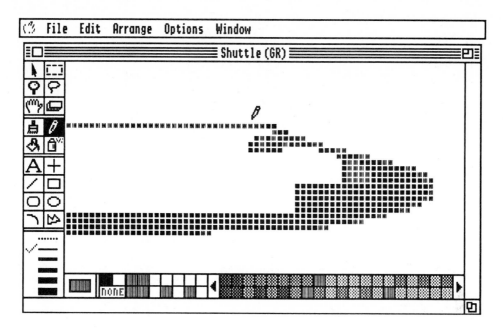

Figure 12-10 Window with graphic in fatbits mode

5 To return to the normal view of your graphic, select the magnifying glass and click anywhere in the document window.

5 To return to the normal view of your graphic, select the magnifying glass and click anywhere in the document window.

Shortcut: *You can always return quickly to the magnifying glass from any other tool. While you are using any other tool, press the Esc key to return to the magnifying glass. The cursor takes the shape of the magnifying glass, and you can use it in the usual way. After you have finished using the magnifying glass, press the Esc key again to return to the previous tool.*

Using the lasso tool

The lasso tool lets you select an irregular-shaped area of the graphic for further action.

To use the lasso tool:

1 Click the lasso icon to select the lasso tool. (See Figure 12-11.)

2 Move the cursor to a location in the document window.

Figure 12-11
Lasso tool

When you move into the window, the cursor turns into a small lasso cursor.

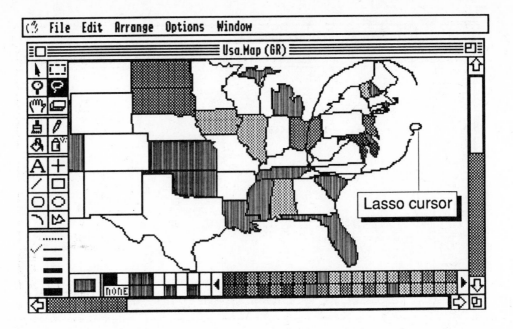

Figure 12-12   Window with lasso outline around object

3 **Hold down the mouse button and drag the mouse to surround the desired area in the document window.**

As you drag the mouse, a line is temporarily drawn on the screen behind the lasso cursor. Continue dragging the mouse until the desired area is completely enclosed by the line.

4 **When you release the mouse button, the graphic element enclosed by the lasso is selected for further action.**

When you release the button, the line snaps in and surrounds any graphic elements inside the area defined by the line. The selected area is surrounded by a dotted line. If you release the mouse button without completely enclosing an area, a line is drawn between the first and last locations of the lasso, and any graphic elements inside that area are selected. (See Figure 12-12.)

You can make changes in an area selected with the lasso in the same way that you manipulate marqueed areas:

- You can drag the selected area to another part of the document. Move the cursor into the selected area. The cursor takes the shape of the arrow pointer. Hold down the mouse button and drag the area to a new location. (See Figure 12-13.) After the area is moved, the elements of the marqueed area become separate objects.

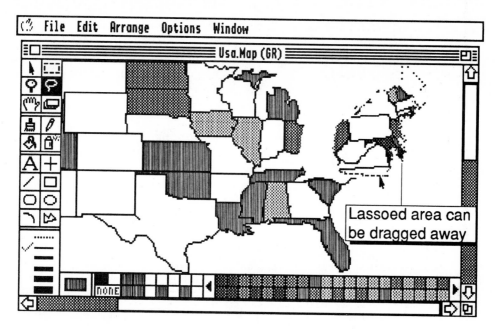

Lassoed area can
be dragged away

Figure 12-13   Lassoed area being moved

- You can move a copy of the lassoed area while leaving the original graphic behind. Hold down the Option key as you drag the selected area away, and the original graphic remains in place as the copy is moved.
- You can select the Cut or Copy commands on the Edit menu to place a copy of the marqueed area on the Clipboard.
- You can select the Clear command to erase the marqueed area. You can also simply press the Delete key to erase the marqueed area.
- You can select the Flip Horizontal, Flip Vertical, Rotate Left, Rotate Right, Nudge Up, Nudge Down, Nudge Left, or Nudge Right commands on the Arrange menu to change the display of the marqueed area. These commands are discussed later in this chapter, under "Changing the arrangement and direction of objects."

Figure 12-14
Grabber tool
icon

Using the grabber tool

The grabber tool (Figure 12-14.) is used to view different parts of the graphic; you can use this tool to slide the entire graphic around on the screen, bringing different parts of the graphic into view.

The scroll bars at the right and bottom of the window can also be used to view different parts of the graphic, but the grabber is particularly useful when you want to move a small distance or want to move diagonally.

You can also use the grabber tool to move around in the graphic when you use the magnifying glass tool. When you use the magnifying glass, you can view and change the fine details of your graphic, but the scroll bars are not available. However, you can still use the grabber tool to move around in the graphic in this magnified view.

To use the grabber:

| 1 | Click the grabber icon (the small hand) to select the grabber tool.

| 2 | Move the cursor into the document window. When you move into the window, the cursor takes the shape of a small hand.

| 3 | Hold down the mouse button and drag the mouse.

As you drag the mouse, the hand moves in the same direction on the screen and drags your graphic in the same direction. (See Figure 12-15.)

Shortcut: *You can always return quickly to the grabber from any other tool. While you are using any other tool, press the Tab key to return to the grabber. The cursor takes the shape of the small hand, and you can use the tool in the usual way. After you have finished using the grabber, press the Tab key again to return to the previous tool.*

Using the eraser tool

The eraser lets you erase parts of your graphic.

To use the eraser:

| 1 | Click the eraser icon to select the eraser tool. (See Figure 12-16.)

| 2 | Move the cursor into the document window.

When you move into the window, the cursor takes the shape of a small white block, representing an eraser.

| 3 | Move the eraser cursor to the area that you want to erase.

| 4 | Hold down the mouse button, and drag the mouse.

As you drag the mouse, the eraser erases any part of the graphic that it passes over. (See Figure 12-17.)

To move the eraser to a new location without erasing any of the graphic, release the mouse button and move the mouse.

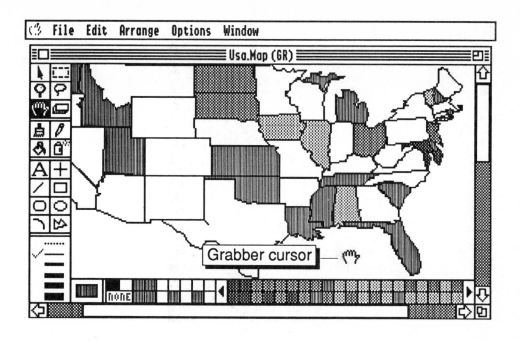

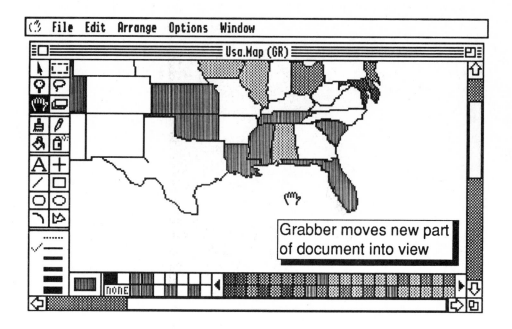

Figure 12-15 Window with hand cursor displayed

Thinking about objects

Figure 12-16
Eraser tool icon

The graphics application creates your graphic on the screen by creating a special kind of graphic element: the paint object. In the past, graphics programs fell into two classes:

- **Paint** programs, which let you edit individual dots on the screen, but which made it more difficult to work with the entire graphic or parts of the graphic;
- **Draw** programs, which let you create objects on the screen that could easily be moved or resized, but which could not be edited in fine detail.

AppleWorks GS combines the best of both kinds of programs by creating paint objects. Like the graphics created by paint programs, the fine details of paint objects can be edited as individual dots on the screen when you use the magnifying glass. Paint objects can also be easily moved, resized, or rearranged on the screen, like the objects created by draw programs.

When do you begin a new object?

An **object** is an element of your graphic that can be selected and manipulated as a separate element. Your graphic consists of a set of these paint objects on the screen.

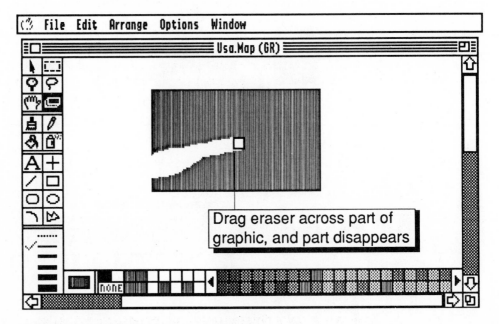

Figure 12-17   Window with object partially erased by eraser

As you work on your graphic, when do you begin each new object?

New objects begin automatically each time you use one of the draw tools. Each element that you draw is a separate paint object. You can select and act on each of those elements separately, if you wish.

For example, if you use the rectangle tool to create three rectangles on the screen, each rectangle is a separate object and each can be selected independently.

When you choose a paint tool, the situation is a bit more complicated. The graphic element that you paint with a paint tool may begin a new paint object, or it may be added to an existing object.

- If the last tool that you used to change the screen was not a paint tool, then the new element that you paint on the screen begins a new paint object.

For example, if you just drew a rectangle with the rectangle tool and then choose to paint a red line with the paintbrush, the red line begins a new paint object.

- If the last tool that you used was a paint tool, the new element that you paint on the screen continues the previous object.

For example, if you choose the paintbrush and then paint three red lines on the screen, all of the lines are included in the same object. If you add two blue lines drawn with the pencil, the three red lines and two blue lines are all included in the same object. All of the elements that you continue to add with paint tools are added to the same object.

- If you click on an object created with paint tools, it is selected for action. If you paint new elements with paint tools, these new elements are automatically added to the same object and become part of that same object.

Generalizations about paint objects

In general, if a graphic element is created with a draw tool, it is always a new object, and it is created as a separate object.

In general, if a graphic element is created with a paint tool, it either continues a previous object (if the last tool that you used was a paint tool) or begins a new object (if the last tool that you used was not a paint tool).

There is an exception to these rules. You always have the option to begin a new paint object at any time.

- **To begin a new paint object at any time, choose the Begin New Paint Object command on the Edit menu.**

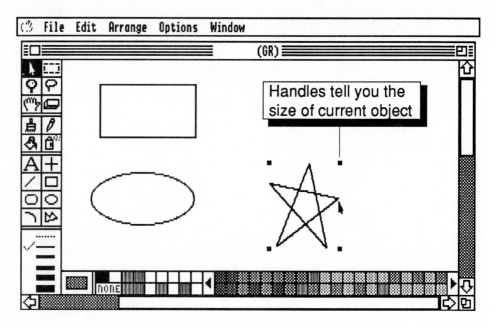

Figure 12-18 Selected objects have handles

After you choose this command, the next element added to the screen begins a new object.

Selecting objects

Objects provide an important advantage to a graphics program: you can act on part or all of the graphics with single commands. For example, you can move, resize, or rearrange objects easily.

Before you can act upon an object, you must **select** it for action.

The arrow pointer tool on the edit tool palette is used to select objects. The methods used to select objects were discussed earlier:

- To select one object, click on the object with the arrow pointer.
- To select multiple objects, Shift-click on the objects.
- To select multiple objects in the same area, use the arrow pointer to draw a selection rectangle on the screen.

Each selected object is displayed with handles at each corner of the object (see Figure 12-18).

After an object is selected, it can be moved, resized, or rearranged on the screen.

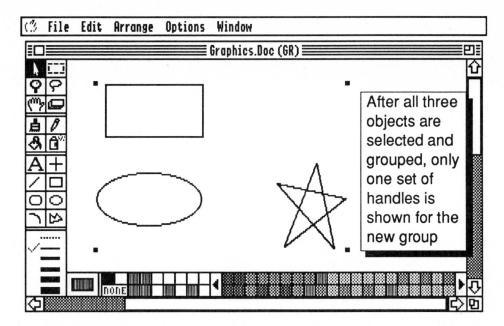

After all three objects are selected and grouped, only one set of handles is shown for the new group

Figure 12-19 Grouped objects

Grouping objects

If you wish, you can join two or more objects into a single object. This is called grouping objects. Grouping objects has an advantage: you can manipulate the entire group with single commands.

To group objects:

1 **Select the objects to group.**

You can click on the first object and Shift-click on the other objects; each object that you select is displayed with handles at each corner of the object. You could also use the arrow pointer to draw a selection rectangle around the desired objects.

2 **Choose the Group command on the Arrange menu.**

The selected objects are joined into a single object, with handles appearing at the four corners of the new object. (See Figure 12-19.)

You can always break the group back into its original objects later.

Shortcut: *You can automatically group new painted graphics with an object created with a draw tool:*

1 Select the object created with a draw tool (such as a rectangle created with the rectangle tool).

2 Select a paint tool (like the paintbrush) and paint in the document window.

As you paint, the new painted element is automatically grouped (autogrouped) with the original object.

Ungrouping objects

You can return to a group later and separate the group back into its component objects. This is called ungrouping.

To ungroup an object:

1 Select the grouped object.

2 Choose the Ungroup command on the Arrange menu.

The group is separated into its original objects. Handles are displayed at the corners of each original object.

Collapsing objects

AppleWorks GS provides a way to permanently group objects; this is called collapsing objects.

To collapse objects permanently into a group:

1 Select the objects that you want to permanently group.

2 Choose the Collapse command on the Edit menu.

The selected objects are permanently grouped, and handles are displayed at the corners of the new object.

Why would you collapse objects, rather than simply group objects? Collapsed objects can be stored more efficiently and occupy less disk storage space. On the other hand, grouped objects offer more flexibility, since they can be ungrouped later if necessary.

Moving objects

One of the most useful advantages of objects is that they can easily be moved and rearranged on the screen. You can easily move a single object or a group of objects. Using the marquee or lasso tool, you can also move part of your graphic on the screen.

Dragging objects to new locations

To move an object or multiple objects:

[1] **Select the object or objects that you want to move.**

You can click on a single object, Shift-click on multiple objects, or use the arrow pointer to draw a selection rectangle.

[2] **Move the arrow pointer so that the tip touches any of the selected graphics.**

[3] **Hold down the mouse button and drag the selected graphics to the desired position.**

As you move the mouse, a dotted rectangle that represents the selected objects moves with the mouse on the screen. This indicates the approximate location where the objects will be placed when you release the button. (See Figure 12-20.)

[4] **Release the mouse button when the graphics are placed correctly.**

Using the Clipboard to move objects

You can use the Clipboard to move objects from one location to another in your document. You can also use the Clipboard to move your graphics to another graphics document, to a picture field in the database, or into the page layout application.

[1] **Select one or more objects that you want to move.**

[2] **Choose the Cut or Copy commands from the Edit menu.**

If you select the Cut command, the selected objects are copied to the Clipboard and are removed from the document. If you select the Copy command, the selected graphics are copied to the Clipboard and the original graphics remain in the original location.

[3] **Move the cursor to the place where you want to move the graphics that are stored on the Clipboard.**

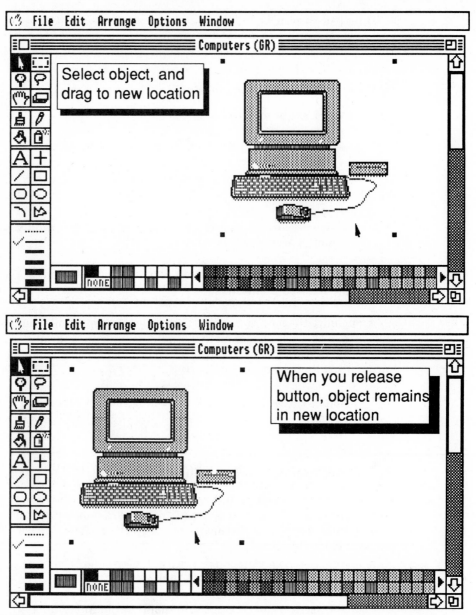

Figure 12-20 Moving a graphic

This destination could be in the same document, or it could be in another graphics document, a database document, or a page layout document.

To move the graphic to another location in a graphics document, click the desired location, and then select the Paste command from the Edit menu.

To move the graphic to a picture field in a database document, open the document, click the field where you want to copy the graphic, and then choose the Paste command from the Edit menu.

To move the graphic to a page layout document, open the document and choose the Paste command from the Edit menu.

4 **After you select the Paste command, the graphic appears at the new location.**

Using control-drag to move graphics

The **control-drag** feature performs an operation similar to the Copy and Paste command, but the operation is shown graphically on the screen.

1 **Select the object or multiple objects that you want to move.**

2 **While the objects are still selected, hold down the Control key and drag the objects to the desired destination. (See Figure12-21.)**

As you control-drag the selected objects, the cursor takes the shape of a lightning bolt and a dotted rectangle represents the current location of the object being moved.

The control-drag operation performs an operation similar to the Copy and Paste commands. The original selected objects remain in their original locations.

Probably the most dramatic use of control-drag is to copy graphics between windows. If you create an object in a graphics window and want to move it to another window, open both windows and resize the windows so that both are visible on the screen.

Then you can use control-drag to directly drag selected objects from one window to another (see Figure 12-22).

In Chapter 15, this technique is shown being used to drag graphics directly from the graphics application into a page layout document.

Nudging objects

You can use the Nudge commands to move your objects slightly on the screen.

1 **Select the object that you want to move.**

2 **Choose the Nudge Up, Nudge Down, Nudge Left, or Nudge Right command on the Arrange menu.**

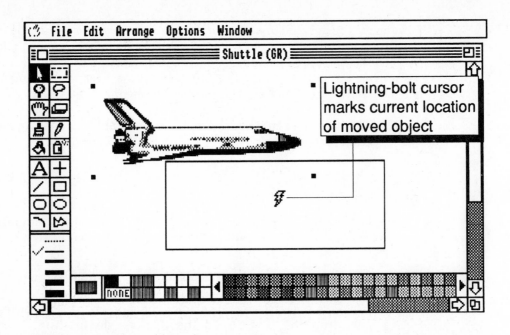

Lightning-bolt cursor marks current location of moved object

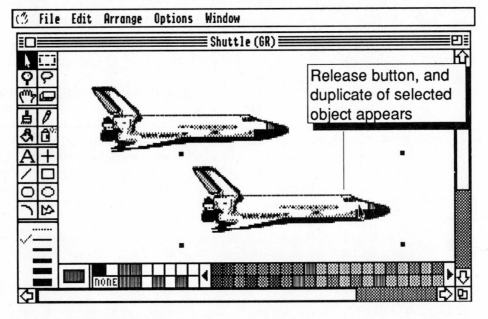

Release button, and duplicate of selected object appears

Figure 12-21 Using control-drag

These commands move the selected objects slightly in the direction indicated. (In more precise terms, the objects are moved one dot or pixel in the indicated direction on the screen.)

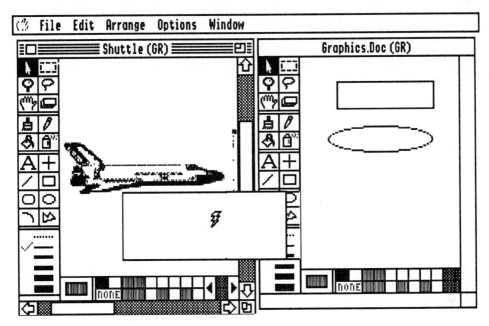

Figure 12-22 Dragging from one window to another

Moving part of your graphic

In some situations, you might not want to move an entire object. Rather, you might want to move only a selected part of an object.

You can move part of your graphic with the marquee or lasso tool.

After you select an area with one of these tools, you can move the cursor into the selected area, hold down the mouse button, and drag the selected area to new locations.

For more information on these tools, see Using the marquee tool and Using the lasso tool earlier in this chapter.

Changing colors and sizes

AppleWorks GS provides powerful features that let you change the color of objects, change the colors in the palette, or automatically shadow objects. You can also resize objects or duplicate objects easily.

Changing the color of an object

You can easily change the color of a selected object. When you first create an object, you click on the pattern palette to select the fill color for the object. You also may select a border color for the object by holding down the Option key and clicking on a color or pattern. Your choices are displayed in the color selection box in the pattern palette.

You can change any of these selections later. You can easily change the fill color or the border color used for an object.

To change the colors used in an object:

1. **Click the object that you want to change.**

Handles appear at each corner of the selected object. The fill color and border color for the selected object appear in the color selection box.

2. **Click on the new color to use as the fill color.**

The new choice is displayed in the color selection box and the color fills the selected object.

3. **If you wish, hold down the Option key and click a new border color.**

The new border color is displayed in the color selection box and appears as the border of the selected object.

Changing the colors on the pattern palette

The pattern palette displays the colors and patterns that you can use in your graphic. The Edit Colors command on the Edit menu provides a powerful tool that lets you change the colors that are available. Since the patterns are mixtures of the colors, the patterns also change when you change the colors.

A complete explanation of this command is provided in Appendix D, Using the Edit Colors command. This section provides a short introduction to the command.

When you choose the Edit Colors command, the Edit Colors dialog box appears (see Figure 12-23).

The colors that you are currently using are displayed at the top of the dialog box. Each of these colors is a mixture of the four colors displayed at the bottom of the box.

The scroll bars at the left represent the mixture of red, green, and blue that are present in each color. (The scroll bars at the right represent an alternative way to encode each color. These are explained in Appendix D, and we can safely ignore them for now.)

To see how any specific color is mixed, let's explore the four colors at the bottom of the dialog box:

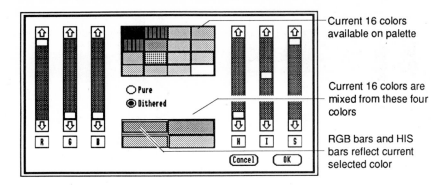

Current 16 colors
available on palette

Current 16 colors are
mixed from these four
colors

RGB bars and HIS
bars reflect current
selected color

Figure 12-23   Edit Colors dialog

- Click the red box. Notice that the scroll box on the Red scroll bar is set to the top of the bar and the other two scroll boxes are at the bottom of the other bars. (The interpretation: The color red is produced by mixing a maximum amount of red pigment and no green or blue pigment.)
- Click the blue box. The color blue is produced by mixing a maximum amount of blue pigment and no red or green pigment.
- Click the green box. The color green is produced by mixing a maximum amount of green, and no red or blue pigment.
- Click the yellow box. Yellow is produced by mixing a maximum amount of red and green, and no blue pigment.

To change the colors available in the pattern palette, all you have to do is change one of the four basic colors:

1   **Click the red, blue, green, or yellow box.**

The scroll boxes on the Red, Green, and Blue scroll bars adjust to reflect the selected color. Watch how the scroll boxes on each of the three color bars are adjusted.

2   **Change the position of the scroll box in one or more scroll bars to new positions.**

You can click the arrows at the top or bottom of a scroll bar, click in the gray area above or below a scroll box, or use the mouse to drag the scroll box. (See Figure 12-24.)

As you move the scroll boxes, the selected color changes, and this change is reflected in the colors seen at the top of the box.

3   **Decide if you want to change the color palette on your graphic or return to the graphic with the palette unchanged.**

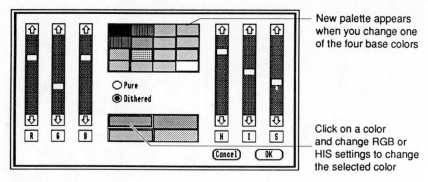

New palette appears when you change one of the four base colors

○ Pure
● Dithered

Click on a color and change RGB or HIS settings to change the selected color

Figure 12-24 Change scroll bar positions

If you click the OK button now, you will be returned to your graphic, and every place where one of the original colors was used, the corresponding new color is now used.

If you want to return to the graphic without changing the palette, click the Cancel button.

Changing the border width of an object

When you draw a geometric shape with one of the draw tools, you can select a desired line width to use for the border of the shape. To change the border width:

| 1 | **Select the object that you want to change.**

A checkmark is displayed to the left of the line width currently used for the border of the shape.

| 2 | **Click on a new line width in the line palette.**

A checkmark appears next to the selected width, and the border of the selected object is displayed in the new selected width.

Adding shadows to objects

A shadow gives three-dimensional appearance to an object. AppleWorks GS can automatically produce a shadow for an object.

To produce a shadow:

| 1 | **Select the object that you want to shadow.**

| 2 | **Choose the Shadow command on the Edit menu.**

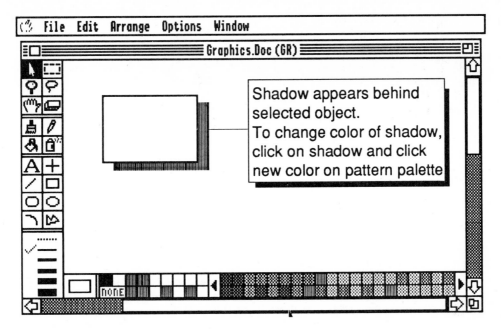

Figure 12-25   Shadowed object

A shadow is automatically drawn for the object (see Figure 12-25).

When the shadow appears, it is displayed as a separate paint object. The shadow is automatically selected when it first appears. It is easy to change the color of the shadow or move it slightly to produce a more dramatic three-dimensional effect.

- **To change the color of the shadow, select the shadow, and click on a new fill color for the shadow.**

- **To move the shadow, select the shadow and drag it to a new position.**

Resizing objects

When an object is selected, handles appear at each corner of the object. The handles are used to resize the object.

To resize an object:

[1]   **Select the object that you want to change.**

Handles appear at each corner of the object.

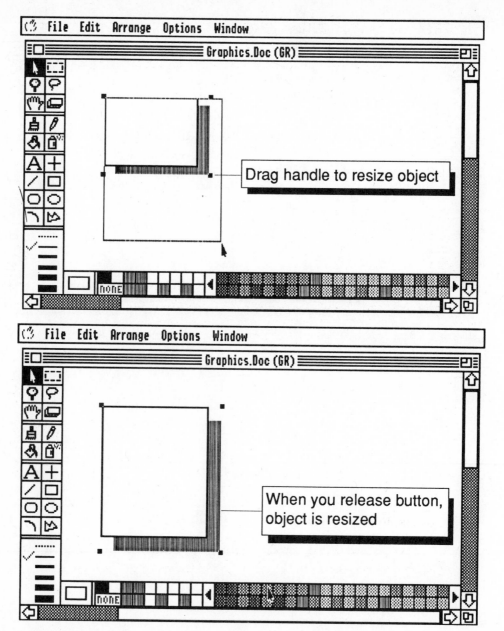

Figure 12-26 Resized object

2   **Move the tip of the arrow to touch one of the handles.**

3   **Hold down the mouse button, and drag the handle to stretch the object. (See Figure 12-26.)**

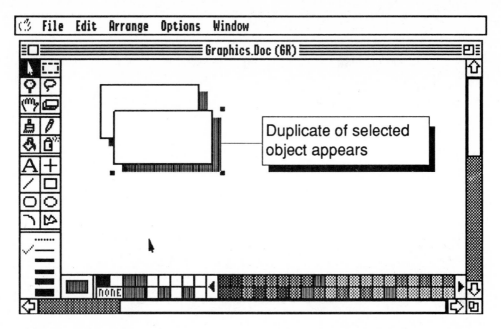

Figure 12-27 Duplicate object

As you drag the handle, a dotted rectangle is displayed that represents the new size of the object. When you release the button, the object takes the new size.

Copying objects with the Duplicate command

AppleWorks GS provides several ways to duplicate objects on the screen: you can use the Copy and Paste command, you can use the control-drag feature, or you can use the Duplicate command. The advantage of the Duplicate command is that it can copy an object with a single command and does not affect the current contents of the Clipboard.

To duplicate an object:

1   Select the object to copy.

2   Choose the Duplicate command on the Edit menu.

A second copy of the selected object appears beside the selected object. (See Figure 12-27.) The duplicate object is selected, and you can move the object or change the color of the object immediately.

Erasing an object completely

The eraser tool can be used to erase part of an object. It's easy to completely remove an entire object.

> **1**   **Click on the object that you want to completely erase.**

> **2**   **Press the Delete key.**

The selected object is removed from the screen.

Changing the arrangement and direction of objects

What happens when two or more objects overlap one another on the screen? AppleWorks GS provides commands to control the arrangement of objects. You can also easily change the direction of an object; for example, if an object is facing left, you can easily flip it horizontally so that it is facing right.

Rearranging a stack of objects

If two or more objects are on the screen, they may overlap one another. In effect, you can think of overlapping objects as being arranged in a stack on the screen. AppleWorks GS provides several commands to rearrange a stack of objects.

To bring any object to the top of a stack:

> **1**   **Select the object that you want to move.**

> **2**   **Choose the Bring To Front command on the Arrange menu.**

The selected object is moved above any overlapping objects and brought to the front of the screen. (See Figure 12-28.)

To send any object to the bottom of a stack:

> **1**   **Select the object that you want to move.**

> **2**   **Choose the Send To Back command on the Arrange menu.**

The selected object is below any overlapping objects and sent to the bottom of the stack.

To bring an object up one layer in the stack:

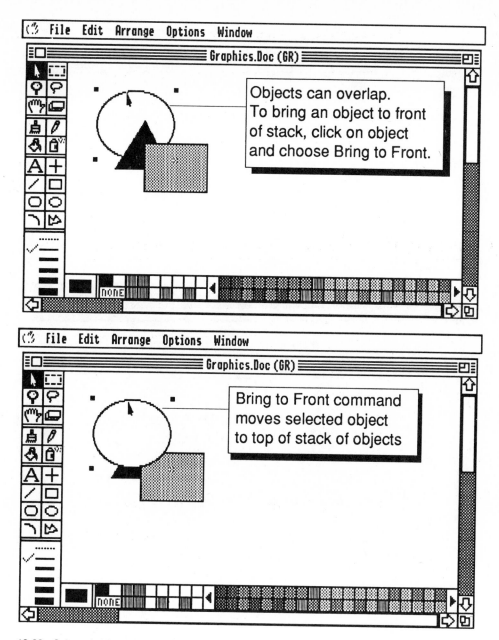

Figure 12-28 Selected objects sent to top and bottom

1 Select the object that you want to move.

2 Choose the Shuffle Up command on the Arrange menu.

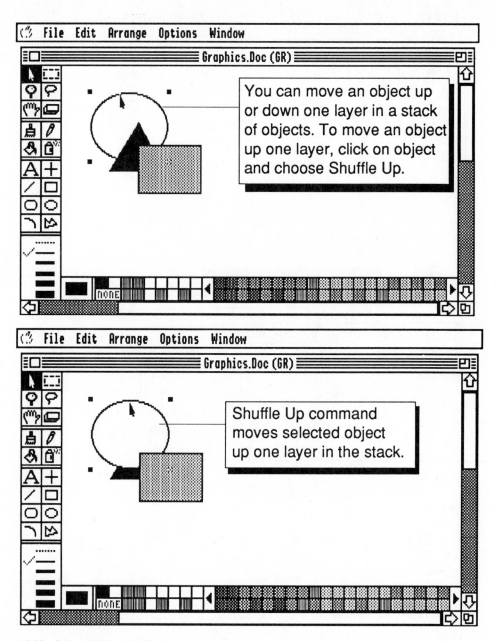

Figure 12-29   Selected object shuffled up one layer

The selected object is moved up one layer in the stack of objects. (See Figure 12-29.)

To move an object down one layer in the stack:

| 1 | **Select the object that you want to move.** |

| 2 | **Choose the Shuffle Down command on the Arrange menu.** |

The selected object is moved down one layer in the stack of objects.

Changing the direction of objects

When you create an object, you might want to change the direction of the object. The graphics application provides commands to let you easily change the direction of an object. If it is facing right, you might want to change it so that it faces left. Another popular choice would be to create a copy of an object and flip it to face in a different direction, producing two copies facing in different directions. By copying objects and changing directions of the copies, you can produce striking graphics with interesting symmetric patterns. (See Figure 12-30.)

To flip an object left or right:

| 1 | **Select the object to flip.** |

| 2 | **Choose the Flip Horizontal command on the Arrange menu.** |

The selected object is flipped left-to-right on the screen.
To flip an object top-to-bottom:

| 1 | **Select the object to flip.** |

| 2 | **Choose the Flip Vertical command on the Arrange menu.** |

The selected object is flipped top-to-bottom on the screen.
To rotate an object 90°:

| 1 | **Select the object to rotate.** |

| 2 | **Choose the Rotate Left command or the Rotate Right command on the Arrange menu.** |

The object is rotated 90° to the left or right. (See Figure 12-31.)

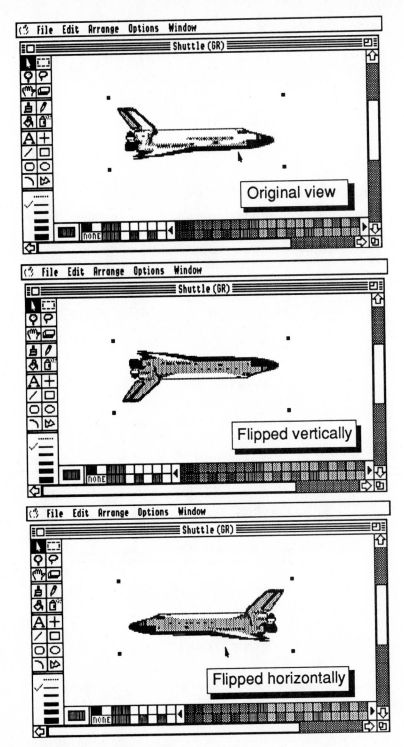

Figure 12-30 Flip horizontally and flip vertically

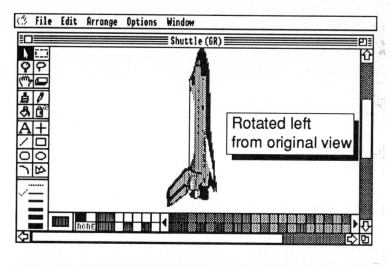

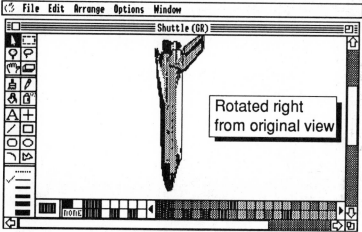

Figure 12-31 Rotate left and rotate right

Hiding the tool and pattern palettes

Hiding the tool palettes

When you open a new graphics document, the tool palettes are all displayed. If you examine the Tools command on the Options menu, a checkmark is displayed to the left of the command.

To remove the tool palette temporarily from the window, choose the Tools command. The palette temporarily disappears, and the checkmark is removed from the command on the Options menu. To return the palette to the window, select the Tools command again.

Hiding the pattern palette

When you open a new graphics document, the color and patterns that are available are shown in the pattern palettes. If you examine the Patterns command on the Options menu, a checkmark is displayed to the left of the command.

To remove the patterns palette temporarily from the window, choose the Patterns command. The pattern palette temporarily is removed, and the checkmark is removed from the command on the Options menu. To return the palette to the window, select the Patterns command again.

Producing illustrations with the graphics application

One of the special uses of the graphics application is to produce **illustrations**, where an illustration can be considered a stylized, abstract version of a graphic. The graphic of the dog used in this book is an example of an illustration.

To produce an illustration with AppleWorks GS, you can start with one version of a graphic, trace and fill certain elements, and then remove the original graphic, leaving behind the stylized abstract tracing.

For example, you could begin with a digitized or scanned image that contains more details than you want in the final illustration, trace and fill the desired elements, and then select and delete the original image. The stylized elements are left behind.

To illustrate the idea, suppose that you want a map of Texas, but you only have available a map of the United States.

1 **Display the original graphic. (See Figure 12-32.)**

2 **Use the pencil tool to trace the outline of Texas, and the paintbucket tool to fill the outline. (See Figure 12-33.)**

3 **Select the original graphic, and press the Delete key.**

The element of the graphic that you traced and filled is left behind, and you can use this illustration as you wish. (See Figure 12-34.)

The stylized picture of the dog used in this book is an example of a traced image. The original image was digitized from a video camera, and then selected parts were traced and filled with black.

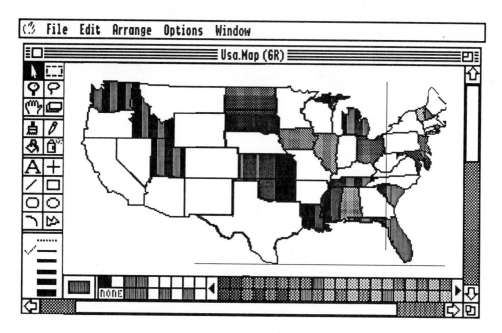

Figure 12-32 Map of US

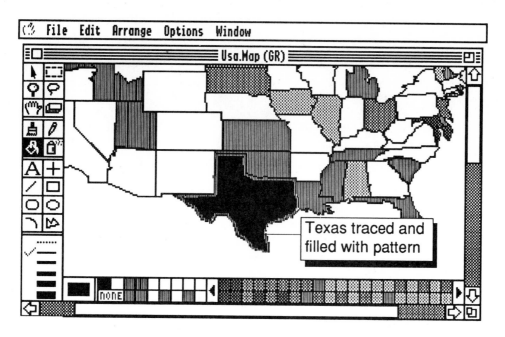

Figure 12-33 Map, with Texas outlined and filled

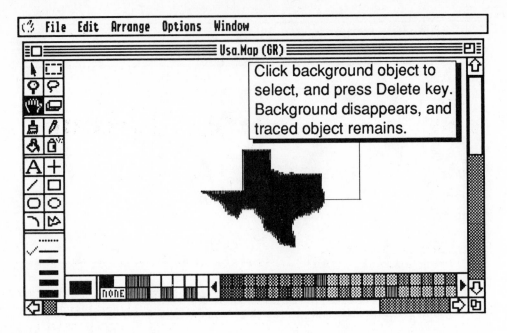

Click background object to select, and press Delete key. Background disappears, and traced object remains.

Figure 12-34   Map of Texas left behind

The next step

This chapter has shown how you can use the powerful editing features in the AppleWorks GS graphics application to produce interesting, professional graphics.

What is the next step?

- Don't forget to save changes to your document. Use the Save As command to assign a name and storage disk for the document, or use the Save command to replace the old version of the document with the current version.
- Print a copy of the document. If you have a color printer like the Imagewriter II, you can print a color copy of the document.
- Incorporate the graphics into a page layout document. Don't forget that the page layout application lets you combine text and graphics into a finished document. You can copy your graphics into a page layout document using the Clipboard or the control-drag feature, or you can import the graphic using the Import File command.

Chapter 13

Creating a New Page Layout Document

About this chapter

The page layout application lets you combine your text and graphics into a finished document. You can place your text or graphics anywhere on the page, arrange your text in columns, and resize graphics to fit a page. As you make each change, you can review the results on the screen and continue to revise the document until each element is placed correctly. When you are happy with the arrangment of text and graphics on the page, you can print a professional-looking document with a striking appearance.

This chapter explains the basic concepts of page layout and introduces the AppleWorks GS page layout application. In this chapter, a new page layout document is created and the use of guides, rulers, and master pages is explained.

The topics in the chapter include

- Page layout concepts
- Creating a new page layout document
- The page layout menu bar
- Viewing the full page
- Working with page icons
- Using master pages
- Using margin and column guides
- Saving and printing page layout documents

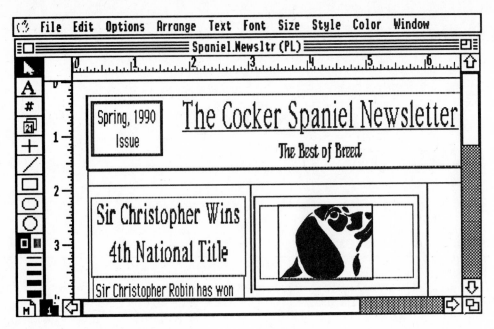

Figure 13-1 Sample page layout document

Page layout concepts

What is page layout? Page layout is the process where text and graphics are combined into a final, completed document.

In the days before electronic page layout, a typical publication like a newspaper was created by arranging text and graphics manually on blank pages. The process was a little like solving a jigsaw puzzle. Text was printed in columns on strips of paper, and the strips were cut into pieces and arranged in place on the blank pages. Space was reserved for pictures and for headlines, and the pieces were arranged and rearranged until finally they all fit and looked right. The pieces were pasted in place, and the final document was produced from the paste-up version.

Electronic page layout lets you perform these tasks much more easily. The AppleWorks GS page layout application lets you create headlines for a page, arrange text in columns, place and resize graphics on the page, and continue to work with the page until you are satisfied with its appearance. (See Figure 13-1.)

To help you create your document, the page layout application provides these important features:

Guides: A guide is a line on the screen that you can move and adjust as you wish. You can place guides on the screen to mark the margins on a page or the location of any desired columns. Guides can be defined as magnetic guides, so that any object placed close to the guide automatically snaps toward the nearest guide. Magnetic guides help you align your objects easily.

Master pages: A master page contains text or graphics or guides that you want to appear on other pages in your document. Master pages let you create a consistent look for your entire document.

Page preview: When you wish, you can display a miniature version of the page on the screen. This lets you preview the appearance of the entire page.

Linked text: You can organize your text into columns, and as you resize the columns, text is automatically rearranged to fit the new sizes of the columns. For example, if you shorten the size of one column, the text that no longer fits in the column automatically flows into the next column.

How is page layout different from word processing?

The page layout application might seem similar to word processing, but there are important differences:

- In page layout you can place your text in any rectangular-shaped area, including side-by-side columns. In word processing, you cannot create side-by-side columns.
- In page layout you can combine text and graphics into a single document. You cannot add graphics to a word processing document.
- In page layout you can use column guides to align your text and graphics neatly in columns.
- In page layout you can create master pages, that contain any information you would like to automatically display on other pages. In a word processing document, you can create headers or footers for each page, but a page layout master page lets you place any desired text or graphic in any location on each page.
- In page layout you can display a miniature version of the page on the screen to preview its final appearance.

In short, the page layout application lets you place text and graphics on an electronic "page" and then produce a final, completed document using both text and graphics. The word processing application is designed to work with text only.

When would you use page layout?

The word processing application is designed to handle your basic text documents. The page layout application is designed to handle documents that include both text and graphics, or documents where you want to arrange your text in columns or other rectangular blocks.

Typical uses of the page layout application might include

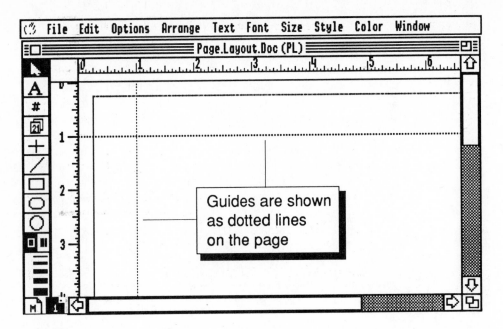

Figure 13-2 Guides

- Producing a school newspaper
- Producing a financial report that includes pie charts
- Producing a science report that includes bar charts
- Producing a newsletter for your company

As with the other AppleWorks GS applications, the use of this application is limited only by your imagination!

New page layout concepts

Page layout introduces several concepts not seen in other applications:

Guides: A guide is simply a marker on a page that sets top and bottom margins, left and right margins, or the location of columns. (See Figure 13-2.)

In a page layout document, a guide is a dotted line that you slide into place. By sliding the guides on a page, you can set margins and column locations and then orient your text and graphics correctly. You can even use magnetic guides, which "snap" your text and graphics automatically into place and help you keep objects aligned in the document.

Master page: A master page is a page that contains information that you want to display on other pages.

You can place a heading, including the page number or today's date, on the master page, and it will automatically appear on every page. Any

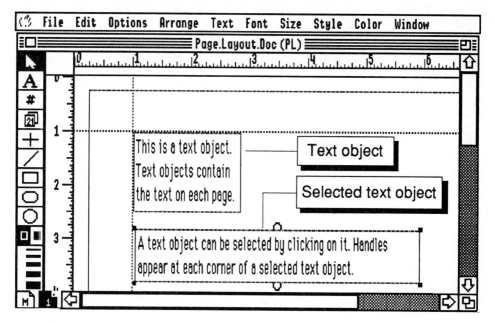

Figure 13-3 Text objects contain the text in your document

text or graphics placed on the master page will appear in the same location on other pages in the document.

You can also place guides on the master page, and they will automatically appear on every other page of the document.

If you want to have different information on left pages and right pages in your document, you can create a Left Master Page to control left pages and a Right Master Page to control right pages.

Text objects: In the graphics application your graphic consisted of one or more graphics objects, and each object could be selected, moved, resized, or otherwise manipulated. Page layout uses both graphics objects and text objects, where a text object is an object that contains the text in your document. (See Figure 13-3.)

You can create text objects two ways:

- You can create a blank text object, where you can enter text by typing from the keyboard, copying text from the Clipboard, or importing text from a saved document.
- If you import a saved document and are not already working with a text object, the imported document is opened into a new text object.

After a text object is created, it can be selected with the arrow pointer, moved, and resized in the same way as graphics objects.

Text stream: As you resize a text object to a different size, some of the text in the object may not be displayed.

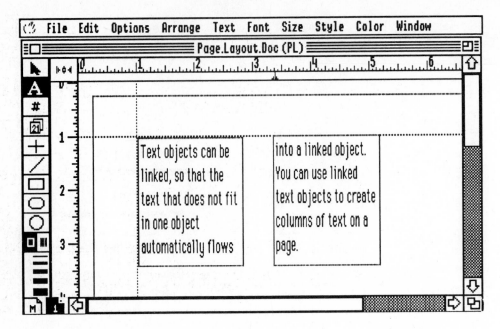

Figure 13-4   Text automatically flows between linked text objects

The text is not lost, even if it is temporarily not visible on the screen. When text is entered into a text object, it is considered a text stream, or a stream of characters. The text object will display as much of the text stream as possible in the current object, but the rest of the stream is remembered.

You can see the rest of the text stream by resizing the text object so that it's larger, or by creating a linked text object, where the stream can be continued.

Linked text objects: You can create a series of rectangular text objects, with text flowing from one object to the next. The text objects are linked. If text does not fit in one text object, it is displayed in the next linked text object in the series.

For example, if you create a text object the size of one column on your page, and all of the text does not fit into that column, you can create a linked text object in a second column, and the rest of the text appears in that linked object. (See Figure 13-4.)

Page layout tools

When you use the AppleWorks GS page layout application, the screen displays a blank page for your text and graphics and a tool palette. The tools include

- **Arrow pointer tool**, used to select objects
- **Text tool**, used to enter or edit text in text objects
- **Page number tool**, used to enter current page number in the document
- **Date tool**, used to enter the current date into the document
- **Horizontal/vertical line tool**, used to draw horizontal or vertical lines
- **Line tool**, used to draw straight lines in any direction
- **Rectangle tool**, used to draw rectangles or squares
- **Round rectangle tool**, used to draw rectangles or squares with rounded corners
- **Oval tool**, used to draw ovals or circles

Planning a page layout document

When you are planning a page layout document, there are three areas to think about:

Pages. How many pages do you need for your document? You can add as many pages as you need, up to a limit of 99 pages.

What elements do you want to appear on other pages? If you want to set margins or place text or graphics on other pages, you can create a master page that contains these elements.

Do you want to place columns in the same place on every page? If so, you can place column guides on the master page to place columns in the same location on other pages.

Text. What text do you want to include in the document? You can use text that you created in the word processor, or you can type text directly into the document You can also use the clipboard to copy information from the database or spreadsheet.

How do you want to arrange the text? You can place text in any location in a page layout document. You can define rectangular text objects at any location on the screen, and this lets you arrange your text in columns or any other desired rectangular area.

Graphics. What graphics do you want to include in the document? You can use graphics created in the AppleWorks GS graphics application or by other popular graphics programs. You can use draw tools to create simple graphics directly in the document.

How do you want to arrange the graphics in the document? You can place the graphics at any location on the page, and you can move or resize the graphic on the page.

As you work with the pages, text, and graphics in your document, you can move elements on the screen at any time, so it isn't necessary to plan your document extensively before you begin. However, it's usually useful to think about these issues a bit before you begin.

Steps toward a page layout document

When you are ready to create a page layout document, the process involves these steps:

- Open a new AppleWorks GS page layout document.
- Select the Choose Printer and the Page Setup commands on the File menu so that the blank page is oriented correctly.
- Place any desired elements on a master page. Place any text, graphics, or guides on a master page if you want to display those elements on other pages in the document. The page number tool and date tool can be used to place the page number or date on each page.
- Place text at desired locations in the document. Create any necessary text objects, enter necessary text, or import the necessary documents. Move and resize the text objects until you are satisfied with the appearance of the page.
- Place graphics at desired locations in the document. Import any desired graphics, and move or resize the graphics until you are satisfied with the appearance of the page.
- Add any desired graphics with the draw tools. You can use the line, rectangle, or oval tools to add simple graphics directly to the document.
- Save the document on a storage disk.
- Print out a copy of the document

This chapter discusses how to open a new page layout document and how to work with pages in the document, including the use of master pages and guides. The next two chapters deal with the use of text and graphics in the page layout document.

Creating a new page layout document

When you are ready to begin a new page layout document, there are two ways that you can create the new document:

- You can create a new document with the New command on the File menu.
- You can create a new document with the Open command on the File menu.

Creating a new document with the New command or Open command is discussed in Chapter 3, AppleWorks GS Common Commands.

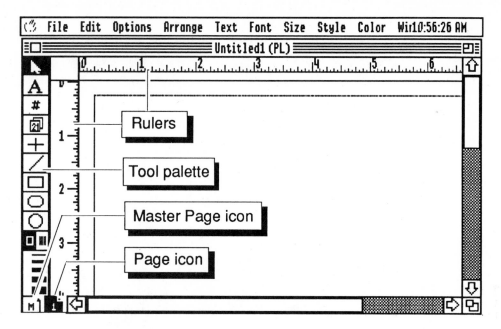

Figure 13-5 New page layout document

The page layout document window

When you open a page layout document, a document window appears on the screen (see Figure 13-5).

The new page layout document window includes features found on all windows, including the title bar, scroll bars, close box, zoom box, and size box.

The document also includes features that are specific to this application:

- At the top of the screen is the **page layout menu bar**, which contains the commands that are available in this application.
- Most of the window is blank. This blank area corresponds to the upper-left corner of the current page. You will place your text and graphics in this area. A **ruler** is displayed at the top of the page and along the left edge of the page.
- The **page layout tool palette** is displayed along the left edge of the window. This palette contains tools to create and edit text objects, enter page number and date, and draw simple graphic objects on the screen.

- The **page icons** at the bottom of the document indicate the number of pages in the document. The highlighted page indicates which page is currently displayed in the window. The page icon labeled "M" indicates a **master page**.

The page layout menu bar

The File menu

The commands on the File menu include New, Open, Close, Save, Save As, Delete File, Import File, Choose Printer, Page Setup, Print, and Quit. (See Figure 13-6.) The use of these commands was discussed in Chapter 3, Apple-Works GS Common Commands. The Print Merge command is dimmed on the File menu, since it is only available in the word processing application.

The Edit menu

The commands on the Edit menu include Undo, Cut, Copy, Paste, Clear, and Select All. (See Figure 13-7.) These commands were described in Chapter 3, AppleWorks GS Common Commands. The additional page layout Edit commands include

Duplicate: This command produces a copy of any selected object.

Insert Page(s): This command generates the specified number of new blank pages for the document.

Delete Page(s): This command removes the specified pages from the document.

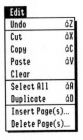

Figure 13-7
Edit menu

The Options menu

The commands on the Options menu let you work with pages, rulers and guides. (See Figure 13-8.)

Fit In Window/Actual Size: This command shrinks the page temporarily and lets you preview the appearance of the entire page on the screen. After you have previewed the page, select the command again to display the document in actual size.

Hide Tools/Show Tools: This command temporarily removes the tool palette from the screen, providing a larger working area on the screen. Select the command again to return the tools to view.

Hide Rulers/Show Rulers: This command temporarily removes the rulers from the screen, providing a larger working area on the screen. Select the command again to return the rulers to view.

Hide Guides/Show Guides: This command temporarily removes the dotted lines that represent guides from the screen, letting you preview

Figure 13-8
Options menu

the final appearance of the page. Select the command again to return the guides to view.

Set Guides: This command displays a dialog box that lets you set margin guides and column guides in the document.

Lock Guides/Unlock Guides: This command lets you temporarily lock guides in place, to avoid accidental movement of the guides. Select the command again to unlock guides.

Magnetic Guides: This command makes a text object or graphics object "snap" to the nearest guide, making alignment of objects easier. When you select the command, a checkmark appears to the left of the command. To remove the "magnetic" feature, select the command again and the checkmark is removed from the command.

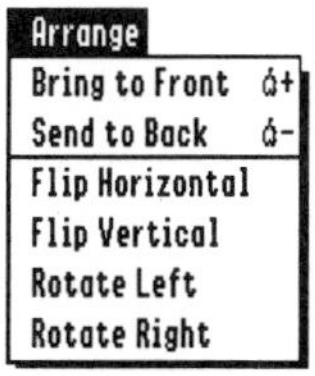

Go To Page: This command lets you display the specified page on the screen.

Set First Page: This command lets you specify the page number assigned to the first page in the document.

Ignore Master Page/Use Master Page: This command specifies that the current page should not display the text, graphics, or guides stored on the master page. Select the command again to return master page information to the current page.

Left/Right Master Pages: This lets you create separate master pages for left pages and right pages in your document. To return to a single master page for all document pages, select the command again.

Figure 13-9
Arrange menu

The Arrange menu

The commands on the Arrange menu let you change the arrangement and direction of objects on the screen. (See Figure 13-9.)

Bring to Front: This command moves the selected object in front of any overlapping objects.

Send to Back: This command moves the selected object behind any overlapping object.

Flip Horizontal: This command flips the selected object left-to-right on the screen. The object is flipped horizontally, producing a mirror-image version of the object.

Flip Vertical: This command flips the selected object top-to-bottom. The object is flipped vertically, producing an upside-down version of the object.

Rotate Left: This command rotates the selected object 90° to the left.

Rotate Right: This command rotates the selected object 90° to the right.

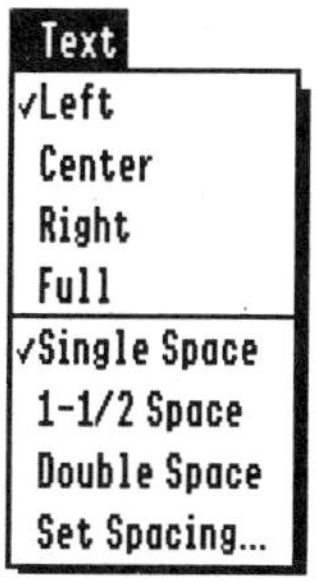

Figure 13-10
Text menu

The Text menu

The commands on the Text menu let you control the alignment and spacing of text in text objects. (See Figure 13-10.)

Font
| Choose Font... |
| Courier |
| √Geneva |
| Helvetica |
| Monaco |
| New York |
| Shaston |
| Times |
| Venice |

Figure 13-11
Font menu

Size
| 8 Point |
| **9 Point** |
| **10 Point** |
| √**12 Point** |
| 14 Point |
| 18 Point |
| 20 Point |
| 24 Point |
| Larger   ⚫> |
| Smaller   ⚫< |

Figure 13-12
Size menu

Style
| √Plain   ⚫T |
| **Bold**   ⚫B |
| *Italic*   ⚫I |
| Underline   ⚫U |
| Outline |
| Shadow |
| Superscript ⚫H |
| Subscript   ⚫L |
| UPPERCASE |
| lowercase |
| Title |

Figure 13-13
Style menu

Left: This command aligns selected text in a text object against the left margin of the object.

Center: This command centers selected text in a text object within the margins of the object.

Right: This command aligns selected text in a text object against the right margin of the object.

Full: This command aligns selected text in a text object against both the left margin and right margins of the object.

Single Space: This command displays selected text in a text object with single spaces between lines.

1 1/2 Space: This command displays selected text in a text object with one and one-half spaces between lines.

Double Space: This command displays selected text in a text object with two spaces between lines.

Set Spacing: This command lets you specify the height (in points) of the spaces used for each line. (There are 72 points per inch.)

The Font menu

The Font menu includes the Choose Font command and a list of available fonts. (See Figure 13-11.) The menu is used to select the font used to display selected text. The use of the Font menu and the Choose Font command was discussed in Chapter 5, Working with Word Processing Documents.

The Size menu

The Size menu includes a list of available font sizes, as well as the Larger and Smaller commands. (See Figure 13-12.) The menu is used to select the size of the font used to display selected text. The use of the Size menu is discussed in Chapter 5, Working with Word Processing Documents.

The Style menu

The Style menu includes a list of available text styles: Bold, Italic, Underline, Outline, Shadow, Superscript, Subscript, Uppercase, lowercase, and Title. (See Figure 13-13.) This menu is used to set the style used to display selected text. The use of the menu is discussed in Chapter 5, Working with Word Processing Documents.

The Color menu

The Color menu displays the sixteen current colors and the Edit Colors command. (See Figure 13-14.) It controls the color used to display selected text. The use of the Edit Colors command is discussed in Appendix D, Using the Edit Colors Command.

The Window menu

The Window menu lists the currently open windows and the Clipboard. The use of this menu is discussed in Chapter 3, AppleWorks GS Common Commands.

Orienting yourself in the document

When you create a new page layout document, you see the upper-left corner of the first blank page in the document.

At the bottom of the screen are page icons labeled "M" and "1." The page icon labeled "M" represents a master page, and the page icon labeled "1" represents the first page in the document.

The page icon labeled "1" is highlighted. That means that you are currently viewing Page 1 of the document in the window. As you view pages on the screen, the icon for the current page on the screen is always highlighted.

Scroll bars are displayed at the right side and bottom of the window. The scroll bars are used to move different parts of the current page into view. (The scroll bars are not used to move to different pages; to display a different page on the screen, you must click on one of the page icons to select the page that you want to display.)

Figure 13-14
Color menu

Seeing the entire page

A good way to begin working with the page layout document is to get an idea about the working area of the entire page. The rulers at the top and left edge of the screen indicate the size of the area displayed, but it is useful to visualize the entire page.

• **To see the entire page, select the Fit in Window command on the Options menu.**

The scale of the document on the screen is changed, and the entire page is displayed on the screen. The current reduced scale is indicated by the rulers; when the full page is displayed, the scale on the rulers is adjusted to reflect the reduced scale. (See Figure 13-15.)

Using this view, you can preview the appearance of the entire page. This will be very useful after you place text and graphics on the page.

You can also perform some editing operations in this reduced view. You can select objects, move objects, and resize objects in full-page view. You can't edit text, however, in this view.

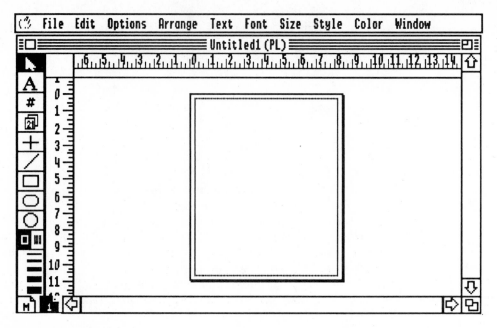

Figure 13-15 Full page view

Note: *If you resize the document window with the Size box, the scale of the display is adjusted again. The document window continues to show the full-page view of the document. For example, if you use the Size box to make the document window much smaller, the size of the page is reduced as well, so that you can still see the full page in the smaller document window.*

Displaying the page actual size

After you have previewed the appearance of the full page, you can again display the page in actual size.

- **To return to actual size, select the Actual Size command in the Options menu.**

  The original view of the page is restored, and you can continue to work on the page.

Setting up the pages in the document

The Page Setup command on the File menu controls the size and orientation of printed pages in a document. It's important that the blank pages on the screen accurately reflect the final printed pages, so it's important to use the Page Setup command to set up blank pages correctly on the screen before beginning your layout.

To set up the blank pages correctly:

1   **Select the Choose Printer command on the File menu.**

The Choose Printer dialog box appears. Specify the correct printer and port and click the OK button. (For more information on this command, see Chapter 3, AppleWorks GS Common Commands.)

2   **Choose the Page Setup command on the File menu.**

The Page Setup dialog box appears. Enter your desired settings and click the OK button. (For more information on this command, see Chapter 3, AppleWorks GS Common Commands.)

After you complete the Page Setup dialog box, you are returned to the page layout document, and the display is adjusted to reflect your settings.

For example, the default Page Setup orientation specifies vertical pages, and the page layout document will display vertical pages on the screen.

If you change this setting and specify horizontal orientation on the Page Setup dialog box, the page layout document will display horizontal pages on the screen.

Working with page icons

At the bottom of the page are the page icons. The page icon that is highlighted represents the page that is currently displayed on the screen. Thus, if the page icon number "1" is highlighted, Page 1 in the document is displayed.

When you begin a new document, a special page icon labeled "M" is displayed to the left of the numbered page icons. This special icon represents the Master Page, which is discussed later in this chapter.

Adding blank pages to the document

When you open a new document, only one numbered page icon is displayed. That means the application is only expecting to work with one page in the document.

Most documents will contain more than one page, so you should add more blank pages to the document. You can always add more blank pages later, so it isn't necessary to add the precise number of pages that you may eventually need.

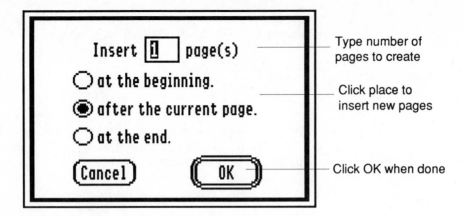

Insert ☐ page(s) ———— Type number of
                        pages to create

○ at the beginning.
                    ———— Click place to
◉ after the current page.   insert new pages

○ at the end.

(Cancel)   ((OK)) ———— Click OK when done

Figure 13-16   Insert pages dialog box

To add pages to the document:

1 **Select the Insert Page(s) command on the Edit menu.**

The Insert Pages dialog box appears (see Figure 13-16).

2 **Type the number of new blank pages to insert and click the place in the document where you want to insert the new pages.**

The maximum number of pages in a page layout document is 99.

3 **Click the OK button.**

New numbered icons that represent the new pages are added to the page icons at the bottom of the window.

Only five numbered page icons can be displayed at one time. If the document includes more than five pages, five numbered icons are displayed, with left and right arrows displayed around the five numbered icons. Click the left arrow to display icons with lower numbers, or click the right arrow to display icons with larger numbers.

You can always add more blank pages later while you are working with your document.

Displaying a specific page

You will work on your document one page at a time. In other applications, you use the scroll bars in the document window to move through a document, but the page layout application uses a different approach. You can use the scroll bars to display the parts of a page that don't fit on the screen at any time, but you use the page icons to move from one page to another.

To display a specific page:

1. **Move the arrow pointer to the bottom of the screen.**

2. **If your document contains more than five pages, the icon that represents the page may not be displayed. Click the left arrow to display page icons with lower numbers, or click the right arrow to display page icons with larger numbers.**

3. **Click the page icon that is numbered with the page number that you want to display.**

The contents of the specified page are shown on the screen.

Note: *When you begin a new document, all of the new pages are blank. Clicking on any of the page icons displays the same blank screen.*

Using the Go To Page command

As the number of pages in a document increase, it becomes less convenient to use the page icons to display a specific page. The Go To Page command lets you quickly jump to a distant page:

To use the Go To Page command:

1. **Choose the Go To Page command on the Options menu.**

The Go To Page dialog box appears (see Figure 13-17).

2. **Type the page number that you want to display, and click the OK button.**

The specified page is displayed, and that page icon is displayed and selected at the bottom of the window.

Specifying the first page number

When you open a new document, the first page is numbered "1." You may have a reason to use a different number for the first page. For instance, you may be producing a larger document in the form of several smaller page layout documents, so you may want to use a number like "15" or "35" for the first page of the current document.

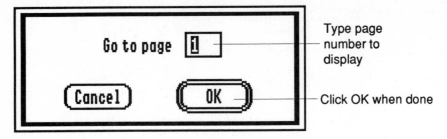

Type page
number to
display

Click OK when done

Figure 13-17 Go to page dialog box

To specify a page number for the first page:

1   **Choose the Set First Page Number command on the Options menu.**

A dialog box appears (see Figure 13-18).

2   **Type the first page number to use in the current document, and click the OK button.**

The number that you entered now becomes the first page number of the document, and the page icons are renumbered at the bottom of the screen.

Removing pages from the document

As you work with your document, you may want to remove an entire page or a range of pages from the document.
To delete pages from the document:

1   **Choose the Delete Page(s) command on the Edit menu.**

The Delete Pages dialog box appears (see Figure 13-19).

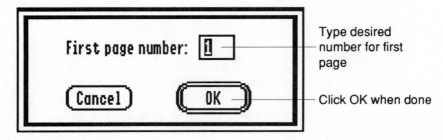

Type desired
number for first
page

Click OK when done

Figure 13-18 Set first page number

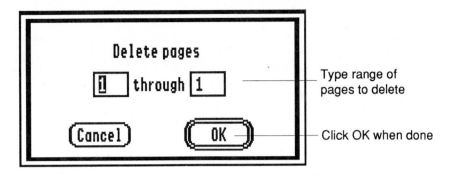

Type range of
pages to delete

Click OK when done

Figure 13-19 Delete pages dialog

2 **Type the number of the first page to delete and the number of the last page to delete.**

All of the pages between the first page number and the second page number will be removed, including those two pages. If only one page should be removed, type the same number in both input boxes.

3 **Click the OK button.**

The specified pages are removed from the document, and the page icons at the bottom of the window are adjusted to reflect the changes.

Thinking about master pages

What is a master page?

A master page contains information that you want to appear on other pages in your document. A master page is created the same way as all other document pages, but anything that you place on a master page appears on other pages as well.

There are three kinds of information that you might want to display on other pages:

- Text. You can place text on a master page, and it is automatically displayed on other pages in the document. You can also place special text on a master page, including the current page number and the current date.
- Graphics. You can place graphics on a master page, and they are automatically displayed on other pages.
- Guides. You can place margin guides or column guides on a master page, and they appear on other pages.

You can create either a single master page or left and right master pages. If you create a single master page, any element placed on the master page appears on all other pages of the document. If you create left and right master pages, elements that are placed on the left master page appear on each left page in the document, and elements that are placed on the right master page appear on each right page of the document.

If you wish, you can choose to have any specific page in your document ignore the information stored on the master pages.

General plan for using master pages

Let's think about how master pages might generally be used. In general the plan would be

1. Think about the information that you want to display on all other pages in the document. Think about whether you want to display some information on all pages, some information on all left pages, or some information on all right pages.
2. Decide if you need one master page, or separate left and right master pages. If you create one master page, the information that you place on the master page appears on all other pages. Separate left and right master pages let you place information that will appear on all left pages or on all right pages.
3. If you need separate left and right master pages, choose the Left/Right Master Pages command on the Options menu to create those pages.
4. Enter the desired text, graphics, or guides on each master page.

Master page icon

A special page icon labeled 'M' is displayed at the left of the page icons. This icon represents the Master Page. (See Figure 13-20.)

- **To display the master page, click the Master Page icon.**

The master page is displayed in the document window, and you can place text, graphics, or guides on this page. Any information that you enter on this page is automatically entered at that same location on every other page.

This lets you create headers or footers for each page or enter any other information that you want to display on every page.

Creating left and right master pages

The Master Page icon lets you create a page that contains information that you want to display on every page of the document.

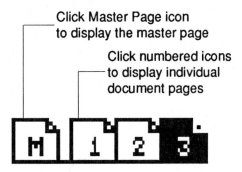

Click Master Page icon
to display the master page

Click numbered icons
to display individual
document pages

Figure 13-20 Master Page icon

If you want to display some information on every left page in the document and different information on every right page in the document, you must create separate left and right master pages.

To create left and right master pages:

1 **Select the Left/Right Master Pages command from the Options menu.**

The page icon labeled "M" is removed from the bottom of the screen; it is replaced by two icons labeled "L" and "R." These two icons represent the left master page and right master page. (See Figure 13-21.)

The Left/Right Master Pages command is replaced by Single Master on the Options menu.

Any information that you have already entered on the master page is automatically transferred to the right master page.

To display left and right master pages:

1 **Click the page icon labeled "L".**

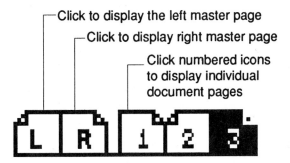

Click to display the left master page

Click to display right master page

Click numbered icons
to display individual
document pages

Figure 13-21 Left, Right Master Page icons

The Left Master Page appears. You can place text, graphics, or guides on this page, and that information is displayed on all left pages.

2   **Click on the page icon labeled "R".**

The Right Master Page appears. You can place text, graphics, or guides on this page, and that information is displayed on all right pages.

Ignoring the master page information

As you work on individual pages in your document, you may not want a specific page to show the information that is controlled by the master page. You can always let a specific page ignore the master page information.

To let a document page ignore the master page:

1   **Click the numbered page icon that represents the page that you want to display.**

The selected page is displayed on the screen.

2   **Select the Ignore Master Page command from the Options menu.**

All master page text, graphics, and guides are removed from this specific document page. The Ignore Master Page command is replaced by Use Master on the Options menu.

To restore the master page information to this specific page, select the Use Master command.

Setting margins and column guides

A good place to begin entering information is to place margin guides and column guides.

Guides are used to help you align your text and graphics correctly on a page. Guides are simply that: guides. They do not control your layout, but they do indicate where margin and column settings occur. You can place your text and graphics anywhere on the document page, regardless of the location of the guides.

There are two kinds of guides that you may use:

- **Margin guides** are used to mark the top, bottom, left, and right margins on a page.
- **Column guides** are used to define and mark columns on a page.

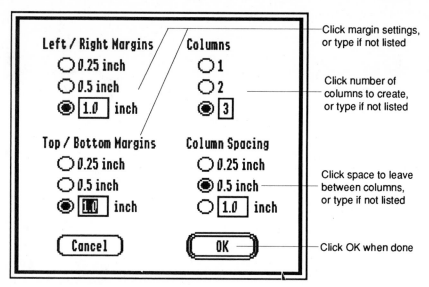

Figure 13-22 Set Guides dialog

Remember: Guides do not prevent you from placing text or graphics anywhere on a page. They simply help you place your text and graphics correctly.

If you set guides on a master page, the column and margin guides are added to every page in the document. If you set guides on a page that is not a master page, the column and margin guides are displayed on the current page only.

If you wish, you can make your guides magnetic. That means that any object placed near a guide is attracted to the guide and automatically moves over and aligns with the guide. (The object "snaps" to the nearby guide.) This helps you align several objects easily.

Entering margin and column guides

Margin guides define the top, bottom, left, and right margins on a page, and column guides define columns on a page.

You can enter margin and column guides manually (see below), but the page layout application provides a command that lets you set both kinds of guide with a single command.

To enter margin and column guides:

1   **Choose the Set Guides command on the Options menu.**

The Set Guides dialog box appears (see Figure 13-22).

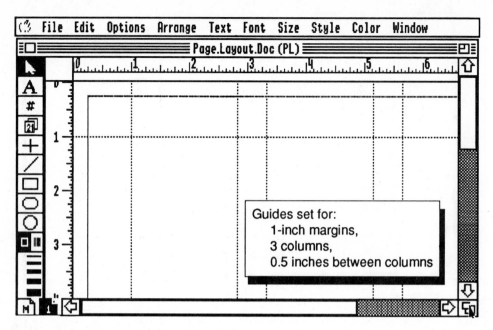

Figure 13-23 Example of margin and column guides

The callout box in the figure reads:

> Guides set for:
> 1-inch margins,
> 3 columns,
> 0.5 inches between columns

The menu bar shows: File Edit Options Arrange Text Font Size Style Color Window

The window title is: Page.Layout.Doc (PL)

2. **Click your desired settings for top, bottom, left, and right margins.**

You can click one of the predefined margin settings, or you can type different settings into the input bars.

3. **Click the number of columns that you want to use on the page.**

4. **Select the number of inches to place between columns.**

You can click one of the predefined settings or type a different number of inches in the input bar.

5. **Click the OK button.**

Your specified guides are displayed as dotted lines on the current page. For example, if you specify top and bottom margins of 1 inch, 3 columns, and 0.5 inch between columns, AppleWorks GS displays the guides like this (see Figure 13-23).

If the current page is a master page, the guides will automatically be displayed on the pages controlled by the master page.

Placing guides manually

You can use the Set Guides command to specify margin and column settings, and the page layout application displays the guides according to your specifications.

You can also place guides manually in the document.

To manually place a guide:

1 **Move the arrow pointer to one of the rulers.**

Move the pointer to the top ruler if you want to create a horizontal guide. Move the pointer to the ruler on the left side of the window to create a vertical guide.

2 **When the tip of the arrow touches the ruler scale, hold the mouse button down.**

The arrow changes to a double-arrow.

3 **Drag the double-arrow from the ruler.**

As you drag the double-arrow in the document, a dotted line that represents the new guide follows the arrow. (See Figure 13-24.)

4 **Drag the guide to the desired location on the page and release the mouse button.**

Notice that the guide extends into the ruler. This lets you place the guide at a specific location. (For instance, if you want a guide placed four inches from the top of the document, the ruler lets you place the guide exactly at that point.)

Moving a guide

After you have placed margin and column guides on a page, you may want to adjust the position of a guide later.

To move a guide:

1 **Place the tip of the arrow pointer on the guide that you want to move, and hold down the mouse button.**

The arrow changes to the double-arrow pointer.

2 **Hold the mouse button down, and drag the guide to a new location. (See Figure 13-25.)**

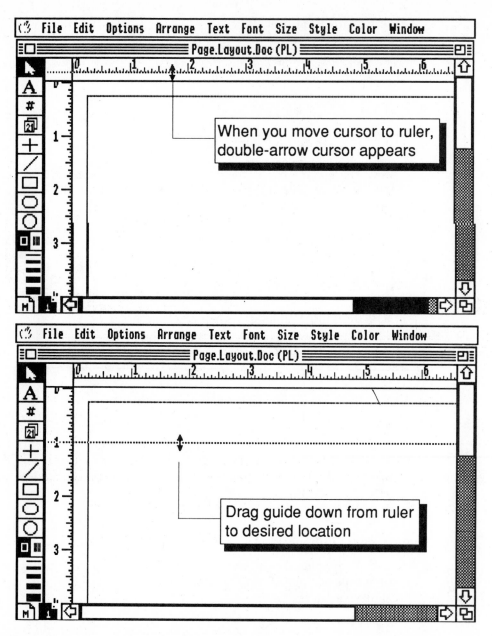

When you move cursor to ruler, double-arrow cursor appears

Drag guide down from ruler to desired location

Figure 13-24 Dragging a guide from top ruler

As you drag a guide, the movement does not affect the placement of text or graphics on the page.

Guides are simply guides: they do not control the placement of the objects. They are simply provided for your guidance as you lay out the page.

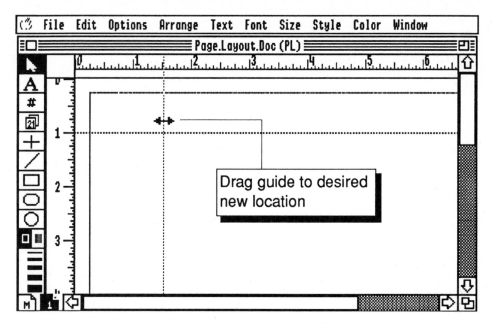

Figure 13-25 You can guide existing guides to a new location

Making guides magnetic

As you place text and graphics on the page, you often want to align the left edges or top edges of objects. For example, you usually want the top edges of two adjacent columns of text to be aligned at the same level.

Magnetic guides help you align objects precisely. When guides are made magnetic, objects automatically are snapped toward the nearest guide. This keeps adjacent objects aligned with each other.

• **To make guides magnetic, choose the Magnetic Guides command from the Options menu.**

All guides are now magnetic, and any object placed near a guide is automatically snapped to the guide.

When you select Magnetic Guides, the command is checked on the menu. To return your guides to their original "nonmagnetic" state, select Magnetic Guides again. The checkmark is removed, and you can now place your objects wherever you like on the page.

Locking guides

You might want to temporarily lock the guides in place, so they are not moved accidentally.

- **To lock guides, select the Lock Guides command on the Options menu.**

Guides are now temporarily locked in place, and you cannot adjust the position of the guides. The Lock Guides command is replaced on the menu by Unlock Guides.

You can select Unlock Guides at any point to release the guides and let you move them again.

Hiding guides

To review the appearance of your document without the dotted lines representing guides, you can hide the guides temporarily.

- **To hide guides, select the Hide Guides command from the Options menu.**

The guides are temporarily removed, and Hide Guides is replaced by Show Guides on the menu.

If you select Show Guides, the guides are restored on the page.

Saving the page layout document

This chapter has introduced the page layout application, and the next chapter will show you how to place text and graphics on the pages of your document.

After you've worked on a page layout document, be sure to save a copy of your work. Remember that AppleWorks GS provides two commands to save your work: the Save As command and the Save command.

Refer to Chapter 3 for a discussion of the Save and Save As commands.

Printing your page layout document

After you place text and graphics on pages in your document, you will want to print a copy of the document.

In this application, you should have chosen the Choose Printer command and the Page Setup command before beginning work. Those two commands are used to set up the blank pages correctly.

To print your page layout document, it is only necessary to select the Print command on the File menu. After you complete the settings on the Print dialog box and click the OK button, your document is printed.

(For more information about printing, see the Choose Printer command, Page Setup command, and Print command in Chapter 3: AppleWorks GS Common Commands.)

The next step

Once you have set up margins and guides and created a basic set of pages for your document, you are ready to place text and graphics on each page. Chapter 14 discusses how to work with text on each page, and Chapter 15 shows you how to use graphics on each page.

Working with Text in Page Layout

About this chapter

After you've created a blank page layout document and placed any desired margin and column guides, you are ready to place text and graphics on the page to produce a finished document.

You can place text in the document by creating text objects. You can create a blank text object and enter text into the object, or you can create text objects by importing text documents created by AppleWorks GS or other programs.

After you create text objects, you can move or resize the objects, and arrange your text on a page as you wish.

You can also place special text, such as the current page number and the current date, in the document at any desired location.

This chapter discusses how to work with text in a page layout document, including these topics:

- Creating a text object
- Entering text into a text object
- Selecting, moving, and resizing text objects
- Text streams and linked text objects
- Importing information from other applications
- Entering the date and page numbers

Adding text to a page

When you are ready to add text to a page in a page layout document, the text is added by creating text objects. A text object is a rectangular area that contains text, but can be selected, moved, and resized like a graphics object.

There are two ways to create text objects:

- You can create a blank text object on the page with the text tool. After a blank text object is created, you can enter text into the object by typing on the keyboard, copying information from the Clipboard, or importing text from other saved documents.
- If you import a document and you are not already working in a text object, text from the saved document is opened in a new text object.

As you enter text in a text object, you can format the text contained in the object using the same formatting commands that are available in the word processing application. As you work with the text object, you can also select the object, move it to a different location on the page, or change the size of the object.

Creating a blank text object

A blank text object is a rectangular area on the page where you can enter text. The object can easily be selected and moved or resized on the page.

To create a blank text object:

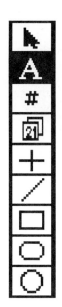

1   **Click the text tool on the tool palette. (See Figure 14-1.)**

When you move into the document, the cursor changes into the I-beam pointer.

2   **Place the I-beam cursor at one corner of a rectangular area where you want to place some text.**

3   **Hold down the mouse button and drag diagonally.**

As you drag, a rectangular text object is created on the page. (See Figure 14-2.) You don't need to be extremely precise about the size or location of the object, since you can move and resize the object later.

4   **Release the mouse button when the text object is drawn on the page.**

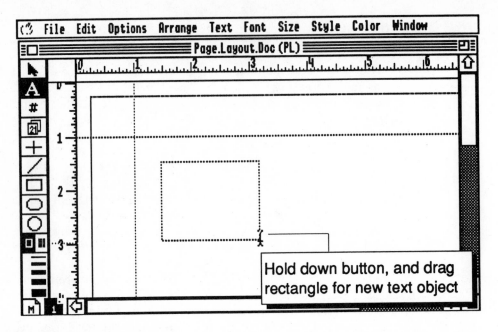

Figure 14-2 Text object on page

The text object is shown as a rectangle, and an insertion point appears in the corner of the object, waiting for you to enter text. (See Figure 14-3.)

The new text object can be moved and resized, as described below.

Tip: *You might want to display and print your text against a colored background. To create a colored background for your text, select a color from the Color menu before creating the text object. When you create the text object, the background of the object will be the selected color.*

Using guides to create a blank text object

The margin and column guides that you place on a page can be used to help you create a text object that fills a defined area. You can quickly create a blank text object that fills the area defined by guides.

1 **Click the text tool to select that tool.**

The cursor takes the form of an I-beam.

2 **Move the I-beam cursor into an area that is bordered by margin or column guides, and click anywhere in the area.**

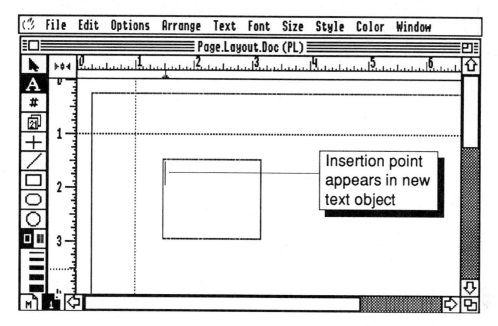

Figure 14-3   Insertion point appears in blank text object

A blank text object is automatically created that is defined by the guides that border the area. An insertion point appears at the upper-left corner of the object. (See Figure 14-4.)

The new text object extends to the nearest guides. If no guides are present on one border of the object, the object extends to the edge of the paper. If no guides have been placed anywhere on the page, the new text object extends to the four edges of the page.

Selecting a text object

A text object can be moved or resized after it is selected.
To select a text object:

1   **Click on the arrow pointer tool in the tool palette. (See Figure 14-5.)**

The arrow pointer is always used to select objects for action.

2   **Select the text object by clicking anywhere inside the object.**

After the text object is selected, handles appear at each corner. The handles are used to resize the text object. Two rounded tabs, called **link tabs**, are displayed at the top and bottom of the text object. (See Figure 14-6.) The link tabs are used to create linked text objects.

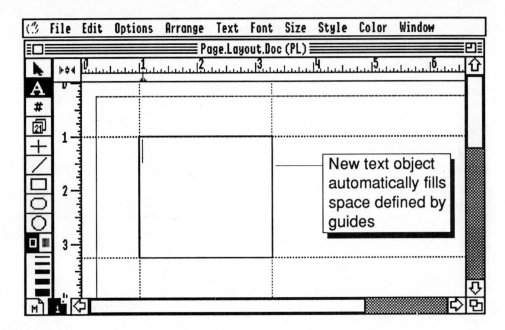

Figure 14-4 Blank text object defined by guides on page

Moving and resizing a text object

You can move or resize the text object using the handles on the selected object.

To move an object:

1. **Click the arrow pointer on the tool palette to select the arrow pointer.**

2. **Click the text object to select the text object.**

Handles and link tabs appear on the selected object.

3. **Move the arrow pointer anywhere inside the selected object.**

4. **Hold down the mouse button and drag the mouse.**

As you drag the mouse, the text object moves across the page. (See Figure 14-7.)

Figure 14-5
Arrow pointer

5. **Release the mouse button when the text object is placed in the desired new location.**

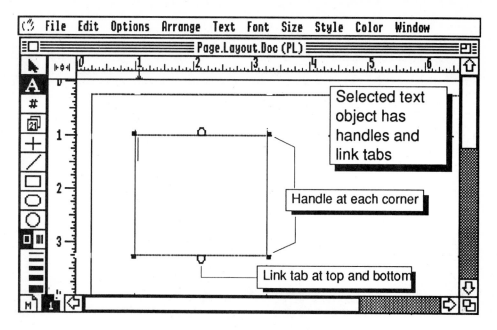

Figure 14-6 Selected text object

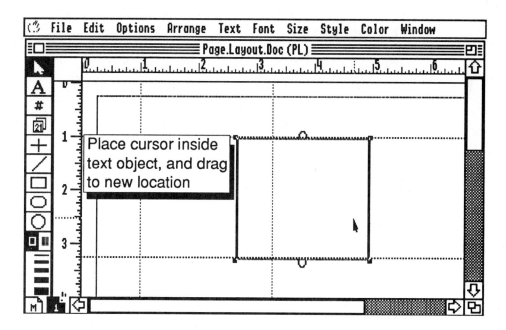

Figure 14-7 Text object can be dragged to a new location

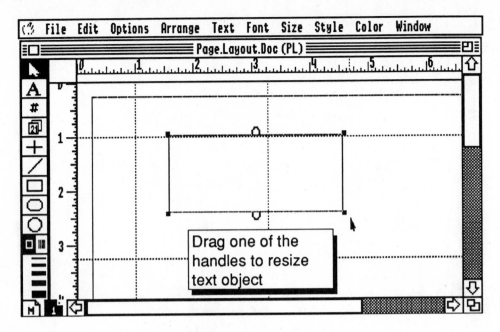

Figure 14-8 Drag one of the handles to resize a text object

To resize a text object:

1 **Select the text object.**

Handles and link tabs appear on the selected object.

2 **Move the arrow pointer to one of the handles at a corner of the object.**

3 **Hold down the mouse button and drag the handle.**

As you drag the handle, the text object is resized on the screen, but the size of the text itself is not changed. (See Figure 14-8.)

The handle is used to resize the object in the same way that the Size box is used to change the size of a window. For example, if you drag down on the lower right handle, the object lengthens. If you drag it to the right, the object widens. If you drag diagonally, both the length and width of the object changes.

Deleting a text object

You can easily remove a text object from the screen.

To delete a text object:

| 1 | Click on the arrow pointer tool to select the tool. |

| 2 | Click on the text object that you want to delete. |

Handles appear on the selected object.

| 3 | Press the Delete key. |

The object and any text contained in the object are removed from the screen.

Typing text into a text object

There are several ways to enter text into a text object: You can type text directly into the object, or you can copy or import existing text into the object.

One way to enter text into a text object is to type the text at the keyboard.

To type text into an object:

| 1 | Click the text tool to select that tool. |

| 2 | Click inside the text object. |

If there is no text in the object, an insertion point appears at the upper left corner of the object.

If there is text in the object, the insertion point appears at the end of the current text. (If you click in the middle of existing text, the insertion point appears at the location where you clicked.)

| 3 | Type text on the keyboard, and it appears at the insertion point. |

As you type, your text is wrapped at the right edge of the text object, so that your text remains inside the box defined by the object. (See Figure 14-9.)

If you type more text than the object can display, the extra text is remembered. All of the text that you type into the object is called the text stream for that object.

Seeing more text: resizing the object

If a text object contains more text than it can display, the rest of the text stream still exists. You simply have to make the adjustments needed to display the rest of the text stream.

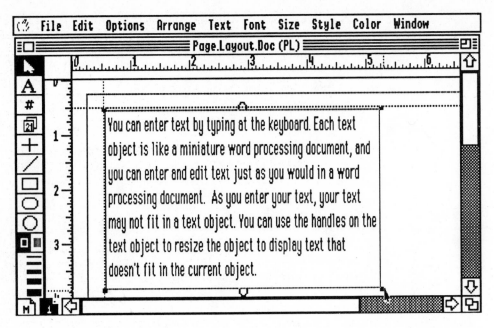

Figure 14-9 Typing text into a text object

[1] **Click the arrow pointer tool, and then select the text object.**

Handles appear at each corner of the selected object. (See Figure 14-10.)

[2] **Drag one of the handles to enlarge the object.**

You can drag the lower corners down or the upper corners up to lengthen the object. You could also drag the corner handles to widen the object. (See Figure 14-11.)

As you enlarge the object, the object readjusts to display as much of the text stream as possible in the new size of the object.

There is another way to display all of the text in a text stream. You can create a series of **linked text objects** to display the stream.

Seeing more text: linked text objects

You may not be able to make a single text object large enough to show all of the text in a text stream. In fact, you generally wouldn't want to make a single text object large enough to show a great deal of text.

Instead, you usually will want to create a number of text objects, arranged in columns or arranged around graphics on the page, with the

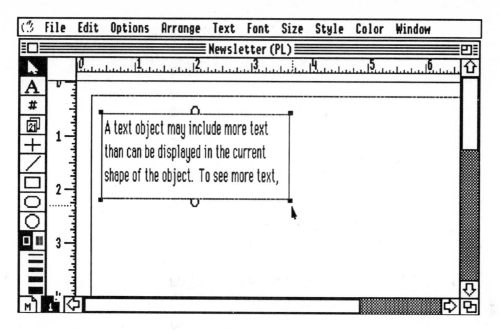

Figure 14-10   A text object might contain more text than can be displayed

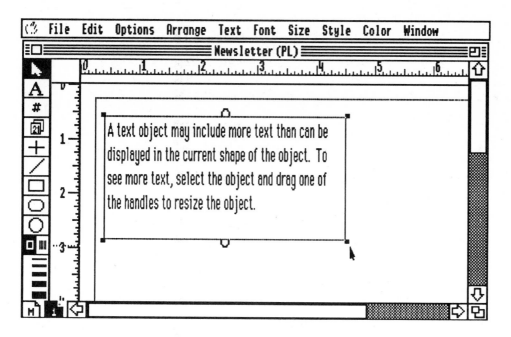

Figure 14-11   A text object can be resized to make text more visible

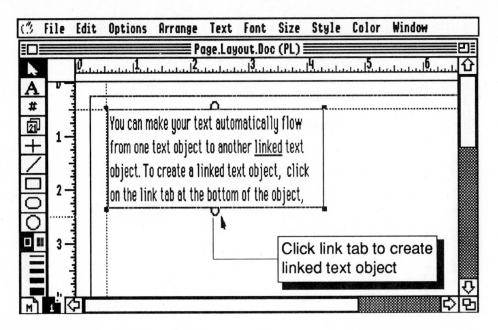

Figure 14-12 Selected text object with link tabs

text flowing from one of the text objects to another. When text flows from one text object to another, they are called linked text objects.

Linked text objects are a series of text objects where text flows automatically from one object to the next.

To create a linked text object:

1. Create a text object on the page.

You may choose to enter text into the object at this point, or you can enter text later.

2. Click on the arrow pointer tool, and click the text object to select it.

When the object is selected, handles and link tabs appear at the top and bottom of the object. The link tabs are used to create linked text objects. (See Figure 14-12.)

3. To create a new object linked to the bottom of this text object, click on the link tab at the bottom of the object.

An icon appears representing a small page of text. This is called the place icon. (See Figure 14-13.)

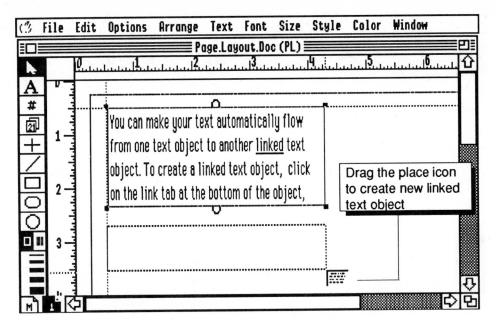

Figure 14-13 Place icon appears after selecting link tab

In the figure: menu bar reads "File Edit Options Arrange Text Font Size Style Color Window". Title bar reads "Page.Layout.Doc (PL)".

Text object contents:

You can make your text automatically flow from one text object to another <u>linked</u> text object. To create a linked text object, click on the link tab at the bottom of the object,

Callout box:

Drag the place icon to create new linked text object

---

4 **Drag the place icon diagonally to create a new text object.**

You can create a new object with a defined size by dragging a rectangle. If you wish, you can also simply click the place icon in an area defined by margin and column guides, and a text object is automatically created that fills the area defined by the nearest guides.

The new text object is now linked to the bottom of the previous text object Any text that did not fit into the previous object flows into the new object and is displayed. (See Figure 14-14.)

To show that the objects are linked, the link tab at the bottom of the previous object and the link tab at the top of the new object are marked with a plus sign.

Seeing still more text . . .

What if all of the text still isn't visible in the two linked text objects?
    You have several options:

- You can select either or both of the text objects and drag the handles to enlarge the objects until all of the text is shown.
- You can create additional linked text objects. Select the second text object, and click on the link tab at the bottom of the object. Drag the text icon to create a third object, and the text that didn't fit into the

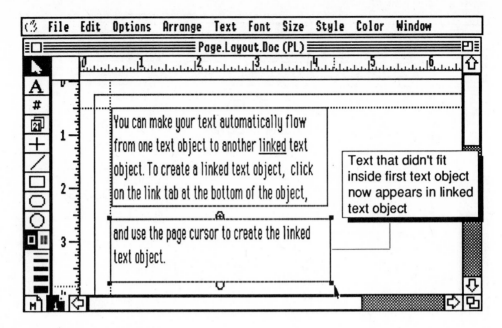

Figure 14-14 Text flows from one linked text object to next object

second object flows into this third object. You can add as many linked text objects as necessary.

Creating columns of text

Linked text objects can be used to create columns of text easily. The general plan to create columns of text would be

- Set column guides to mark the location of the desired columns.
- Create a text object that matches the dimensions of the first column. You can drag a rectangle on the screen, or simply click the text tool in the first column. When you click the text tool in a column, an object defined by the column guides and margin guides is automatically created.
- Click the link tab at the bottom of the first text object.
- Use the place icon to create a linked object in the next column.
- Click the link tab at the bottom of the second column object, and create any other necessary column objects.
- After the necessary linked columns have been created, you can return to the first object and enter text. It will automatically flow from the first object to the other linked text objects. (See Figure 14-15.)

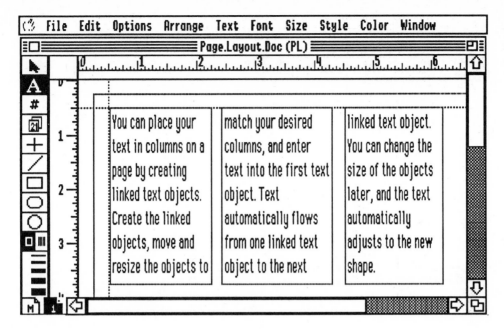

Figure 14-15 Demonstration of columns of text

Using the Clipboard to enter information

One way to enter text into a text object is to type the text at the keyboard. You can also enter information from other AppleWorks GS documents into an existing text object by copying the information from the Clipboard.

Placing information on the Clipboard

The Clipboard can be used to transfer a copy of information from one document to another, or from one location in a document to another location within the document.

To place information on the Clipboard, select the information that you want to transfer, select the Cut or Copy command on the Edit menu.

The selected information is placed on the Clipboard. You can now move to another location in the document or to a different document and use the Paste command to transfer the information from the Clipboard to a new location.

Copying information from the Clipboard

The Clipboard lets you easily bring text from other applications into a text object.

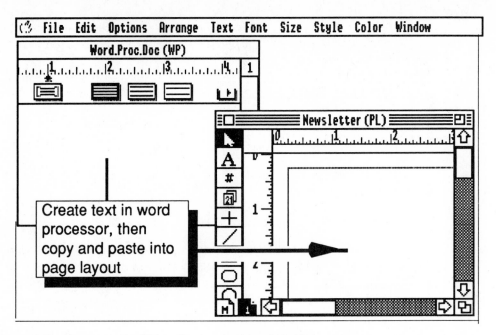

Figure 14-16   You can use the Clipboard to copy text into a text object

1. **Place selected information on the Clipboard.**

Remember that you can select information in other applications and use the Cut or Copy command to place selected information on the Clipboard. When you leave the other application and enter page layout, the information remains on the Clipboard.

2. **Select the text tool on the tool palette.**

3. **Click in the text object where you want to insert the information from the Clipboard.**

An insertion point appears at the location where you click.

4. **Choose the Paste command from the Edit menu.**

The information stored on the Clipboard is inserted at the location of the insertion point. (See Figure 14-16.)

What information can be copied from the Clipboard?

You can use the Clipboard to paste text information into a text object from other AppleWorks GS applications.

- If the information was copied from a word processing document, all formatting is copied and the text is displayed as it appeared in the word processing document.
- If the information was copied from a database, the information is displayed as a table that is similar to that seen in the database List view.

Database information is displayed in a special format: each field in a record is separated from the next field by a tab, and each record is separated from the next by a return character.

- If the information was copied from a spreadsheet, the information is displayed as a table, very similar to the display seen in the spreadsheet document.

Each spreadsheet cell in a row is separated from the next cell by a tab, and each row of information is separated from the next by a return character.

Using saved text documents in page layout

In addition to typing text into an object or copying text from the Clipboard, you can also use the contents of other saved documents in a page layout document.

There are two ways to use saved documents:

- You can import the contents of a saved text document into an existing text object.
- You can import the contents of a saved text document into its own text object.

Copying saved documents into an existing object

If you have created a text object, you may want to copy an existing saved document into that object. In a sense, you can "pour" the contents of a saved document into an existing text object at the current location of the insertion point.

To import text into an existing text object:

1. Select the text tool on the tool palette.

2. Click in the text object where you want to insert the information from a saved document.

An insertion point appears at the location where you click.

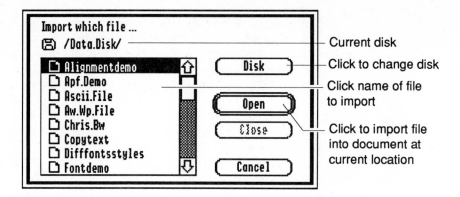

Figure 14-17 Import File dialog box

3 **Choose the Import File command from the File menu.**

The Import File dialog box appears (see Figure 14-17).

Select the desired file from the document list box. The contents of the file are inserted into the text object at the location of the insertion point.

For more information on Import File, see Chapter 3, AppleWorks GS Common Commands, and Chapter 18, Transferring Information.

Creating new objects from saved documents

Instead of copying the contents of a saved document into an existing object, you may want to simply create an entirely new object that contains the contents of a saved document.

Before performing this operation, be sure that there is no insertion point currently placed in a text object. If there is an insertion point that is currently active, the document that is imported will be copied at the location of the insertion point, as described in the preceding section.

To import a document into its own text object:

1 **Choose the Import File command from the File menu.**

The Import File dialog box appears. Select the desired file from the document list box.

After you select the desired file, you are returned to the page layout document, and the place icon representing a small page of text appears.

2 **Move the place icon to the location where you want to place the new text object.**

3 **Create the new text object by dragging the place icon diagonally on the screen.**

If you wish, you can click the place icon on the screen, and a text object is automatically created that extends to the nearest guides on the page.

The contents of the document are displayed in the new text object. You may need to resize the text object or create linked text objects to display all of the text in the document.

What documents can be imported?

The documents that can be imported on a specific storage disk are automatically displayed when you select the Import File command.

The page layout application can import the following saved documents:

- AppleWorks GS word processing documents
- Classic AppleWorks word processing files
- MultiScribe GS documents
- Files saved in ASCII text format

When a document is imported, all formatting information is imported. However, the size of the text object may alter the display of the document. You can move or resize the document, create linked text objects to display the entire contents of the file, or use any of the usual text-editing commands to make changes in the text.

Formatting text: rulers and fonts

Text objects can be formatted

As you type text into a text object or copy text into a text object, the ruler displayed at the top of the window is changed (see Figure 14-18):

- A tab well is displayed to the left of the ruler. This tab well contains icons for left tabs, decimal tabs, and right tabs.
- An indentation marker is displayed on the ruler that marks the amount of space that the first line of the current paragraph is indented from the left edge of the object.

Each text object can be considered a miniature version of a word processing document. Each paragraph in the text object can be formatted in much the same way that word processing documents can be formatted.

You can set the amount of space that text should be indented from the left edge of a text object, set tabs for use within each paragraph. You can change the font, size, style, or color of selected text in an object. You can also set the spacing and alignment for each paragraph in an object.

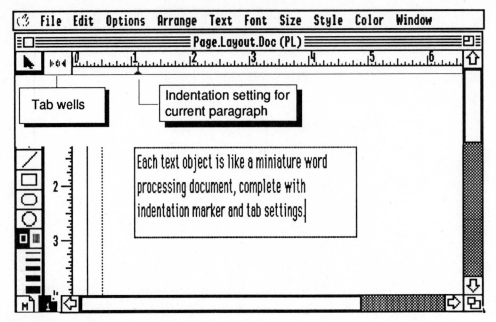

Figure 14-18 Indentation marker and tabs for text object

Setting indentation

When you click in a text object, the ruler displays an indentation marker. This indentation marker sets the amount of space that the first line of the current paragraph is indented.

You can adjust that marker to specify the amount of space that text should be indented from the left edge of the object.

To set the indentation marker:

1   **Click the text tool to select that tool.**

2   **Select the text in an object that you want to format.**

To format a single paragraph, click the I-beam cursor anywhere in the paragraph. (See Figure 14-19.)

To format the entire text stream, click the I-beam cursor in the text object and then choose the Select All command on the Edit menu.

To select more than one adjacent paragraphs, click in the first paragraph and drag down through the adjacent paragraphs to highlight the paragraphs.

3   **Move the cursor to touch the indentation marker.**

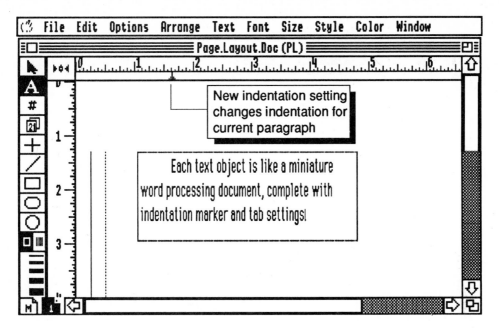

Figure 14-19 Setting indentation for text object

When it touches the indentation marker, the cursor takes the shape of the arrow pointer.

| 4 | **Drag the indentation marker to the desired location on the ruler.** |

The selected text is adjusted to match the new setting. The first line of each selected paragraph is indented to match the setting.

Setting tabs

When you click in a text object, the ruler displays any tabs that are in effect for the object. You can set new tabs or move existing tabs on the ruler.

The tab settings are made in the same way that tabs are adjusted in a word processing document.

To set tabs in a text object:

| 1 | **Click the text tool to select that tool.** |

| 2 | **Select the text in an object where you want tabs to apply.** |

Tab settings are paragraph-based. That means that each paragraph can have its own tab settings.

To set tabs in a single paragraph, click the I-beam cursor anywhere in the paragraph.

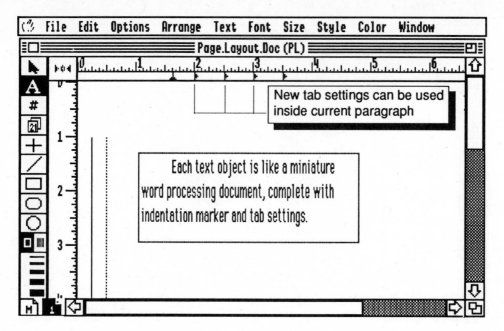

Figure 14-20 Setting tabs for text object

To set the same tabs for the entire text stream, click the I-beam cursor in the text object and then choose the Select All command on the Edit menu.

To set the same tabs for more than one adjacent paragraphs, click in the first paragraph and drag down through the adjacent paragraphs to highlight the paragraphs.

3 Move the cursor to the tab wells, and drag the first tab that you want to use from a well.

You can use left tabs (where text begins at the tab setting and extends to the left of the setting), decimal tabs (where the decimal point of numbers are aligned at the tab) or right tabs (where the right edge of text is aligned with the tab).

4 Place the desired tab at the desired location on the ruler. (See Figure 14-20.)

Once a tab is placed on the ruler, you can always move it easily.

To move any existing tab, move the cursor to the tab on the ruler, and drag the setting to the right or left to a new position.

To remove a tab, simply drag the tab icon down off the ruler.

Changing spacing and alignment

The spacing and alignment of text is set in much the same way as they are set in a word processing document.

To change spacing and alignment:

1 **Click the text tool to select that tool.**

2 **Select the text in an object that you want to format.**

Spacing and alignment settings are paragraph-based. That means that each paragraph can have its own tab settings.

To format a single paragraph, click the I-beam cursor anywhere in the paragraph.

To format the entire text stream, click the I-beam cursor in the text object and then choose the Select All command on the Edit menu.

To format more than one adjacent paragraphs, click in the first paragraph and drag down through the adjacent paragraphs to highlight the paragraphs.

3 **Select the desired settings from the Text menu.**

You can select single, 1 1/2, or double spacing for selected text. You can select left, center, right, or full justification for alignment. (See Figure 14-21.)

You may also select the Set Spacing command on the Text menu to determine the number of points to use for each line. This is known as **leading**. This lets you control line spacing much more precisely than using simple double spacing. The Set Spacing command lets you display your text on lines that are slightly larger than the text. This display gives your document a more professional appearance.

Changing fonts, sizes, styles, and color

Each text object is similar to a small word processing document, and you can control the fonts, sizes, styles, and colors of your text using the standard word processing procedures.

To change the text display:

1 **Click the text tool to select that tool.**

2 **Select the text in an object that you want to change.**

Highlight the text that you want to change by dragging the text tool over the desired text.

To select the entire text stream, click the I-beam cursor anywhere in the object, and then choose the Select All command on the Edit menu.

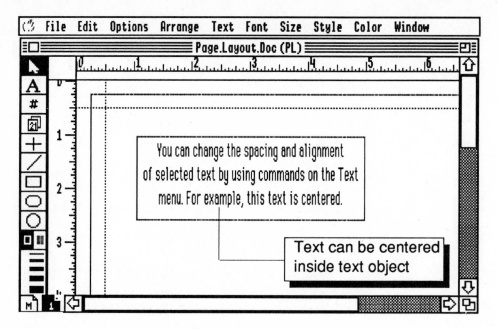

Figure 14-21 New spacing and alignment for text

3 **Select the desired settings from the Font, Size, Style, and Color menus.**

As you make each selection, the highlighted text reflects your choice. (See Figure 14-22.)

Special text items: page number and date

The tool palette contains two special icons: one for page numbers and one for the current date. These icons let you place the current page number or the current date at any location in the document.

You can place the date or page number on specific pages in the document. You can also place the date or page number on a master page; in that case, the correct date or page number is automatically displayed on other pages in the document.

Displaying the page number

The tool palette includes a special page number icon that can be used to display the current page number on any page. (See Figure 14-23.)

To display the current page number:

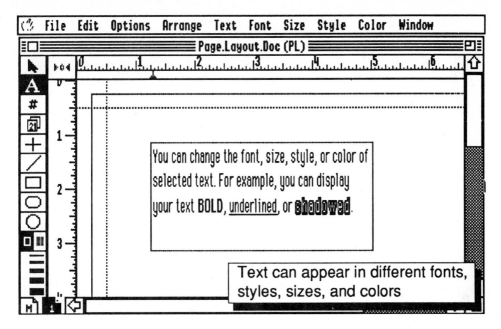

Figure 14-22   New fonts, sizes, styles for text

1   **Click the page number icon.**

The cursor takes the shape of a small number sign.

2   **Move the cursor to the location where you want to place the page number of the current page.**

3   **Click the location where you want to display the page number.**

When you click the icon, the page number of the current page appears where you clicked. (See Figure 14-24.)

If you click the page number icon on a master page, the correct page number appears automatically on other pages in the document. If you click the page number on a numbered page, the page number appears only on that page.

Figure 14-23
Page number
icon

Displaying the date

The tool palette includes a special date icon to display the current date on any page in the document. (See Figure 14-25.)

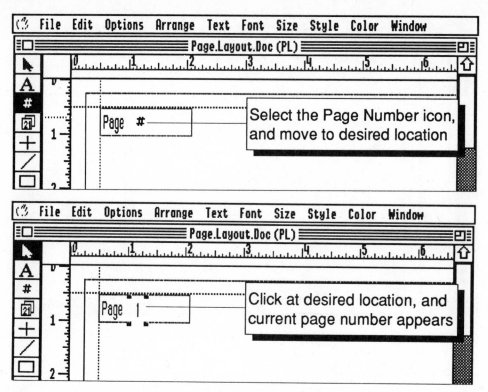

Figure 14-24 Click the page icon where you want to display the page number

Figure 14-25
Date icon

To display the current date:

1. **Click the date icon.**

The cursor takes the shape of a small calendar page.

2. **Move the cursor to the location where you want to place the current date.**

3. **Click the location where you want to display the date.**

When you click the icon, the current date is read from the clock inside your Apple IIGS, and the date appears where you clicked. (See Figure 14-26.)

If you place the date on a master page, the date appears automatically on other pages in the document. If you place the date on a numbered page, the date appears only on that page.

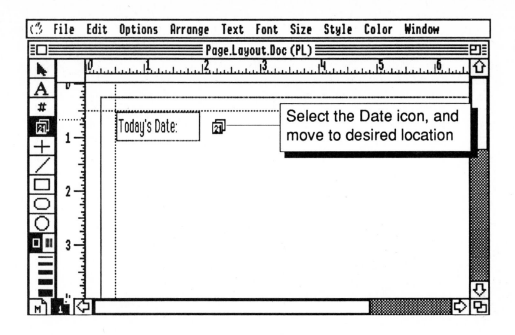

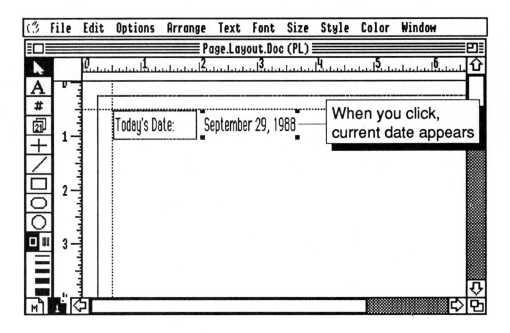

Figure 14-26 Click the date icon where you want to display the current date

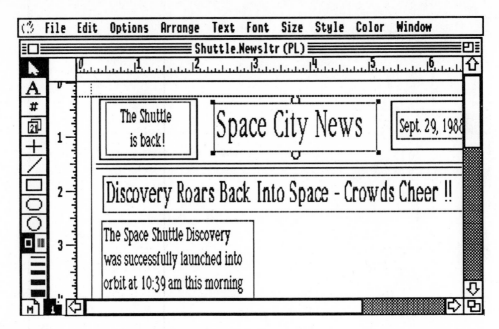

Figure 14-27 You need to add graphics to finish a document

The next step

After you have placed text on the page you could save and print the document — but graphics would add an important additional element to the document.

For example, Figure 14-27 shows a newsletter with an interesting design, but a graphic of a shuttle spacecraft would improve it a lot! In Chapter 15 we will discuss how to import graphics into a document and combine graphics with text to produce a professional-looking finished document.

Before moving to the next chapter, don't forget to save your work with the Save As command. (Refer to Chapter 3 for more information about saving your document.)

Working with Graphics in Page Layout

About this chapter

The page layout application lets you combine text with graphics to produce a completed document.

This chapter describes how graphics can be imported from other AppleWorks GS documents and other applications. It also shows you how to use the page layout drawing tools on the tool palette.

The topics in this chapter include

- Using graphics in page layout
- Using the Clipboard to import graphics
- Using Control-drag to copy graphics
- Importing saved graphics
- Moving graphics objects
- Resizing graphics objects
- Rearranging graphics objects
- Adding graphics with the draw tools

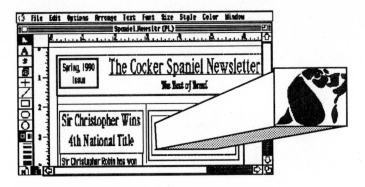

Figure 15-1 A completed document uses both text and graphics

Using graphics in page layout

Page layout lets you combine text and graphics in a single document. While you can create a page layout document without graphics, graphics help you present a much more pleasing and professional document. (See Figure 15-1.)

In many ways, using graphics is much easier than using text, since there is no question of creating new graphics objects or linked objects with graphics. In addition, using graphics objects in a page layout document is very similar to using similar objects in a graphics document.

Typical graphics operations

When you use graphics in a page layout document, these are some of the most important operations that you would perform:

- Bringing graphics objects into the document. The first step in using graphics is transferring a copy of the graphic to a specific page. You can transfer graphics from the AppleWorks GS graphics application, or you can use graphics created and saved from other programs.
- Placing the objects in an appropriate location. You can always change the location later, since you can move graphics objects easily on the page.
- Resizing graphics objects on the screen. When you bring a graphic into a document, you often need to change the dimensions of the graphic so that it fits a specific location on a page. You can resize your graphics easily to new dimensions on a page.
- Using the draw tools to add simple graphics. You may want to add lines between your columns or place boxes around the graphics on the page. You can add these simple graphics easily using the draw tools on the tool palette.

Using the Clipboard to enter information

An important way to enter graphics into a page layout document is to transfer a graphic from the Clipboard into the page layout document.

Placing a graphics object on the Clipboard

The Clipboard can be used to transfer a copy of a graphic from one document to another, or from one location in a document to another location within the document.

To place a graphic on the Clipboard, select the graphic that you want to transfer, and then select the Cut or Copy command on the Edit menu.

The selected graphic is placed on the Clipboard. You can now move to another location in the document or to a different document and use the Paste command to transfer the graphic from the Clipboard to a new location.

What graphics can be copied to the Clipboard?

You can transfer graphics to a page from other AppleWorks GS applications that use graphics.

- You can select graphics in an AppleWorks GS graphics document, copy it to the Clipboard, and then paste it into a page layout document.
- You can select the contents of a picture field in a database record, copy the field to the Clipboard, and then paste it into a page layout document.
- You can select a graphics object on one page of a page layout document, copy the object to the Clipboard, and then paste the object at another location.

Copying graphics from the Clipboard

Once you have placed a graphic on the Clipboard, you can copy it to a page in a page layout document. (See Figure 15-2.)

1 | **Place selected graphics on the Clipboard.**

Remember that you can select graphics in other applications and use the Cut or Copy command to place the selected graphic on the Clipboard. When you leave the other application and enter page layout, the graphic remains on the Clipboard.

2 | **Move to the page in the page layout document where you want to copy the graphic.**

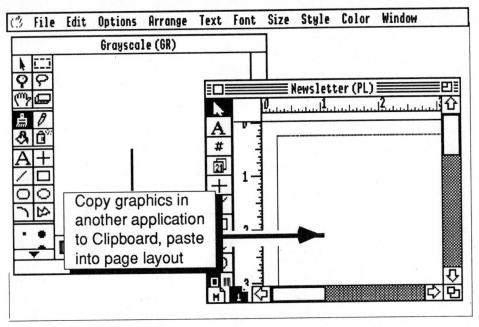

Figure 15-2 You can use the Clipboard to copy graphics into a document

Open the page layout document and move to the desired page.

3 | **Choose the Paste command from the Edit menu.**

The graphic appears on the page. The object is selected, with handles at each corner. The selected object can be moved, and the handles can be used to resize the object.

Example: Copying from a graphics document

You can create a graphic in the AppleWorks GS graphics application and then copy that graphic into a page layout document. (See Figure 15-3.)

1 | **Open an AppleWorks GS graphics document.**

2 | **Select the graphics objects that you want to transfer to the page layout document.**

If you want to transfer the entire document, use the Select All command on the Edit menu to select the entire document.

3 | **Choose the Copy command on the Edit menu.**

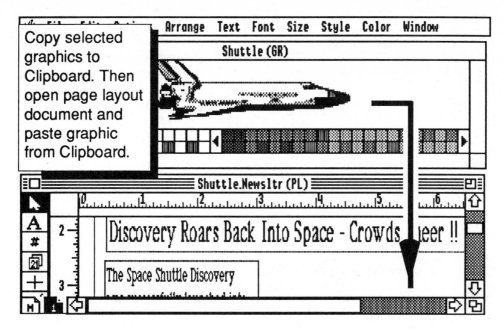

Figure 15-3 You can copy graphics created in the graphics application

4 Open the page layout document and display the page where you want to copy the graphic.

5 Select the Paste command on the Edit menu.

Example: Copying from a database document

You can also copy the graphics stored in a picture field in a database and use the graphic in a page layout document. (See Figure 15-4.)

1 Open an AppleWorks GS database document.

2 Choose Form view and move to the record that contains the graphic that you want to transfer.

3 Select the picture field that contains the graphic that you want to transfer.

4 Choose the Copy command on the Edit menu.

5 Open the page layout document and display the page where you want to copy the graphic.

6 Select the Paste command on the Edit menu.

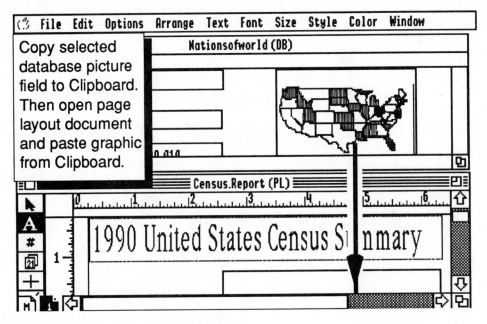

Figure 15-4 Copying from database via Clipboard

Using Control-drag to copy graphics

The Control-drag feature lets you easily move graphics from a graphics document into the page layout document. By opening two windows on the screen (with one containing the graphic and the other containing the page layout document), you can directly drag the graphic into the page layout document. (See Figure 15-5.)

[1] **Open a graphics document that contains the graphics that you want to transfer.**

[2] **Open the page layout document and display the page where you want to copy the graphic.**

You can display the page in actual size, or you can use the Fit In Window command to view the full page on the window.

[3] **Resize both windows so that both are visible on the screen.**

[4] **Select the graphic that you want to copy.**

[5] **Hold down the Control key and the mouse button, and drag the selected object from the graphics document across to the other document.**

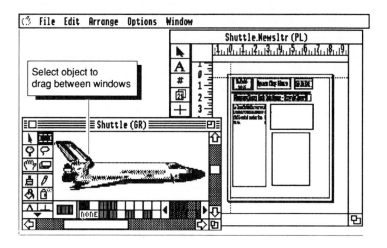

Select object to drag between windows

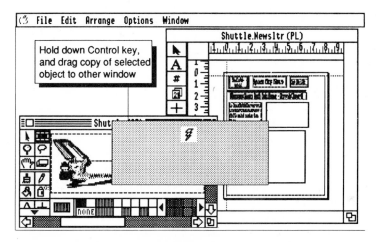

Hold down Control key, and drag copy of selected object to other window

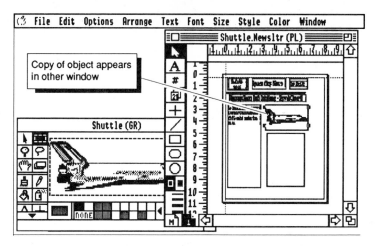

Copy of object appears in other window

Figure 15-5   You can visually copy graphics into a page layout document using Control-drag

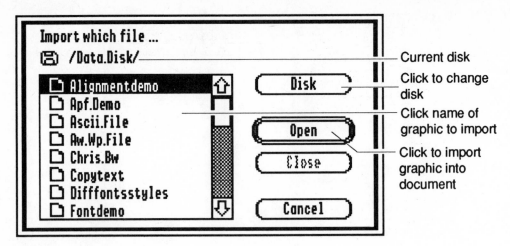

Figure 15-6   Import File dialog box

As you drag the graphic, the cursor takes the shape of a lightning bolt, the Control-drag symbol.

6 │ **When the lightning bolt is moved to the location where you want to copy the graphic, release the mouse button and Control key.**

The graphic is displayed in the page layout document.

Copying graphics from saved documents

There is one major alternative to copying graphics from the Clipboard. You may have created and saved a graphics document within Apple-Works GS, or you may have created and saved a graphic with other programs. You can import a saved graphics image into a page layout document, so you can use these previously-saved documents.

Importing a saved graphic document

If you have created and saved a graphics document, you can bring the graphic into your page layout document.

To import a graphics document at full size

1 │ **Choose the Import File command from the File menu.**

The Import File dialog box appears (see Figure 15-6).
Select the desired file from the document list box.

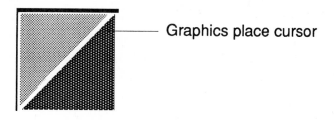

Graphics place cursor

Figure 15-7   Place icon

After you select the desired file, you are returned to the page layout document, and the place icon representing the corner of a graphic appears (see Figure 15-7).

2   **Move the place icon to the location where you want to place the new graphics object.**

3   **Click the place icon at the desired location.**

When you click the icon, the contents of the graphics document are displayed on the page.

The new graphic is a single graphics object. The new object is selected, with handles displayed at each corner. You can move the object on the page or use the handles to resize the object.

To import a graphic scaled to a smaller size

1   **Choose the Import File command from the File menu.**

The Import File dialog box appears. Select the desired file from the document list box.

After you select the desired file, you are returned to the page layout document, and the place icon representing the corner of a graphic appears.

2   **Move the place icon to the location where you want to place the new graphics object.**

3   **Hold down the mouse button and drag a rectangle on the page. (See Figure 15-8.)**

When you release the mouse button, a rectangle appears on the page, and the imported graphic is displayed in the rectangle. (See Figure 15-9.) The graphic fits inside the rectangle. It is not scaled, but is reshaped to fit the shape of the rectangle.

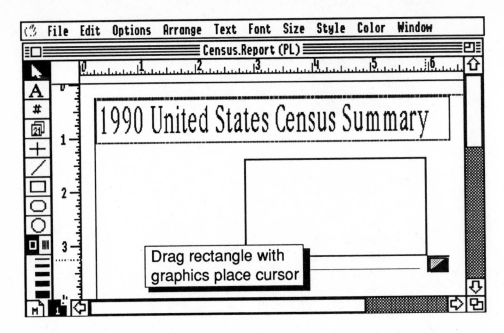

Figure 15-8 Drag a rectangle with place icon

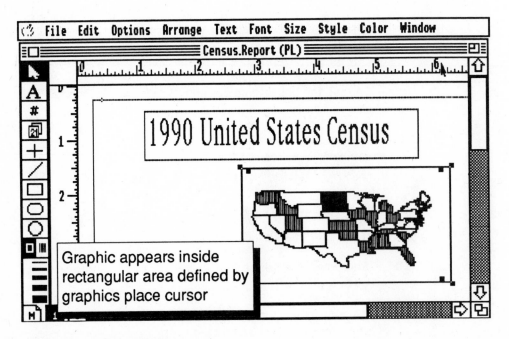

Figure 15-9 Graphic displayed inside rectangle

The new graphic is a single graphics object. The new object is selected, and handles are displayed at each corner. You can move the object on the page or use the handles to resize the object.

What graphics can be imported?

The documents that can be imported on a specific storage disk are automatically displayed when you select the Import File command.

The page layout application can import the following saved graphics documents:

- AppleWorks GS graphics documents
- Graphics stored in Paint (PNT) format
- Graphics stored in Apple Preferred Format (APF)
- Graphics stored in PICT format
- Graphics stored in Screen format (640 and 320)

Working with graphics objects

After you place one or more graphics objects on a page, you may want to change the size or arrangement of the objects later.

Selecting a graphics object

Before you can act on a graphics object, you must select the object for further action.

To select a graphics object:

1   **Click the arrow pointer tool on the tool palette.**

This tool is used to select objects.

2   **Click on the graphics object that you want to select.**

The object is selected and handles are displayed at each corner of the object.

Moving a graphics object

You can move a graphics object from its original location on a page. (See Figure 15-10.)

To move a graphics object:

1   **Click on the graphics object that you want to move.**

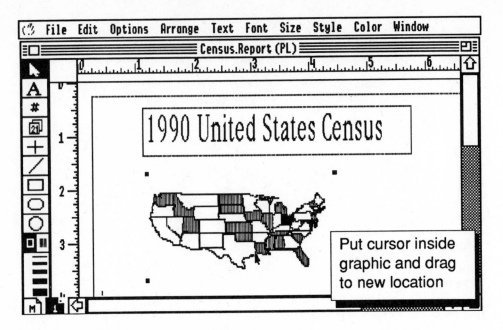

Figure 15-10 You can drag a graphic to a new location

The object is selected and handles are displayed at each corner.

2 | **Move the arrow pointer into the object.**

3 | **Hold down the mouse button, and drag the object to a new location.**

When you release the mouse button, the object remains in the new location. If you have selected magnetic guides, the object will snap to the nearest guide if you place it close to the guide.

Note: *You can move objects when the screen is displayed in full-page view. Select the object by clicking on it, and then drag it to a new location.*

Resizing a graphics object

You can change the dimensions of a graphics object from its original size on a page. (See Figure 15-11.)

To resize a graphics object:

1 | **Click on the graphics object that you want to resize.**

The object is selected and handles are displayed at each corner.

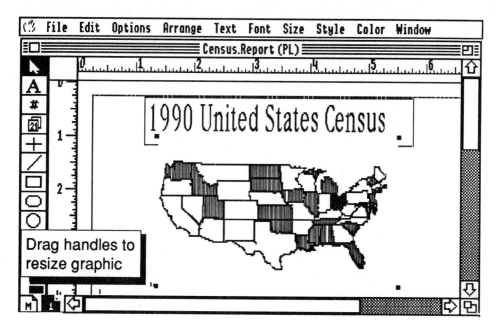

Figure 15-11 You can resize an object by dragging a corner handle

2 **Move the arrow pointer to one of the four handles.**

3 **Hold down the mouse button, and drag the handles to resize the object. As you drag the handle, a rectangle is displayed that shows the new dimensions of the object.**

When you release the mouse button, the object assumes the new size that you defined.

Caution

If you resize a graphics object, the image may be distorted into a different shape, stretched or shrunken to fit the new size that you defined.

Deleting a graphics object

You can easily remove a graphics object from the screen.
To delete a graphic:

1 **Select the object to delete.**

2   Press the Delete key.

Duplicating a graphics object

You can easily generate a second copy of a graphics object on a page:
To duplicate a graphic on a page:

1   Select the object to duplicate.

2   Choose the Duplicate command on the Edit menu.

A second copy of the selected graphic is displayed next to the original object.

Changing the arrangement and direction of objects

Each page in a page layout document consists of a group of objects on the screen. These objects can be rearranged on the screen in the same way that objects were rearranged in a graphics document. You can control the arrangement of overlapping objects or change the direction of objects on the page.

Rearranging a stack of objects

Two or more objects on a page may overlap one another. You can rearrange the stack of objects so that each object is in the desired position.
To bring any object to the top of a stack:

1   Select the text object or graphics object that you want to move. (See Figure 15-12.)

2   Choose the Bring To Front command on the Arrange menu.

The selected object is moved above any overlapping objects and brought to the front of the screen.
To send any object to the bottom of a stack:

1   Select the text object or graphics object that you want to move.

2   Choose the Send To Back command on the Arrange menu.

The selected object is below any overlapping objects and sent to the bottom of the stack of object.

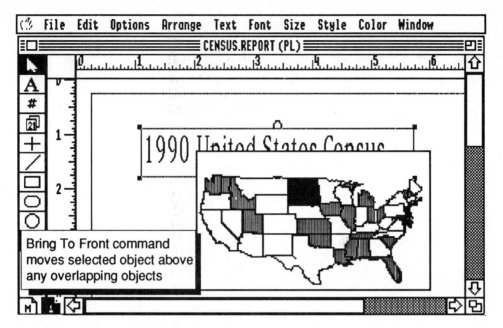

Figure 15-12 Selected objects can be sent to top or bottom

Changing the direction of objects

You can change the direction that a graphics object is facing. If it is facing right, you might want to change it so that it faces left. You can also flip an object top-to-bottom or rotate the direction of an object. (See Figure 15-13.)
To flip an object left or right:

1. **Select the object to flip.**

2. **Choose the Flip Horizontal command on the Arrange menu.**

The selected object is flipped left-to-right on the screen.
To flip an object top-to-bottom:

1. **Select the object to flip.**

2. **Choose the Flip Vertical command on the Arrange menu.**

The selected object is flipped top-to-bottom on the screen.
To rotate an object 90°

1. **Select the text or graphics object to rotate.**

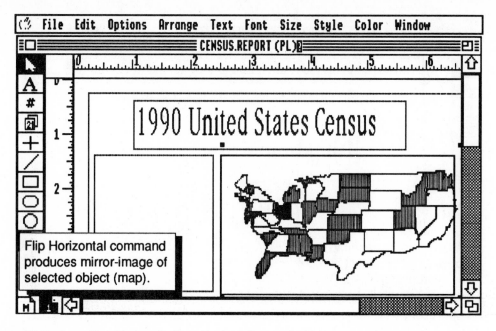

Figure 15-13 A graphics object can be flipped horizontally or vertically

[2] **Choose the Rotate Left command or the Rotate Right command on the Arrange menu.**

The object is rotated 90° to the left or right. (See Figure 15-14.)

Note: *You may want to display text rotated 90° to the left or right. The easiest way to display rotated text is:*

[1] **Create and format the text in an AppleWorks GS graphics document.**

[2] **Copy the text from the graphics document to the page layout document. When you copy the text into the page layout, it is now regarded as a solid graphics object.**

[3] **Select and rotate the text in the same way that you would rotate any other graphics object.**

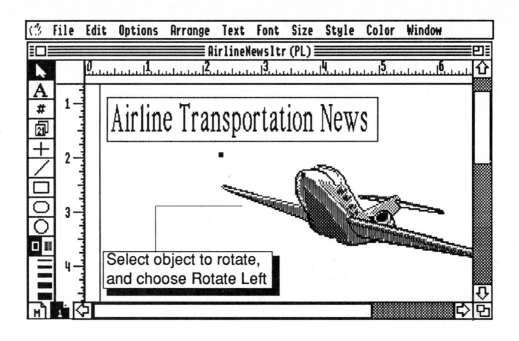

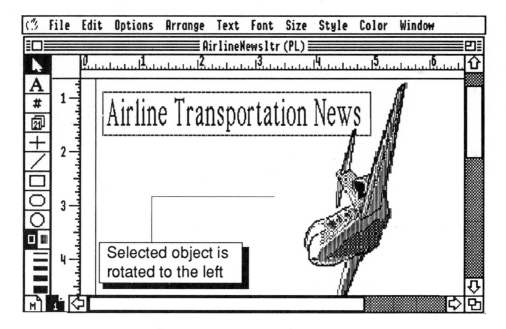

Figure 15-14 A graphics object can be rotated left or right

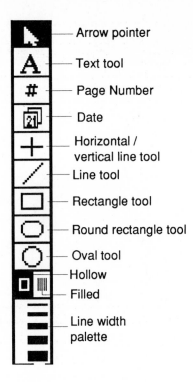

Figure 15-15   Tool palette

Adding graphics with the draw tools

You can add simple graphics to a page with the draw tools provided on the tool palette. These tools are similar to the draw tools used in the graphics application.

These tools can be used to add lines to separate columns, create lines beneath headlines, place boxes around graphics, or add other simple graphics.

Draw tools on the palette

The tool palette (Figure 15-15) includes the following draw tools:

- **Horizontal/vertical line tool:** Used to draw a horizontal or vertical line.
- **Line tool:** Used to draw a straight line in any direction. If you hold down the Shift key while drawing the line, the lines is constrained and can only be drawn in 45° increments.

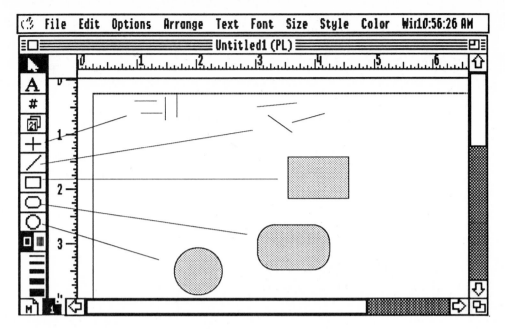

Figure 15-16 The draw tools are used to draw lines and shapes on the the page

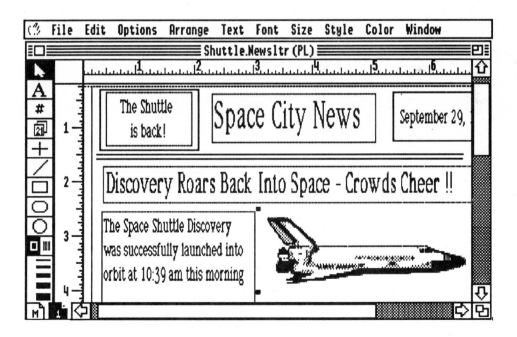

Figure 15-17 A completed document

- **Rectangle tool:** Used to draw a rectangle or square. Hold down the Shift key as you draw the rectangle to constrain the tool and only draw squares.
- **Round rectangle tool:** Used to draw a rectangle or square with rounded corners. Hold down the Shift key as you draw the rectangle to constrain the tool and only draw squares.
- **Oval tool:** Used to draw an oval or circle. Hold down the Shift key as you draw the oval to constrain the tool and only draw circles.

Using the draw tools

To use the draw tools, you should follow these steps:

1   **Select the tool that you want to use.**

2   **Select the color that you want to use from the Color menu.**

3   **Click the Filled icon or the Hollow icon.**

If you click the Filled icon, the object will be filled with the selected color. If you select the Hollow icon, the the interior of the object is left transparent.

4   **Click the line width to use for the borders of the objects.**

5   **Move into the document window and draw an object with the desired dimensions.**

The tools are used in the same way as the similar tools are used in the graphics application. (See Figure 15-16.)

The next step

After you have placed and arranged the text objects and graphics objects on each page of your document, be sure to save your work with the Save As command on the File menu. (Refer to Chapter 3 for information on the Save As command.)

Finally, you can print out a final version of the document on your printer, and admire the polished appearance of the final product! (See Figure 15-17.)

Chapter 16

Starting Off in Telecommunications

About this chapter

Telecommunications lets you connect your computer to a second, remote computer and transfer information between the two computers.

This chapter introduces key concepts about telecommunications and leads you through the steps needed to prepare for a telecommunications session. In Chapter 17, a typical communications session is discussed.

The topics in this chapter include

- Telecommunications concepts
- Hardware and software connections
- Why use telecommunications?
- Communications services
- A word about modems
- Setting hardware parameters
- Setting communications parameters
- Adding numbers to the phone list

Telecommunications concepts

The AppleWorks GS telecommunications application lets you connect your computer to another computer (called the remote computer) and transfer information back and forth. The two computers are usually located at some distance from each other, with the two computers connected by the telephone system.

Think about what that means — you can connect your computer to a remote computer across town, across the country, or around the world. In the most common situation, you would use the AppleWorks GS telecommunications application to connect your Apple IIGS to a much larger, more powerful remote computer to transfer information from the remote computer to your system.

Why would you want to connect your computer to a remote computer? A variety of commercial and free services are available to you. By connecting to a remote computer, you have access to hundreds of free programs for your computer, financial and news information, and a very large amount of other information.

In addition, your computer is usually not the only other computer that is connected to the large remote computer. It may be connected with many other smaller computers, and you can interact with other computer users who are connected to the large computer.

How is your computer connected to the remote computer?

You don't need a lot of equipment to connect your computer to a remote computer. You already have access to the two most important components: your computer and AppleWorks GS.

In general, telecommunications involves two kinds of connections:

- **Hardware connections** between the computers. Some computer hardware is required to physically connect your computer to the remote computer. If the two computers are close to each other, a simple cable is all that you need. If the two computers are farther apart, you need a special piece of equipment called a modem that connects your computer to the telephone system; when both computers are connected to the telephone system, the telephone line serves as the cable that connects the two computers.
- **Software connections** between the computers. Some computer software is required to manage the transfer of information between computers. The AppleWorks GS telecommunications application is an example of this kind of software, and you don't need any other software beyond AppleWorks GS.

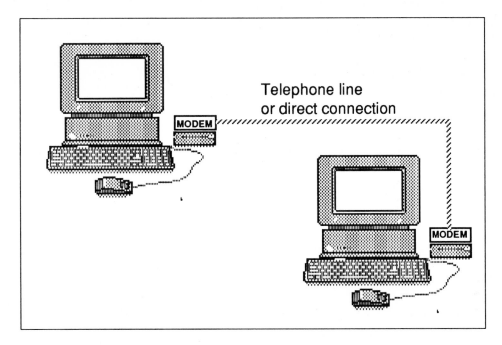

Figure 16-1 Computers can transfer information over the telephone lines

Making the hardware connection

Your Apple IIGS needs some hardware equipment to connect it to the remote computer.

If the remote computer is near your Apple IIGS, the connection can be as simple as a cable to connect the two computers. For example, if the second computer is in the same room or on the same desk, a cable from one of the serial ports on your Apple IIG can connect it to a second computer and serve as the hardware connection.

If most cases, the remote computer is some distance away; it may be across town or across the country. To connect your Apple IIGS to a remote computer at a distance, your Apple IIGS must be equipped with a **modem**.

A modem is a connection between a computer and the telephone system that allows computer information to be sent over telephone lines. After you install a modem in your Apple IIGS, you can send information over the telephone lines. That means that you can connect your Apple IIGS to any other computer that is also equipped with a modem and connected to the telephone system.

Figure 16-1 demonstrates how a modem is used to connect your Apple IIGS to a remote computer.

The modems turn the computer signals into a form that can be transmitted via the telephone system. When you send a signal from your computer to a second computer:

Your computer's signals are translated by your modem into a form that can be sent over the telephone lines.

Your computer's signals are sent to the second computer over the telephone lines.

The second computer's modem receives the signals and transmits them to the second computer.

Making the software connection

A modem lets you send and receive information between your Apple IIGS and any other computer equipped with a modem. You also need telecommunications software to manage the transfer of information, and your AppleWorks GS telecommunications application will handle your communications needs.

When you connect with a large remote computer, you'll often use these common communications terms:

- **log on:** When you connect to the larger computer, you will usually have to provide an identification number or password. This is called **logging on** to the computer system.
- **on-line:** After you have successfully connected your computer to the remote computer, you are on-line. That means that you are connected and in communication with the other computer.
- **download:** You'll often transfer files "down" from the larger system to your Apple IIGS. This is called **downloading** files.
- **upload:** You may occasionally transfer files from your Apple IIGS to the remote computer. Sending files "up" to the larger computer is called **uploading** files.
- **log off:** When you are finished with a communications session, you will break off the connection. This is called **logging off** the remote computer system. Logging off is often accomplished by hanging up the telephone connection.
- **off-line:** When you aren't communicating with the remote computer, you are off-line. You are obviously off-line before and after a communications session. AppleWorks GS also lets you temporarily suspend a session while you are connected and perform some off-line activities, like opening or saving files.

Why would you use telecommunications?

Most of the AppleWorks GS applications have obvious uses. The word processing application is obviously used to create text document, and the graphics application is used to create graphics on the screen.

It may not be obvious what you might use telecommunications for. Communications is one of the lesser-used computer applications, but it is increasingly popular and important.

A brief list of common ways that you could use telecommunications include

- Transferring information from a large database to your computer
- Reading information posted on bulletin boards
- Download public-domain software
- Sending messages with electronic mail
- Interacting with other users in a conference
- Using "chat mode" to swap messages with other computer users

On-Line Databases

You can transfer information from large **databases** into your computer. There are many large databases that are available from commercial services. These range from general-interest databases to specialized databases. For example, there are specialized medical, legal, and education databases.

You can search for information among the large databases, and then transfer desired information to your computer for further use. For example, you can search for information in the Reader's Guide to Periodicals, in ERIC (an education research database), in MEDLINE (a medical database), or LEXIS (a legal database). These searches can be completed much more quickly than traditional searches with printed reference materials.

Bulletin boards

You can read information posted on computer **bulletin boards**. An electronic bulletin board works much the same way as a printed bulletin board. Users can post notices for other users or can read notices posted by others. Bulletin boards are good sources of information on new hardware and software, conference notes, job announcements, etc.

Public domain software

Many services maintain large collections of **public domain** software or **shareware** software. Public domain software can be used freely; the authors of shareware software request a small fee if you keep and use the software.

These programs can be downloaded to your computer and saved for future use. This can be an important source of new software to expand your software collection.

Electronic mail

You can send information to specific computer users with **electronic mail**. Electronic mail (also known as E-mail) can be used like a printed mail service. You are assigned a specific account, and you can send and receive messages from specific people using the system.

If you send a message to a specific user and they are not currently connected to the computer, the service saves the message. When the other user logs on to the service, they can read the mail from you and send a message back to you. Commercial services like MCI-Mail are an increasingly important method for transmitting information.

Computer conferences

You can communicate with other users in a **conference**. A conference is an on-going discussion on a specific topic. Conferences are widely available on a variety of topics, and conferences on popular topics may continue for days, weeks, or much longer.

You can think of a conference as an infinite memo, where users keep posting new comments on previous contents. You can read recent messages in the conference, ask questions, or add your own comments and responses. Most conferences let users interact at the same time, so that you can comment on another user's comments immediately after it is posted.

Chat or CB mode

Chat or CB mode is like a conference, except that there is no specific topic. It's similar to using a citizens' band (CB) radio. You can exchange comments with other computer users who are currently on the system. Chat mode messages are usually not saved; the interaction is live and transient, just like using a CB radio.

Special interest groups

Many services group information into clusters arranged by some common topic or factor. For instance, the Apple-related information may be grouped in an Apple Special Interest Group, or Apple SIG. Information services may maintain SIGs on a large number of topics, such as different brands of computers, different programming languages, or other similar topics.

A sampler of computer information services

Many information services provide some or all of the above activities. Typical examples are listed below in alphabetical order:

AppleLink Personal Edition

AppleLink Personal Edition is an Apple-specific service jointly provided by Apple Computer and Quantum Computer Services. This service lets you search for information on Apple computers, software, and services.

BIX (Information: 603-924-9281)

The Byte Information Exchange (BIX) is technically oriented; if you like Byte magazine, you'll like BIX. BIX is excellent for discussions of new hardware and software, and it's a good source of new public domain software.

CompuServe (Information: 800-848-8199)

CompuServe maintains extensive databases, including information on business, finance, medicine, education, science, law, news, popular entertainment, and sports. CompuServe also maintains extensive software files and Special Interest Groups, including an Apple II SIG (MAUG).

Connect (Connect, Inc. 408-973-0110)

Connect is a new service that provides databases and other communications services. The service is an Apple spin-off that markets two software products to provide easy access: MacNet for general access to the service, and Governet, aimed at government users.

Dialog (Information: 415-858-2700)

Dialog is a very well-established information service. The service is education-oriented and includes about 50 general-interest databases and specialized databases in science, social science, and medicine.

Einstein (Addison-Wesley, 415-854-0300)

This service was introduced in 1987 and is designed to teach on-line search techniques. Einstein includes reference databases and full-text databases, including regional newspapers and UPI, AP, and TASS newswires).

Genie (Information: 800-638-9636)

Genie maintains extensive databases, including information on business, finance, medicine, education, science, law, news, popular entertainment, and sports. It also maintains extensive software files and Special Interest Groups, including an Apple II SIG (Apple II Roundtable).

MIX (McGraw-Hill, 800-622-6310)

MIX is a new service, designed to promote electronic mail and conferences among students and teachers in K-12 education.

Source (Information: 800-336-3330)

The Source maintains extensive databases, including information on business, finance, medicine, education, science, law, news, popular entertainment, and sports. It maintains extensive software files and Special Interest Groups, including an Apple II SIG (Applesig).

A word about modems

When you are ready to begin a communications session, you have two of the most important pieces of equipment that you need: your Apple IIGS and AppleWorks GS. However, you also need a modem for your Apple IIGS if you want to connect to a remote computer via the telephone system.

Kinds of modems

There are several common kinds of modems, and any of these may be used to connect your Apple IIGS to the telephone system. Three common kinds are

- **Acoustic modem.** This modem provides two cups where a standard telephone handset can be inserted. These modems are inexpensive and were common in the early 1980s; they are less common now. Acoustic modems translate information into electronic sounds that are transferred through the handset into the telephone system. This method can produce more mistakes during the transfer of information than direct-connect modems.
- **Direct-connect modem.** These modems connect your computer directly to the telephone system. There are two types of direct-connect modems:
- An **external modem** consists of an external box, which connects to a slot in your computer and is directly connected to an available telephone jack.
- An **internal modem** is contained entirely inside your computer. It may consist of a single interface card, or it may be built directly into the computer. A telephone wire connects the internal modem to an available telephone jack.

Hayes-compatible modems

Modems produced by the Hayes Computing Company were introduced during the early development of microcomputers and quickly became a standard modem. Most modems produced by competing modem manufacturers still advertise that they are "Hayes-compatible." Hayes modems include several built-in commands to perform simple operations, and most modems are still careful to include those built-in commands.

Modems and baud rate

One important characteristic of a modem is its **baud rate**. The baud rate is the speed that the modem can transfer information.

Examples of typical baud rates are 300 baud, 1200 baud, 2400 baud, and 9600 baud. The baud rate corresponds to the number of bits that the modem can transfer per second. You can estimate the number of characters per second by dividing the baud rate by 10. Thus, a modem transferring information at 300 baud can transfer about 30 characters per second, or about 2-3 seconds per line.

An inexpensive modem might operate at only one rate, such as 300 baud. A more expensive modem might operate at several baud rates, such as 2400 baud, 1200 baud, or 300 baud. As you might expect, a modem that can transfer information at higher baud rates is more expensive than a modem that transfers information more slowly.

What determines the baud rate that you can use? Usually you will want to use your modem's fastest baud rate, but one important rule may prevent this: both your computer and the remote computer must use the same baud rate. Thus, if you have a modem that can operate at 2400 baud, 1200 baud, or 300 baud, and the other computer has a 300 baud modem, both of you must use 300 baud as the transfer rate.

Why use a faster modem?

There are two important reasons to use the fastest possible baud rate. First, it's more convenient. If you use 300 baud, you will quickly discover that you can read the information being transferred faster than the computers are able to transmit it.

Second, many commercial services charge by the amount of time that you are connected (the connect-time), so a faster modem will reduce charges. However, some services charge a higher rate if you use a faster modem, so this advantage might be lessened. Faster modems are also more expensive to purchase than slower modems.

Using a communications program

When you have a modem for your Apple IIGS, you are ready to use the Apple-Works GS communications application to connect to a remote computer.

When you're ready to begin a communications session, you need to provide certain information to your communications software. Any communications program requires several pieces of information to make a successful connection:

- The telephone number of the second computer system.
- Information about the specific modem in use and how it is connected to your computer. In AppleWorks GS, this information is called the **hardware parameters**.
- Information about the way that information will be exchanged, such as the baud rate being used. In AppleWorks GS this information is called the **communication parameters**.

You need to determine this information before you start. Once you have this information, you are ready to begin the actual communications session.

When you begin the session, you will enter a communications program that will manage the session for you. Virtually all communications programs let you

- Specify the type of hardware that you are using.
- Enter the communications parameters that you are using.
- Enter and dial the telephone number of the other computer.
- Send information, such as text files, to the remote computer.
- Receive and save information sent from the remote computer.

The AppleWorks GS telecommunications application is your communications program, and it provides these basic features, as well as special additional features. For instance, AppleWorks GS maintains a special list of phone numbers that let you dial a number with a single keystroke, and it can automatically redial a telephone number if it is busy.

Starting the telecommunications application

When you are ready to begin a communications session, you should launch the AppleWorks GS telecommunications application in the same way that you launched other applications. In other applications, you launched each application to create a new blank document.

You should perform a similar operation in the telecommunications application. The new telecommunications document that you create will be used to save the hardware settings, communications settings, and telephone numbers that you enter. You can save this telecommunications document and open it again for later sessions, and you will not have to enter the information again.

Launching the telecommunications application

When you are ready to begin a communications session, you should launch the telecommunications application and create a new telecommunications document.

There are two ways that you can create a new communications document:

- You can create a new document with the New command on the File menu.
- You can create a new document with the Open command on the File menu.

See Chapter 3, AppleWorks GS Common Commands, for more information about using the New Open commands.

The telecommunications document window

When you open a new telecommunications document, a new window appears on the screen (see Figure 16-2).

This document window contains the elements found in all windows, including a title bar, Close box, Zoom box, Size box, and scroll bar.

The window includes several elements that are specific to this application:

- The **telecommunications menu bar**, which contains the commands needed to enter hardware settings, communications parameters, and manage the transfer of information.
- The **communications status bar**, which displays a message about the current status of the communications session.

The telecommunications menu bar

The telecommunications menu bar at the top of the screen contains the commands needed to enter necessary hardware and communications information and manage the transfer of information.

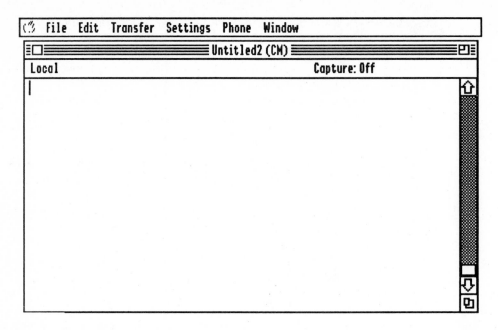

Figure 16-2   New telecommunications document

Figure 16-3
File menu

File menu

The commands on the File menu include New, Open, Close, Save, Save As, Delete File, Import File, Choose Printer, Page Setup, Print, Print Merge, and Quit. (See Figure 16-3.) These commands are found on the File menu in all AppleWorks GS applications and are described in Chapter 3, AppleWorks GS Common Commands.

The Choose Printer, Page Setup, Print, and Print Merge commands are dimmed on the menu; they are not available in this application. This application is used to transfer information between computers. The information can be saved on a storage disk and printed from the word processing application later.

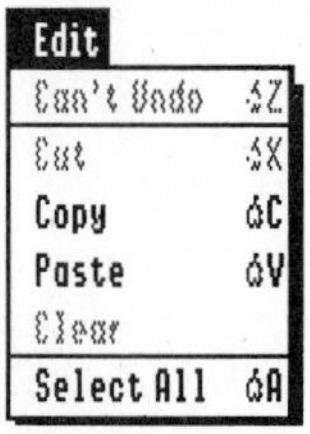

Edit menu

The commands on the Edit menu include **Copy**, **Paste**, and **Select All**. (See Figure 16-4.) These commands are described in Chapter 3, Apple-Works GS Common Commands.

Transfer menu

Figure 16-4
Edit menu

The Transfer menu commands manage the transfer of files and other information between the two computers. (See Figure 16-5.)

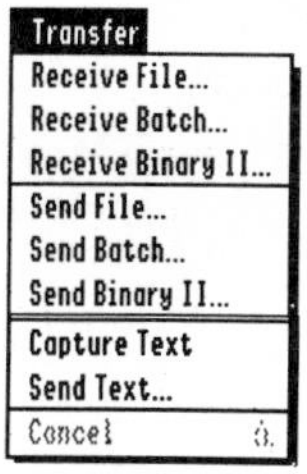

Figure 16-5
Transfer menu

Receive File: This command sets your computer to receive a single file from the remote computer.

Receive Batch: This command sets your computer to receive one or more files from the remote computer. The names of the files are determined by the remote computer.

Receive Binary II: This command sets your computer to receive one or more files sent from the remote computer in a special format, Binary II. This format includes special information beyond the actual contents of the document; for example, the Binary II format of a file contains information about the application that created the file.

Send File: This command lets you specify and send a specific file to the remote computer.

Send Batch: This command lets you specify and send one or more files to the remote computer.

Send Binary II: This command lets you specify and send one or more files to the remote computer; the files are sent in the special Binary II format. (See Receive Binary II above.)

Capture Text/End Text Capture: This command controls a special recorder that can temporarily store the information that is displayed on the screen. The information is stored in a temporary area called the Capture Text buffer. When you choose Capture Text, the recorder begins storing information and the command is replaced by End Text Capture on the Transfer menu. When you choose End Text Capture, the recorder stops storing information and you can store the information that is in the Capture Text buffer permanently on disk.

Send Text: This command lets you specify and send a text file to the remote computer.

Cancel: This command lets you interrupt the current transfer operation.

Settings menu

The Settings menu commands let you enter hardware settings and communications parameters for the session. (See Figure 16-6.)

Show Control: This command displays any control characters that are included in text being transferred from the remote computer. When you select this command, a checkmark appears to the left of the command, and any control characters are displayed. (For example, the control character Control-C is displayed as ^C.) If you select the command again, the checkmark is removed and control characters are not displayed in text.

Edit Line: This command controls the display of an edit line above the status bar in the document window. When you select this command, a checkmark appears to the left of the command, and an edit line is displayed.You can use this edit line to type and edit a line of text before sending it to the remote computer. The line of text in the edit line is not sent to the other computer until you press the Return key. If you select

Figure 16-6
Settings menu

the command again, the checkmark is removed from the command, and the edit line is removed from the window.

Status Bar: This command controls the display of the status bar in the document window. When you open a new document, a checkmark is displayed to the left of the command, and the status bar is displayed. The status bar displays the current status of the session; as you are dialing, connected, or disconnected, an appropriate message is displayed. The amount of text currently stored in the Capture Text buffer is also shown. If you select the command again, the checkmark is removed from the command, and the status bar is removed from the window.

Local: This command lets you temporarily interrupt the communications session and type information that is not immediately transferred to the other computer. When you choose the command, a checkmark appears to the left of the command, and "Local" is displayed on the status bar. The text that you type while Local is selected is not sent to the remote computer. When you choose the command again, the checkmark is removed and communications with the other computer resumes.

Hardware: This command lets you specify information about the hardware that you are using, including the modem and the port or slot to which it is connected.

Communication: This command lets you specify information about the rules observed during the transfer of information, including the baud rate and other communications parameters.

Phone menu

Figure 16-7
Phone menu

The commands on the Phone menu control the telephone connection with the remote computer. Using these commands, you can store the telephone numbers of remote computers, dial a number, break the connection, or set your computer to act as the remote computer. (See Figure 16-7.)

Autodial: This command lets your computer redial a number that was busy on the previous try. When you select this command, a checkmark appears to the left of the command and a busy number is automatically redialed after waiting a specified number of seconds. The number of seconds is specified in the Communications dialog box. If you select the command again, the checkmark is removed and a busy number is not automatically redialed.

Dial: This command lets you enter a list of telephone numbers for remote computer systems, store special communications parameters for different remote computers, and define "fast-dial" codes for different numbers that let you dial a number with a single keystroke.

Hangup: This command ends a communications session by breaking the connection with a remote computer.

Answer Phone: This command lets your computer act as a remote computer. When you select this command, your computer will wait for another computer to dial in and connect. After the connection is made, you can transfer files and information using the Transfer commands.

Setting the hardware parameters

Before you can successfully connect to a second computer, you will have to enter two kinds of information into your communications software. This information specifies

- the **hardware parameters**, which is information about the specific hardware that you are using, and
- the **communications parameters**, which are the "rules" to be followed when information is exchanged between the two computers.

When you save the telecommunications document, these settings are saved for future use, so you will only have to enter this information once.

Setting these parameters is one of the most complicated parts of telecommunications: it isn't really hard, but it may seem complicated and confusing, since the terms may not be familiar to you.

What hardware parameters must you specify?

The AppleWorks GS communications application needs three pieces of information about your hardware:

- **Modem:** What modem are you using? Are you using a Hayes modem, Apple Modem, or another type?
- **Serial device:** If you're using an external modem, which port is your external modem connected to?
- **Slot:** If you're using an internal modem, which slot holds your modem?

Entering the hardware parameters

Before you can connect to a remote computer, you must enter the hardware parameters for your system.

To enter the hardware parameters:

1 **Select Hardware from the Settings menu.**

The Hardware dialog box appears (see Figure 16-8.)

2 **Click on the modem that you are using, and click on External Modem or Internal modem.**

(Click the No Modem button if the two computers are directly connected by cable.)

3 **If you are using an external modem, click on the serial device in use. If you are using an internal modem, click on the slot in use.**

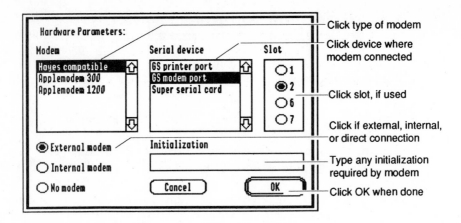

Figure 16-8 Hardware dialog box

4 **If necessary, type any text characters that are required to initialize your modem into the input bar.**

Some modems may require a special series of characters sent at the beginning of a session. If your modem requires this initialization string, type it into the Initialization input box. (Consult the documentation for your modem to determine if the initialization string is needed.)

5 **Click the OK button when the information is correct.**

Setting the communications parameters

The communications application also needs to know what rules both computers will observe during the session.

For example, you must specify the baud rate used by the computers. Rules like these are collectively known as communications protocols. When you connect your Apple IIGS to different remote systems, different protocols might be used by different systems.

What communications parameters must you specify?

The AppleWorks GS communications application needs several pieces of information:

- **Baud rate:** How fast will information be transferred? Typical baud rates are 300, 1200, 2400, 4800, and 9600.

- **Parity:** Parity is a system used to check whether information is being transferred correctly. Parity may be odd, even, or none.
- **Data bits:** How many bits of information are transferred to specify each character? Possible choices are 7 or 8.
- **Stop bits:** How many bits are sent to separate characters? The choices are 1 or 2.

The above information is required for a successful connection. Several other pieces of communication information may also be supplied; these are not absolutely required, but the correct settings should be entered if possible:

- **Generate line feeds:** When you send a file to the remote computer or receive a file, should a carriage return be placed at the end of each line? (Some files already contain these carriage returns, so it isn't necessary to generate new line feeds.)
- **XON/XOFF:** Should the XON/XOFF protocol be used? This is a special protocol used by some systems to signal the end of each packet of information. This helps to ensure that information is being sent and received correctly.
- **Echo:** Should a copy of information be sent to your computer as well as the other computer? (This is also called full duplex, or "echoing.") Some systems automatically echo the information, while others require that you specify this option.

How do you know the correct communications parameters?

The hardware parameters are easy to enter: you know which modem you are using and the slot where it is connected. But how do you determine the communications parameters?

The communications parameters must be agreed on before a session begins, and it is generally the remote computer that determines the parameters. If you wish to connect to a commercial service on a distant remote computer, the service will supply documentation that includes the communications parameters to use.

Likewise, if you want to use a bulletin board running on a local computer system, the service should provide preliminary information that includes the parameters to use for a successful connection.

Entering the communications parameters

To enter the communications parameters into AppleWorks GS:

1 **Choose the Communications command from the Setting menu.**

The Communications dialog box appears (see Figure 16-9).

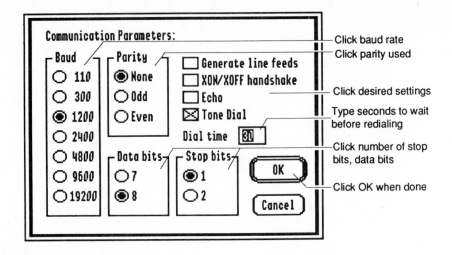

Figure 16-9 Communications dialog box

2. Click on the appropriate baud rate, parity, number of data bits, and number of stop bits.

3. If you want to generate line feeds during transfer of files, use the XON/XOFF protocol; or echo signals to your computer, check the appropriate check boxes.

4. If your modem uses tone-dialing, check the Tone Dial box. If your modem uses pulse-dialing, leave this box unchecked.

5. If you want to automatically redial a busy number, enter the number of seconds to wait before redialing.

This value is used with the Autodial command on the Settings menu. If you select the Autodial command, a busy number is automatically redialed after the number of seconds that you have entered here.

6. When the appropriate settings have been entered, check the OK button.

What if different remote computers use different parameters?

It is very likely that different services or remote computers will use slightly different parameters.

You can handle this problem in two ways:

- Before connecting to a new service or remote system, return to the Communications dialog box and change the settings to the required new settings.
- Enter and save the telephone number of each service or remote system in the communications Phone List.

When a number is saved in the Phone List, the specific parameters for that number are saved with the telephone number. When you dial the number later, the correct parameters are automatically used. Using the Phone List is described in the next section.

Using the Phone List

The final piece of information that AppleWorks GS needs before a communication session is the telephone number of the remote system. You can enter the telephone number directly into AppleWorks GS when you are ready to connect to the remote system, but AppleWorks GS provides a more convenient way to enter and save the telephone numbers of systems and services. Once the numbers have been saved, you will not need to enter them again later. You will also be able to conveniently dial the number with a single keystroke.

When you save the communications document, this Phone List is saved, along with the hardware parameters and communications parameters for the session.

Entering numbers into the Phone List

The AppleWorks GS Phone List contains a list of numbers of remote computers that you might want to phone. For each remote computer, you can enter its phone number, any special communications parameters for this remote computer, and a "fast-dial" code that lets you dial the number with a single keystroke.

To enter a number into the Phone List:

1. **Select Dial from the Phone menu.**

The Dial dialog box appears (see Figure 16-10).

2. **Type a name to use for the telephone number, a single character to use for fast-dialing, and the telephone number to add to the list.**

The fast-dial character can be used to dial the number later with a single keystroke. To dial the number later, you simply hold down the Option key and press the fast-dial code character.

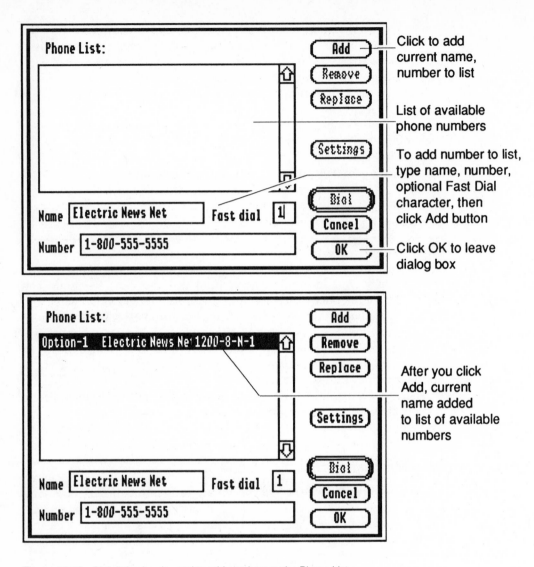

Figure 16-10 Dial dialog box is used to add numbers to the Phone List

3 **If the service has special communications parameters, click the Settings button.**

If you do not click the Settings button, the number will use the communications parameters that you specified in the last section.
If this number has different settings, click the Settings button. The same Communications dialog box that was discussed in the last section is displayed. Click the specific settings for this telephone number, and then click the OK button.

4 Click the Add button when the information is correct.

The fast-dial character, name, and current communications settings are displayed in the Phone List scroll box.

Changing the communications parameters for a specific number

The communications settings are coded in the scroll box to the right of the name. They are coded in this format: Baud rate–number of data bits–parity–number of stop bits. For example, the code "1200–8–N–1" means that the service uses 1200 baud, 8 data bits, no parity, and 1 stop bit.

You can always return to the Phone List and change the communications settings used with a specific telephone number.

To change the specific parameters used with specific number:

1 Click on the name of the service in the Phone List scroll box.

The entry is highlighted and selected.

2 Click the Settings button.

The same Communications dialog box is displayed as discussed earlier in "Setting the communications parameters."

3 Click the appropriate settings for this specific number, and click the OK button.

The specific parameters that you entered are now saved with this specific number.

To remove a number from the phone list

1 Select Dial from the Phone menu.

The Dial dialog box appears (see Figure 16-11).

2 Click on the name of the number that you want to remove from the list.

The name is highlighted in the list box, and the name, number, and fast-dial character are displayed in the input bars at the bottom of the box.

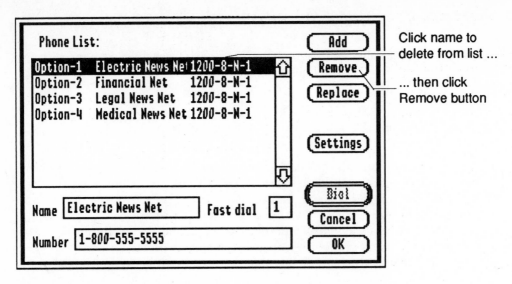

Figure 16-11 Dial dialog box is used to remove numbers from the Phone List

3 **Click the Remove button.**

The telephone number is removed from the list.

To replace a number on the phone list

1 **Select Dial from the Phone menu.**

The Dial dialog box appears (see Figure 16-12).

2 **Click on the name of the number that you want to replace on the list.**

The name is highlighted in the list box, and the name, telephone number, and fast-dial character are displayed in the input bars at the bottom of the dialog box.

3 **Type in a new name, telephone number, or fast-dial character for this number.**

If a special setting is required for this number, click the Setting button and select the correct settings for this specific number.

4 **When the information for the number is correct, click the Replace button.**

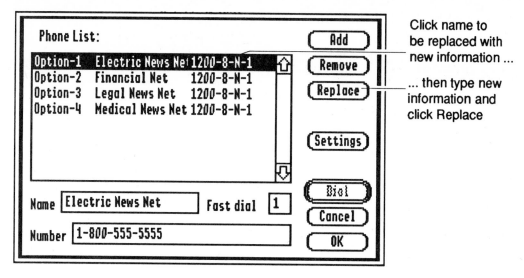

Figure 16-12 Dial dialog box is used to replace an old number with a new number

The new information for the telephone number is substituted for the old information on the list.

Saving the communications document

After you have entered your hardware parameters, communications parameters, and Phone List information, don't forget to save your telecommunications document.

A telecommunications document saves the current environment: the hardware and communications settings, and the information stored in the Phone List. It is very important to store this information, so that you will not have to enter the information again in the future.

Refer to Chapter 3 for instructions on how to use the Save As and Save commands.

The next step

Once you have created and saved a telecommunications document that contains your hardware and communications settings, you can connect to a remote computer and transfer information.

The next chapter discusses how to manage a communications session. It discusses how to connect with the remote computer and how to send and receive files from the remote computer.

Chapter 17

Managing a Communications Session

About this chapter

This chapter discusses how to conduct a typical communications session. The topics in the chapter include

- Opening a saved communications document
- Connecting with a remote computer
- Transferring text
- Transferring files
- Ending a session
- Using your computer as a remote computer

Opening an existing document

When you are ready to connect your computer to a remote computer, you can retrieve a saved telecommunications document that contains your hardware parameters, communications parameters, and the Phone List that you created earlier.

To open a saved telecommunications document:

1. Select the Open command on the File menu.

2. Click on the name of the document that you want to open.

3. Click on the Open button in the dialog box.

Connecting to the remote computer

To establish a connection with a remote computer, you must dial the number of the computer. Before you can make a successful connection, the remote computer must be expecting the call and prepared to acknowledge the call. (If you would like to use your computer as a remote computer, see "Using your computer as a remote computer" later in this chapter.)

After you dial the remote computer and a successful connection is made, the remote computer will respond that you are successfully connected.

Dialing the remote computer's number

1. Select Dial from the Phone menu.

The Dial dialog box appears (see Figure 17-1.)

2. Click on the name of the number that you want to dial.

The name is highlighted in the list box, and the name, number, and fast-dial character are displayed.

3. Click the Dial button.

The number is dialed.

If the remote computer is available and the number is not busy, a successful connection is made and an appropriate message appears on the screen.

Phone List:
Option-1 Electric News Net 1200-8-N-1
Option-2 Financial Net 1200-8-N-1
Option-3 Legal News Net 1200-8-N-1
Option-4 Medical News Net 1200-8-N-1
Add
Remove
Replace
Settings
Dial
Cancel
OK
Name Electric News Net
Fast dial 1
Number 1-800-555-5555
Click name to be dialed
Click to dial selected number

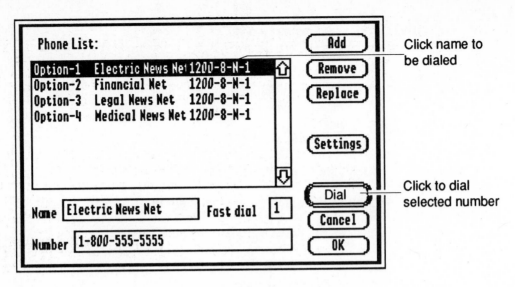

Figure 17-1 Dial dialog box is used to dial number of remote computer

Usually the remote computer will request some identification from your computer, such as an identification number or password. Figure 17-2 shows a typical opening dialog with the remote computer.

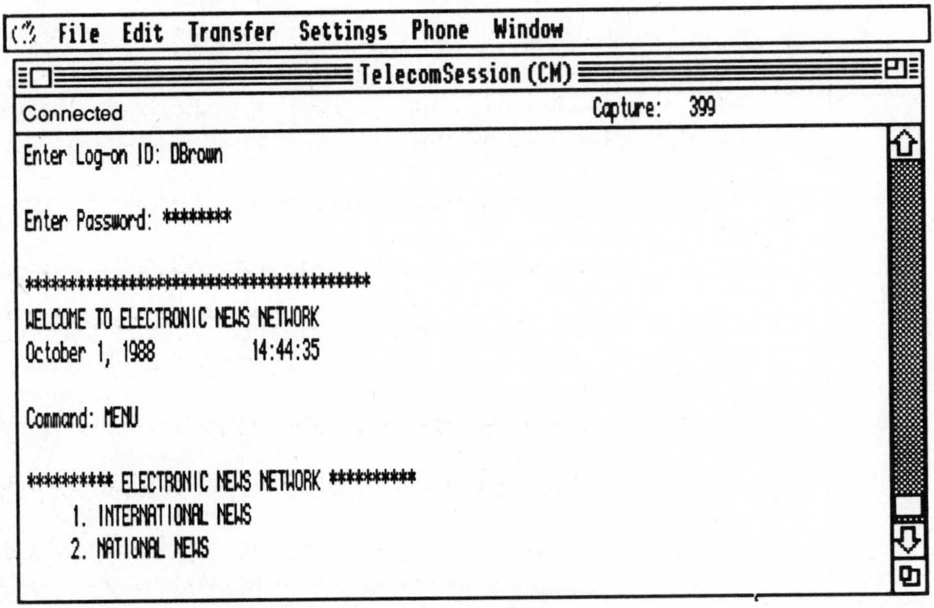

File Edit Transfer Settings Phone Window
TelecomSession (CM)
Connected
Capture: 399
Enter Log-on ID: DBrown
Enter Password: *******
****
WELCOME TO ELECTRONIC NEWS NETWORK
October 1, 1988 14:44:35
Command: MENU
********** ELECTRONIC NEWS NETWORK **********
1. INTERNATIONAL NEWS
2. NATIONAL NEWS

Figure 17-2 Typical opening dialog in communications session

Fast-dialing a number

When you enter a number into the Phone List, you can specify a fast-dial character for the number. This lets you dial the number with a single keystroke at any time.

To fast-dial a number:

1 **Hold down the Option key.**

2 **Press the fast-dial character for the number.**

The fast-dial character was specified when you entered the telephone number in the Dial dialog box.

The number is dialed and a connection is made.

Autodialing a number

The Autodial feature lets the computer automatically redial a busy number. When you completed the Communications dialog box earlier, you specified the number of seconds to wait before redialing a busy number.

To redial a busy number:

1 **Select the Autodial command from the Phone menu.**

A check mark appears to the left of the Autodial command.

2 **Dial a telephone number.**

If the telephone number is busy, the telecommunications application automatically redials the number.

The number of seconds that the application waits before redialing is specified by selecting Communications on the Settings menu.

Transferring text

One important application of communications is **transferring text** information from one computer to the other. AppleWorks GS lets you receive text sent from a remote computer and send text to the remote computer.

You can transfer text in several ways:

- You can type text directly into the Telecommunications document. As you type the text, the text is sent to the other computer.
- You can type text into the Edit Line. When you press the Return key at the end of the line, the line of text is sent to the other computer.

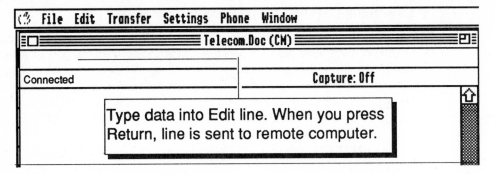

Figure 17-3   Edit Line in use

- You can capture text as it is sent from the second computer, using the Capture Text command. After the text is captured, you can save it in a text file on your disk.
- You can send a text file to the other computer using the Send Text command.

Sending text from the Edit Line

If you type from the keyboard directly into the telecommunications document, each character is sent to the other computer as you type it.

You may want to prepare an entire line of text before it is sent, and then send the entire line at one time. You can display and use an edit line at the top of the document to prepare a line of text for transmission.

To use the edit line:

$\boxed{1}$ **Select the Edit Line command from the Settings menu.**

An input bar appears at the top of the screen. This input bar is called the edit line.

$\boxed{2}$ **Type your desired text into the edit line. (See Figure 17-3.)**

You can use the usual mouse commands, keyboard commands, and Clipboard commands to prepare a line of text.

$\boxed{3}$ **When the line is complete, press the Return key.**

The line of text appears in your document window and is sent to the other computer.

Capturing text from the remote computer

During the session, your computer and the remote computer exchange information by sending text messages back and forth. As text is sent back and forth, the text appears in your document window.

When the document window is full, the text at the top of the window scrolls off the top of the window. You can use the window's scroll bars to review the previous 256 lines of text, but you may want to save parts of the text transmission in a more permanent form.

The Capture Text command lets you control a recorder in your computer's memory. You can turn on the recorder at any time and "capture" desired parts of the transmission. When you turn the recorder off, you can save the captured text in permanent form as a document on a storage disk, and you can use the word processing application to examine and print the document later.

To capture text that is being transmitted:

1 **Select the Capture Text command from the Transfer menu.**

If you have selected the Status Bar command from the Settings menu, the message "Capture: On" appears on the status bar. The Capture Text command is replaced on the menu by End Text Capture.

2 **Continue the communications session.**

As information appears in the document window, the text is temporarily saved in your computer's memory. It is temporarily saved in a special storage area called the Capture Text Buffer. (See Figure 17-4.)

3 **When you no longer wish to save the information being transferred, select the End Text Capture command on the Transfer menu.**

The status bar displays the message "Capture: Off."
The Save As dialog box appears, and you can specify a name and a storage disk to store the text that was captured.

4 **Complete the Save As dialog, and click the OK button.**

The text that has been captured is saved on the specified disk. You can review and print the text later with the word processing application.

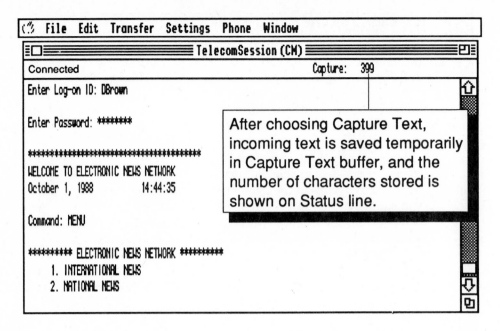

Figure 17-4 Capture Buffer in use

Reviewing the text in a session

As you capture the text in a session, the text is displayed in the document window. The document window contains a scroll bar; you can use the scroll bar to review part of the session.

After the document window fills, information will begin to scroll off the top of the window, just as information in a word processing document scrolls off the top of the window.

You can use the scroll bar to review the previous 256 lines of this session. (See Figure 17-5.)

The previous 256 lines are saved in a Review Buffer, and you can use the scroll bars to see the contents of this buffer.

How does this Review Buffer compare with the Capture Text Buffer? If you have selected the Capture Text command and are capturing text, the Capture Text Buffer is recording the text during the session. The Review Buffer may contain a maximum of 256 lines; the amount of text that can be stored in the Capture Text Buffer is much larger. However, you cannot use the scroll bars to see more than the previous 256 lines. To see the entire Capture Text Buffer, you can end text capture, save the Capture Text Buffer, and open the word processing application to see the entire buffer.

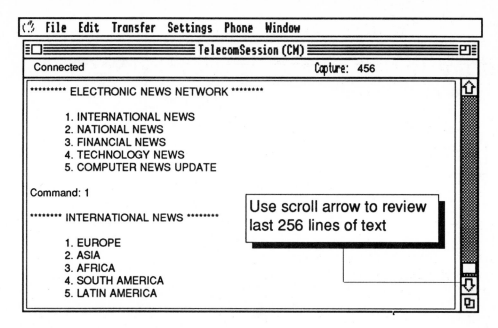

Figure 17-5   Use scroll bars to review text in Review Buffer

Sending text to the other computer

You can send an entire text file to the other computer with the Send Text command. A text file is a file saved in the ASCII text format. When you save a document in this format, only the actual characters in the document are saved; special features like fonts and styles are not stored when a document is saved in ASCII text format.

When should you use the Send Text command? This command lets you send an ASCII text file to the remote computer, and it sends these simple files in the simplest way. However, the Send Text command does not let you use special rules called protocols to check that the information was transmitted correctly. Two popular error-checking protocols are called the Xmodem and Ymodem protocols. To send text files using error-checking protocols like Xmodem or Ymodem, use the Send File command or Send Batch command; for more information on these commands, see "Transferring Files" in the following section.

To send a text file:

1   **Select the Send Text command from the Transfer menu.**

A dialog box appears, and displays the names of the text files available on the current disk (see Figure 17-6).

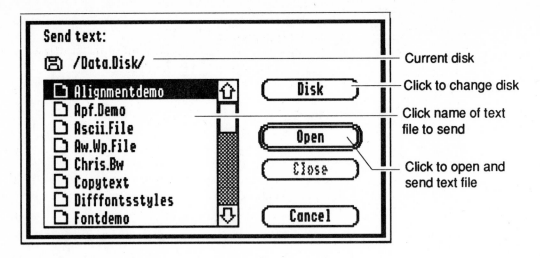

Send text:

🖫 /Data.Disk/ ————————————————— Current disk

☐ Alignmentdemo ⬆ (**Disk**) ————————— Click to change disk

☐ Apf.Demo ——————————— Click name of text
☐ Ascii.File file to send
☐ Aw.Wp.File (**Open**)
☐ Chris.Bw
☐ Copytext (**Close**) ————————————— Click to open and
☐ Difffontsstyles send text file
☐ Fontdemo ⬇ (**Cancel**)

Figure 17-6   Send Text dialog box

> **2**   **Click on the name of the text file that you want to send, and click the Send button.**

The specified text file is sent to the other computer.

Transferring files

Another important use of telecommunications is the transfer of entire files from one computer to another. You may want to send several different kinds of files, including

- Text files, stored in ASCII text format. Only the characters in a document are stored; special characteristics like fonts and styles are not stored.
- Binary files, which can store graphics information, programs, or documents with special information. A special format called Binary II format stores both the actual content of the document and other information, such as the file type and length of the file.

AppleWorks GS provides these commands to handle file transfers:

- **Send Text command.** This command lets you send an ASCII text file to the other computer. This command was discussed in the previous section.

- **Send File command.** This command is used to select and send a single file to the other computer.
- **Receive File command.** This command is used to receive a file being transmitted to you from the other computer.
- **Send Batch command.** This command is used to select one or more files and then send the batch of files to the other computer.
- **Receive Batch command.** This command lets you receive one or more files from the other computer.
- **Send Binary II command.** This command is used to select and send files in the special Binary II format to the remote computer.
- **Receive Binary II command.** This command lets you receive files in the special Binary II format from the remote computer.

When would you use the different commands?

AppleWorks GS provides several different commands to send and receive files, and it's important to understand which commands should be used to handle different situations.

- Use the Send Text command to send a text file. The text file is sent to the remote computer, but no special error-checking protocols can be specified.
- Use the other commands to send and receive files using special error-checking protocols. When you send files to the remote computer, you may select either Xmodem or Ymodem to check the accuracy of the transmission. When you receive files, you may select the Xmodem, Ymodem, or Xmodem CRC protocols. Both your computer and the remote computer should use the same protocol during the transfer.
- Use the Send File or Receive File commands to send or receive single files.
- Use the Send Batch or Receive Batch commands to send or receive a specified group of files in the same transmission.
- Use the Send Binary II or Receive Binary II commands to send or receive files using the special Binary II format. This format stores not only the simple data in a document, but also special information like the file type and length. This format is particularly useful, since it lets you transfer graphics or database files that can be used immediately by specific applications.

Sending a file to the remote computer

You can specify and send one file to the remote computer with the Send File command on the Transfer menu.

To send a file:

1 **Select the Send File command from the Transfer menu.**

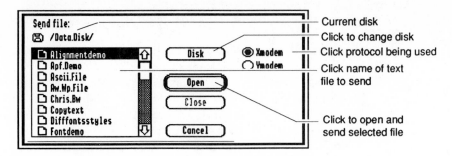

Figure 17-7 Send File dialog

A dialog box appears and displays a list of the files available to send. (See Figure 17-7.)

2 **Select the file that you want to send.**

3 **Click the protocol to use for the transmission.**

As files are transmitted, special rules (called protocols) can be used to ensure that the files have been sent correctly. This box lets you specify either the Xmodem or Ymodem protocols. Be sure that both your computer and the remote computer that is receiving the file are set to use the same protocols.

4 **Click the Open button.**

The Open button opens the specified file and sends the file to the other computer.

Receiving a file from the remote computer

You can prepare your computer to receive a file from the other computer with the Receive File command.

To receive a file:

1 **Select the Receive File command from the Transfer menu.**

A dialog box appears (see Figure 17-8).

2 **Type a name for the file into the input bar.**

3 **Click the protocol that both computers are using for this transmission.**

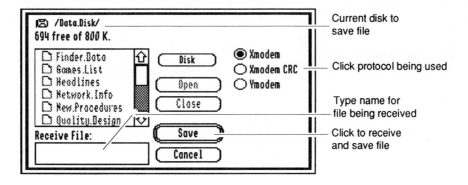

Figure 17-8 Receive File dialog

As files are transmitted, special rules (called protocols) can be used to ensure that the files have been sent correctly. This box lets you specify either the Xmodem, Ymodem, or XModem CRC protocols. Be sure that both your computer and the remote computer that is sending the file are set to use the same protocols.

4 **Click the OK button.**

When the file has been sent from the other computer, it is saved on the specified disk with the specified name.

Sending a batch of files

This command lets you select one or more files on your computer and send the files in a batch to the other computer.
To send a batch of files:

1 **Select the Send Batch command from the Transfer menu.**

The Send Batch dialog box appears (see Figure 17-9).
This dialog box displays a list of the files currently selected to send. When you first select this command, no files are currently selected.

2 **Click the Add button in the dialog box.**

A second dialog box appears and displays the files available to send from the current disk. (See Figure 17-10.)
To see the files on other disks, eject the current disk, insert a new disk, and click the Disk button.

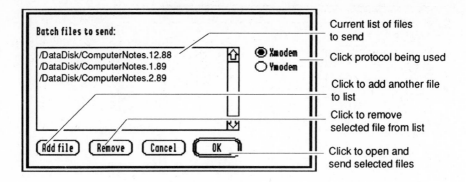

Figure 17-9   Send Batch dialog

    3   **Click on the name of the file that you want to add to the list being sent, and then click the Open button.**

The selected file is added to the list of files to send to the other computer.

    4   **To add another file to the list of files being sent, repeat steps 2 and 3.**

Continue to add files until you have created the desired list of files to send to the other computer.

    5   **To remove a file from the list being sent, click on the file name, and then click the Remove button.**

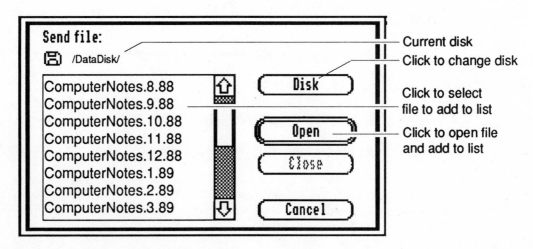

Figure 17-10   Display Available Files dialog

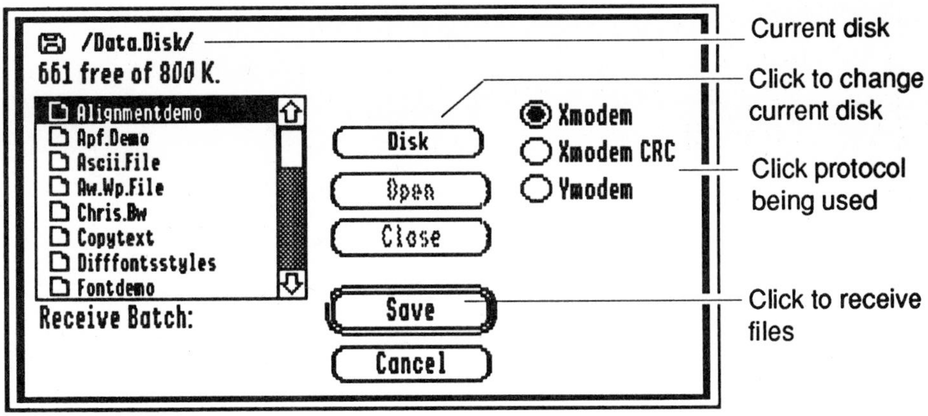
/Data.Disk/
661 free of 800 K.
Alignmentdemo
Apf.Demo
Ascii.File
Aw.Wp.File
Chris.Bw
Copytext
Difffontsstyles
Fontdemo
Receive Batch:
Disk
Open
Close
Save
Cancel
Xmodem
Xmodem CRC
Ymodem
Current disk
Click to change current disk
Click protocol being used
Click to receive files

Figure 17-11 Receive Batch dialog

After you click the Remove button, the selected name is removed from the list of files to send.

6 **To send the files to the other computer, click on the OK button.**

When you click on the OK button, the files are sent to the other computer in the order that they are listed in the dialog box.

Receiving a batch of files

You can set your computer to receive a batch of files from the remote computer with the Receive Batch command.

To receive a batch of files:

1 **Select the Receive Batch command from the Transfer menu.**

A dialog box appears (see Figure 17-11).

2 **Click on the transfer protocol being used by the other computer.**

3 **Specify the disk where the files should be saved.**

The dialog box displays the current disk (or folder). The files being received will be stored on that disk. To select a different disk, click the Disk button until the name of the desired disk is displayed.

4 **Click the OK button.**

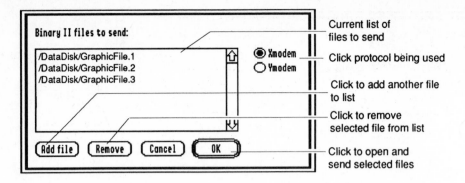

Figure 17-12   Send Binary II dialog

When the files have been sent from the other computer, they are saved on the specified disk. The files are saved with the same names used on the other computer.

To send a Binary II file

This command lets you send files in the Binary II format to the remote computer. This file contains not only the actual data stored in the document, but also special information like file type and file length. This extra information lets a specific application use the document more easily.

1   **Select the Send Binary II command from the Transfer menu.**

The Send Binary II dialog box appears (see Figure 17-12).
This dialog box displays a list of the files currently selected to send.

2   **Click the Add button in the dialog box.**

A second dialog box appears and displays the file available to send from the current disk. (See Figure 17-13.)

3   **Click on the name of the file that you want to add to the list being sent, and then click the Open button.**

The selected file is added to the list of files to send to the other computer.

4   **To add another file to the list of files being sent, repeat steps 2 and 3.**

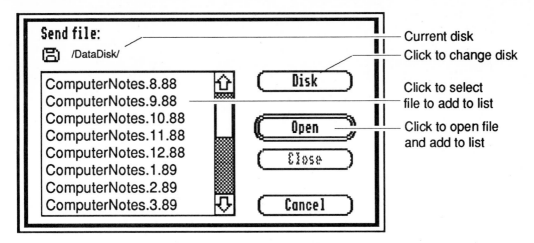

Figure 17-13 Available files displayed

Continue to add files until you have created the desired list of files to send to the other computer.

[5] **To remove a file from the list being sent, click on the file name, and then click the Remove button.**

After you click the Remove button, the selected name is removed from the list of files to send.

[6] **To send the files to the other computer, click on the OK button.**

When you click on the OK button, the files are sent to the other computer in the order that they are listed in the dialog box.

To receive a Binary II file

You can set your computer to receive a batch of files in the Binary II format from the remote computer with the Receive Binary II command.
To receive a batch of files in Binary II format:

[1] **Select the Receive Binary II command from the Transfer menu.**

A dialog box appears (see Figure 17-14).

[2] **Click on the transfer protocol being used by the other computer.**

[3] **Specify the disk where the files should be saved.**

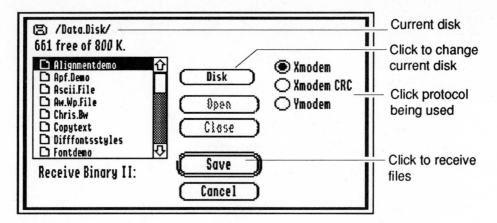

Figure 17-14   Receive Binary II dialog

The dialog box displays the current disk (or folder). The files being received will be stored on that disk. To select a different disk, click the Disk button until the name of the desired disk is displayed.

4   **Click the OK button.**

When the files have been sent from the other computer, they are saved on the specified disk. The files are saved with the same names used on the other computer.

Ending a session

When you are ready to end a communications session, the remote computer may provide a special procedure to end the session. You may be asked to log off the remote computer in a special way.

You can break off a communications connection by hanging up the phone line, in much the same way that you hang up your telephone to break a connection.

To break the connection, select the Hangup command on the Phone menu. This disconnects your computer from the remote computer and ends the communications session.

Using your computer as the remote system

If you wish, you can arrange for your computer to act as the remote computer. You can connect it to the telephone system, and then wait for another computer to dial your number and establish a connection.

To make your computer the remote computer:

| 1 | **Select Answer Phone from the Phone menu.**

A checkmark appears to the left of the Answer Phone command.

| 2 | **Wait for an incoming call.**

Your computer is now acting as a remote computer for other computers to call. To stop receiving calls, select the Answer Phone command again, and the checkmark is removed from the command.

The next step

The previous chapters have demonstrated the six AppleWorks GS applications. You can use each of these applications independently, but it's important to realize that you can easily transfer information from document to document inside AppleWorks GS.

In the following chapter, you will learn:

- how to transfer information between documents created by the same application
- how to transfer information between documents created by different applications
- how to import information from programs other than AppleWorks GS
- how to export AppleWorks GS information to other programs

Chapter 18

Transferring Information in AppleWorks GS

About this chapter

AppleWorks GS lets you transfer information between documents created by the same application or between documents created by different applications.

In addition, you can bring information from files created by other programs into AppleWorks GS documents, or prepare AppleWorks GS documents so that they can be used by other programs.

This chapter surveys the ways that you can transfer information between documents within AppleWorks GS, import information from other programs, or export AppleWorks GS documents to other programs.

The topics in this chapter include

- Using the Clipboard to transfer information
- Using Control-drag to transfer information
- Using Import File to import information
- Using Save As options to export information

Transferring information

When you create a document, you may later want to transfer part of the information in the document to another document. The second document may be created by the same AppleWorks GS application, or it might be created by another application. For example, you might want to transfer some of the text in one word processing document into a second word processing document, or you might want to transfer it into a database or page layout document.

On other occasions, you might want to transfer the entire contents of a document into a second AppleWorks GS document. For example, you might create a word processing document, and then you may want to transfer the entire contents of that document into a second document. You may create a graphics document, and then you may want to transfer the entire document into a page layout document.

On still other occasions, you might want to save your AppleWorks GS documents in a form that can be used by other programs. AppleWorks GS provides commands that can handle each of these situations:

- You can use the Clipboard to transfer part or all of a document to a second AppleWorks GS document.
- You can use the Control-drag feature to graphically drag part or all of one document from one location to another.
- You can use the Import File command to paste the contents of an entire file into a document.
- You can use Save As options to save your AppleWorks GS documents in a format that can be used by other programs.

Using the Clipboard to copy information

The Clipboard is a special part of memory that temporarily stores a selected part of a document, and it can store text or graphics. The Clipboard is used with the Cut, Copy, and Paste commands on the Edit menu to copy selected information from one location to another inside AppleWorks GS.

Copying information with the Clipboard

The Clipboard can be used to transfer information from one location to another within the same document, or to a location in a different document.

To transfer information with the Clipboard:

1 **Select the text or graphics that you want to transfer.**

The information may consist of a block of text in a word processing document, selected fields in a database, selected cells in a spreadsheet, selected text or graphics objects in a graphics or page layout document, or selected text in a telecommunications document. Any information in a document that can be selected can be transferred with the Clipboard.

2 | **Select the Cut or Copy command on the Edit menu.**

If you select the Cut command, the selected information is removed from the document and copied to the Clipboard. If you select the Copy command, a copy of the information is placed on the Clipboard, and the original copy is left in place.

3 | **Move to a new location.**

This new location might be in the same document, or it might be in a different document.

4 | **Select the Paste command on the Edit menu.**

The contents of the Clipboard are copied to the new location.

If you copy information from one document to another, it is important to understand that different applications handle the actual transfer of information somewhat differently. The following sections describe how information is transferred from each AppleWorks GS application to other applications.

Copying information from a word processing document

You can use the Clipboard to transfer text information from a word processing document to a database, spreadsheet, graphics, or page layout document. You can also copy text from a word processing document to the telecommunications application to send to the remote computer.

Since you can transfer information from word processing to the database or the spreadsheet, you may find that this is a convenient way to prepare information for a database or spreadsheet document. The word processing application provides convenient text-editing commands, and it is somewhat easier to enter information into a word processing document. (See Figure 18-1.)

To copy data from word processing into a database:

1 | **Prepare a word processing document that contains the information that you want to enter into a database.**

The information should be arranged in a table and should observe these rules:

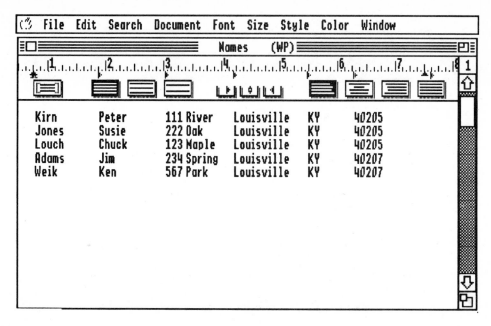

Figure 18-1 Database entries created in a word processing document

- Press the Tab key between each field entry.
- Press the Return key at the end of each record entry.

| 2 | Select the information that you want to transfer to the database and choose the Copy command on the Edit menu. |

| 3 | Open the database document, and display the document in List view. |

| 4 | Click the first cell where you want to begin to copy the information from the Clipboard, and select the Paste command on the Edit menu. |

The information is copied from the Clipboard. Information is copied into the first selected field until the first Tab character is reached; the next information is copied to the next field in the same record until the second Tab character is reached, and so forth. When the Return character is reached, information is copied into the next record.

Static text fields can display formatted text. Use Copy and Paste to copy formatted text from a word processing document into a selected static text field.

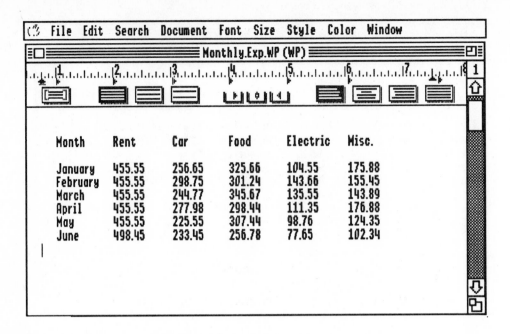

Figure 18-2 Spreadsheet entries created in a word processing document

If the Paste command tries to paste information of one type into a database field that is defined to use a different type, the database field is left blank.

To copy data from word processing into a spreadsheet:

1. **Prepare a word processing document that contains the information that you want to enter into a spreadsheet. (See Figure 18-2.)**

The information should be arranged in a table and should observe these rules:

- Press the Tab key between each cell entry.
- Press the Return key at the end of each row of information.

2. **Select the information that you want to transfer to the spreadsheet and choose the Copy command on the Edit menu.**

3. **Open the spreadsheet document.**

4   **Click the cell where you want to begin to copy the information on the Clipboard, and select the Paste command on the Edit menu.**

The information is copied from the Clipboard. Information is copied into the first cell until the first Tab character is reached; the next information is copied to the next cell in the same row until the second Tab character is reached, and so forth. When the Return character is reached, information is copied into the next row of the spreadsheet.

To copy text from word processing into a graphics document:

1   **Select the text that you want to transfer to a graphics document.**

2   **Choose the Copy command on the Edit menu.**

3   **Open the graphics document.**

4   **Select the Paste command on the Edit menu.**

Each line of the selected text is copied into its own text object. Remember that a text object in a graphics document can only be one line long.

To copy text from word processing into page layout:

1   **Select the text that you want to transfer to a page layout document.**

2   **Choose the Copy command on the Edit menu.**

3   **Open the page layout document to the desired page.**

4   **Use the Paste command to copy the text into the document.**

You can use the Paste command in two ways. If you select the Paste command without selecting a text object, the text is copied from the Clipboard into a new text object. If you select a text object and place an insertion point inside the text object before choosing the Paste command, the Paste command copies the text at the location of the insertion point.

To copy text from word processing into telecommunications:

1   **Select the text in a word processing document that you would like to transmit to the remote computer during a communications session.**

2   **Choose the Copy command on the Edit menu.**

3   **Open the telecommunications application.**

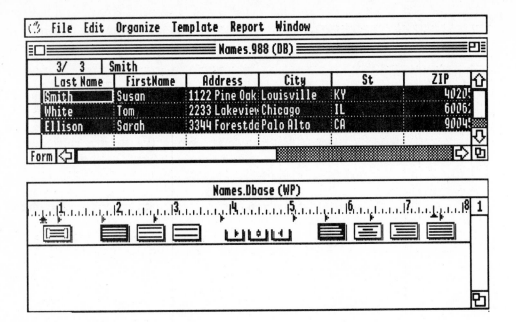

Figure 18-3 Database entries selected

---

4 | **Connect to the remote computer and begin the session.**

5 | **Select the Paste command when you want to send the text to the other computer.**

When you select Paste, the text appears in your window and is sent to the other computer.

Copying information from a database document

You can use the Clipboard to transfer information from a database document to a word processing, spreadsheet, graphics, or page layout document. You can also copy information from a database document to the telecommunications application to send to the remote computer.

In general, the information is transferred from the database to other applications in the form of a table copied from List view in the database.

To copy data from a database into word processing:

1 | **Display the database in List view.**

2 | **Select the database information that you want to copy, and choose the Copy command. (See Figure 18-3.)**

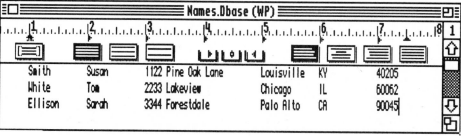

Figure 18-4 Database entries copied into a word processing document

3 Open the word processing document and click at the desired insertion point.

4 Select the Paste command on the Edit menu.

The information is copied from the Clipboard into the word processing document. A Tab character is placed after each field entry, and a Return character is placed after each record. (See Figure 18-4.)

To copy data from a database into a spreadsheet:

1 Display the database in List view.

2 Select the database information that you want to copy, and choose the Copy command.

3 Open the spreadsheet document and click the cell where you want to begin copying information.

4 Select the Paste command on the Edit menu.

The information is copied from the Clipboard into the spreadsheet. The first field entry is placed in the selected cell, the next field entry in the record is placed in the next cell in the same row, and so forth. Each field entry from the database is placed in a cell, and each record begins a new row in the spreadsheet.

To copy data from a database into a graphics document:

[1] **Select the database information that you want to copy, and choose the Copy command.**

You could select and copy the contents of text or picture fields to the Clipboard.

[2] **Open the graphics document and select the Paste command on the Edit menu.**

The selected information is copied from the Clipboard into the graphics document. If you selected text information, the information is displayed in the graphics document as one or more text objects; each line of text is displayed as one text object. If you copied graphics from a picture field, the graphic is displayed as a graphics object.

To copy data from a database into page layout:

[1] **Select the database information that you want to copy, and choose the Copy command.**

You might select and copy text information, or you might select and copy graphics from a picture field.

[2] **Open the page layout document and move to the desired page.**

[3] **Select the Paste command on the Edit menu.**

The information is copied from the Clipboard into the page layout document.

If you select a text object and place an insertion point in the object before selecting Paste, the Paste command copies text information as a table at the insertion point. A Tab character is placed after each field entry, and a Return character is placed after each record.

If you did not select an insertion point, the Paste command copies text into a new text object, with a Tab character between field entries and a Return character at the end of each record.

Graphics contained in picture fields are copied to the page as separate graphics objects.

To copy data from a database into telecommunications:

[1] **Display the database in List view.**

[2] **Select the database information that you want to copy, and choose the Copy command.**

The information in picture fields cannot be transferred into a telecommunications document.

3 **Open the telecommunications application and connect to the remote computer.**

4 **When you are ready to transmit the information, select the Paste command on the Edit menu.**

The information is copied from the Clipboard into the telecommunications window and is sent to the other computer, with a Tab character placed between each field entry and a Return character at the end of each record.

Copying information from a spreadsheet document

You can use the Clipboard to transfer information from a spreadsheet document to a word processing, database, graphics, or page layout document. You can also copy information from a spreadsheet document to the telecommunications application to send to the remote computer.

In general, the information is transferred from the spreadsheet to other applications in the form of a table that resembles the spreadsheet format.

To copy data from a spreadsheet into word processing:

1 **Select the spreadsheet information that you want to copy, and choose the Copy command. (See Figure 18-5.)**

2 **Open the word processing document and click at the desired insertion point.**

3 **Select the Paste command on the Edit menu.**

The information is copied from the Clipboard into the word processing document. A Tab character is placed after each cell entry, and a Return character is placed after each row in the spreadsheet. (See Figure 18-6.)

To copy data from a spreadsheet into a database

1 **Select the spreadsheet information that you want to copy, and choose the Copy command.**

2 **Open the database document and display the database in List view.**

3 **Click the database cell where you want to begin to copy the information.**

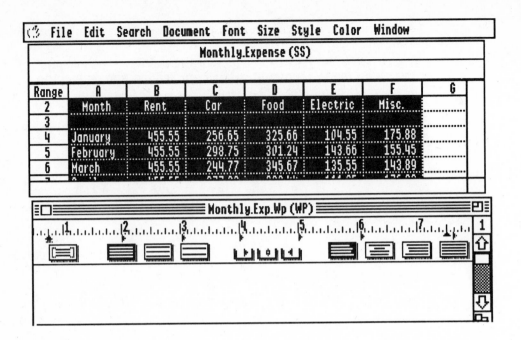

Figure 18-5 Spreadsheet entries selected

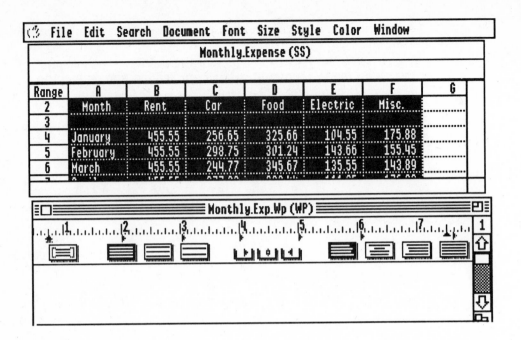

Figure 18-6 Spreadsheet entries copied into a word processing document

4   **Select the Paste command on the Edit menu.**

The information is copied from the Clipboard into the spreadsheet. The first cell entry is placed in the selected database field, the next cell entry is placed in the next database field in the same record, and so forth. At the end of each row of spreadsheet information, information is copied into the next record in the database.

If the Paste command tries to copy data of one type into a field defined to store a different type of data, the field is left blank.

To copy data from a spreadsheet into a graphics document:

1   **Select the spreadsheet information that you want to copy, and choose the Copy command.**

2   **Open the graphics document, and select the Paste command on the Edit menu.**

The selected information is copied from the Clipboard into the graphics document. The information is displayed in the graphics document as one or more text objects; each row of spreadsheet data is displayed as one text object.

To copy data from a spreadsheet into page layout:

1   **Select the spreadsheet information that you want to copy, and choose the Copy command.**

2   **Open the page layout document and move to the desired page.**

3   **Select the Paste command on the Edit menu.**

The information is copied from the Clipboard into the page layout document.

If you select a text object and place an insertion point in the object before selecting Paste, the Paste command copies the spreadsheet information as a table at the insertion point. A Tab character is placed after each cell entry, and a Return character is placed at the end of each row.

If you did not select an insertion point, the Paste command copies the spreadsheet information into a new text object, with a Tab character between cell entries and a Return character at the end of each row.

To copy spreadsheet data into telecommunications:

1   **Select the spreadsheet information that you want to send to the remote computer, and choose the Copy command.**

2   **Open the telecommunications application and connect to the remote computer.**

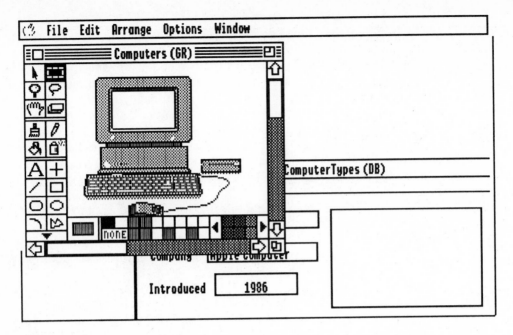

Figure 18-7 Graphics entries selected

| 3 | When you are ready to transmit the information, select the Paste command on the Edit menu. |

The information is copied from the Clipboard into the telecommunications window and is sent to the other computer, with a Tab character placed between each cell entry and a Return character at the end of each row.

Copying information from a graphics document

You can use the Clipboard to transfer information from a graphics document to a database or page layout document. (A word processing, spreadsheet, or telecommunications document cannot display graphics.)

To copy from a graphics document into a database document:

| 1 | Select the graphics that you want to copy, and choose the Copy command. (See Figure 18-7.) |

| 2 | Open the database document and display the database in Form view. |

| 3 | Move to the desired record and select the picture field where you want to copy the graphic. |

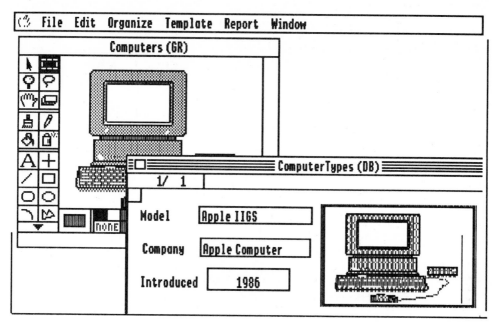

Figure 18-8 Graphic entries copied into database document

> 4 | **Select the Paste command on the Edit menu. (See Figure 18-8.)**

To copy graphics into page layout:

> 1 | **Select the graphics that you want to copy, and choose the Copy command.**

> 2 | **Open the page layout document and move to the desired page.**

> 3 | **Select the Paste command on the Edit menu.**

The graphics object is copied from the Clipboard into the page layout document.

Copying from page layout and telecommunications

Page layout documents are similar to word processing and graphics documents. Text can be copied following the same rules as text copied from a word processing document, and graphics are copied following the same rules as graphics copied from a graphics document.

The telecommunications document is a simple text document. You can copy text from the telecommunications document following the same rules as text copied from a word processing document.

Using Control-drag to copy information

The Control-drag feature is a special feature of AppleWorks GS that lets you copy information from one location to another and see the movement displayed graphically on the screen.

You can use this Control-drag feature in any of the situations described in the previous section as a replacement for the Copy and Paste commands.

To use Control-drag:

1. Open a window that contains the information that you want to transfer.

2. Resize the window so that it occupies only a part of the screen.

3. Open a window that displays the document where you want to copy the information.

4. Resize the second window so that you can see the contents of both windows on the screen at once.

5. Click in the window that contains the information that you want to copy.

This window becomes the active window. The active window is always displayed at the top of an overlapping stack of windows, and the title bar of the active window displays horizontal stripes.

6. Select the information that you want to copy.

7. Hold down the Control key and the mouse button, and drag the selected information over into the destination window.

As you drag the selected information from one window to the other, the cursor takes the shape of a lightning bolt. (See Figure 18-9.)

8. Release the Control key and the mouse button when the lightning bolt is in the destination window.

The selected information is displayed in the destination window.

You can then click the Zoom box on the destination window, to display the destination window on the full screen, and make any desired changes to the information that was copied.

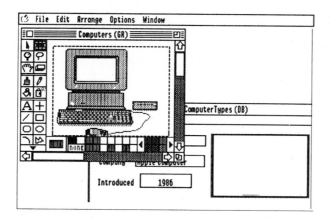

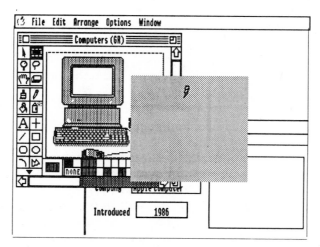

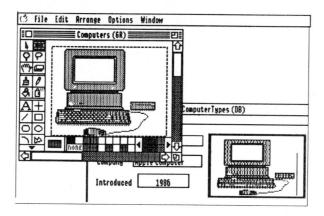

Figure 18-9   You can visually move information using Control-drag

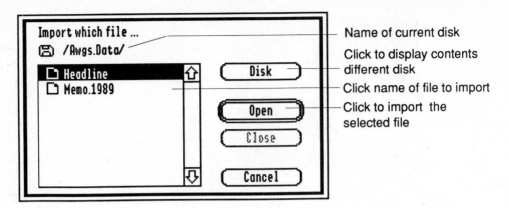

Figure 18-10   Import File dialog

Copying entire files into a document

The Copy and Paste commands let you easily transfer part of one document into another document. Sometimes you might want to copy the entire contents of one document into a second document.

The Import File command lets you copy an entire file or document into the current document. In effect, the Import File command performs a "paste" operation, but what is pasted is not the contents of the Clipboard — it's the contents of a selected file or document.

Each AppleWorks GS application can import specific kinds of files. Documents can be imported that were produced by AppleWorks GS applications, as well as documents produced by AppleWorks, MultiScribe GS, and some graphics applications. You can also import files stored as ASCII text files.

Using the Import File command

The Import File command pastes the contents of a selected document at a specified location in the current document.

To use the Import File command:

1   **Choose the Import File command on the File menu.**

The Import File dialog box appears (see Figure 18-10).
The document list box shows the files that can be imported from the current disk. To see the contents of other disks, click the Disk button.

2   **Click the name of the document that you want to import.**

|3| **Click the Open button.**

The contents of the selected document are pasted into the current document at the current location.

Importing files into a word processing document

When you choose the Import File command inside a word processing document, the Import File command pastes the contents of the specified file at the current location of the insertion point.

The word processing application can import the following files:

- AppleWorks GS word processing documents
- Classic AppleWorks word processing files
- MultiScribe GS word processing files
- Text files saved as ASCII text files

When you import other AppleWorks GS word processing documents or MultiScribe GS documents, the text fonts, styles, sizes, and colors are all imported. Graphics from MultiScribe GS documents are not imported.

Some styles are imported with classic AppleWorks files. Boldface, underline, superscript, and subscript styles are imported. Margin settings and spacing are also imported. Any merge fields in the file are treated as ordinary text; to use a classic AppleWorks file as a merge document, you must add new merge fields. For more information on merge fields, see Chapter 8, Merge Documents and Mailing Labels.

Importing files into a database document

When you choose the Import File command inside a database document, you can import both text and graphics into the document.

The database application can import text files saved as ASCII text, with the text in the file entered into fields in the database. You can also import a graphics document into a selected picture field.

To import the text information into database fields:

|1| **Display the database in List view and select the cell where you want to begin copying the information in the text file.**

|2| **Choose the Import File command on the File menu.**

A dialog box asks for the format in which the field entries are stored in the file (see Figure 18-11).

After you click the format used to store information in the file, the text in the file is copied into the database fields.

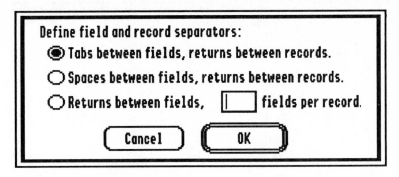

Figure 18-11 Import Into Database dialog box

To import graphics into the database:

1. **Select the picture field where you want to import the graphic.**

2. **Choose the Import File command.**

The Import File dialog box displays graphics documents that can be imported. The database application can import graphics files stored in one of these formats:

- AppleWorks GS graphics documents
- Apple Preferred Format (APF)
- Paint (PNT) format
- PICT format
- Screen format (320 or 640)

3. **Select the graphics document that you want to import, and click the OK button.**

The selected graphic is displayed in the picture field.

Importing files into a spreadsheet document

When you choose the Import File command inside a spreadsheet document, you can import ASCII text files into the document. The ASCII text files can contain information stored in several different formats. You must specify the format when the file is imported.

To import the text information into a spreadsheet:

1. **Select the spreadsheet cell where you want to begin copying the information in the text file.**

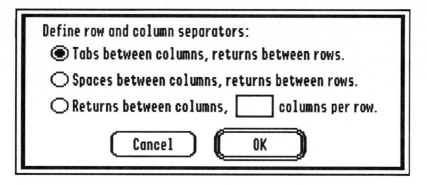

Figure 18-12   Import Into Spreadsheet dialog box

2   **Choose the Import File command on the File menu.**

A dialog box asks for the format in which the spreadsheet entries are stored in the file (see Figure 18-12).

After you click the format used to store information in the file, the text in the file is copied into spreadsheet cells.

Importing files into a graphics document

When you choose the Import File command inside a graphics document, you can import the contents of other AppleWorks GS graphics documents or graphics produced by other programs.

To import graphics into a graphics document:

1   **Choose the Import File command on the File menu.**

The Import File dialog box displays graphics documents that can be imported. The graphics application can import graphics files stored in one of these formats:

- AppleWorks GS graphics documents
- Apple Preferred Format (APF)
- Paint (PNT) format
- PICT format
- Screen format (320 or 640)

2   **Select the graphics document that you want to import, and click the OK button.**

The selected graphic is displayed in the current graphics document.

Importing files into a page layout document

When you choose the Import File command inside a page layout document, you can import text stored in word processing files, as well as graphics produced by AppleWorks GS or by other programs.

The page layout application follows a combination of rules observed by the word processing application and the graphics application.

To import text into a page layout document:

1	**Move to the page where you want to import the text.**

2	**Place an insertion point inside a text object if you wish.**

If you place an insertion point in a text object, the imported text will be pasted at the location of the insertion point. If you do not place an insertion point, a new text object will be created, and the imported text will be copied into the new text object.

3	**Choose the Import File command on the File menu.**

The Import File dialog box displays the text files that can be imported. The page layout application can import the following files:

- AppleWorks GS word processing documents
- Classic AppleWorks word processing files
- MultiScribe GS word processing files
- Text files saved as ASCII text files

4	**Select the text file that you want to import, and click the OK button.**

The selected file is copied into the page layout document.
To import a graphics document into page layout:

1	**Move to the page where you want to import the graphic.**

2	**Choose the Import File command.**

The Choose File dialog box displays the graphics documents that can be imported. The page layout application can import graphics files stored in one of these formats:

- AppleWorks GS graphics documents
- Apple Preferred Format (APF)
- Paint (PNT) format
- PICT format
- Screen format (320 or 640)

| 3 | Select the graphics document that you want to import, and click the OK button. |

The selected graphic is displayed on the current page of the document.

Importing files into telecommunications

When you choose the Import File command inside a communications session, the imported file is displayed in the document window and is transmitted to the remote computer.

To import text into telecommunications:

| 1 | Launch the telecommunications application and connect with the remote computer. |

| 2 | When you are ready to transmit a file, choose the Import File command on the File menu. |

The Import File dialog box displays documents that can be imported. The telecommunications application can import files stored in one of these formats:

- AppleWorks GS word processing documents
- Classic AppleWorks word processing files
- MultiScribe GS word processing files
- Text files saved as ASCII text files

| 3 | Select the document that you want to import, and click the OK button. |

The selected document is displayed in the document window and is transmitted to the remote computer.

Exporting files to other programs

The previous sections discussed importing information, or bringing information into an AppleWorks document. In some cases, you might want to export the information in your document; that is, you might want to provide the information to other computer users who are using programs other than AppleWorks GS. In fact, you might even want to provide the information to people using computers other than the Apple IIGS.

AppleWorks GS normally saves your work in a special format that is used by this program. This special format stores not only the text and numbers in your documents, but also a great deal of information about formatting, fonts, styles, and so forth. Other programs simply can't understand this format.

Fortunately, most of the AppleWorks GS applications let you save documents in a format that can be used by other programs (or even other computers).

For example, you can save text information as ASCII files, which save the text in a document, but none of the special formatting information. ASCII files can be understood by many other programs. You can even send ASCII text files to other computers using the telecommunications application, where the files can be used by other programs on the other computers.

Graphics documents can be saved in Apple Preferred Format, which is a format that can be used by other Apple II graphics programs.

In the word processing application, you can save your documents as ASCII text files, which can be exported and used by many other word processing programs.

In the database application you can save your database as an ASCII file, with tab characters placed after each field entry and a Return character placed at the end of each record.

In the spreadsheet application you can save your data as an ASCII text file, with tabs placed after each cell entry and a Return character placed at the end of each row.

The graphics application lets you save your graphics in Apple Preferred Format (APF). The page layout application does not let you save a page layout document in any other format. The telecommunications application lets you save files as ASCII text files.

Saving documents as ASCII text files

The word processing, database, and spreadsheet applications let you save documents as ASCII text files. The basic information from a document is saved in an ASCII text file, but fonts, styles, and other special formatting information is not saved.

When you have entered the desired information into a word processing document, database document, or spreadsheet, it is easy to save the information as an ASCII text file.

To save a document as an ASCII text file:

1 **Select the Save As command from the File menu.**

The Save As dialog box appears (see Figure 18-13).

2 **Type a name to use for the document.**

3 **If the desired storage disk is not displayed, click the Disk button until the desired disk is displayed.**

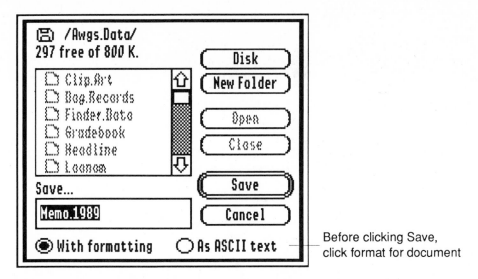

```
 ⊟ /Awgs.Data/
297 free of 800 K.                   ( Disk )
 ▢ Clip.Art            ⇧           ( New Folder )
 ▢ Dog.Records
 ▢ Finder.Data                       ( Open )
 ▢ Gradebook
 ▢ Headline                          ( Close )
 ▢ Loanam          ⇩
Save...                            (( Save ))
[Memo.1989]                          ( Cancel )
⦿ With formatting    ○ As ASCII text
```

Before clicking Save, click format for document

Figure 18-13   Save As dialog

4   **Click the Save As ASCII button, and click the OK button.**

The document is saved as an ASCII text file with the specified name on the specified disk.

If the document is a database document, a tab character is placed after each field entry, and a Return character is placed at the end of each record.

If the document is a spreadsheet document, a tab character is placed after each cell entry, and a Return character is placed at the end of each row.

Saving graphics in Apple Preferred Format

You can save your graphics documents in Apple Preferred Format, which is a format that can be used by other Apple II graphics programs.

To save your graphics in APF:

1   **Create the desired graphics document.**

2   **Select the Save As command from the File menu.**

The Save As dialog box appears (see Figure 18-14).

3   **Type an appropriate name for the document.**

4   **If the desired storage disk is not displayed, click the Disk box until the desired storage disk is displayed.**

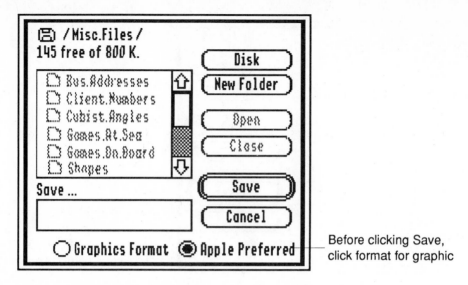

Disk

New Folder

Open

Close

Save

Cancel

Before clicking Save,
click format for graphic

Figure 18-14   Save As dialog box for graphics

5   **Click the Apple Preferred button, and click the OK button.**

The document is saved in the Apple Preferred Format with the specified name on the specified disk.

A final word

This book has shown you how to use AppleWorks GS to handle most of your important computer applications. You've seen how to create word processing documents, how to organize information in the database, how to perform calculations and generate charts with the spreadsheet, how to produce color graphics and then combine those graphics with text in a page layout document, and how to communicate with other computers. Finally, in this chapter you've seen how to transfer text and graphics between different AppleWorks documents and how to use AppleWorks GS with files produced by other programs.

As you use AppleWorks GS, you might like more detailed information about certain specialized topics, such as using classic AppleWorks documents, AppleWorks formulas and functions, or the specialized Edit Colors command. The following appendices contain more information on these topics.

For now, you're well-prepared to begin to use the power of AppleWorks GS in your home, school, or office. Good luck . . . and have fun with Apple-Works GS!

Appendix A

Using Classic AppleWorks Files

AppleWorks GS is designed to let you directly use any files that you may have created with classic AppleWorks. This appendix summarizes special information about any changes or limitations to your AppleWorks data that may occur when you use those files with AppleWorks GS.

Opening classic AppleWorks files

When you choose the Open command on the File menu, the Open File dialog box appears (see Figure A-1).

Classic AppleWorks files are displayed in the document list box. Files created by the AppleWorks word processor, database, or spreadsheet are represented by distinctive icons to the left of the file name. (See Figure A-2.)

Each type of classic AppleWorks file can be opened by the analogous AppleWorks GS application. The AppleWorks GS word processing application can open classic AppleWorks word processing files, the database application can open classic AppleWorks database files, and the spreadsheet application can open classic AppleWorks spreadsheet files.

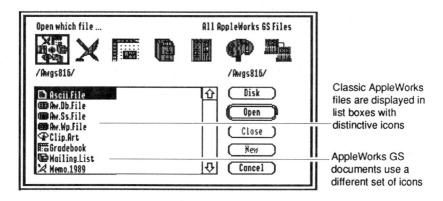

Figure A-1 Open File with AppleWorks files

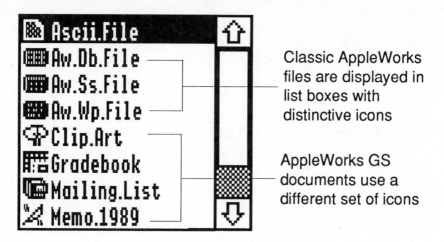

Classic AppleWorks files are displayed in list boxes with distinctive icons

AppleWorks GS documents use a different set of icons

Figure A-2   AppleWorks icons

Remember that the document list box displays all files that can currently be opened. If the AllTypes icon is selected at the top of the dialog box, all classic AppleWorks files are displayed in the list box. If the word processing icon is selected, only classic AppleWorks word processing files are displayed. If the database icon is selected, only classic AppleWorks database files are displayed. If the spreadsheet icon is selected, only classic AppleWorks spreadsheet files are displayed.

To open a classic AppleWorks file, use the same method used to open an AppleWorks GS file:

1   **Click on the name of the file to select the file.**

2   **Click the Open button on the dialog box.**

You could also simply double-click on the file name to select and open the file.

Opening classic AppleWorks word processing files

When you open a classic AppleWorks word processing file, the text contained in the file is displayed in a new word processing window. Many of the formatting options that you may have specified in the file are retained and displayed in the window. For example, if you had inserted the codes for boldface or underlining in the file, your text is now displayed on the screen as bold or underlined.

The following table lists the formatting retained in the new document:

Bold, underline, subscript, superscript
Single, double, or triple spacing
Left, center, or right justification
Margin settings
Sticky spaces
Forced page breaks

Header or footer information in the document is printed as text at the top or bottom of each page. Any merge fields that you have added to the original document are treated as ordinary text. If you want to use the document as a merge document, you must add AppleWorks GS merge fields. See Chapter 8, Mail Merge and Mailing Labels, for more information.

Text is displayed in 12-point Geneva when the document is opened.

After the document is opened, you can modify the text in any way. When you save the document, you can save it as an AppleWorks GS document and treat it as any other document in the future.

Opening classic AppleWorks database files

When you open a classic AppleWorks database file, a new definition form is created, and all of the categories in the file are converted to AppleWorks GS fields.

The fields are arranged left-justified along the left edge of the definition form. The arrangement is similar to the original arrangement of categories that you see in Single-Record Layout in classic AppleWorks.

The information in the database is transferred to the AppleWorks GS database document. All information is treated as text.

After the document is opened, you can rearrange fields, add fields, or modify the document as you would any other database document.

Opening classic AppleWorks spreadsheet files

When you open a classic AppleWorks spreadsheet file, the contents of the spreadsheet are displayed in a new AppleWorks GS spreadsheet window.

The following lists the formatting retained in the document:

Cell formatting
Default cell format
Column width
Titles

The most important changes are seen in classic AppleWorks formulas. A crucial change applies to relative and absolute references in formulas. In classic AppleWorks spreadsheets, no information is stored with the formula to indicate if references are relative or absolute. All references are stored as relative references. As a result, when classic AppleWorks formulas are transferred to the new document, all references must be displayed as relative references. This will have no impact on the values displayed on the original spreadsheet, but may have serious consequences if you copy or move formulas from their original location in the spreadsheet. Carefully check all formulas in the spreadsheet before copying or moving formulas!

For more information on absolute and relative references, see Appendix B, AppleWorks GS Formulas.

AppleWorks GS may also add parentheses to the formula. Classic AppleWorks evaluates operators in a formula with a different order of precedence from AppleWorks GS. As a result, parentheses may be added to retain the original meaning in the new version of the formula. AppleWorks GS also retains information about whether automatic or manual recalculation is selected.

Importing classic AppleWorks word processing files

The Import File command on the File menu can be used to paste the entire contents of a classic AppleWorks word processing file at the current location in an AppleWorks GS word processing or page layout document.

When you select Import File, a dialog box appears that lists the documents that may be imported into the current document. You can import classic AppleWorks word processing files into the AppleWorks GS word processing, page layout, or telecommunications documents.

When you select a classic AppleWorks word processing file, the contents of the selected file are pasted into the document, with formatting retained as described earlier. The only difference is that the text is displayed in the font currently in effect at the insertion point, rather than 12-point Geneva.

Appendix B

AppleWorks GS Formulas

The AppleWorks GS spreadsheet and database applications share several common features. In both applications, you can enter specific data values in specific locations. In a spreadsheet you can enter specific data values into specific cells, and in a database you can define data-entry fields and enter specific pieces of information into those fields in each record.

Both applications also provide a special feature: they let you enter a formula in a cell or field to automatically display a value that is calculated from the other values in the application:

In a spreadsheet, you can enter a formula into an individual cell, and the formula displays a value for the cell that is based upon other values in other cells. If you enter into a spreadsheet cell the formula "=A1+A2+A3", that cell will display the sum of the values in cells A1, A2, and A3.

Typical spreadsheet formulas might be:

= A1 + B2 + D4	(displays sum of the three cells)
= sum (A1..A10)	(displays sum of cells from A1 through A10)

In a database, you can define **calculated fields**. A calculated field contains a field formula that automatically displays a value based on other values in the record. For example, if you create a calculated field that contains the formula "[field1]+[field2]+[field3]", that field will display in each record the sum of the values found in field1, field2, and field3 in that record.

Typical database field formulas might be

[field1]+[field2]	(displays the sum of the two fields)
avg([field1],[field2],[field3])	(displays average of three fields)

In each application the formula is constructed in a similar way. A formula in a spreadsheet can include specific constant values, it can refer to the values in other cells, or it can include functions that perform calculations on the other. In a database, the formula can include specific constant values, it can refer to the values in other fields, or it can contain functions that perform calculations on the other values.

Elements of a formula

Spreadsheet formulas and calculated field formulas both contain similar elements:

Formulas in both applications can contain either **constant** or **variable** values. Constant values are values that do not change as you use the application. A typical formula may contain numeric constants (like the number 34 or the number 2010) or text constants (like the string 'Seattle').

Formulas also may contain **variable** values, which are references to values found in fields or cells that may change as you use the application. A spreadsheet formula may contain a reference to values stored in one or more additional cells, and a database field formula may contain a reference to one or more additional fields in a record.

A formula may also include one of the built-in AppleWorks GS functions that are described in Appendix C, AppleWorks GS Functions. The only restriction on the use of these functions is that a function requiring a range of spreadsheet values may not be used in a database field formula. These functions include NPV, IRR, HLOOKUP, and VLOOKUP.

Constant values, variable values, functions . . . these are the basic elements of a formula. A formula may contain one other crucial component: the **operators** that combine the constants, variables, and functions into an expression. Operators are symbols like the plus sign that act on the constants, variables, and function values to produce a final value for the formula. AppleWorks GS provides the familiar arithmetic operators (+, −, *, /) to use in a formula, as well as range of other relational and logical operators.

References in spreadsheet formulas

One of the most powerful features of a spreadsheet formula is the ability to calculate values based on the values stored in other cells. As with any powerful feature, however, it is possible to misuse the power and produce critical errors. If you are going to base an important decision on the numbers in a spreadsheet, it is very important to understand exactly how a spreadsheet formula refers to other cells.

When you include a reference to another cell in a spreadsheet formula, the reference may be one of two kinds: an **absolute** reference or a **relative** reference. Both kinds of reference will produce exactly the same result if the formula is not moved or copied to a different location. However, if you do move or copy the formula to a different location, very different results are seen.

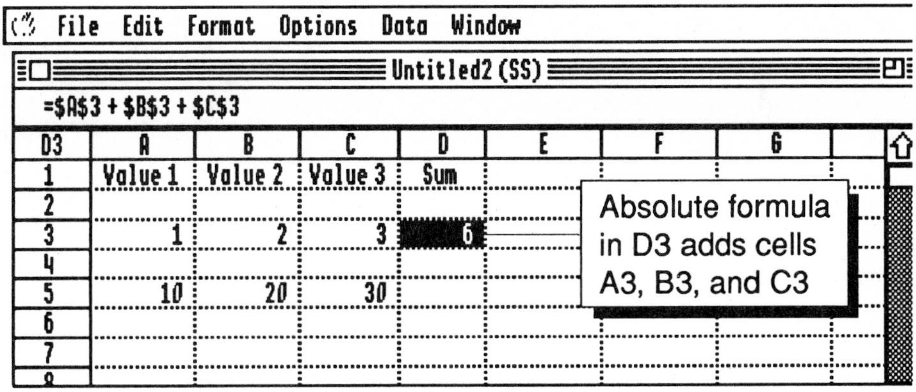

```
=$A$3 + $B$3 + $C$3
```

D3	A	B	C	D	E	F	G	
1	Value 1	Value 2	Value 3	Sum				
2								
3	1	2	3	6				
4								
5	10	20	30					
6								
7								

Absolute formula in D3 adds cells A3, B3, and C3

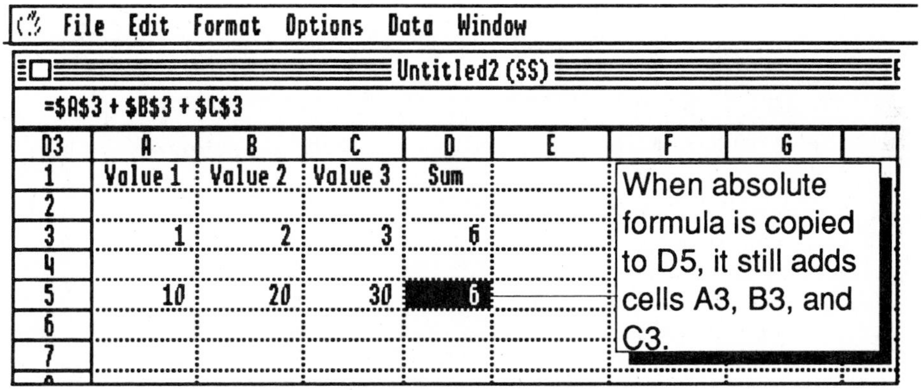

(% File   Edit   Format   Options   Data   Window

```
=$A$3 + $B$3 + $C$3
```

D3	A	B	C	D	E	F	G	
1	Value 1	Value 2	Value 3	Sum				
2								
3	1	2	3	6				
4								
5	10	20	30	6				
6								
7								

When absolute formula is copied to D5, it still adds cells A3, B3, and C3.

Figure B-1   Absolute reference

If a cell is referred to by an absolute reference, the formula uses the value in that precise cell always, no matter where you move the formula later. This can be very important to you, since you may want to move a formula to a new location later. For example, if formula cell B1 contains an absolute reference to cell A1, the formula is "locked" onto cell A1, and it will always use the value in A1. If you move the formula from B1 to F1 later, the formula will still use the value in cell A1. (See Figure B-1.)

On the other hand, if a formula cell refers to a second cell by a **relative** reference, the formula uses the value of the cell found in the same relative location (compared to the formula cell) if you move the formula later. For example, if a formula in cell B1 refers to cell A1 by relative reference, it isn't "locked" onto that specific cell . . . it only remembers that it should use the value of the cell found just to the left. If you move the formula to cell F1 later, the formula will use the value found in cell E1 (the cell now found just to the left). (See Figure B-2.)

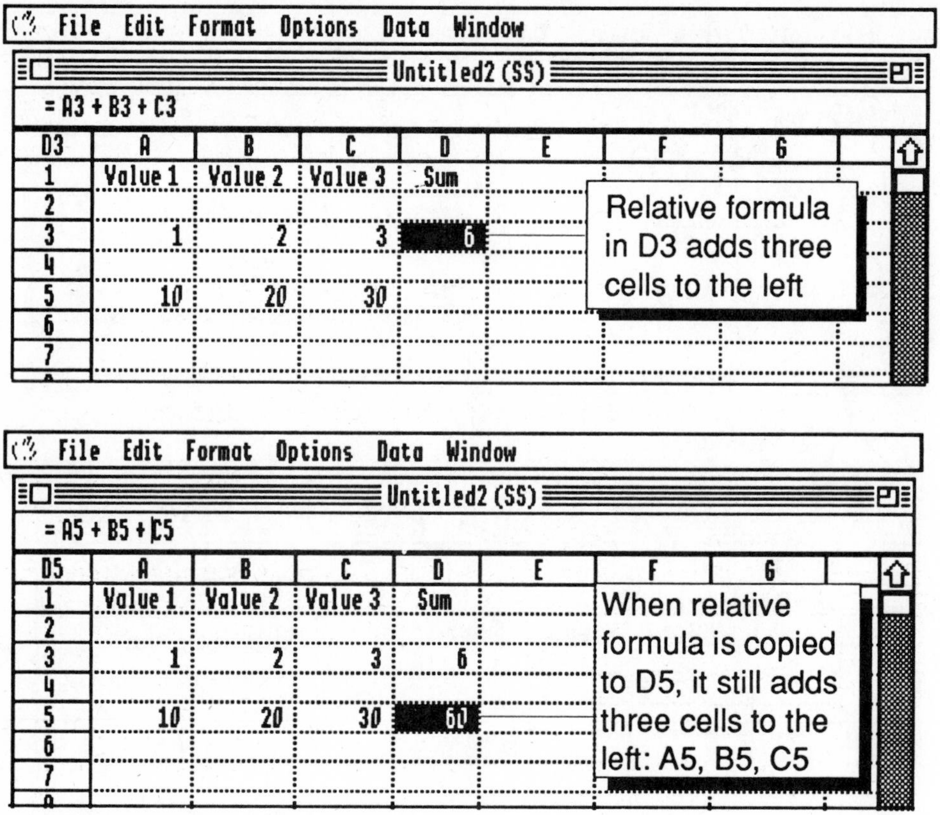

Figure B-2 Relative reference

Both absolute reference and relative reference have important uses, but it's important to use the right reference for a given situation.

How do you create a relative reference?

A relative reference is the easiest kind of reference to create, since relative references are the type you use most often.

To enter a relative reference into a formula:

- **Type the cell coordinates (such as A1) into the formula.**

- **Click on the cell, and the cell coordinates are automatically entered into the formula.**

For example, if you type the formula "=A1" into cell B1, the reference to cell A1 is a relative reference. The formula refers to the cell in the same row as cell B1 and located one column to the left. If you copy this formula into a different cell, it no longer refers to cell A1; rather, it refers to the cell in the same row as the new cell and located one column to the left.

How do you create an absolute reference?

If you enter an absolute reference into a cell, the formula is "locked" onto the cell, and the value in that precise cell will be used wherever you move the formula.

To create an absolute reference, type the $ character before the element of the reference that you want to remain unchanged when you copy the formula to another location.

For instance, if you type the formula **=$A$1** into cell B1, the formula will always refer to the value in cell A1, even if you copy the formula into a new location. You can interpret this to mean "use the value in the cell always in column A and always in row 1."

If you place the $ character before both the column reference and the row reference, the formula refers to the cell in the same row and same column, regardless of the location of the new cell. When this reference is copied to another cell, the reference will always refer to the original cell.

Mixing references

The distinction between a relative reference like A1 and an absolute reference like $A$1 is clear. There is one other possibility: it is possible to create a cell reference that is partly absolute and partly relative, and these can be useful at times.

For instance, you could type a reference like $A1 or A$1 in a formula; these references are partly absolute and partly relative. The part of the coordinate that follows the $ character is absolute, and the other part of the coordinate is relative.

How do you interpret these mixed references? One important fact to remember is that all four versions of this reference (A1, $A$1, $A1, A$1) all produce the same result in the original formula cell — they all refer to cell A1. The only difference is seen when the formula is copied to a new location. The formula that contains the absolute reference $A$1 will still refer to cell A1, but all of the other versions would refer to different cells.

- If the formula contains the relative reference A1, the formula now refers to the cell that is in the same relative position to the new cell that A1 occupied with respect to the original cell.
- If the formula contains the mixed reference $A1, the formula now refers to the cell in column A (which is the absolute part) and the same number of rows away that A1 was from the original cell.
- If the formula contains the mixed reference A$1, the formula now refers to the cell in row 1 (the absolute part) and the same number of columns away that A1 was from the original cell.

Moving spreadsheet formulas

When you create a formula in a spreadsheet cell, references to other cells may be either absolute or relative; the results displayed in that original cell will be the same. The effect of absolute or relative references is seen only when you copy the formula into another location or move the formula to another location.

AppleWorks GS provides several methods for copying or moving formulas:

- You can use the Fill command to copy the contents of a cell to a range of cells. If the original cell contains a formula, the formula is copied to the other cells in the range.
- You can use the Clipboard commands to cut or copy a formula in a cell, and then paste the formula into another selected cell. When you use the Clipboard, the formula is copied in its original form to the other cells in the range, with all absolute and relative references retained in their original forms. You can also use Control-drag to move a selected range from one location to another, and this has the same effect as a Clipboard copy-and-paste operation.
- You can use the Move command to move a selected cell or range from one location to another. This command has a very different effect on relative references. The Move command assumes that you want the formula to display the same results in the new location as in the original location. How can this be accomplished? When you move the selected range, all relative references are adjusted so that they still refer to the original referenced cells. For example, suppose that a formula in cell B1 contains a relative reference to cell A1. If you move this formula with the Move command, the formula in the new location still refers to cell A1. In effect, the Move command temporarily turns all relative references into absolute references, moves the formula, and then returns the references to relative references.

References to database fields

By comparison, the references found in database formulas are much tamer. A database formula can refer to the values found in other fields in the record, but there is no concept of absolute or relative references.

The database formula could contain numeric or text constants, or it could include the AppleWorks GS built-in formulas, and or it could refer to other database fields.

To create a calculated field:

1   **Create or select a field on the definition form.**

2   **Select the Field Formula command on the Edit menu.**

3   **When the Field Formula dialog box appears, enter the formula into the formula input bar.**

- You can type the name of the field into the formula bar. If you type the field name into a formula, be sure to surround the field name with square brackets.
- You can click on the name of the desired field in the Fields list box. The name is automatically entered at the current cursor location in the formula, surrounded by square brackets.

Operators

The constant and variable values in a spreadsheet or database formula are combined with operators to produce a value for the formula.

AppleWorks GS provides three kinds of operators: arithmetic operators to perform numeric calculations, comparison (or relational) operators to compare values, and logical operators to manipulate logical (true/false) values.

The arithmetic operators which are available in AppleWorks GS are listed in the following table, in decreasing order of precedence:

Symbol	Name	Use	Operation
-	unary minus	-value	Reverses the sign of the value
+	unary plus	+value	Retains the sign of the value
^	exponentiation	value1 ^ value2	Raises value1 to power of value2
*	multiplication	value1 * value2	Multiplies value1 by value2
/	division	value1 / value2	Divides value1 by value2
+	addition	value1 + value2	Adds value1 to value2
-	subtraction	value1 - value2	Subtracts value2 from value1

Comparison operators are used with logical functions like the if function to establish logical values. They can be used to test if one value is equal to, less than, or greater than a second value. The comparison operators available include

Symbol	Name	Example	Operation
=	Equals	if (value1=value2...	Tests if value1 is equal to value2
<>	Not equals	if (value1<>value2...	Tests if value1 is not equal to value2
>	Greater than	if (value1 > value2...	Tests if value1 is greater than value2
>=	Greater than or equal to	if (value1 > =value2	Tests if value1 is greater than or equal to value2
<	Less than	if (value1 > value2.	Tests if value1 is less than value2
<=	Less than or equal to	if (value1 > value2	Tests if value1 is less than or equal to value2

All of the comparison operators in this table have lower precedence than any of the numeric operators.

A logical operator performs an operation on expressions that evaluate to true or false. This table summarizes the AppleWorks GS logical operators:

Symbol	Name	Example	Operation
&	Logical and	if (value1&value2...	Tests if value of both value1 and value2 are true. Returns true if both are true; otherwise returns false.
|	Logical or	if (value1 | value2...	Tests if value of either value1 or value2 is true. Returns true if either is true; returns false if both are false.
~	Not	~ value...	Reverses the logical value of value.

Order of Precedence

When an expression is evaluated, the order of precedence of operators defines the order in which the operations are performed. For example, in AppleWorks GS the multiplication operator (*) is ranked higher in precedence than the binary addition operator (+). That means that multiplication operations are performed before any addition operations are performed. For example, in the expression 5+4*2, AppleWorks GS would evaluate this expression as 40, since multiplication is performed before addition.

This table summarizes the order of precedence of the AppleWorks GS operators:

Operators

~	−	+		(unary operators, used before a single value)
^				
*	/	%		
+	−			(binary operators, used between two values)
<	>	<=	>=	
=	<>			
&				
|				

If an expression contains operators of equal predecence, the expression is evaluated left-to-right, unless another sequence is forced by the use of parentheses.

Appendix C

AppleWorks GS Functions

A formula in a spreadsheet cell or a database calculated field can include constant values (like the number 34 or the text value 'Park Place') or references to values in other cells or fields. A formula can also include functions to perform calculations based on those values. AppleWorks GS provides more than 70 functions to perform calculations on the values in your spreadsheet or database.

For example, you can use a simple function like the **sum** function to total values, or you could use a function like the **stdv** function to calculate the standard deviation of values. You could even use one of the financial functions like the **pmt** function to quickly calculate the payments required to repay a loan.

This appendix presents a summary of the built-in functions that can be used in a database or spreadsheet formula.

Parts of a function

What is a function? A function is just an operation, and the operation that a particular function performs is indicated by its name. Most functions require one or more values to operate on. For example, the **sum** function totals the values that are provided to it. The values that are provided to a function are called the function **arguments**.

When you use a function in a database or a spreadsheet formula, you must include

- the function name (like sum)
- any required function arguments, surrounded by parentheses

For example, to use the sum function in a formula, you must include the name sum, followed by the values to be totalled surrounded by parentheses.

Constants and variables

As you enter the elements of a formula or the arguments for a function, it's important to realize that the values fall into two broad categories:

Constants: A constant is a numeric or text value that does not change. For instance, the number 345 and the text value 'Houston' are examples of constants. A text value is surrounded by quote marks; either single or double quote marks may be used.

Variables: A variable value can change at different times as you use an application. For example, a reference to another field in a database formula or a reference to another cell in a spreadsheet formula is an example of a variable value. As the values in the other fields or cells change, the value of the variable will change.

What kinds of values are used as function arguments?

Different functions can operate on different kinds of values, so different functions require different function arguments. For example, the **sum** function can operate on numeric values, but it can't operate on text values.

The kinds of arguments that may be required for different functions fall into several categories: numeric value, numeric list, a range of spreadsheet values, text, text list, logical value, logical list, date, and financial values.

A word about expressions

When we talk about function arguments, the term **expression** is used often. An expression is simply any calculated value.

Some expressions are obviously calculated values, but other expressions are less obvious. For example, **2+2** is obviously a calculated value, so it's an expression. On the other hand, the value **2** is also a calculated value — the value is 2, and it's an expression as well. Expressions can also involve text values. Several AppleWorks GS functions can operate on text values.

In general, an expression is any calculated value, regardless of whether the calculation involves one value or more than one value. Examples of expressions are

```
4+3-1
6*5+78
56
'New York'
```

Number values

A function may require a **number** (or numeric value) as an argument. Any expression that evaluates to a numeric value would be acceptable.

A numeric value may be provided as a constant or a variable value. A numeric constant would simply be a number, while a variable would be a reference to a spreadsheet cell or a numeric database field.

For example, the SIN function is a trig function that requires a numeric argument; it calculates the sine value of the numeric value that is provided. You could provide the numeric argument:

- as a constant ...SIN(4)
- as an expression ...SIN (20/5)
- as a variable ...SIN (A1), where cell A1 contains the value 4

The resulting value is the same in all cases.

Numeric list

A function may require a list of numeric values as an argument. You can supply the list:

- as a **list of numeric values**, separated by commas. For example, the function SUM(43,67,A1) returns the sum of the values 43, 67, and the value in cell A1.
- as a **range of numeric values** in a spreadsheet. A range is indicated by listing the first cell, followed by two dots, followed by the last cell in the range. For example the function SUM(A1..A10) returns the sum of the values in cells A1 through A10, inclusive. Some functions require that the numeric values be provided as a spreadsheet range.

Text values

A function may require a text value as an argument. A text value is a sequence of alphanumeric characters. A text value may be a constant (with the characters surrounded by single or double quote marks) or a variable (database text field or spreadsheet text cell.)

Text values are known more formally as **string** values, since they consist of a string or sequence of characters.

Text list

A function may require a list of one or more text values, with each value separated by commas from the next. This list is more formally known as a **string list**.

For example, the CONCAT function is used to join two or more text values together into a single text value. The function takes a list of text values as its argument and returns a single text string that consists of the text values joined together (concatenated).

Logical value

A logical value is an expression that evaluates to True or False. Apple-Works GS encodes the value True as the numeric value 1, and the value False as the numeric value 0. If an expression does not evaluate to the value 0, it is regarded as True.

Some AppleWorks GS functions require one or more logical values as arguments, and return the value True or False.

Logical list

A function may require a list of one or more logical values. For instance, the OR function requires a list of logical values as its arguments. If any of the logical values on the list have the value True, then the value of the function is True.

Date

A function may require a date as an argument. A date is entered as a text value, surrounded by quote marks. Examples of strings are '9/15/89' or 'January 15, 1989'.

Providing the right type of values

In many cases you can use references to spreadsheet cells or database fields as function arguments. When you refer to a cell or a field, it's important that that cell or field contains data of the appropriate type. If a function requires a numeric value, be sure to refer to fields or cells that contain numeric values. If you refer to values of the wrong type, the function will still attempt to evaluate the result, but it's much better to provide data of the correct type.

Functions by category

The following list summarizes the built-in AppleWorks GS functions that can be used in spreadsheet formulas or in the formulas for database calculated fields.

The functions are grouped by category, including

Arithmetic functions:

abs, exp, frac, inf, int, ln, log, mod, product, random, round, sgn, sqrt

Trig functions:

acos, asin, atan, cos, degrees, pi, radians, sin, tan

Statistical functions:

avg, count, max, min, stdv, sum, var

String (text) functions:

concat, len, lower, null, position, proper, substr, upper

Conversion functions:

asc, chr, string, val

Date functions:

date, day, month, numdate, today, weekday, year

Logical functions:

and, false, if, isblank, isempty, iserror, isna, isnumber, isstring, not, or, true

Financial functions:

fv, irr, npv, pmt, pv, rate, term

Special-purpose functions:

alert, choose, error, hlookup, na, vlookup

The rest of this appendix provides a list of AppleWorks GS functions, the type of arguments that each function requires, a brief description of the function, and several examples illustrating how the function might be used.

Many of the functions accept references to spreadsheet cells or database fields. When a spreadsheet reference is possible, typical cell values like A1 or A1..A10 are used as illustrations; when you use the function, any cell reference can be substituted for these examples. Similarly, when a database field can be used as an argument, the illustrations use examples like [fieldname] or [field1]; when you use the function, you would substitute your actual field names for those examples.

Arithmetic functions

ABS(NUMBER)

Returns absolute value of **number**.
   Examples:

   abs(–1) returns 1.
   abs(1) returns 1.
   abs(0) returns 0.
   abs(A1) returns the absolute value of the value in spreadsheet cell A1.
   abs([fieldname]) returns the absolute value of the value in database field specified.

EXP(number)

Returns the value of the constant e raised to the power of **number**.
   Examples:

   EXP(–1) returns 1.718.
   EXP(0) returns 1.
   EXP (1) returns 2.718.
   EXP(A1) or EXP ([fieldname]) returns value of e, raised to numeric value found in spreadsheet cell A1 or database field.

FRAC(number)

Returns the fractional part of **number**.

Examples:

frac(3.5) returns 0.5.
frac(2.75) returns 0.75.
frac(A1) or frac ([fieldname]) returns the fractional part of the value in
spreadsheet cell A1 or database field.

INF

Returns the value infinity.

INT(number)

Returns the integer part of **number**.
  Examples:

INT(3.5) returns 3.
INT(2.75) returns 2.
INT(A1) or INT ([fieldname]) returns the integer part of the value in
spreadsheet cell A1 or database field.

LN(number)

Returns the natural logarithm of **number**.
  Examples:

LN(1) returns numeric value 0.
LN(100) returns numeric value 4.605.
LN(0) or LN of negative number returns ERROR.
LN(A1) or LN([fieldname]) returns natural log of value in spreadsheet
cell A1 or database field.

LOG(number)

Returns the base 10 logarithm of **number**.
  Examples:

LOG(1) returns numeric value 0.
LOG(100) returns numeric value 2.
LOG(0) or LOG of negative number returns ERROR.
LOG(A1) or LOG([fieldname]) returns common log of numeric value
found in spreadsheet cell A1 or database field.

MOD(number1, number2)

Returns the remainder of **number1** divided by **number2**.

Examples:

MOD(10,3) returns numeric value 1.
MOD(3,0) returns value ERROR.
MOD(A1,A2) returns remainder when spreadsheet cell A1 is divided by cell A2.
MOD([field1],[field2]) returns remainder when database field1 is divided by database field2.

PRODUCT(numeric list)

Returns the product of all the numbers on **numeric list**.
Examples:

PRODUCT(2,3,4,) returns 24.
PRODUCT(A1..A10) returns the product of the values found in the spreadsheet range from A1 through A10, inclusive.
PRODUCT([field1], [field2],...) returns the product of the values found in database fields.

RANDOM(number)

Returns a random number between 0 and (**number** – 1). If the argument is 0 or 1, then returns a random value greater than or equal to 0 and less than 1.
Examples:

RANDOM(50) returns a random number between 0 and 49, inclusive.
RANDOM(0) or RANDOM(1) returns a random number greater than 0 and less than 1.
RANDOM(A1) or RANDOM([fieldname]) returns a random number between 0 and the value in spreadsheet cell A1 or database field, minus 1.

ROUND(number1,number2)

Returns **number1** rounded up to the **number2** of decimal places specified by the second argument.
Examples:

ROUND(3.1416, 2) returns 3.14.
ROUND (1.5, 0) returns 2.
ROUND(A1, 1) returns the value in spreadsheet cell A1, rounded to 1 decimal place.
ROUND([fieldname],1) returns value in database field specified, rounded to one decimal place.

SGN(number)

Returns the sign of **number**. If the number is positive, returns 1. If the number is 0, returns 0. If the number is negative, returns –1.
Examples:

SGN(2) returns 1.
SGN(-2) returns –1.
SGN(0) returns 0.
SGN(A1) or SGN ([fieldname]) returns the sign of the value in spreadsheet cell A1 or database field.

SQRT(number)

Returns the positive square root of **number**. If the number is negative, the function returns ERROR.
Examples:

SQRT(16) returns 4.
SQRT(–1) returns ERROR.
SQRT(A1) or SQRT([fieldname]) returns the square root of the value in spreadsheet cell A1 or database field.

Trigonometric functions

ACOS(number)

Returns in radians the arccosine of **number**.
Examples:

ACOS(–0.5) returns 2.094 (2_/3 radians).
ACOS(A1) or ACOS([fieldname]) returns the arccosine of the value in spreadsheet cell A1 or database field.

ASIN(number)

Returns in radians the arcsine of **number**.
Examples:

ASIN(-0.5) returns –0.524 (–_/6 radians).
ASIN(A1) or ASIN([fieldname]) returns the arcsine of the value in spreadsheet cell A1 or database field.

ATAN(number)

Returns in radians the arctangent of **number**.
  Examples:

  ATAN(1) returns 0.785 (pi/4 radians).
  ATAN(A1) or ATAN([fieldname]) returns the arctangent of the value
  in spreadsheet cell A1 or database field.

COS(number)

Returns the cosine of **number** (entered in radians).
  Examples:

  COS(1.047) returns 0.5.
  COS(A1) or COS([fieldname]) returns the cosine of the value in spreadsheet cell A1 or database field.

DEGREES(number)

Returns in degrees the value of **number** (entered in radians)
  Example:

  DEGREES(3.1416) returns 180, the number of degrees equivalent to
  3.14 (pi) radians.

PI

Returns an approximation of the mathematical constant pi.

RADIANS(number)

Returns value in radians equivalent to **number** entered in degrees.
  Example:

  RADIANS(180) returns the value 3.14 (an approximation of pi).

SIN(number)

Returns the sine of **number** (entered in radians).
  Examples:

  SIN(0) returns 0.(sin of 0 radians).
  SIN(pi/2) returns 1.(sin of pi/2 radians).
  SIN(A1) or SIN([fieldname]) returns the sine of the value in spread-
  sheet cell A1 or database field.

TAN(NUMBER)

Returns the tangent of the **number** (entered in radians).
Examples:

TAN(pi/4) returns 1 (tangent of pi/4 radians).
TAN(A1) or TAN([fieldname]) returns the tangent of the value in spreadsheet cell A1 or database field.

Statistical functions

AVG(numeric list)

Returns the average of **numeric list**.
Examples:

AVG(1,3,5) returns 3, the average of the list.
AVG(A1..A10) returns the average of values in cells A1 through A10.
AVG([field1], [field2], . . .) returns the average of the values in database fields.

COUNT(list)

Returns the number of cells or fields containing values.
Examples:

COUNT(A1..A10) returns the number of spreadsheet cells that contain values in the range A1 through A10, inclusive.
COUNT([field1], [field2], . . .) returns the number of database fields that contain values among the fields listed.

MAX(numeric list)

Returns the maximum value in **numeric list**.
Examples:

MAX(2, 10, 4, 6) returns 10.
MAX(A1..A10) returns the maximum numeric value found in the range of spreadsheet cells from A1 through A10.
MAX([field1], [field2], . . .) returns the maximum value in database fields specified.

MIN(numeric list)

Returns the minimum value in **numeric list**.

Examples:

MIN(2, 10, 4, 6) returns 2.
MIN(A1..A10) returns the minimum numeric value found in the range
of spreadsheet cells from A1 through A10.
MIN([field1],[field2], . . .) returns the minimum value in database fields
specified.

STDV(numeric list)

Returns the standard deviation of the values in **list**.
Examples:

stdv(2, 7, 9, 10, 27) returns 9.46.
stdv(A1..A10) or stdv([field1],[field2], . . .) returns the standard deviation of the values found in spreadsheet cells or in database fields.

SUM(numeric list)

Returns the sum of the numbers in **numeric list**.
Examples:

sum(1,3,5) returns 9.
sum(A1..A10) or sum([field1], [field2], . . .) returns the sum of the values
found in spreadsheet cells or database fields.

VAR(numeric list)

Returns the variance of the numbers in **numeric list**.
Example:

VAR(A1..A20) returns the variance of the values in spreadsheet cells
A1 to A20.

String functions

CONCAT(string list)

Returns a single string produced by joining the **string list**.
Examples:

CONCAT("hello", " world") returns the single string "hello world".
CONCAT(A1,A2,A3) returns a single string that combines the values
in spreadsheet cell A1,A2, and A3.

CONCAT([field1], [field2], [field3]) returns a single string that combines the values in the database fields specified.

LEN(string)

Returns a number that represents the length of **string**.
Examples:

LEN("Cat") returns 3.
LEN(A1) or LEN([fieldname]) returns the length of the string value in spreadsheet cell A1 or database field.

LOWER(string)

Returns **string** with all characters in lowercase.
Examples:

LOWER("CAT") returns string "cat".
LOWER(A1) or LOWER([fieldname]) returns string in spreadsheet cell A1 or database field, with all characters converted to lowercase.

NULL

Returns a null string ("").

POSITION(string1, string2)

Returns a number corresponding to the position where **string1** first occurs in the **string2**.
Examples:

POSITION("d", "abcde") returns the value 4, the position where the first argument first occurs in the second string.
POSITION("world", "Hello world") returns the value 7.
POSITION(A1, A2) returns the location of cell A1's string value within cell A2's string value.
POSITION([field1], [field2]) returns the location of field1's string value within field2's string value.

PROPER(string)

Returns a string with the first character in the **string** converted to upper case and all other characters lower case.
Examples:

PROPER('shelley') returns 'Shelley'.
PROPER(A1) or PROPER([fieldname]) returns the string found in

spreadsheet cell A1 or database field, with the first character converted to upper case, and all other characters converted to lower case.

SUBSTR(string, Start, Length)

Returns the substring specified by the two numeric arguments, **start** and **length**. The first argument is a **string**, from which a substring will be extracted. The argument **start** specifies the starting position of the substring and the **length** argument specifies the length of the substring.
Examples:

SUBSTR("Hello world", 7, 5) returns "world".
SUBSTR("abcdefg", 3, 2) returns "cd".
SUBSTR(A1, 3, 5) returns the substring found beginning at position 3 and extending for 5 characters within cell A1's string value.
SUBSTR([fieldname], 3, 5) returns the substring found beginning at position 3 and extending for 5 characters within the field's string.

UPPER(string)

Returns **string** with all characters in uppercase.
Examples:

UPPER('shelley') returns 'SHELLEY'.
UPPER(A1) or UPPER([fieldname]) returns the string found in cell A1 or database field, with all characters converted to upper case.

Conversion functions

ASC(string)

Returns the ASCII value of the first character in **string**.
Examples:

ASC("A") returns 65, the ASCII value of the character "A".
ASC("alphabet") returns 97, the ASCII value of the character "a".
ASC(A1) or ASC([fieldname]) returns the ASCII code of the first character in spreadsheet cell A1 or database field.

CHR(number)

Returns the string value corresponding to the ASCII value specified by **number**.

Examples:

chr(65) returns "A", the character represented by ASCII value 65.
CHR(A1) or CHR([fieldname]) returns the character represented by the ASCII code of the value in spreadsheet cell A1 or database field.

STRING(number)

Returns a string equivalent of the numeric argument.
 Examples:

STRING(43) returns the string "43".
STRING(A1) or STRING([fieldname]) returns the string equivalent of the numeric value in spreadsheet cell A1 or database field.

VAL(string)

Returns the numeric equivalent of the **string** argument.
 Examples:

VAL("43") returns the numeric value 43.
VAL(A1) or VAL([fieldname]) returns the numeric equivalent of the string value in spreadsheet cell A1 or database field.

Date functions

DATE(number)

Returns the string date equivalent of **number**. The numbering system begins on Jan. 1, 1900, so that the number 1 returns the date "Jan. 1, 1900", the value 2 returns "Jan. 2, 1900", and so forth.
 Examples:

DATE(10894) returns the date "Oct. 29, 1929".
DATE(32873) returns the date "Jan. 1, 1990".
DATE(A1) or DATE([fieldname]) returns the date equivalent of the numeric value in spreadsheet cell A1 or database field.

DAY(string)

Returns a number representing the day portion of the date represented by **string**.

Examples:

DAY(Jan. 24, 1988) returns 24.
DAY(Jan 1, 1989) returns 1.
DAY(A1) or DAY([fieldname]) returns the day part of the date in spreadsheet cell A1 or database field.

MONTH(string)

Returns a string for the month portion of the date represented by string. The date may be expressed in these forms: 12/25/90; 12/25/1990.; Dec. 25, 1990; December 25, 1990.
Examples:

MONTH('Jan. 24, 1989') returns "Jan."
MONTH(A1) or MONTH([fieldname]) returns the month portion of the date in spreadsheet cell A1 or database field.

NUMDATE(string)

Returns an integer value for the date represented by **string**. Jan. 1, 1900 is assigned the numeric value 1. The date may be expressed in these forms: 12/25/90; 12/25/1990.; Dec. 25, 1990; December 25, 1990.
Examples:

NUMDATE(Jan. 1, 1900) returns the value 1.
NUMDATE(Jan. 1, 1989) returns the value 32508.
NUMDATE(A1) or NUMDATE([fieldname]) returns the numeric equivalent of the date string value in spreadsheet cell A1 or database field.

TODAY

Returns a string representing today's date.
Example:

today() returns "Jan. 1, 1989", or a similar string that corresponds to the current date.

(If the date is incorrect, set the date using the Apple IIGS Control Panel.)

WEEKDAY(string)

Returns a string representing the weekday for a date provided as a **string**.

Examples:

WEEKDAY('June 21, 1989') returns "Wednesday".
WEEKDAY(A1) or WEEKDAY([fieldname]) returns the weekday of the date in spreadsheet cell A1 or database field.

YEAR(string)

Returns a number representing the year portion of a date provided as a **string**.
Examples:

YEAR('Jan. 1, 1990') returns 1990.
YEAR(A1) or YEAR([fieldname]) returns the year of the date in spreadsheet cell A1 or database field.

Logical functions

AND(logical list)

Returns True if all values in **logical list** are true.
Example:

AND(A1=B1, C1=D1) returns True if the value in cell A1 equals the value in cell B1 and the value in cell C1 equals the value in cell D1.

FALSE

Returns numeric value 0. FALSE takes no arguments.

IF(logical expression, expression1, expression2)

If the **logical expression** is true (or evaluates to any value other than 0), this function returns the value of **expression1**; otherwise, it returns the value of **expression2**.
Examples:

if(A1<90, "B", "A") returns the value "B" if the value in cell A1 is less than 90; otherwise, it returns the value "A".
if(A1=B1, 10.5, 12.75) returns the value 10.5 if the value in cell A1 is equal to the value in cell B1; otherwise, it returns the value 12.75.

ISBLANK(expression)

Returns the numeric value 1 (true) if **expression** is a null string.

Example:

ISBLANK(A1) returns value 1 if cell A1 contains no value.

ISEMPTY(expression)

Returns true (the numeric value 1) if the specified cell, field, or expression is empty.
Examples:

ISEMPTY(A1) returns true if the cell A1 contains no value.
ISEMPTY([Field1]) returns true if the field named Field1 contains no value.

ISERROR(expression)

Returns the value 1 (true) if the **expression** evaluates to ERROR.
Examples:

ISERROR(SQRT(A1)) returns 1 (true) if the value in cell A1 is less than 0, since attempting to evaluate the square root of a negative value produces an error.

ISNA(expression)

Returns the value 1 (true) if the **expression** is the special NA value.
Examples:

ISNA(A3) returns true (the value 1) if the cell A3 contains the special value NA.

ISNUMBER(expression)

Returns true (numeric value 1) if the value of the expression is a **number**.
Examples:

ISNUMBER(A1) returns true if the cell A1 contains a number value.
ISNUMBER([fieldname]) returns true if the database field contains a **number**.

ISSTRING(expression)

Returns true (numeric value 1) if the value of the **expression** is a string.

Examples:

ISSTRING(A1) returns true if the cell A1 contains a string value.
ISSTRING(Field1) returns true if the field named Field1 contains a string.

NOT(expression)

Returns the value true (numeric value 1) if the value of the expression is zero (the value false).
Examples:

NOT(A1) returns value 1 if value in spreadsheet cell A1 evaluates to 0; otherwise returns value 0.
NOT([field]) returns value 1 if value in database field evaluates to 0; otherwise returns value 0.

OR(logical list)

Returns true if any of the values on the **list** are true.
Examples:

OR(1+1=2, 2+254) returns true, since the first argument is true.
OR(A1=B1, C1=D1) returns true if the value in cell A1 equals the value in cell B1 or the value in cell C1 equals the value in cell D1.

TRUE

Returns the numeric value 1 (true).

Financial functions

The following functions require more explanation than the previous functions. These functions are used to calculate financial values, and the purpose of the function arguments and the value that is returned require special attention.

FV(payment, rate, term)

Calculates the future value of an investment.
The first argument, **payment**, is the payment or the amount of the periodic investment. The payment should be entered as a negative value. A leading dollar sign is optional. The second argument, **rate**, is the interest rate; the rate may be entered as a percent value (such as 10%) or

a decimal value (such as 0.10). The third argument, **term**, is the number of periods making up the term of the investment.
    Example:

FV(–5000,8%,20) returns the future value of an investment of $5000 at an annual rate of 8% after 20 years.

IRR(guess, numeric range)

Calculates the internal rate of return on a series of irregular periodic cash flows (stored in spreadsheet in **numeric range**).
    The internal rate of return is the rate that causes the net present value of an investment to equal the cost of the investment. The **guess** parameter is your best guess of the approximate rate of return; the IRR function uses this guess as the starting point for its calculations. You can enter the guess parameter as a decimal value or as a percentage; the values 10% or 0.10 would be treated as the same value. Use IRR to compare the attractiveness of investment opportunities.
    Example:

IRR(0.10, A1..A10) returns the internal rate of return on an investment that pays the periodic values stored in spreadsheet cells A1 through A10. The guess value is .1, meaning that you think the rate is approximately 10%.

NPV(rate, numeric range)

Returns the net present value of future payments. **Rate** represents a discount rate; you can enter **rate** as a percent value (such as 10%) or a decimal value (such as 0.10). The **numeric range** is a list of future credits and debits. Income is represented by positive values in the list, and payments are represented by negative values in the list. The future payments are assumed to occur at equal time intervals, and the first payment is assumed to occur at the end of the first time interval.
    Example:

NPV(12%, A1..A10) describes the net present value of three future payments of the numeric values contained in spreadsheet cells A1 through A10, invested at a constant interest rate of 12%.

PMT(pv, rate, term)

Calculates the periodic payment necessary to amortize a loan across a fixed number of periods. **Pv** is the present value or principal amount of the loan; enter **pv** as a positive value with an optional leading dollar sign. **Rate** is the interest rate of the loan; you can enter rate as a percent value (such as 10%) or a decimal value (such as 0.10). **Term** is the number of periods that make up the term of the loan.

Example:

PMT(10000,10.5%,240) returns the monthly payment on a loan of $10,000 at an interest rate of 10.5% for 240 months.

Calculates the periodic payment necessary to amortize a loan across a fixed number of periods.

PV(payment, rate, term)

Calculates the present value of a series of equal periodic payments or of a single investment. **Payment** is the amount of the investment or periodic payment; enter **payment** as a negative value, with an optional leading dollar sign. **Rate** is the discount rate; you can enter **rate** as a percent value (such as 10%) or a decimal value (such as 0.10). **Term** is the number of periods that make up the term of the investment.

Example:

PV(10000,8%,10) returns the present value (the value today) of a payment of $10000 invested at an annual rate of 8% for 10 years.

RATE(fv, pv, term)

Calculates the interest rate of return on an investment involving constant, equal periodic payments or a single lump-sum payment. **Fv** is the future value of the loan; enter **fv** as a positive value with an optional leading dollar sign. **Pv** is the present value of the investment; enter **pv** as a positive value, with an optional leading dollar sign. **Term** is the number of periods that make up the term of the investment.

Example:

RATE(10000,2000,5) returns the rate of return of an investment that has a present value of $2,000, a future value of $10,000 over 5 periods.

TERM(payment, rate, fv)

Returns the number of periods required to amortize a loan involving constant periodic payments. **Payment** is the periodic payment; enter payment as a negative value, with an optional leading dollar sign. **Rate** is the interest rate of the loan; you can enter **rate** as a percent value (such as 10%) or a decimal value (such as 0.10). **Fv** is the future value of the loan; enter **fv** as a positive value, with an optional leading dollar sign.

Example:

TERM(–1000,8%,50000) returns the number of periods required to amortize a loan of $50,000 at 8% with payments of $1,000 per period.

Special purpose functions

Alert(string)

Returns an alert box with **string** displayed in box.
  Examples:

IF (ISERROR(A1), ALERT ("ERROR IN CELL A1"), NULL) returns an alert box with the message "ERROR IN CELL A1" if an error is found in spreadsheet cell A1.

CHOOSE(number, list)

Returns the numeric value in **numeric list** that is in the position specified by **number**.
  Examples:

CHOOSE(2, 5, 6, 8,) returns the value 6 (the second value on the list).
CHOOSE(3, A1..A10) returns the third value in the list of spreadsheet cells from A1 through A10 (ignores empty cells in ranges).
CHOOSE(3, [field1], [field2], . . .) returns the third value of the list of values found in the specified database fields.

ERROR

Returns the value Error.
  HLOOKUP(value, range, offset)
  Looks up value in a table contained in the spreadsheet range. Finds largest value in first row of the **range** that is less than or equal to **value**, and then returns the value found **offset** rows below. (Assumes that the first row of the range is sorted in increasing order.)
  Example:

HLOOKUP(2, A1..D4,3) returns value found using this search method:

finds largest value in row A1 to D1 that is less than or equal to 2,
finds cell 3 rows down from top of range (the offset value), and returns the value in that cell.

NA

Returns the value "NA."

VLOOKUP(Value, range, offset)

Looks up **value** in a table contained in the spreadsheet **range**. Finds largest value in first column of the **range** that is less than or equal to **value**, and then returns the value found **offset** columns to the right. (Assumes that the first column of the range is sorted in increasing order.)

Example:

VLOOKUP(2, A1..D4,3) returns value found using this search method:

finds largest value in columns A1 to A4 less than or equal to 2, and then finds cell 3 columns to the right in the range (the offset value), and returns the value in that cell.

Appendix D

Using the Edit Colors Command

AppleWorks GS lets you use 16 colors at any one time. These colors can be selected from many more colors that the Apple IIGS can display. In addition, the graphics application lets you use patterns created from the 16 colors.

The Edit Colors command lets you change the colors available for use in an AppleWorks GS application. The Edit Colors command is available on the Color menu in the word processing and page layout applications, or on the Edit menu in the database and graphics application. The command is not available in the spreadsheet or telecommunications applications.

When you open an application, the application is set to use 16 default colors. The Edit Colors command lets you change these default colors. If you change the 16 default colors inside the graphics application, the related patterns in the pattern palette are automatically changed to reflect the new colors.

Selecting the Edit Colors command

You can choose the Edit Colors command inside the word processing, database, page layout, or telecommunications application.

To select the Edit Colors command:

1. **Move the arrow pointer to the menu bar and identify the location of the command.**

In the word processing or page layout application, the command is found at the top of the Color menu. In the database or graphics application, the command is found on the Edit menu.

2. **Select the Edit Colors command.**

The Edit Colors dialog box appears (see Figure D-1).

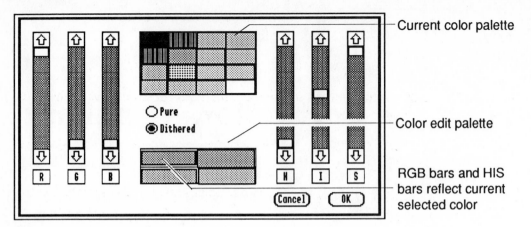

Figure D-1 Edit Colors dialog box

This dialog box corresponds to a color editor. This color editor contains the components that you need to change the colors that are displayed within this particular document.

- The color editor has five major components:
- The RGB control bars (on the left side of the box)
- The HIS control bars (on the right side of the box)
- The current color palette, which displays the 16 current colors
- The color edit palette, where you select the color that you want to edit
- Selection buttons to select Pure or Dithered colors

The RGB control bars and the HIS control bars are used to create new colors. By sliding the scroll boxes up and down, new colors are produced and substituted for existing colors on the palette. The RGB and HIS control bars represent alternative ways to edit colors. Either set of control bars can be used to edit selected colors.

The current color palette displays the current 16 shades and colors available for use. As you edit colors, the colors displayed on the palette will change to reflect your changes.

The color edit palette lets you select the current color that you want to change.

The Pure and Dithered buttons let you select which of two ways colors should be generated on the screen.

An approach to follow

When you use the Edit Colors command, you can follow these steps:

1 **Select Pure or Dithered to select one of two ways to create colors.**

2 **Select a color to edit on the color edit palette.**

3 **Adjust the RGB or HIS control bars to create a substitute color for the selected color.**

As you adjust the control bars, the current palette displays the effects of the change.

4 **If you wish, select another color to edit and adjust the control bars for that color.**

5 **When you have adjusted all of the colors that you want to change, click the OK button.**

You are returned to the document, and the new color palette replaces the old color palette. If your document contains colors from the previous color palette, each color that was displayed in the old color palette will be replaced by the color that now occupies its position on the new palette.

Selecting pure colors or dithered colors

If you could look very closely at your Apple IIGS screen, you would find that the screen display is made up of rows and columns of fine dots. The screen display is generated by determining the color of each dot on the screen. (There are 200 rows of dots and 640 columns of dots on the Apple-Works GS screen.)

AppleWorks GS can create the current color palette in two ways:

- AppleWorks GS can create the palette using only two pure colors. The resulting palette contains 16 shades composed of mixtures of the two colors. (Black and white are two of the shades. Black is the absence of color, and white is the mixture of all colors.)
- AppleWorks GS can produce the palette using four pure colors and using the process called dithering. Dithering produces more colors on the palette than just using pure colors.

How can dithering produce more colors than the simple pure colors? Your eyes can be tricked into seeing other colors by mixing colors on the screen. The dithering process places columns of one pure color on the screen alternated with columns of a second pure color. Your eyes interpret this as a third color. This third color is called a dithered color.

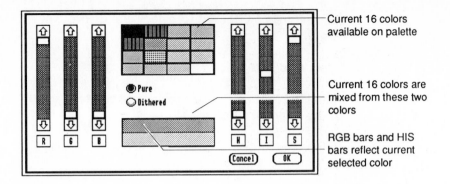

Figure D-2   Pure colors dialog box

When you use the color editor, the first decision to make is: Do you want to create the color palette from pure colors or dithered colors?

- If you want to create 16 shades from two pure colors, click the Pure button in the dialog box. The color edit palette at the bottom of the dialog box is changed to display the current two colors, and the color palette at the top of the box shows the shades that would be available if you click the OK button at this point (see Figure D-2).
- If you want to create 16 shades and colors from four pure colors, click the Dithered button in the dialog box. The color edit palette at the bottom of the dialog box is changed to display the current four pure colors, and the color palette at the top of the box shows the shades that would be available if you click the OK button at this point (see Figure D-3).

Remember: Clicking the Pure button will let you create a palette that is composed of shades of two colors, while clicking the Dithered button

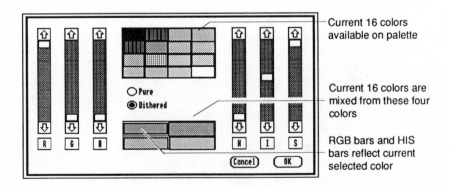

Figure D-3   Dithered colors dialog box

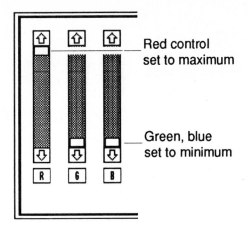

Red control
set to maximum

Green, blue
set to minimum

R G B

Figure D-4   Red on RGB control bars

will create a palette that contains more colors, but fewer shades of each color.

The RGB and HIS control bars

The RGB control bars at the left side of the dialog box and the HIS control bars at the right side of the dialog box represent different ways to edit a color. You can use either system to edit a color. When you adjust the settings on one set of control bars, the controls on the other set are automatically adjusted to the same color.

The RBG control bars represent every color as a mixture of red (R), green (G), and blue (B). For example, pure red is represented by the maximum amount of red and a minimum amount of green and blue. (The scroll box on the R control bar is adjusted to its maximum position, and the scroll boxes on the G and B control bars are adjusted to their minimum positions. See Fig D-4.)

The HIS control bars represent each color as a hue setting (the Hue control bar), an intensity setting (the Intensity control bar), and a saturation setting (the Saturation control bar). The Hue control bar is used to select a specific color; as you scroll this bar, all possible pure colors are displayed. The Intensity control bar selects the brightness of the color. The Saturation control bar selects the richness of the color (how deep or pastel a color appears).

It doesn't matter which method you use to edit a color: when you generate a color by changing the settings on the RGB control bars, the HIS control bars change to reflect the same color. Similarly, if you ad-

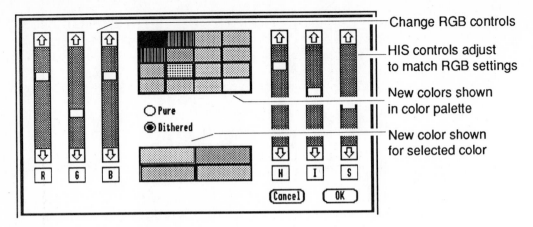

Change RGB controls

HIS controls adjust to match RGB settings

New colors shown in color palette

New color shown for selected color

Figure D-5 Edited color control bars

just the HIS control bars, the RGB control bars change to reflect the same color.

Editing a selected color

After you click the Pure or Dithered button, you are ready to actually edit the colors on the palette.

To change one of the colors:

| 1 | **Click one of the colors on the color edit palette.**

If you selected Pure colors, you can choose one of two colors. If you selected Dithered colors, you can choose one of four colors.

| 2 | **Change the selected colors by adjusting either the RGB control bars or the HIS control bars.**

As you adjust the control bars, the selected color in the color edit palette changes to match the new settings on the control bar. In addition, the color palette at the top of the dialog box also changes to reflect the effects of the new color. (See Figure D-5.)

| 3 | **If you wish, repeat steps 1 and 2 to edit other colors on the color edit palette.**

Remember, it doesn't matter whether you edit the selected color with the RGB control bars or the HIS control bars. They are simply two ways of representing the same color. Beginners might find the HIS model easier to use. You can adjust the Hue scroll bar until the desired color is displayed, and then adjust the Intensity and Saturation control bars to generate the desired shade of the color. (As you move the HIS control bars, the RGB control bars are automatically adjusted to reflect the same color.)

Making the new color palette active

When you return to the application, the new color palette that you have generated is active. Each color that was displayed in the old color palette will be replaced by the color that now occupies its position on the new palette.

- **To make the new palette active and return to the application, click the OK button.**

To return to the application without replacing the old palette with the new palette, click the Cancel button.

Special example: Grayscale palette

For some applications, you may want to display an image in shades of gray, rather than use the more standard color palette. For example, you might digitize or scan a black-and-white image and import the image into the graphics application. If you display the image using the default color palette, the image is displayed with false colors. While the effect is interesting, you may want to display the image in its original shades of gray.

The method is based on this idea: We will create the grayscale using the HIS control bars. When the Saturation control bar is set to its minimum (lowest) setting, all colors are gray, so all of the colors on the palette should be created with the Saturation control bar at this setting. The Intensity control bar controls the brightness of the color; this control bar will generate shades of gray. The Hue control bar is not relevant; no matter what it is set for, the color will be gray if the Saturation control bar is set to its minimum setting.

To change the color palette to display shades of gray:

1 **Click the Dithered button.**

2 **Click on the upper-left color in the color edit palette.**

- Move the Saturation control bar to its minimum (lowest) setting.
- Move the Intensity control about 1/5 from the bottom of the scroll bar.

3   **Click on the upper-right color in the color edit palette.**

- Move the Saturation control bar to its minimum (lowest) setting.
- Move the Intensity control about 2/5 from the bottom of the scroll bar.

4   **Click on the lower-left color in the color edit palette.**

- Move the Saturation control bar to its minimum (lowest) setting.
- Move the Intensity control about 3/5 from the bottom of the scroll bar.

5   **Click on the lower-right color in the color edit palette.**

- Move the Saturation control bar to its minimum (lowest) setting.
- Move the Intensity control about 4/5 from the bottom of the scroll bar.

The color palette now displays different shades of gray, including black and white. When you return to the application, this palette will be active and the application will display text and graphics using this grayscale palette.

To create different shades of gray, adjust the intensity control to different settings.

Index